Finding Them Gone: Visiting China's Poets of the Past

Translations by Red Pine & Travel Writings by Bill Porter

TRAVEL WRITINGS (AS BILL PORTER)

South of the Clouds: Travels in Southwest China

The Silk Road

Road to Heaven: Encounters with Chinese Hermits

Yellow River Odyssey

Zen Baggage: A Pilgrimage to China

CHINESE POETRY

The Collected Songs of Cold Mountain

The Mountain Poems of Stonehouse

Guide to Capturing a Plum Blossom by Sung Po-jen

In Such Hard Times: The Poetry of Wei Ying-wu

CHINESE POETRY ANTHOLOGIES

Poems of the Masters: China's Classic Anthology of T'ang and Sung Dynasty Verse

The Clouds Should Know Me by Now:Buddhist Poet Monks of China (with Michael O'Connor)

BUDDHIST, ZEN, AND TAOIST TEXTS

Lao-tzu's Taoteching: With Selected Commentaries from the Past 2,000 Years

P'u Ming's Oxherding Pictures and Verses

The Zen Teaching of Bodhidharma

The Heart Sutra: The Womb of Buddhas

The Diamond Sutra: The Perfection of Wisdom

The Platform Sutra: The Zen Teaching of Hui-neng

The Lankavatara Sutra: Translation and Commentary

Bill Porter /Red Pine

Finding Them Gone

Visiting China's Poets of the Past

Copper Canyon Press

Port Townsend, Washington

Work on this book was made possible by a fellowship from the John Simon Guggenheim Foundation and the financial support of Yin Yun (see Day 25).

Copper Canyon Press is in residence at Fort Worden State Park in Port Townsend, Washington, under the auspices of Centrum. Centrum is a gathering place for artists and creative thinkers from around the world, students of all ages and backgrounds, and audiences seeking extraordinary cultural enrichment.

LIBRARY OF CONGRESS CATALOGING-IN-PUBLICATION DATA

Red Pine, 1943–
Finding them gone : visiting China's poets of the past / Bill Porter/Red Pine.
   pages   cm
ISBN 978-1-55659-489-2 (paperback)
1. Poets, Chinese. 2. Chinese poetry – History and criticism. 3. Literature and society – China. I. Title.
PL2277.R43 2015
895.109 – dc23

2015017126

9 8 7 6 5 4 3 2 FIRST PRINTING

COPPER CANYON PRESS
Post Office Box 271
Port Townsend, Washington 98368

www.coppercanyonpress.org

To W.S. Merwin

YELLOW SEA

EAST CHINA SEA

1 Beijing
Tienchin
Shihchiachuang

Yellow River

2 Chingchou
2 Changchiu
Chinan **2**
Yushan **3**
▲ *Taishan*
1 Chufu

Kaifeng
Chengchou
Tunghsu
3 Weishih
4 Hsincheng
Loyang **5**
▲ *Sungshan*
6 Juchou
▲ **6** *Yuntaishan*

CHINA

Yangchou
Nanking
Tangtu **23**
24 Hsuancheng
23

Shanghai
Suchou
24 Huchou
Hsiamushan
25 ▲
Hangchou **26**
Shaohsing **28**
Ningpo
Tungshan **27**
29 ▲ Tientai
▲ *Tientaishan* **30**

Chiuchiang
21 ▲ *Lushan*
21
Poyang Lake
Shangiao
Yingtan **22**
22
22 Linchuan
Huangkang **18**
Echou **17**
Chienshan
Wuhan **18**
17 Anlu
Hsuishui **20**
Nanchang
Wantsar **20**
Shangli
Pingchiang **19**
Yuehyang **20**
Milo
Milo R. **19**
19
Tungting Lake
Yuan R.
Changsha
Hsiang R.

Hsiangyang
Han R.
16

Lepingli **15**
Yichang **14**
14
Three Gorges

Paiticheng **13**
Wanchou
Yangtze R.
Chungching

Sian
Paochi **8**
7 **7**
CHUNGNAN MTNS.
CHINLING MTNS.
Wei R.
Han R.

Yellow R.

Chiangyou
Shehung
Suining **12**
Anyueh
Santai **11**
11
12
9
Chialing R.
Fuchiang R.
Chengtu **10**
9 **10**
Min R.

Numbers refer to travel days.

● town
▲ mountain

100 miles
200 km
100
0

N

CONTENTS

Finding Them Gone: Visiting China's Poets of the Past

I checked out of the Beijing Friendship Hotel at five thirty, before the sun was up. The Friendship was where all the "foreign experts" from the Soviet Bloc and Third World stayed back in the day when China's Communist Party ruled a Communist country. It was where my Chinese publisher always put me up. He was once a bureau chief in the Ministry of Education, and I was, in an odd way, a "foreign expert." Besides, I couldn't turn down free lodging, especially garden-surrounded lodging in a city like Beijing.

Once I reached the street, I headed for the nearest subway station. It was only a two-minute walk, but this was the end of August. I was already perspiring. When I saw a taxi waiting at the curb, I threw my pack in the front, climbed in the back, and asked the driver to take me to South Station. That was where the new bullet trains left from, and I had a ticket on the first one of the day headed south. My train was scheduled to leave at seven, and I figured I would need an hour to get there. But I had never been on a road in Beijing before sunrise. Once we were on Third Ring Road, we were going one hundred kilometers per hour, in Beijing. It felt unreal.

As I looked out the car window at the predawn skyline, I could see the distinctive pagoda of Tienning Temple. Dating back to 1083, it was the oldest structure in Beijing. I was actually looking for another tower, a tower that disappeared before the pagoda was built. It would have been a few hundred meters to the north in the ward recently reclaimed by the Taoists of White Cloud Temple. It was called Youchou Tower—Youchou being an old name for Beijing. One day in 696, Ch'en Tzu-ang climbed to the top and wrote one of the most famous poems in the Chinese language, "Climbing Youchou Tower Song" 登幽州臺歌:

> I don't see the ancients who came before me
> I don't see those yet to come
> facing the endlessness of Heaven and Earth
> I am so overcome I cry

前不見古人，後不見來者。念天地之悠悠，獨愴然而下。

According to the earliest commentary on the *Shihching*, or Book of Poetry, "poetry is what the heart holds dear put into words" 在心為志, 發言為詩. Of course, the poems Chinese poets wrote weren't always from the heart. The Chinese have had their share of head poets. But there were plenty of poets like Ch'en Tzu-ang, and I wanted to thank as many as I could for sharing their hearts. I had put together a thirty-day itinerary to visit their hometowns and graves, and this was Day 1. As quickly as Youchou Tower and Ch'en Tzu-ang's poem came to mind, they vanished in the first rays of the morning sun. A few minutes later I was at the station. It looked more like an airport terminal. It was huge: 60,000 tons of steel huge. I paid the driver the 44RMB (the exchange rate was 6RMB to 1USD) it cost me to be an hour early and hoisted my backpack onto my shoulders. Unlike Chinese airport terminals, there were no free baggage carts waiting outside. If there was air-conditioning inside, I didn't feel it. The temperature was expected to hit a hundred that day. I walked past the ticket windows and the ticket-vending machines and the convenience stores and the still-closed doors of KFC and Burger King and looked up at the billboard-sized train schedule. Once I saw my train listed, I headed toward my designated gate. When I was within viewing distance, I sat down on one of the metal benches, alongside a few other early arrivals.

My clothes were still damp, not from perspiration but from washing them the night before, which didn't happen until after ten. Earlier that evening I participated in a panel discussion about China's hermit tradition sponsored by a real estate company. My stays in Beijing were like that: one appearance or interview after another, involving odd, if not mysterious, concatenations. It was the price authors paid if they wanted to sell books, which I did, of course. It turned out that the people most interested in the books I wrote lived in China, not in America. The income made a huge difference. I no longer qualified for food stamps. Damp clothes were a small inconvenience. Besides, that morning they made me feel cooler.

Once the gate opened, I followed my fellow passengers down the escalator onto the platform. There were a dozen trains lined up waiting to begin another day zipping across the Middle Kingdom. Their white fuselages shimmered in the early morning light. They were so clean someone must have washed them during the night. My train was bound for Shanghai, 1,300 kilometers away, and it was scheduled to get there in five and a half hours. It was pulling sixteen cars, and I was perspiring again by the time I reached the car at the front. I had asked my publisher to arrange for a seat behind the engineer. I'd seen pictures on the Internet of the glass enclosure and was looking forward to the view of hurtling down the tracks from behind the engineer's shoulder. But it was not to be. As the attendant in charge of the five seats in the front cabin escorted me inside, I saw that the clear glass of the engineer's

High-speed trains waiting to leave Beijing's South Station

enclosure had been replaced by frosted glass. Apparently the engineers didn't feel comfortable with people staring over their shoulders while going 350 kilometers an hour. I later learned there was a button the engineer could push to change the glass from clear to frosted. I still don't understand how it worked, but it worked.

I sat down, and the attendant asked me whether I would like a cup of coffee — not tea, coffee. I suppose it was the drink foreigners were expected to ask for, and I didn't disappoint her. A few minutes later, she brought the coffee along with a small box of complimentary snacks that included packages of dried seaweed, dried dates, dried peas ("from America"), hawthorn candy, something labeled Instant Donkey-Hide Gelatin, and a mint — presumably to mask donkey-hide breath. As I sat there thus ensconced and cared for, the train pulled out of the station. The engineer didn't waste any time picking up speed. Within five minutes Beijing was a memory. The digital readout in the front of the car indicated we were going over 300 kilometers per hour. Outside, the fog, if that was what it was, limited visibility to a few hundred meters. All I could see were plastic-canopied fields: suppliers to the greengrocers of Beijing.

Out of curiosity I got up and walked down the corridor to the dining car. It was located in the middle of the train. All the seats were occupied, apparently by people looking for more room than their own seats afforded. At the far end of the car, there was a counter selling snacks and drinks and microwave meals. If nothing else, my curiosity was satisfied. I walked back to my seat and resumed my survey of the Yellow River floodplain. A flatter landscape would be hard to find. Nearly all of North China was made of Yellow River mud, the detritus of a million years of floods.

The coffee eventually had its usual effect, and I visited the first-class toilet, which was a room unto itself – quite the upgrade from the usual craphole that emptied onto the tracks. Not only was the room spotless, there was soft toilet paper. There was even a sink with hot and cold water. While I was enjoying this pleasure dome, the train stopped briefly in Chinan, the capital of Shantung province. As soon as it pulled out of the station, I returned to my seat and prepared for my stop. Thirty minutes later, I got off in Chufu. Two hours and 500 kilometers after leaving Beijing, I found myself in 500 BC.

I was one of four passengers who disembarked. Everyone else was bound for the twenty-first century. Waiting for me at the station exit was my friend Eric Lu Ch'ang-ch'ing. Eric had worked in China's travel industry for three decades and had teamed up with my friend Andy Ferguson in organizing Zen tours to China. While it wasn't a major source of revenue for either, it was far more rewarding than guiding people to such tourist sites as the Underground Army or the Great Wall. Eric's home was in Chinan, and he was taking the day off to drive me around Confucius's hometown.

We didn't waste any time. We headed southeast, toward Mount Nishan, where Confucius was born in 551 bc. It was only thirty kilometers away, and the road was decent. The countryside was a refreshing change from Beijing. The last kilometer along the Yi River was *more* than refreshing. It was memorable. The pavement was covered with cypress branches. Farmers were letting passing cars do their work for them: crushing the small balls lining the branches so that they could collect the seeds and sell them for use in essential oils. The fragrance would have cured a cold.

Not far beyond the branch-lined section of the road there was a turnoff. We followed it uphill 200 meters to the foot of Nishan and joined six other cars inside a parking lot. I was surprised to see so many cars. It was a weekday. Still, Confucius's birthplace did qualify as a tourist site. At the ticket window, I paid the senior-citizen entry fee. Eric showed his tour guide ID and paid nothing. Instead of walking through the entrance, we entered through the exit. I wanted to begin where Confucius was abandoned by his mother, shortly after he was born.

The reason, according to the only records we have on the subject, had to do with his appearance. As he grew up, people remarked on his large, bulging forehead. Maybe there were other physiological aspects that didn't make it into the history books. Or maybe the reason he was abandoned had to do with his conception. His father was eighty, and his mother was twenty when she gave birth. Once again, the only records we have tell us his parents "made love in the fields." I'm not sure why his parents chose the fields or whether "the fields" meant something else – outside the bounds of convention or propriety, perhaps. The story about being abandoned also sounded suspicious. The founder of the dynasty during which Confucius lived was also abandoned by his mother.

Instead of perishing, the infant survived. He was nursed by a tigress that had just given birth to cubs, and the cave was protected by an eagle. As we entered the cave, Eric and I lowered our heads and followed a path of raised stones someone had placed there to keep the feet of visitors above the water that flowed out of the rocks. Inside, there was just enough room for a large flat rock, which must have served as the infant's crib.

After seeing what there was to see, we exited and followed a path of stone steps up the mountain. It was more of a hill than a mountain, and I wondered if that was why Confucius's mother named her son Ch'iu, meaning "hill." Halfway to the top, the stone steps were replaced by moss-covered dirt, and the open vegetation was replaced by the shade of thousand-year-old cedars. The path ended at the Nishan Academy where Confucius supposedly taught. I say "supposedly" because it was so far from Chufu, I doubt he ever came here for anything more than summer retreats. Confucius's career as a teacher took place in town, not in the countryside. The academy's one small building was full of benches and desks and was someone's idea of a country school for children – not the sort of place where the Sage's adult disciples would have studied. Still, it provided the sort of setting in which one could imagine Confucius speaking the line that begins his *Analects:* "To learn and to put what one learns into practice, is that not happiness?" And what did he teach? Ritual and music were his favorite subjects, and both included poetry.

Leaving the academy, we followed the main path downhill toward the entrance. Along the way we stopped at two shrine halls whose courtyards were overgrown: one was built to honor Confucius's parents and the other to honor the spirit of the mountain. Among the ancient cedars in the second courtyard stood a stele recording the restoration of the shrine to Nishan. It was dated 1342. In the same courtyard, there were four other visitors. One of them walked over and introduced himself. He said he owned Chinese translations of two of my books and asked me to pose with him and his friends for a photo. I never knew where the people who read my books were going to turn up. The Chinese were once again taking interest, if not

Confucius's grave

pride, in their past, and even a Westerner's view of that past was somehow worth reading about. I wasn't about to complain and smiled when the photographer reminded us to say "ch'ieh-tzu" (eggplant), as the pronunciation of the word produced the same effect as saying "cheese." Another popular alternative was "ch'ien," meaning "money," which usually turned smiles into laughs.

Just then, we heard the bullhorn of an actual tour group, which we passed as we headed downhill. On the way, we stopped briefly at River View Pavilion. This was where Confucius was said to have stood one day – contemplating the flowing waters of the Yi River – and sighed, "Alas, we too pass on like this, not stopping day or night!" (*Analects*: 9.16). I had always imagined Confucius standing like Heraclitus, looking down at the current. The river, it turned out, was 300 meters away and obscured by a forest. Faced with such an anomaly, I shrugged. I was just a pilgrim.

We returned to the road and followed the Yi back to Chufu. Thirty minutes later, we crossed the river's ever-flowing current and entered the old part of town. I was reminded of Confucius's sigh again. It was true. We were like a river. One moment this thought, the next moment another. And yet trying to find a "we" in all this was as arbitrary and unreal as the river Heraclitus kept trying to step into. Besides, what was all this "passing on," anyway? The thought crossed my mind as quickly as we did the Yi.

Once across, we turned west and drove parallel to the river on Raindance Altar Road. This section of the Yi once formed the city's south moat. A block later, we stopped to inspect what was left of the altar for which the road was named. Again, according to the *Analects* (11.25), one day Confucius asked his disciples what they would like to do if they could do whatever they wished. While the others expressed their desires for worldly fame and power, Tseng Hsi said he would like to go to Raindance Altar with a group of friends, bathe in the river, and return home singing. Confucius sighed and told his disciples, "I'm with Tseng Hsi."

It was an old ritual, bathing at the end of spring on the third day of the third lunar month. It has since been refocused and associated with visiting ancestral graves. Westerners in China call it Grave Sweeping Day. The name in Chinese is "Ch'ing-ming" (Purification Day), which reflects its origins as a celebration of cleansing and renewal. Eric and I got out and walked over to the place where Tseng Hsi and, presumably, Confucius did exactly that. Whatever the site might have been in the past, it was now a ten-meter-high dirt mound covered with vegetation. I looked for a way to the top, but the base was surrounded entirely by a stone balustrade meant to prevent access, and beyond that by a dense ring òf cedars. I walked around the mound without finding an opening. No doubt, a long time had passed since anyone danced on top or bathed in the ever-passing river below, let alone walked home singing. The Yi flowed on, and so did we.

Next on the itinerary was the Duke of Chou Shrine in the northeast part of town. Chufu was the capital of the ancient state of Lu, which was given to the duke as his fief when he helped found the Chou dynasty around 1050 BC. The duke was Confucius's hero, the man on whom he modeled himself, and the shrine built in the duke's memory was where Confucius came to study the rites and ceremonies he considered an essential part of good government. In some accounts, the duke was also linked to the same two books attributed to Confucius, namely, the Book of Poetry and the *Book of Changes.* No doubt the time he spent here was crucial to Confucius's education and to the development of his own views.

The shrine was not a major tourist destination – or even a minor one. Eric and I were the only visitors. As we walked down the path leading to the main hall, we passed dozens of thousand-year-old cedars and a number of stone steles, including one inscribed with the *Chinjenming* (Words of the Golden Man). The text was attributed to Huang-ti (c. 2600 BC), the Yellow Emperor, and was seen by some as the inspiration for Lao-tzu's *Taoteching.* The inscription was mostly worn away, but I could still read the lines near the beginning: "Don't talk too much, or you'll be sorry. Don't do too much, or you'll regret it." It was full of one-liners like these, and I don't know why it hasn't been translated into English. Or maybe it has, and I simply haven't heard about it – perhaps by someone in the fortune cookie business. Since there wasn't much more of the text that we could make out, we continued up the steps to the lone shrine hall.

Just outside the entrance, we stopped to inspect another stele that recorded the history of the shrine. It was broken in two, and only the bottom half remained. On the back, a recent inscription recorded the reason why: in November 1966, 200 Red Guards, led by T'an Hou-lan and Mao's private secretary Ch'en Po-ta, whom many consider the main architect of the Cultural

Revolution, came to Chufu and began destroying whatever they could. The Duke of Chou's shrine was one of their victims. At least they left the cedars. It was a lovely place. As we walked around, we were followed by a yellow-crested woodpecker (oddly, not in any Chinese bird book I've seen) and a dozen sparrows curious as to what we were doing in their world.

We concluded that the place was deserted because it was lunchtime, which reminded us it was lunchtime. We drove back to the town's old North Gate and ate at a hotel restaurant. There, too, we were the only guests. Apparently, the absence of tourists was simply due to the absence of tourists. Meanwhile, Eric ordered a small banquet: smoked tofu, for which the town was famous, cold green beans in a sesame sauce, stir-fried slices of beef and tomato, *shao-ping* pastry stuffed with garlic tops, rice noodles, and cold beer. It was enough food for four or five people. The Chinese are embarrassed if there isn't food left on the table. My own sentiments being just the opposite, I always end up eating too much.

Once we managed to push ourselves away from the table, we returned to Eric's car and drove north several blocks until a barrier blocked the way. The road ahead led to the Confucius Forest, where any resident of Chufu related to Confucius or sharing his surname had the right to be buried, though only for a few months. Strange but true. There were more than 30,000 people in Chufu who claimed to be descendants. While Eric waited in his car, I got into a pedicab and continued past the barrier. At the main gate I got out and paid the entry fee and walked through the forest's ancient archway. On the other side, the old gauntlet of trinket stands was gone. There was now a line of electric carts to take visitors on a tour of the grounds. Having been there before, I walked past the carts and continued beneath two more archways and across a small stone bridge that spanned the dry streambed of the Ssu River. The river had been diverted to prevent flooding. On the other side was a shrine hall, and on the far side of that was the walkway leading to where Confucius was buried.

The Sage's grave was a simple affair: a small grass-covered mound with two stone markers. On the older one were carved the words *Hsuan Kung* 宣公 (Exalted Lord), which referred to his elevation to sagehood by imperial decree 2,000 years ago. I waited until the handful of visitors departed. When I was finally alone, I poured the Exalted Lord two cups of George T. Stagg, the most exalted offering I could come up with, and another cup for myself. I'm not sure what Confucius would have thought of the bourbon: the sweetness of the corn, the spiciness of the rye — neither grain existed in ancient China. I knew he wasn't opposed to such beverages. In the *Analects* (10.8) it says of

Chussu Academy in Chufu

Confucius, "He set no limit when it came to alcohol, as long as he didn't make a scene." My sentiments, exactly. In this case, the cups were so tiny that there was no danger of either of us violating his dictum. I scattered his share on the stele and on his grave, downed mine, then returned to Eric's waiting sedan.

We had one more stop in Chufu – the reason that I had decided to begin my pilgrimage here in the first place – the Chussu Academy, named for the Chu and Ssu Rivers between which it was located. It was where Confucius compiled the Book of Poetry. Unfortunately, road construction was in progress, and our attempt to reach it by the normal route was unsuccessful. We stopped to ask directions from some farmers harvesting corn (grown for animal feed and not for distilling whiskey), and they directed us to a dirt road that approached the academy from the rear. When we finally reached the front gate, it was not only closed, it was barred from the inside. I was crushed. I concluded that the road construction had given the caretaker a reason to stay home. No one was expecting visitors. Out of habit, I banged on the gate anyway, and the poetry gods smiled. The caretaker was napping in the guardhouse, and the banging woke him up.

As the huge wooden gate creaked open, we once more found ourselves alone. Except for the caretaker, some wild birds, and a few chickens, the place appeared to be deserted. The two shrine halls were empty, too, and the steles outside the halls were also barren. They had been worn by centuries of wind and rain and were impossible to read. While we were looking around, I spotted a young woman in one of the side halls. I walked over and asked her what she was doing there, which probably sounded odd, coming from a foreign tourist. But if she was surprised, she didn't show it. She was assigned, she said, to help get the place ready for its impending transformation into a lecture hall. She knew a lot about the place. She said the front shrine hall dated back to the Ming dynasty and was built on the original site of the school where Confucius taught his disciples. The side hall where she was working was where he lived while he was editing the Book of Poetry.

For over 2,000 years the Chinese have been reading and reciting and memorizing and quoting the 300 or so poems Confucius collected in his anthology. Lately, though, some scholars have begun questioning our understanding of them, trying to separate the poems from the moral or philosophical agendas through which they have been interpreted over the centuries. Ironically, such doubts have been made possible by Confucius himself, in the form of a text written around 300 BC titled *Kungtzulunshih* (Confucius on Poetry). Unfortunately, only pieces of this text have come to light (stolen from the Kuotien archaeological site, sold on the black market, resold by a Hong Kong antique dealer, and currently in the possession of the Shanghai Museum). Although the order of the pieces is problematic, enough has been deciphered to convince scholars that we can no longer claim to understand the original meaning of many of the poems – or at least why Confucius included them. What *was* the teaching he was trying to convey? He was, after all, primarily a teacher.

Even where we do think we understand the original meaning of the poems, they don't necessarily impress with their literary art. Martin Kern has called the book "the living dead of Chinese poetry, occupying its mandatory place at the beginning of our anthologies where it blocks, rather than opens, the pathway to those later texts for which alone it is worth learning Chinese."[1] It's true. The poems in the Book of Poetry represent a far simpler form of literary art than those composed over a thousand years later during China's Golden Age of Poetry. But they were still poems. And that was why I was here, to honor the art. Despite being full of dull stuff, the book included dozens of poems like "Humble Door" 衡門:

---

1. Martin Kern, "Lost in Tradition: The *Classic of Poetry* We Did Not Know," in *Hsiang Lectures on Chinese Poetry*, vol. 5, ed. Grace S. Fong (Montreal: Centre for East Asian Research, McGill University, 2010), 29.

Behind my humble door
I can live in peace
beside this trickling stream
I can live with hunger

If I'm to eat fish
must it be a bream from the river
if I'm to take a wife
must it be a countess from Ch'i

If I'm to eat fish
must it be a river carp
if I'm to take a wife
must it be a Sung princess

衡門之下，可以棲遲。泌之洋洋，可以樂饑。
豈其食魚，必河之魴？豈其娶妻，必齊之姜。
豈其食魚，必河之鯉？豈其娶妻，必宋之子。

It doesn't amount to much, but it served to remind readers of the virtue of contentment — a virtue of which we can never be reminded too much. This, of course, was one of the aspects of poetry considered important in ancient China: its usefulness in advancing moral values. The poems in the Book of Poetry were also about love, as poems are everywhere, as in "The Countryside Is Home to Vines" 野有蔓草:

The countryside is home to vines
with sparkling drops of dew
and home to a beautiful girl
with clear and lovely eyes
meeting unexpectedly
my wishes are fulfilled

The countryside is home to vines
with shimmering drops of dew
and home to a beautiful girl
with lovely and clear eyes

meeting unexpectedly
how good to be with you

野有蔓草，零露漙兮。有美一人，清揚婉兮。邂逅相遇，適我願兮。
野有蔓草，零露瀼瀼。有美一人，婉如清揚。邂逅相遇，與子偕臧。

Admittedly rudimentary, but still better than anything I've written on those rare occasions when I've been spurred to express such feelings. And it does what poetry does everywhere: it gives the human heart a voice.

Whether or not we can still claim to understand the poems in the Book of Poetry, we can't help but recognize the role they played in the development of Chinese civilization. Even though we might not know what some of the poems mean or why Confucius chose them for inclusion, his efforts helped to give poetry an importance it has never enjoyed in the West – and probably never will. Confucius made speaking from the heart an essential part of Chinese culture. Ever since then, no one was allowed to serve in government in China who could not write a poem. It was part of the entrance requirements. Confucius made sure Li Pai (701–762) and Tu Fu (712–770) wrote poems, and they, too, came to Chufu to pay their respects.

Eric and I thanked the young woman for showing us where the history of poetry began in China – at least the book part of it. After returning to the highway, we headed north and crossed the Ssu River. The road was new and a pleasure to drive on. Ten minutes later, we saw a sign for Stone Gate Mountain National Forest Park, my last destination of the day. The arrow pointed us onto another good road, which was not always a good sign. Sometimes it meant "big tourist site ahead." And, of course, a national park qualified. A minute later, we passed another sign. It said, Car Camping. People were car-camping in China? That was new. A few minutes later, we passed another sign. This one was for a huge complex of buildings still under construction. It was the new campus of Far Eastern Polytechnic College. That explained the new road. Like mushrooms after a rain, private colleges were springing up everywhere in China. The country's new economy needed something more than farmers and factory workers, and there weren't enough public colleges. Ironically, it was in Chufu, with Confucius, that public education began in China. There had been teachers before, but none whose students were not members of the nobility. In his honor, Confucius's birthday, September 28, is celebrated as Teachers' Day.

A few minutes later, we pulled into the Stone Gate Mountain parking lot. I paid the entry fee, Eric flashed his tour guide ID, and we began walking up a trail of stone steps. Cicadas were singing, magpies were squawking, doves were cooing, and once more we were alone. It was Wednesday. Everyone was either in school or at work or car-camping. The trail followed a stream up the mountain, and the air felt cool. Just as the steps approached the entrance to a Buddhist monastery, we turned left onto another trail then turned left again. Ten minutes after starting out, we reached our destination. It was a good thing I had been there before. There were no signs. The trail we took ended at a pavilion built on a large outcrop of rock whose layers had been weathered to form waves. Between the waves were pools of water, and in ancient times the place was called Terrace of Pools. Nowadays, it's called Terrace of Jewels.

The view was grand: the pavilion floating on waves of rock, the valley below, and Stone Gate's southern ridge on the other side of the valley spread out like a painting. That was where Confucius reportedly edited the *Yiching* (*Book of Changes*), in which he took the earlier works of Fu Hsi and the Duke of Chou and added to them a moral compass for navigating the ever-changing river of life. He once said, "I don't compose. I only transmit." He was also China's first great editor.

I chose the northern and not the southern ridge because this was where China's two greatest poets once spent the night. On the stone slab beneath the pavilion's roof, I set out the same three small porcelain cups I set out earlier at Confucius's grave. I bought them the week before at a flea market in Beijing, the one held every Thursday and Saturday at Paokuo Temple. They were the kind of cups used at family sacrifices and perfect for the offering I brought. If there was one thing China's poets liked to do it was drink. With that in mind, I took out the small silver flask I had filled with bourbon the night before. I brought two bottles of whiskey with me from America: an eighteen-year-old Willett and the 2011 George T. Stagg release—the last of the Guggenheim money that made my trip possible. I decided to begin with the Stagg. At 142.6 proof, I had no doubt it would make me some friends in China's poetry heaven. I poured three shots. One for Li Pai, one for Tu Fu, and one, of course, for me. Since Eric was driving, he was limited to inhaling the fumes.

It was easy to imagine the two men sitting here watching the sun cross the sky followed by the moon. They drank all day and into the night and finally fell asleep under the same blanket. The year was 745, and it was about the same time of year, when everyone in China was waiting for summer to give way to fall. This was the second time they met, and it would be the last. Commemorating the occasion, Li Pai wrote "In Eastern Lu Seeing Off Tu Fu at Stone Gate" 魯郡東石門送杜二甫:

> Our drunken parting has lasted for days
> and now we've climbed to the Terrace of Pools
> when will we travel this Stone Gate Road
> and raise these golden cups again
> with autumn falling on the Ssu
> and dawn lighting Tsulai
> tumbleweeds going separate ways
> let us drain this wine we hold

> 醉別復幾日，登臨遍池臺。何時石門路，重有金樽開。
> 秋波落泗水，海色明徂徠。飛蓬各自遠，且盡手中杯。

The Ssu was the river we passed when we left Chufu, the river that flowed just north of the Chussu Academy and that used to flow past Confucius's grave. Tsulai was the name of a nearby peak to the northeast between Stone Gate and Taishan, China's most sacred mountain. After watching a few clouds pass by, I drained my cup then sprinkled Tu Fu's and Li Pai's in the pools. The day was getting late. I put the cups away, and Eric and I headed back down the mountain.

Over the years, Tu Fu wrote ten poems to Li Pai. Two years after their meeting at Stone Gate — when Tu Fu was living on the Wei River near the capital of Ch'ang-an, and Li Pai had been banished from the court and was wandering south of Nanking along the east shore of the Yangtze — Tu Fu wrote "Thinking of Li Pai on a Spring Day" 春日憶李白, in which he compared his friend to the two most famous poets of the fifth and sixth centuries:

> The poetry of Li Pai has no equal
> the etherealness of his thoughts is unique
> purer and fresher than Yu Hsin's
> more refined and unrestrained than Pao Chao's
> on the Wei's north shore beneath flowering trees
> or east of the Yangtze below evening clouds

where will we share that cup of wine
and discuss the art of words again

白也詩無敵，飄然思不群。清新庾開府，俊逸鮑參軍。
渭北春天樹，江東日暮雲。何時一樽酒，重與細論文。

Where, indeed? Apparently, in another lifetime. Back on the highway, we headed north again. But Eric soon turned east, wanting to take me to Chinan via the eastern route around the sacred peak of Taishan. This led us past Tsulai Mountain. It was lit by the sunset, rather than the dawn, as in Li Pai's poem. I suddenly recalled a poem by Confucius in which he referred to the small peak at the base of Tsulai known as Liangfushan. The poem was found in a collection of clan memorabilia hidden in the walls of the family home during the great book burning of 213 BC. It was titled "Song of the Hill" 丘陵之哥：

The hill I climb
its slopes are steep
the Tao of Harmony rises ahead
but only gets farther away
having lost the path home
and beset by hardships
I lament and reflect
with Taishan before me
standing majestic
and Liangfu in between
its trails choked with thorns
and no way around
and me with no axe
and more troubles every day
I can't stop sighing
my tears form a stream

登彼丘陵，峛嶷其阪。仁道在邇，求之若遠。
遂迷不復，自嬰屯蹇。喟然回慮，題彼泰山。
鬱確其高，梁甫回連。枳棘充路，陟之無緣。
將伐無柯，患茲蔓延。惟以永歎，涕實潺湲。

For Confucius, the sacred peak of Taishan represented the Tao, and the steep slopes of Liangfu and the thorn-choked paths leading past it from Chufu represented the unfortunate times in which he was born. If only he had an axe. But he did. Only it turns out it was a writing brush. I was glad I remembered the poem.

As we continued past Taishan, the road was lined with farmers selling walnuts and watermelons. It was the end of summer and still hot. It had been a long day, and I fell asleep. Two hours later, Eric dropped me off at my hotel. I had asked him to make a reservation for me at a place across the street from Paotuchuan Park, which I planned to visit the next morning. But the hotel told him they didn't accept foreigners. Forty years earlier, foreigners could stay in only a few select hotels in any given city. Now they can stay almost anywhere, but there are still exceptions. So Eric made a reservation for me at Motel 168. It was a disappointing alternative, but it didn't matter. I was exhausted and barely had the energy to shower, much less wash my clothes.

Lying in bed, I thought: "One day down, twenty-nine to go." It was the self-imposed parameter of my trip. Such parameters had made my writing possible in the first place. I'd never written anything other than letters until I began working at English-language radio stations, first in Taiwan then in Hong Kong. It was my job in Hong Kong that pushed me over the edge: traveling in China for extended periods, then converting my travel notes into a series of two-minute "fluff pieces." My first trip was from the mouth of the Yellow River to its source and resulted in over 200 pieces of fluff. Unbelievably, the programs were such a success I was asked to do more, and I wrote and recorded similar series about my travels along the Silk Road and among China's hill tribes and to every historical site I could think of. It was a relentless way of traveling and also of writing: six weeks on the road followed by twelve weeks in Hong Kong getting far enough ahead to take another six-week trip. That was how I learned to write. Admittedly, it was exhausting, and I wouldn't recommend to anyone either the way I travel or the way I write. Fortunately, the end was in sight — at least the travel part: twenty-nine days away.

Left: Terrace of Pools on Stone Gate Mountain

As far as I was concerned, the sun could have come up later. Another hour or two of sleep would have been welcome. At least my first destination wasn't far: Paotuchuan Park, less than 300 meters from my hotel. Before heading out, I had the good sense to put new insoles in my shoes. I bought them years ago from a lady on a street somewhere in China and had been carrying them around so long I forgot about them. The soles of my canvas shoes, the ones I replaced every summer at Payless for $9.99, had become so thin I could feel the cracks in the sidewalks. The insoles made a huge difference. It was like walking on carpet. My feet felt happy. For a traveler, few things are more important than happy feet.

It was nearly eight o'clock when my feet and I entered Gushing Springs Park, which is what Paotuchuan means in English. Chinan is known as the City of Springs, but for many years the city's nickname had become a joke. When I first passed through on my way up the Yellow River in 1991, the city's springs had stopped flowing, and the water in its parks had to be pumped in. The aquifer that made the springs possible had been damaged by underground construction. I was happy to see the springs gushing again, but they weren't why I was there. Nor was I there to join the early morning exercise groups doing their routines to music. I wound my way instead through the park's maze of walkways toward the place where a poet once lived.

Suddenly I stopped. The walkway I had been following led to a pond, and swimming in the pond were two spotted seals. Since I was the only one who stopped to stare, the novelty must have worn off for everyone else. I tried to take a photo, but my lens kept fogging up. I forgot to mention the heat, the heat and the humidity. It climbed into the upper nineties that day, and I was constantly wiping my forehead and wringing out my bandanna. Once I managed to record something I could show to others, not unlike a photo of a flying saucer, I moved on.

The reason I was visiting the park was just ahead: the memorial hall built where Li Ch'ing-chao (1084–1155) once lived. Her statue was just inside the gate and was flanked by pink and lavender blooms of crepe myrtle and yellow sprays of forsythia. Sitting on a stone bench off to the side, an old man was playing a two-string fiddle known as a *nan-hu*. I stopped to listen, as did an old lady employed to pick up cigarette butts and trash with a long-handled device. The old man's music carried us both off to the northern frontier, her to where her husband was guarding a remote outpost and me to the ruins of a Buddhist temple whose hidden cache of manuscripts I hoped to find. Not until the musician reached the end of his song did the woman and I resume our more modest missions.

Inside the hall, I walked through a series of rooms that displayed the highlights of Li Ch'ing-chao's life. In one, she was a child impressing her elders with her skill at composing verse extempore. In another, she was a young woman cataloguing the collection of antiques she and her husband had acquired. In yet another, her life's perambulations were summarized on a map.

Chinan was the biggest city in that part of China and the last city the Yellow River passed through before it started looking for the sea. Li Ch'ing-chao spent a good deal of her youth here, and it was from Chinan that she sailed upriver to Kaifeng, 600 kilometers to the southwest, to join her father, who was serving at the Sung court. The map also showed her flight from Chinan in 1128 after the Jurchens invaded North China and sacked Kaifeng. She loaded her and her husband's collection of antiques into eight carts and managed to get them all the way to Nanking, where her husband had preceded her to become that city's new mayor. Unfortunately, soon after she arrived, he died, and she was forced to rely on the generosity of relatives and friends – relatives and friends who were not all that generous. A red line on the map continued from Nanking zigging and zagging throughout the lower reaches of the Yangtze. Li spent the rest of her life wandering its waterways looking for a new home she never found. No one knows where she died or where she was buried, only that she lived to be seventy-two. They were turbulent times, and she was flotsam on the waves.

While I was following her journey on the wall, I heard music playing over the loudspeakers. A woman was singing, and the voice sounded familiar. When I asked the hall's caretaker, she said it was Ts'ai Ch'in, and the song was one of Li Ch'ing-chao's. Ts'ai Ch'in was one of my favorite singers when I lived in Taiwan. She had a rich voice and was always pushing it into new territory. She was once a guest on my weekly interview program in my previous incarnation as a radio journalist, and she sat next to me one night at the annual radio station banquet. I still remember my frontal lobes melting. She had the longest, most beautiful hair. Her apartment was only two blocks from my wife's, but our paths never crossed again. The caretaker said the CD wasn't for sale. Instead, she sold me a copy of Li Ch'ing-chao's poems and turned to the one I had just heard. It was one of her lyric poems – composed to a set melody and meant to be sung. The melody in this case was "Ju-meng-ling" 如夢令, which meant something like "dreamscape." The title, though, only referred to the melody and did not necessarily have anything to do with the poem:

> I recall that sunset by the river pavilion
> so drunk I forgot the way home
> exhilaration fading rowing back late
> losing my way in a sea of lotus flowers
> struggling through
> struggling through
> I startled a whole sandbar of egrets

常紀溪亭日暮，沈醉不知歸路。興盡晚回舟，誤入藕花深處。
爭渡，爭渡，驚起一灘鷗鷺。

In the final hall, Li was sitting alone in her room. The sign said, Wandering Destitute. She was writing another poem for which she is still remembered. It was a quatrain titled "Summer Day" 夏日:

> Alive a hero among men
> dead esteemed among ghosts
> Hsiang Yu is in my thoughts today
> refusing to escape to the Yangtze's east shore

生當作人傑，死亦為鬼雄。至今思項羽，不肯過江東。

Having lost too many battles in his quest for the throne, the warlord Hsiang Yu (d. 202 BC) refused to cross the Yangtze to safety. Cornered, he turned and faced his enemies and died on the river's west shore. His grave was across the river from where Li composed this poem. She couldn't help wondering whether she should have stayed in Chinan instead of taking refuge on the Yangtze's safer east shore where her life was not what she had envisioned. Unable to return home and unable to make a new home as an émigré, she spent the rest of her life in transit. I read another poem from this final phase of her life, one she composed to the tune "P'u-sa-man" 菩薩蠻 (Bodhisattva from Numan):

The wind is soft the sun is faint it's still early spring
I put on a lined shirt and my mood improved
I felt a chill when I first awoke
and my plum petal makeup was smeared
as for where I'm from
I only forget when I'm drunk
the incense I burned while I slept
its traces are gone but not the wine's

風柔日薄春猶早，夾衫乍著心情好。睡起覺微寒，梅花鬢上殘。
故鄉何處是，忘了除非醉。沈水臥時燒，香消酒未消。

That was all the time I had. I had a morning train to catch and hurried to the park exit. It was rush hour, and there wasn't an empty taxi in sight. There were, however, alternatives. I crossed the street to a bus stop and five minutes later climbed aboard air-conditioned public transportation. What a difference that made. The temperature outside was already in the nineties. My air-conditioned respite, however, was brief and ended one block short of the train station. I had a ticket for the 9:22 express to Chingchou, which was where Li Ch'ing-chao and her husband spent ten idyllic years after he and his family were banished from court in 1107.

I was fifteen minutes early, but the train was an hour late. Normally, I preferred buses. Buses left on time, more or less. But they were slower, and Chingchou was 200 kilometers away. Trains normally left on time, too, but only from their station of origin. Relying on a train that came from somewhere else was always a gamble. This time I lost and arrived in Chingchou an hour later than planned. Normally that would have been okay, but I had a return ticket on the 12:36. Instead of having two hours in Chingchou, I had one. Sometimes I planned my itineraries with unwarranted precision.

As I walked out of the station, I looked for the usual assortment of touts and drivers, but the exit was deserted. The Chingchou train station, like a lot of new stations in China, was far from the old part of town. In fact, it was bordered on three sides by cornfields and orchards. There were, however, a few taxis waiting on the road below, so I hurried down the steps and started to get into one. As I did, two other people got in from the other side. Apparently, people in Chingchou shared rides into town then switched to other, cheaper, transportation. While I was considering what to do, I saw another

Statue of Li Ch'ing-chao at her memorial hall in Changchiu

taxi delivering someone else to the station. Before it pulled away, I flagged it down and had it to myself. I told the driver I was in a hurry. Twenty minutes later I was at my destination, Fankungting Park, named for a magistrate who served in Chingchou thirty years before Li Ch'ing-chao moved here.

Since my time at the park was going to be brief, I asked the driver to wait for me then hurried down a long flight of steps. The park consisted of a ring of hills surrounding a small lake and a few scattered pavilions. As I reached the bottom of the steps, I was glad to see a sign pointing toward Kueilaitang, or Homecoming Hall. That was where Li and her husband lived during his banishment. Those turned out to be their happiest years together. Free from the distractions of life at court, they were able to focus on their mutual passion: collecting antiques and recording the inscriptions they found on them.

Unfortunately, the hall was in a walled compound on the far side of the park. I alternated between walking as fast as I could and jogging, and it *still* took me five minutes. When I entered the gate, I would have sighed if I weren't out of breath. The compound consisted of three small, more or less empty halls. One hall contained nothing but a plaster of paris statue of the poet playing the zither for her husband, and another their bed. The third hall was her studio. Its name was on the wall outside. Li Ch'ing-chao called it her Yi-an Studio. She liked the name so much, she also used it as her sobriquet: Yi-an Chu-shih, the Easily Contented Scholar. Both names, that of their residence (Kueilaitang) and that of her studio, came from a poem by T'ao Yuan-ming, who was a hero to both Li and her husband. Like T'ao, they yearned for a simpler life. Unfortunately, they were too well connected to the centers of wealth and power. After ten years in and around Chingchou, her husband and his family were rehabilitated, and they returned to the capital.

Her studio included only a table and a chair. But the walls were covered with more than paint. There were copies of her poems and stills from movies about her life. The Chinese loved her. It was in her studio that she wrote her famous essay on lyric poetry, the verse form in which she had few peers. She wrote that lyric poetry was not simply the combination of words and melody but a form of poetry in which the tonal quality of each word was as important as its meaning. A lyric poem was a song. Li also wrote that lyric poetry should arise from real events but should reflect on the past as well. She didn't always follow that last requirement, but such was the reputation she achieved; lyric poets ever since have framed their compositions in the light of her rules.

The only thing over which I lingered was a calligraphic rendering of her poem "Summer Day" – the same poem I had seen earlier on one of the walls of her memorial hall in Chinan. But in this case the calligraphy had been freshly mounted and was being sunned on the grass in the courtyard. That was pretty much it. Despite my initial disappointment, I was actually relieved there was so little to see and hurried back across the park and up the steps to where I hoped my taxi was waiting. It was. But my driver wasn't alone. She had phoned her nineteen-year-old nephew thinking he could practice his English on the way to the train station. At least it distracted me from the time. We arrived with only minutes to spare. The driver, though, wanted to take a picture of her nephew with me on the steps, which took time I wasn't sure I had. Once she confirmed that one of the photos was okay, I waved goodbye and ran inside. Just as I reached the platform so did the train.

After working my way down the aisle, I had to roust a young man from my seat. The train was packed with students heading back to colleges and universities. It was Thursday, August 30, and classes were scheduled to begin the following Monday. Like students everywhere, each held some sort of electronic device. As a result, the car was strangely quiet. Everyone was pecking away, texting family and friends or playing video games. Ninety minutes later, I gave my seat back to the fellow I'd rousted and got off in Changchiu.

It wasn't a big town, and not many trains stopped there. Once again, there was a shortage of taxis. And once again, people shared. While I was walking down the street in search of a taxi of my own, a car pulled up next to me. It wasn't a taxi, but the driver asked me where I wanted to go. I told him Paimochuan, Hundred Springs Park. He said he would take me for 10RMB, and we were there in less than ten minutes. I paid the driver and asked him to wait. I told him I had other plans. At least this time I didn't have to hurry: there was no train to catch.

Like Fankungting in Chingchou, Paimochuan was another park laid out around a lake, and on the far side was another Li Ch'ing-chao memorial hall.

There were three such halls in China, and I had already visited the other two. Near the park entrance, a man was selling the heroes of Chinese opera made of colored sugar, and an old lady was selling books from the Communist period. I stopped to ask the woman whether she had any poetry by Mu Tan or Ai Ch'ing, my favorite poets of that otherwise unfortunate era. She shook her head, and I continued on, past bumper cars and a carousel whose horses were galloping to the most discordant music, which was thankfully drowned out by cicadas in full chorus. Before I knew it, I was standing in front of a bronze statue of Li Ch'ing-chao. It was based on a portrait of her when she was thirty-one. Next to the statue a plaque in English called her the greatest exemplar of the "euphemistic school of poetry." I loved the word "euphemistic." The Chinese phrase was *wan-yueh*, "graceful and to the point." On the wall behind the statue, carved in golden calligraphy, was an example of her euphemistic style, which she wrote to the melody "Sheng-sheng-man" 聲聲慢 (Sheng-Sheng Idle):

I keep searching the horizon
cold through and through
desolate and forlorn
while the weather keeps changing
it's so hard to feel at peace
how can a few cups of weak wine
ward off the evening wind
the geese overhead
a newly broken heart
and yet these are old friends

Piles of chrysanthemums cover the ground
flowers that withered and fell
no one can pick now
I watch from a window
hoping for darkness
the paulownia in another drizzling rain
drop after drop
until dusk
how can the word *sorrow*
do such a scene justice

尋尋覓覓，冷冷清清，淒淒慘慘戚戚，乍暖還寒時候，最難將息。
三杯兩盞淡酒，怎敵他晚來風急。雁過也，正傷心，卻是舊時相識。
滿地黃花堆積，憔悴損，如今有誰堪摘。守著窗兒，獨自怎生得黑。
梧桐更兼細雨，到黃昏，點點滴滴。這次第，怎一個愁字了得。

Her memorial hall was on the far side of a large pond. It was built on the site of her old home, where she was born and grew up. Behind the small hall that contained her statue, I followed a trail of stone slabs placed to keep people's shoes from getting wet. Due to recent rains, the five springs that formed the pond's Meihuachuan, or Plum Blossom Spring, were overflowing into the adjacent lake.

Next to the walkway, there was a shallow section of the pond where people could fill bottles with souvenir water. I did the opposite. I took out my flask and filled one of my small porcelain cups with bourbon and toasted the maiden of the euphemistic school. I took a sip then poured the rest into the pond. It's hard to find a good drinking companion, and I know Li Ch'ing-chao would have enjoyed the whiskey. Despite the sorrow that dogged her life, she was, after all, the Easily Contented Scholar.

I continued on and entered her old home. Decorating one of the walls of her reconstructed bedchamber was her poem "Reflection" 感懷, written in

One of several gushers at Plum Blossom Spring in Changchiu

1121 in Laichou, where her husband had been appointed magistrate after his rehabilitation and prior to his being recalled to the capital.

> Dreary window wobbly desk no good books
> I've ended up like poor Kung-lu
> from local wine and strings of coins
> and what fills the days with laughter
> I've retreated behind my door to write
> in this perfumed dwelling full of artful thoughts
> I've found true friends in the silence
> Sir Void and Mister Nothing

寒窗敗几無書史，公路可憐何至此。青州從事孔方君，終日紛紛喜生事。
作詩謝絕聯閉門，燕寢凝香有佳思。靜中吾乃得至交，烏有先生子虛子。

Kung-lu was the personal name of Yuan Shu, who tried to become emperor, following the fall of the Han dynasty, and ended up starving to death. Mister Nothing and Sir Void were two characters in an ode by the poet Ssu-ma Hsiang-ju (179–117 BC) and recalled similar useless yet sagacious characters in the work of Chuang-tzu. Li loved to cloak her life, as well as her poetry, in such images from the past. One of the caretakers told me that over the entrance at the other end of the park was a plaque with her father's calligraphy, but I had seen enough.

I walked back the way I came and paused to take a photograph of her statue. A drunken man in a suit who was being escorted by several other men in suits approached me and asked who she was. I couldn't help laughing, to which he took offense. I told him I was astonished that he didn't know the identity of his country's most famous poetess. It was cruel of me to admonish him like that, and I felt the sting he must have felt. He said nothing more and rejoined his friends. I, too, turned and left. Me and my big mouth.

I'd asked the driver to wait because I needed transportation back to Chinan. There wasn't another train for four hours, and a bus wouldn't have worked either. I wanted to make a stop in the countryside outside Chinan. I also thought I might hire him for the next two days – days that were going to involve a lot of uncertain roads as well as an overnight stay in the middle of nowhere. Relying on public transportation for that part of my journey would have been impossible. So I showed him my map and the route I had planned.

He thought about it for a minute then came up with the figure of 1,500 RMB or $250. It was about what I was hoping to pay, and off we drove.

On our way out of Changchiu, he pulled over next to a van waiting at the side of the road. The driver turned out to be his wife. She reached out her window and handed me a GPS device to give her husband. His surname was Lu, and he had never heard of the place I wanted to visit on the way to Chinan, much less the ones I wanted to visit the following day. I was impressed by his foresight.

With that out of the way, we headed for my final destination, which was in an area east of Chinan known as Licheng. I wanted to visit a memorial hall built in honor of another composer of lyric poetry — Li Ch'ing-chao's male counterpart — and I had a map that I had printed off the Internet. From Changchiu we took Highway 102 west, and when we reached the expressway that led to the Chinan airport, we started wandering around. And we wandered around for an hour, even *with* the GPS. It turned out the map I printed was missing a critical piece of information. I had failed to include one of the characters that made up the name of the village near the memorial hall. I typed "Feng-cha" instead of "Ssu-feng-cha." So whenever we stopped to ask directions, which we did half a dozen times, all we got were blank looks. Meanwhile, it was getting closer and closer to five o'clock when places such as memorial halls closed. The road gods, though, took pity on me — as they have time after time during my wanderings across China. Two women selling lotus roots on the side of the road knew exactly where it was. Five minutes later, we were there. We never would have found it without their help. It was down a nondescript dirt road and surrounded on all sides by farmland. Given the location, I was surprised there was anything at all. It was just an old, walled compound. The gate, though, was open, and it was five minutes to five.

Just inside the gate, half a dozen men were sitting under a pavilion. They were farmers, and their work for the day was done. Their bicycles were propped against the pavilion's railing, and they appeared to be waiting for the place to close. When I approached, the only man wearing a clean shirt stood up and asked me what I was doing there. I told him, and he said the memorial hall didn't close until 5:30, so I had plenty of time. I took that as a comment on the memorial hall — that thirty minutes would be more than enough. It turned out he wasn't a farmer. He was the caretaker, and he led me to the administration office to register. The place didn't get many visitors. I was only the second person that day, and there were no names in the register for the previous two days.

Hsin Ch'i-chi

The man then handed me a brochure, pointed me toward the three exhibition halls at the back of the compound, and returned to his friends. In front of the halls stood a warrior carved out of stone. It was the poet Hsin Ch'i-chi as a young man. He was born here in 1140 and grew up in a North China that had been conquered by the same Jurchens from whom Li Ch'ing-chao had fled. The Jurchens were a nomadic people who lived in northern Manchuria and who helped the Chinese defeat another nomadic group, the Khitans, who lived in southern Manchuria. Once the Khitans were out of the way, the Jurchens continued south and occupied all of North China.

Just past Hsin's statue were the exhibition halls. They echoed as I walked through them. It was as though funds were earmarked for the buildings but not for anything to put inside them. One of the halls included a few period pieces: a loom and a spinning wheel, a grain thresher and a brick oven-bed – the kind people in North China relied on to survive winters until quite recently.

Another hall had a series of panels depicting the events of Hsin Ch'i-chi's life. The event that brought him to the attention of his compatriots occurred when he was twenty-two. He joined a local army of resistance and urged others to do the same. Among those who followed his lead was a monk who turned out to be a traitor. One night the monk absconded with the commander's personal seal, the one he used to authenticate documents. When the commander discovered his seal missing he threatened to kill Hsin, since he had introduced the monk. Hsin said if he didn't come back with the seal in three days, he would gladly offer up his head. The next day, he rode straight into the enemy camp, located the monk, and brought back the missing seal along with the monk's head. The statue outside displayed the heroic demeanor with which he has been cloaked ever since. It was the image of a patriotic knight-errant, an image that has resonated with a lot of young men throughout Chinese history.

Eventually, Hsin joined the imperial forces and ended up in the same area as Li Ch'ing-chao – in and out of Hangchou, where the Sung court relocated after the invasion. If he wrote poems as a young man, they haven't survived. But as he grew older, he left behind hundreds, such as this one, which he wrote in 1188 to the tune "Ch'ou-nu-er" 醜奴兒 (Ugly Slave):

I didn't know the taste of sadness in my youth
I loved to climb towers
I loved to climb towers
and in my poems I forced myself to speak of sadness

Knowing the taste of sadness now too well
I start to speak of it but stop
I start to speak of it but stop
and say instead "What a chilly autumn day"

少年不識愁滋味，愛上層樓，愛上層樓，為賦新詞強說愁。
而今識得愁滋味，欲說還休，欲說還休，却道天凉好個秋。

In the last hall, there were several editions of his poems in a glass case but no copies for sale. In another case, there were several volumes containing articles from a Hsin Ch'i-chi conference held in Chinan in 1987. Apparently that was when the exhibition halls were built. Since I didn't see an appropriate place for an offering, I decided to save Hsin's share of whiskey for his grave. But it was 1,000 kilometers away, and I couldn't help wondering whether I would make it that far. The heat and the pace of my itinerary were beginning to wear on me, and it was only my second day.

As we pulled back onto the paved road, I made a note of the location for future reference: 300 meters north of the G20 expressway and 200 meters west of county road X053. Despite the train delay at the beginning of the day, and my mistaken map at the end of it, I had somehow managed to see everything I had hoped to. I thanked the road gods. Unfortunately they, too, called it quits at 5:30. As we entered Chinan, we hit rush-hour traffic. It took over an hour to drive the twenty-five kilometers from Licheng back to my place of rest.

I gave Mr. Lu 250RMB for his part of the day's excursion. He was happy with the amount, though when we returned to the subject of the next two days, which included an overnight in a town he had never heard of, the price rose from 1,500RMB to 1,800RMB. And it included a "friend" who, he said, would take over for him when he got tired. I told him I would think about it and call him later. After he left, I flagged down three taxis. Their drivers all wanted at least 1,800RMB for the first day and the same amount for the second day. Obviously, I was out of touch with the going rate – at least for big-city taxis. I called Mr. Lu and asked him to pick me up at seven o'clock the next morning. I needed to get an early start if I was going to visit all the places I hoped to before sundown.

With the next day's transportation arranged, I walked down the street looking for a place to eat. Finally, something easy. Less than a hundred meters from my hotel I entered the Tsaopao Paotzupu, which specialized, as its name indicated, in *pao-tzu*s (steamed buns). Naturally, I ordered a couple. I also ordered a dish that included some kind of wild vegetable mixed with a combination of soy pulp and eggs. I wished I had asked how they made it. It was superb. And it came with a plate of crepes. I also ordered shrimp with baby cabbages. Equally delicious. But trying to finish such a meal was one of the problems of traveling alone. I resolved to order less.

Meanwhile, back at Motel 168, I also resolved to avoid motels. I'm not sure why they're called "motels." They certainly aren't "motor hotels." They're simply cheap hotels, and they were springing up everywhere in China. I suppose this is because their rooms are functional, like motel rooms in America, and people are traveling more than they did before. At least the room was clean. And the air-conditioner worked. But the linoleum floor and the vinyl-covered furniture and the modular shower with so little room to turn around in that I gouged myself on one of the fixtures combined to form a disappointing end to an otherwise exhilarating day. What I really wanted was a bath, but hotels – and motels – in China were switching to shower stalls. I could see the sense in it, but baths weren't about sense. I was two days into my trip, and already I was whining.

Before I put Day 2 to sleep, I looked at the brochure the caretaker at the Hsin Ch'i-chi Memorial Hall had given me. It included a poem Hsin composed to the tune "Lin-chiang-hsien" 臨江仙 (Immortal at the River):

> I have so much planned for my sixty-third year
> it's hard to have regrets so soon
> the faults of my sixty-second year are clear
> I'll correct them beginning today
> and think about this again tomorrow
>
> When faults exceed virtues only wine can help
> why didn't I learn this sooner

as I put an end now to last year
let me drink with my guests while I'm "indisposed"
and write poems in reply while I'm drunk

六十三年無限事，從頭悔恨難追。
已知六十二年非。隻應今日是，後日又尋思。

少是多非惟有酒，何须過後方知。
從今休似去年时。病中留客飲，醉裏和人詩。

It was a New Year poem. The Chinese count their age from New Year's Day, not from their birthdays. Hence, it was an occasion for celebration and also for commiseration – in either case, wine. A few months after he wrote this, Hsin was called out of retirement – "indisposed" being a euphemism. I resolved to double his share of whiskey, assuming I found a place to share it with him. And with that I wished Chinan's lyric, euphemistic bards sweet dreams.

Mr. Lu arrived at seven o'clock. It was the only time I would be "on schedule" that day, or the next, but at least Day 3 *began* when it was supposed to. I got in the car's front seat. Sitting in the back was Mr. Lu's "friend," someone to take over the driving when he got tired. I imagined a pal who had nothing better to do. His pal turned out to be a very attractive young woman. Perhaps that explained why his price was as low as it was. This was going to be a paid vacation. I couldn't but wonder, though, what this woman was doing with *him*. I made no attempt at seeking an explanation. I was glad to set off on what I expected would be two difficult, but important, days trying to track down five poets in the middle of nowhere.

By leaving Chinan early, we at least missed the morning rush-hour traffic. But when we had the option of switching to an expressway, Mr. Lu stayed on the old highway. According to our arrangement, he agreed to follow a route of expressways I outlined for him on my map and to pay for all road tolls and gas. Since expressway tolls were much higher than those for local highways, when he saw an opportunity to stay on the local highway, he took it. It was my fault. I was tired from the previous two days and wasn't paying attention. I should have anticipated that. Chinese taxi drivers are among the cleverest people I've ever met. They know a lot more than the roads.

Once I realized what was going on, it was too late to turn back. We muddled on for another hour through local traffic. Finally, we saw a sign for an expressway entrance, and this time we followed it. It was a short reprieve. We had to exit thirty minutes later in order to cross the Yellow River. I wanted to visit Yushan, on the river's north shore. From the expressway exit, it was twenty kilometers to the bridge and another twenty to Yushan. I thought we could get there in an hour, maybe less. Mr. Lu and I were both counting on his GPS. But once we were across the river, it didn't recognize any of the names on the map I had printed off the Internet – unlike the previous day's, this map was correct. Nor were there signs for Yushan or any of the towns nearby. Apparently, none were important enough to warrant a sign, much less a direct road. Since Yushan was to the southwest, we took turns going west then south then west then south, stopping every ten minutes to ask directions. The directions were not always in agreement, but we persevered, and after two hours we finally arrived.

Like Nishan, Yushan was just a hill. And like Nishan, there was a surrounding wall and a gate where visitors paid an entry fee. The gate was open,

Spirit way to Ts'ao Chih's grave at the foot of Yushan

and over its archway were the words I was looking for: Grave of Ts'ao Chih. As I walked through, I found myself alone. Given the difficulty reaching the place, I wasn't surprised. The caretaker wasn't expecting anyone. He was sitting inside the ticket office eating lunch and said I was the first visitor that day. Most people, he said, came on Saturdays and Sundays. I was there on a Friday. After selling me an entry ticket he returned to his lunch, and I began my self-guided tour. It was just after eleven. I had hoped to get here by nine. Once again, I was a victim of looking at maps and plotting distances and assuming the road gods – and my driver – were on my side.

At least I was there, at Ts'ao Chih's grave, of which there are three. This one, sanctioned by officialdom, was where the poet asked to be buried. I followed the short walkway to the tombstone at the base of the mountain. On either side of the path were memorial pillars and mythical beasts, all carved out of large blocks of stone. It was the sort of "spirit way" usually reserved for a king or an emperor. I read an inscription on a stele next to the tombstone that outlined Ts'ao Chih's life and the periodic efforts over the centuries at honoring the site with shrine halls and pavilions. Although this was his official grave, not many scholars concurred. An excavation of the site in the early 1950s yielded some bones but no skull, and the bones subsequently and inexplicably disappeared. Still, it was a place to make an offering, and I acquainted the grave mound's resident spirit with another one, from Kentucky. I limited myself to a single cup, which I simply splashed on the tombstone. Given the heat, I didn't pour one for myself.

After paying my respects, I followed another path to a pavilion on top of the hill. I wanted to survey Ts'ao Chih's estate. Along the way, I came to a sign that pointed to a cave where China's first Buddhist hymns were composed. Yushan and the countryside around it constituted the last and largest of the fiefs given to Ts'ao Chih. He only lived here briefly in 229, but while he was here, he heard music coming from this cave. In addition to poetry, he was equally skilled in music. He wrote down the melodies he heard then added words. According to the account on the sign, his hymns made their way to the Wei-dynasty capital of Loyang, where they were used in court ceremonies and even in monasteries. Although Ts'ao Chih's hymns have since been lost, the sign extolled them as the first successful merging of Sanskrit and Chinese in song and as the inspiration for similar hymns in Korea and Japan. To honor such a development, Buddhist organizations from elsewhere in East Asia were helping finance the construction of a large shrine hall at the foot of the mountain.

Stopping to read the account at least gave me a chance to catch my breath. After wiping the sweat from my forehead, I continued up the path in what must have been hundred-degree heat. When I finally reached the pavilion at the summit, I sat down on a cement bench in the pavilion's shade. I wiped my forehead once more and looked out at the landscape. Just beyond the foot of Yushan was the Yellow River, about 300 meters away and as muddy as ever. Over the course of the past million years, it had oscillated like an unmanned fire hose and had filled in the sea with mud as far north as Beijing and nearly as far south as Shanghai. It was the Yellow River that made North China possible. Its present course was one of its favorites. It was the same course it took when Ts'ao Chih was alive. All the land I could see from the top of the hill once belonged to him. Among all the great Chinese poets of the past, he alone was a man of such means. He could have been king. But he drank too much, and he was star-crossed when it came to love.

Ts'ao Chih was born in 192, the third son of Ts'ao Ts'ao, one of China's most famous kings. After the breakup of the Han dynasty, Ts'ao Ts'ao gained control of North China but was never able to conquer the South. Hence, he called himself a king and not an emperor. Of his twenty-five sons, Ts'ao Chih was his favorite, and he attempted several times to make Ts'ao Chih his heir. Ts'ao Chih, though, was either drunk or too dismissive of imperial protocol to avail himself of such opportunities. Despite such flaws, if that was what they were, he still hoped to serve in some capacity and expressed such sentiments in "Dew on the Leek" 薤露行:

> There's no end to Heaven and Earth
> light and shade take turns
> people live but awhile
> suddenly we're dust in the wind
> I hoped to perform meritorious deeds
> to devote myself to my lord
> to assist my king with my talents
> with an open and unbiased heart
> swimming things honor dragons of the deep
> running things honor a unicorn
> if creatures can recognize virtue
> why not the gentlemen at court
> in the works compiled by Confucius
> the royal way is abundantly clear
> I offer this modest brush of mine
> to promote sweetness and style

天地無窮極，陰陽轉相因。人居一世間，忽若風吹塵。
願得展功勤，輸力於明君。懷此王佐才，慷慨獨不群。
鱗介尊神龍，走獸宗麒麟。蟲獸猶知德，何況於士人。
孔氏刪詩書，王業粲已分。騁我徑寸翰，流藻垂華芳。

Obviously, Ts'ao Chih's talents were not those of a warrior or a ruler but of a poet. He was terribly innocent. As long as his father was alive, his innocence was indulged. When his father died in 220, his elder brother, Ts'ao P'i, became king. Ts'ao P'i didn't share his father's appreciation for his younger brother and was jealous and fearful of his potential. As soon as Ts'ao P'i ascended the throne, he sent Ts'ao Chih away from the capital to live on a series of distant estates — though not so distant that he couldn't keep an eye on him. Ts'ao P'i also executed or banished his brother's friends and supporters and even killed another brother who he feared might conspire with Ts'ao Chih to overthrow him. From 221 until his death in 232, Ts'ao Chih was repeatedly forced to move from one place to another. He likened himself to a tumbleweed, as in his poem "Alas" 吁嗟篇:

This tumbleweed alas
in the world yet alone
forever cut off from its roots
day and night never resting
east and west down the Seven Highways
north and south beyond the Nine Byways
meeting a gust of wind
suddenly blown into the clouds
thinking to explore the ways of Heaven
I suddenly fell into a deep abyss
a whirlwind carried me to safety
back toward the fields I once knew
but heading south I was blown north
heading east I was blown west
where in this world can I stay
I'm here then I'm gone
drifting across the Eight Rivers
flying past the Five Peaks
wandering without a home
my hardships known to none
I wish I were orchard grass
burned up in the autumn fire
of course such an end would be painful
but I could then rejoin my old roots

吁嗟此轉蓬，　居世何獨然。　長去本根逝，　宿夜無休閒。
東西經七陌，　南北越九阡。　卒遇回風起，　吹我入雲間。
自謂終天路，　忽然下沈淵。　惊飇接我出，　故歸彼中田。
當南而更北，　謂東而反西。　宕宕當何依，　忽亡而復存。
飄颻周八澤，　連翩歷五山。　流轉無恆處，　誰知吾苦艱。
願為中林草，　秋隋野火燔。　磨滅豈不痛，　願與根荄連。

Alas, his roots wouldn't have him. And so he spent the last decade of
his life traveling back and forth across the Yellow River floodplain. Yushan
was Ts'ao Chih's final estate, which probably explains the grave here with
his name on it. He didn't die here, though. He died in Huaiyang. And south
of that town he has another grave. During the depredations of the Cultural

Revolution, it was opened and found to contain only the poet's clothes. Burying a person's clothes in one place and the body in another was an ancient custom stretching at least as far back as 5,000 years, to the Yellow Emperor. It provided people with another place to pay their respects. The consensus among scholars nowadays is that Ts'ao Chih's real grave isn't at Yushan or Huaiyang but south of Kaifeng between the towns of Chihsien and Tunghsu. That was where he spent most of his final decade. It was 300 kilometers from Yushan and was where we headed next.

After driving back to the bridge and the expressway on the other side, we turned southwest, toward Kaifeng. Knowing I wouldn't need to make a decision regarding our direction or the road for several hours, I took a nap. I even convinced Mr. Lu to roll up the windows and turn on the air-conditioning. And so I dozed off thinking about Ts'ao Chih. I kept coming back to his heart, which was, I concluded, the reason for his excessive drinking and for his poor relationship with his elder brother.

When he was thirteen, he fell in love with the twenty-three-year-old Lady Chen, who had been given to his brother as spoils of war. The following year, she bore her husband a son, who would later become emperor. Ts'ao P'i, though, tired of Lady Chen. As soon as their father died, he not only made himself king, he made himself emperor. He then ordered Lady Chen to commit suicide and elevated one of his concubines to become his empress. He also ordered Ts'ao Chih to leave the capital. The following year, Ts'ao Chih wrote his most famous poem, "Homage to Lady Chen." After Ts'ao Chih's death, her son had the title changed to avoid disgracing his mother's memory. Ever since then, it has been known as "Ode to the Spirit of the Lo" 洛神賦, the Lo being the river that flowed through Loyang as well as the name of the spirit of the drowned daughter of Nu Wa, mythical mother of the Chinese race. The conceit that gave the poem its voice was a dialogue between the earthbound poet and Lady Chen's departing spirit. The poem is over 130 lines long, and this is how it ends:

> As she passed that northern isle
> and crossed those southern hills
> and turned her alabaster neck
> and clear and lovely eyes
> her crimson lips then parted
> laying bare our knotted web
> "The ways of spirit and mortal differ

alas our youthful years didn't match"
lifting her sleeve she wiped her eyes
as tear after tear streaked her robe
"This happy moment must end forever
I leave alas for a different land
I offer my endless love
and these earrings from the Southland.
Into the realm of shadows I fade
but my heart remains with my lord"
suddenly I saw her no longer
her spirit vanished and the light disappeared

於是越北沚，過南岡，紆素領，回清陽，動朱唇以徐言，陳交接之大綱。
恨人神之道殊兮，怨盛年之莫當。抗羅袂以掩涕兮，淚流襟之浪浪。
悼良會之永絕兮，哀一逝而異鄉。無微情以效愛兮，獻江南之明璫。
雖潛處於太陰，長寄心於君王。忽不悟其所舍，悵神宵而蔽光。

In many of his poems, Ts'ao Chih flies off into the clouds to dwell among the Taoist immortals on the Cinnabar Hills or in the Islands of the Blessed. Here, though, he is pinned by love to the world in which we all dwell. And yet, he never gave up trying to reach those pure, ethereal realms extolled by Taoists. Clearly, he was influenced by the elegiac flights of Ch'u Yuan, who lived 500 years earlier in what Lady Chen refers to here as "the Southland." Like Ch'u Yuan, Ts'ao Chih hoped his pure counsel would bring peace to the land. And like Ch'u Yuan, he failed. He died from illness at the age of forty and was buried in the countryside east of Tunghsu.

Four hours after leaving Yushan, we took the Tunghsu exit, which connected us with a local highway that led us east to Changchih, where we then turned north. The final four kilometers, we passed through a series of three villages all named Chiputsun, or Seven Step Village. All the houses were made of mud bricks—as they had been for the past 3,000 years. Some, though, had tiled fronts. The advances of civilization were reaching the countryside in Honan province ever so slowly. Finally, we reached the third village. To distinguish it from the others, it was called Rear Seven Step Village. This was where Ts'ao Chih's grave was located and also where his brother planned to execute him.

It was the one story about Ts'ao Chih just about every Chinese has heard. It seems that Ts'ao P'i was convinced his younger brother was planning to rebel and decided to confront him at the estate to which he had sent him. Despite finding no military preparations or other signs of rebellion, Ts'ao P'i was determined to execute his brother then and there. However, instead of simply ordering his brother killed, he proposed a challenge: if before Ts'ao Chih walked seven steps he could compose a poem about brotherly love without using the word "brother," the emperor would spare him. Ts'ao Chih then composed his famous "Poem in Seven Steps" 七步詩:

> Cooking beans to make soup
> we strain the pods for the broth
> the stalks heat the pot from below
> and the beans fill the pot with tears
> growing from the very same root
> why are you burning to hurt me

煮豆持作羹，漉豉以為汁。其向釜下然，豆在釜中泣。
本是同根生，相煎何太急。

Ts'ao Chih's poem was what the Chinese called a *shih:* a verse with equal line lengths and alternating-line rhymes — like the poems that made up the *Shihching* (Book of Poetry). And he would have sung it, as poets writing in this style still do today. Ts'ao Chih also wrote *fu,* or odes, that included lines of varying length that were not necessarily sung. And he wrote *yueh-fu,* or ballads, that were a little like both. His greatest contribution to Chinese poetry, though, were his *shih.* But instead of the four-syllable lines of the Book of Poetry, he used five-syllable lines. That single extra syllable gave him room to do much more, and he became one of China's great masters of this new poetic form that would dominate Chinese poetry for the next 500 years and beyond. Of course, Chinese is a tonal language, and the combination of tones is equally important. It wasn't only Ts'ao Chih's use of the five-syllable line that set him apart but also his sense of song. He was a musician, as most Chinese poets were until modern times.

And there we finally were, where Ts'ao Chih saved his life with a poem about beans. Mr. Lu stopped outside the gate of the village's only walled compound. Over the gate were the words again: Grave of Ts'ao Chih. It was just after five o'clock. I got out and gave the gate a push, but it was locked. Through the crack where the two halves met, I could see several men talking beneath a pavilion. I knocked as loud as I could, and several villagers

Ts'ao Chih's grave at Seven Step Village

yelled on my behalf. A minute later, a man appeared and unlocked the gate. As I walked inside, half the village followed. I can't imagine many foreigners had visited before.

The compound included about an acre of land, all of it dirt, except for a few dozen poplars in need of a good rain. The walls only enclosed the front half of the compound. The back half merged with several farmhouses and the playground of Seven Step Village Elementary. In the middle of the grounds was a lone, dilapidated pavilion with a stele underneath that recorded the history of the site. After reading what parts I could, I walked over to the grave. In front of the mound were a cement incense trough and a cement altar. I saw some incense burning and asked the caretaker whether any of Ts'ao Chih's descendants lived in the village. He said some people in Tunghsu claimed to be related, but no one in the village. He lit incense out of respect every evening before going home.

Not long after Ts'ao Chih was buried here, the grave's location was forgotten. The reason wasn't a lack of respect but the Yellow River. One of its periodic floods obliterated the site, along with everything else in this region. When the floodwaters receded and people came back to reclaim their land, the grave mound was no longer visible. It was buried beneath mud, and it stayed buried until 1470, when another flood exposed its interior stone doors, which bore the inscription Grave of Ts'ao Chih. Since the grave's rediscovery, several shrines had been built on the site. One by one they too were swept away by floods. Given the relative remoteness of the place, I wasn't surprised that no plans seemed to be underway for a new one.

After setting out my own offering and letting the fragrance of the whiskey make its way to the spirit world, I picked up one of the cups and raised it in honor of the poet with the broken heart. I also offered one to the caretaker. As he downed his share, his eyes widened with surprise. It was the Stagg. While he smacked his lips in approval, I finished my cup and poured the third cup on the grave. I stayed long enough to take a few photographs and to amuse the crowd of villagers with a brief account of why I was there, traveling through China drinking with poets whose poetry I loved. It didn't matter that they were dead. I wasn't. And what was life for anyway if not to thank those who made our lives happier? Such was my spiel. It was six o'clock when we left.

After navigating twenty kilometers of rush-hour country traffic on a series of bad roads, we reached Tunghsu at seven. Tunghsu wasn't on the itinerary. The itinerary called for visiting the grave of another poet west of there before ending the day, but Tunghsu was as far as we got. Although it wasn't much of a town, I was hoping to find a hotel. As we drove down Liberation Road, Mr. Lu pointed out the Yingpin, or Welcome Guesthouse. I was hoping for something better and asked him to continue on to what looked like the town's main intersection. It was manned by traffic police, and I got out and asked one of the policemen to recommend a place for the night. He pointed back to the Yingpin. It was the town's one and only one-star option. After dropping me off, Mr. Lu and his companion left to spend the night elsewhere. At least the Yingpin was sufficiently old that my bathroom had a bathtub. I don't remember dinner, but I do remember filling the tub with hot water and thinking that any day ending with a hot bath was a good day.

Mr. Lu and his friend picked me up at the hotel at eight. The sky had clouded up during the night, and the temperature was only in the eighties. The difference was noticeable. As we headed toward my first destination of the day, it was almost pleasant, as long as the car windows remained open and we kept moving. From Tunghsu, we drove through the countryside in a southwesterly direction. Thankfully, all the roads were paved. It was another zigzag journey with frequent stops to ask directions. The place I was looking for was forty kilometers from Tunghsu, and it took an hour to get there, which was good, considering how uncertain we were of whether the roads we took were the right roads. Our uncertainty ended when a farmer said the next village was Juanchuang (Juan Manor). Sure enough, just north of Juan Manor, I saw what I was looking for and asked Mr. Lu to pull over. I got out and walked through a field of corn and then a field of bell peppers toward a grave mound. A stone stele off to the side confirmed that this was, indeed, the grave of Juan Chi (210–263).

Juan Chi followed Ts'ao Chih as the second major poet of the third century. Like Ts'ao Chih, he was a member of the aristocracy. His father served as an official at the court of Ts'ao Chih's father, and various family members served during the reigns of Ts'ao Chih's brother and nephew. However, as Juan Chi was growing up, control of the court began to shift from the Ts'ao clan to the Ssu-ma clan. Many historians view this as the most dangerous period at court in all of Chinese history, which is saying a lot. Assassinations and executions were common. Juan Chi had close ties to both clans, which placed him in a precarious position. Many of his friends and relatives were killed for nothing more than their associations. Juan Chi managed to avoid a similar fate by getting drunk or feigning madness whenever pressed for political views or expressions of allegiance.

The madness and drinking came easy. Juan Chi was the most prominent member of a group of eccentrics known as the Seven Sages of the Bamboo Grove. In addition to his seemingly dysfunctional lifestyle, he was also known for his music. One of his compositions for the zither, "Wine Crazy," is still played today. His fame, though, rested on his poetry, in particular a series of eighty-two poems he titled *Songs from the Heart* 詠懷, distinguished both by their honesty and by their metaphorical overlay that enabled Juan to survive such honesty. In front of his tombstone, I poured us both an early morning shot of elixir and read aloud the poem that begins his collection:

Late at night unable to sleep
I sat up and played my zither
moonlight shone through the curtains
a cool breeze ruffled my robe
in the distant wilds a lone goose cried
above the north woods a circling bird called
this way then that searching for something
while anxious thoughts troubled my heart

夜中不能寐，起坐彈鳴琴。薄帷鑒明月，清風吹我襟。
孤鴻號外野，翔鳥鳴北林。徘徊將何見，憂思獨傷心。

On the surface, Juan's poems seem simple and serene. The simplicity and serenity, though, disappear when one considers his images. The lone goose and circling bird, for example, express the tension between cultivating virtue in the wilds and serving at court — the court at the time being located in the northern part of Loyang. It was the old Confucian conundrum: to put one's talents in the service of the state or to cultivate one's virtue in seclusion. Like Ts'ao Chih, Juan Chi hoped to serve, but he saw no safe perch.

Grave of Juan Chi

In such a setting, one poem didn't seem enough. So I read number 21 in the same series:

The moment today I think about still
the sun's chariot was about to depart
pulling back my sleeve I grasped my sword
looking up I watched the clouds advance
in the clouds I saw an ink-black crane
calling with all its heart
disappearing into a darkening sky
never to be heard in this world again
unwilling to consort with pigeons
or to join the flock at court

於心懷寸陰，義陽將欲冥。揮袂撫長劍，仰觀浮雲征。
雲間有玄鶴，抗志揚哀聲。一飛沖青天，曠世不再鳴。
豈與鶉鷃遊，連翩戲中庭。

Here Juan Chi admires the crane, which represents the liberated Taoist immortal, and disdains the pigeons wheeling in unison over the capital and covering the court with their crap. Transcendence was his lifelong passion. Even if he didn't succeed in his quest, the poetry such a quest inspired was treasured by all the great poets of the T'ang and Sung dynasties. Poets such as Li Pai and Tu Fu modeled their own *Songs from the Heart* on Juan's. I couldn't help wondering why he wasn't better known. Maybe it was the mask of madness and drunkenness he wore. Or maybe it was all those metaphors he hid behind.

I didn't really need an answer. I drained my cup, emptied his on his grave, then inspected the steles lined up on either side of the mound. They were new and had been placed there over the past two decades by his descendants. Someone remembered. Seeing a farmer working nearby, I walked over and asked whether there was anything else connected with Juan Chi in the area. He said there used to be a shrine hall just south of the grave mound, but it was destroyed during the Cultural Revolution. There were still a few Juan family graves in the grove of trees where the shrine hall once stood, he said, but that was it. I thanked him and walked back to Mr. Lu's car. I was done with the grave but not with Juan Chi. My next destination was where he lived, which was the town of Weishih thirty kilometers to the west.

Like Tunghsu, Weishih was a county seat surrounded by farmland, and all the roads that led us there were country roads. It took us an hour to drive those thirty kilometers. Weishih, though, looked more prosperous. Maybe it was just market day. The streets were crowded, and so were the sidewalks. That Weishih had sidewalks also distinguished it from Tunghsu. It was already an ancient town when Juan Chi lived here. As we drove down the main street, we stopped a few times to ask directions. For a change, everyone we asked knew what we were looking for, and we were there in a matter of minutes.

Juan Chi lived at the northeast corner of the town's East Lake. The home was long gone, and the only thing that marked the spot was a cement dais with Juan's statue on top. Underneath were the words Hsiao T'ai (Droning Tower). There were a dozen steles on either side. Like those at the grave, they were recent and had been placed there by Juan Chi's descendants from as far away as Singapore. Also, decorating the sides of the dais were copies of poems written by visitors in the past, including two poets on my list, Chia Tao and Su Tung-p'o. It turned out I was one in a long line of pilgrims.

Juan Chi's Droning Tower, or what was left of it, was off to the side, reduced to a dirt mound. It wasn't more than six or seven meters high, but it still took me a minute to climb to the top, which I managed to do by grabbing hold of tree roots exposed by erosion. The hill once served as the tower's base. The original tower was built of bricks and wood to a height of thirty meters, and it had been rebuilt several times. The most recent version was destroyed during World War II.

I should mention that I only recently found out what such a tower was used for. In my earlier translations of the word *hsiao*, I invariably opted for "whistle" rather than "drone." It seemed to make sense, and all the dictionaries agreed. However, once I began looking deeper, I discovered that in the mouths of Taoists *hsiao* had a very different meaning and involved breathing out in a way that could be heard for miles. Such droning was done from

Remains of Juan Chi's Droning Tower

the top of a hill or a raised platform. None of the Taoists I've spoken with, however, have been able to tell me how to do it. Either the regimen behind such a skill has died out, or such knowledge is transmitted in secret.

In Juan Chi's day droning was considered an art worthy of any gentleman interested in a life beyond the crowd. Juan's contemporary Ch'eng Tzuan (231–273) wrote a long poem about it titled "Ode to Droning," 嘯賦, which was later collected in the sixth-century literary anthology known as the *Wenhsuan.* Ch'eng began by describing how practitioners climb to a height and focus their thoughts on what is subtle and distant with such intensity that they become oblivious of themselves. Once this is achieved, they give rise to:

> a sound not dependent on an instrument
> a technique free of tools
> using what one has at hand
> focusing the mind and controlling the breath
> you move your lips and a tune appears
> you open your mouth and a sound comes forth
> whatever you meet or encounter
> inspires a response in song
> it isn't discordant when it's loud
> it doesn't sound weak when it's faint
> it's purer and more piercing than a flute
> softer and more refined than a zither
> ethereal enough to reach the realm of spirits
> subtle enough to probe the deepest depths
> creatures all dance and tap their feet
> phoenixes prance and flap their wings
> ....
> know then the wonder of droning
> is the pinnacle of sounds

聲不假器，用不借物，近取諸身，役心御氣。
動脣有曲，發口成音，觸類感物，因歌隨吟。
大而不洿，細而不沈，清激切於箏笙，優潤和於瑟琴。
玄妙足以通神悟靈，精微足以窮幽測深。
百獸率儛而抃足，鳳皇來儀而拊翼。。。
乃知長嘯之奇妙，此音聲之至極。

According to scholars, it was something akin to the overtone singing still practiced by certain Central Asian pastoral tribes such as the Tuvans. The focus, though, was on the generation of *ch'i* and not on the sound itself. It was part of Taoist training. Standing there where Juan Chi once practiced this art, I read poem 5 of his heartfelt series:

> Those early years of my life
> I indulged in music and song
> I traveled west to Hsienyang
> where I met the rich and the famous
> but before the revelry ended
> suddenly the sun slipped away
> I spurred my horse and headed home
> and gazed on the rivers of Loyang again
> having squandered a fortune of gold
> I was pressed to meet even simple expenses
> to the north stretched the road to Taihang
> but not for someone as lost as me

平生少年時，輕薄好弦歌。西游咸陽中，趙李相經過。
娛樂未終極，白日忽蹉跎。驅馬復來歸，反顧望三河。
黃金百鎰盡，資用嘗苦多。北臨太行道，失路將如何。

Juan Chi doesn't hide behind metaphors in this poem but takes on the persona of someone who seeks transcendence through the pursuit of pleasure. He imagines himself traveling to Hsienyang, the ancient capital of the defunct Ch'in dynasty, just west of the modern city of Sian. Hsienyang was sufficiently removed from Loyang in time and space that it was safe to use as a setting for his critique of excess. In the court of the past, Juan joins its pleasure-seekers and squanders his fortune. He finally returns home impoverished and unable to escape the tedium to which he is now heir. All he can do is look in vain toward the Taihang Mountains north of Loyang on the other side of the Yellow River. That was where Juan Chi and his six friends established their famous Bamboo Grove: the never-never land of the third century. It was on my itinerary, but not that day. I clambered down from Juan Chi's dirt hill and resumed my journey.

From Weishih, we continued west toward Hsincheng. It was fifty kilometers away, and my next destination was on the other side. Hsincheng was one of China's oldest cities. It was where the Yellow Emperor first established the dominion of the Han Chinese over North China around 2600 BC. I didn't have time, though, for the Yellow Emperor and had planned to drive straight through. But the road we hoped would lead us through the center of town was under construction. We had to circle around from the south. That road *also* turned out to be under construction. It took us nearly two hours to reach Hsincheng's western outskirts, where every road was also being torn up, including the one I was hoping would lead me to my next poet. The city was making its move into the twenty-first century all at once.

This was one of those times when close was not good enough. We kept stopping to ask, but the directions didn't agree. We followed them all, and eventually one of them turned out to be right. We finally reached the village of Tungkuossu, or East Wall Temple. The temple was gone, but I was hoping the residence of one of its native sons would still be there, or at least something marking the site. Mr. Lu parked, and I went looking for it. An old man walking along the roadside directed me to the local primary school and followed me into the schoolyard.

This was the birthplace of Pai Chu-yi (772–846), whose poems nearly everyone in China once memorized and understood. When Pai's grandfather was serving as a local official east of Loyang, he became friends with a man who was serving in Hsincheng and paid the man a visit. He liked the area so much that he moved his family to this village. This was where his grandson was born, and I was hoping there would be something left of the place – which isn't as absurd as it might sound, at least not in China, where poets are among the most respected members of its civilization. I thought maybe there would be some sort of memorial hall or shrine.

Inside the school's front gate, my self-appointed guide proceeded to tell me about the place. He turned out to be the village headman and also the former principal of the school, which was named, appropriately, Pai Chu-yi Elementary. He said the original homesite was now the school playground, which included two basketball courts and half a dozen ping-pong tables. Commemorating the site's historical importance was a billboard with various bits of information about the village's famous resident. While it didn't say anything I didn't already know, it *did* include two poems I hadn't read before. Pai Chu-yi was one of China's more prolific poets, leaving behind over 3,000 poems. One of the poems on the billboard was titled "Grass" 草. It was Pai Chu-yi's earliest surviving poem, written when he was sixteen, and was about seeing off a friend:

The grass that covers the plain
every year it withers and thrives
brush fires can't burn it up
when spring winds blow it reappears
its subtle fragrance reclaims the old paths
its sunlit color reconnects distant towns
here where I see my friend off again
it fills our parting with its efflorescence

離離原上草，一歲一枯榮。野火燒不盡，春風吹及生。
遠芳侵古道，晴翠接荒城。又送王孫去，萋萋滿別情。

In the final couplet, Pai borrowed his phrasing from Ch'u Yuan's "Summoning a Hermit" 招隱士: "My noble friend has left but hasn't yet returned / spring grass meanwhile spreads its efflorescence" 王孫遊兮不歸, 春草生兮萋萋. He was comparing his friend to a would-be recluse. I was amazed to think that at sixteen, Pai had already identified the dialectic that would dominate his own life: to serve or not to serve. The billboard also included a second poem, "Spending the Night in Jungyang" 宿滎陽 — Jungyang being an old name for Hsincheng, around whose chaos we had just driven. Pai Chu-yi stopped there one night in 828 on his way to Loyang and left this behind:

Jungyang was where I was born
I was still young when we moved away
after forty years of rambling
I'm sleeping in Jungyang again
I was eleven or twelve when we left
this year I'll be fifty-six
I recall playing as a child
as if it were before my eyes
but once we left we lost our place
no relatives live here anymore
the town and its markets aren't all that have changed
the hills and valleys are different
only the waters of the local rivers
still follow their old thoughtless course

生長在滎陽，少小辭鄉曲。迢迢四十載，復到滎陽宿。
去時十一二，今年五十六。追思兒戲時，宛然猶在目。
舊去失處所，故里無宗族。豈惟變市朝，兼亦遷陵谷。
獨有溱洧水，無情依舊綠。

Honan was the flattest province in China. Armies swept across it at will, as did floods. Pai Chu-yi's father finally moved the family to a safer place, and his son finished growing up elsewhere. I didn't pull out the bourbon. Not for someone that young. Nor would a schoolyard have been the right spot. I planned to visit other places where Pai Chu-yi lived, places where he would appreciate some liquid inspiration from across the sea. I thanked my guide and waved to the schoolchildren who were looking out of their classroom windows, wondering what planet I was from. I had disrupted their classes. Fortunately, leaving was easier than arriving. Thanks to our guide's directions, Mr. Lu had no trouble finding his way back to the old highway that led west, away from Hsincheng.

I was happy to be back on mud-free pavement. The smoothness of the road could have put me to sleep, and I had to remind myself to pay attention. My next stop was less than ten kilometers away. As we approached the town of Hsintien, I saw a sign. That was new. An actual sign. We turned onto a country road and three kilometers later pulled up outside a memorial hall built to honor Ou-yang Hsiu (1007–1072).

This was also the location of Ou-yang's grave, but it wasn't where he was first buried. He died in Fuyang, 300 kilometers to the southeast, and was buried there. He had fallen in love with that city's West Lake during an earlier assignment and retired to Fuyang in 1071. It was an all-too-brief retirement: he died the following year. Three years later, the emperor ordered Ou-yang's body moved closer to the capital to make visits easier. Once this spot outside Hsintien was chosen, it became the family burial ground. It still holds the graves of Ou-yang Hsiu's third and last wife, his four sons, and a grandson. Although the old shrine hall and even the trees were leveled during the Cultural Revolution, the place had been recently restored, and the grounds were quite lovely.

I followed a winding cedar-lined path to the very back of the grounds and set out my usual offering in front of Ou-yang's grave and the grave of his wife. While the fragrance rose to the heavens, I read him a poem that he composed to the tune "Picking Mulberries" 采桑子. It was the last of ten poems he wrote in Fuyang just before he died. Having served there as a mere

Graves of Ou-yang Hsiu and his wife

magistrate twenty years earlier, he returned in the red-wheeled carriage of a retired high official. And yet, he couldn't help sigh:

> Having long been enchanted by West Lake
> I've returned in this crimson carriage
> on the drifting clouds of fame and fortune
> twenty springs gone in the blink of an eye
> like a crane I've come back from a distant journey
> but the people who live in this city
> everyone I meet is new
> no one recognizes the magistrate who served here so long ago

平生為愛西湖好，來擁朱輪。富貴浮雲。俯仰流年二十春。
歸來恰似遼東鶴，城郭人民。觸目皆新。誰識當年舊主人。

Of China's major poets, Ou-yang Hsiu was a rare bird in that his career was so successful. He got along with everyone, even his political opponents, and he served in senior positions in the courts of several emperors. His accomplishments also distinguished him. He was simultaneously one of the dynasty's greatest statesmen, historians, essayists, calligraphers, and, of course, poets. Equally remarkable was that he grew up in relative poverty and without a father's guidance. Like the Confucian philosopher Mencius, he had a devoted mother.

After paying my respects at his grave, I moved on to the exhibition halls that told the story of his life. In one hall there was a painting of him listening to the night wind and composing his "Ode to the Sounds of Autumn" 秋聲賦:

> Alas
> plants and trees have no feelings
> their time comes and they wither
> among creatures only we humans
> are sensitive to such things
> our minds burdened by a hundred cares
> our bodies wearied by ten thousand tasks
> something moves us
> and it shakes our marrow
> especially when we consider what we can't do
> or we worry about what we can't understand
> how quickly our skin becomes wrinkled
> or how silently our hair turns white
> but why am I comparing something so fragile
> with something as glorious as a plant or a tree
> when I think how they're battered and beaten
> how I hate the sounds of autumn

嗟呼，草木之無情，有時而飄零。人為動物，惟物之靈。
百憂感其心，萬物勞其形。有動於中，必搖其精。
而況思其力之所不及，憂其智之所不能。
宜其渥然丹者為槁木，黟然黑者為星星。
奈何以非金石之質，欲與草木而爭榮。
念誰為之戕賊，亦何恨乎秋聲。

Ou-yang's poetry had an openness and casualness that reflected his personality. He never let the rules of poetic meter or form stand in the way of a good line. As I continued through the halls, I was surprised that for such an out-of-the-way place the displays were so well done. I was impressed by one in particular. It was a piece of calligraphy by Su Tung-p'o (1037–1101). Along with Ou-yang Hsiu, Su was one of China's most famous calligraphers. In fact, Su was Ou-yang's protégé. In 1091, twenty years after his mentor's death, Su wrote out Ou-yang's "Record of Drunkard's Pavilion" 醉翁亭記. And here it was, preserved in the exhibition hall's glass case.

When officials were out of favor, assuming they weren't executed, they were posted far from the capital, the distance depending on the severity of the judgment against them. Ou-yang Hsiu suffered a number of such rustications, but they were of the 500-kilometer variety. For more severe judgments, officials were sent 1,000 or even 1,500 kilometers away. On one of his 500-kilometer "assignments," Ou-yang was sent to serve as magistrate of Chuchou, not far from Nanking. He often hiked along the stream that flowed from the top of nearby Langyashan and liked the scenery so much that he built a pavilion beside the stream. He commemorated its construction with an inscription that ended:

The birds know the joys of the mountains and forests, but they don't know the joys of the people. And the people know the joys of accompanying the Magistrate on his hikes, but they don't know the joy their joy gives the Magistrate. He who can share the joy of others while drunk and describe it while sober, this is the Magistrate. And who is the Magistrate? Ou-yang Hsiu of Luling.

然而禽鳥知山林之樂，而不知人之樂。人知從太守遊而樂，而不知太守之樂其樂也。醉能同其樂，醒能述以文者，太守也。太守謂誰。廬陵歐陽修也。

Su Tung-p'o's rendering of this inscription is one of China's most famous calligraphic treasures. Copies have been carved on stone since the Ming dynasty, and a rubbing of one such carving was on display in the case before me. Calligraphy was such a powerful art, a brush-dance on paper or silk. I tried my hand—and arm—at it, but I could never muster the strength or the focus. In the 1970s, when I was living in the farming village of Bamboo Lake on a mountain north of Taipei, I ground my ink and practiced every day. And once a week I came down the mountain and joined four fellow students for a lesson at the home of Chuang Yen. Chuang was curator of the Palace Museum's painting and calligraphy collection and the most famous calligrapher in Taiwan. Every week he reviewed our work then unrolled one of the museum's treasures on his living room table to inspire our submissions for the following week. After a year, I gave up. I was not a brush dancer. There was no room for hesitation or reflection. It was a performance art. And here in front of me was one of the greatest performances by one of China's greatest calligraphers. I tried to take a photograph, but the reflection from the display case made that impossible. I gave up and headed back to the car.

As I walked back through the grounds, I was gratified to find a statue of Ou-yang Hsiu's widowed mother teaching her son calligraphy. Lacking the means to send her son to school, let alone to hire tutors, she broke off a reed and taught her son to write characters in the sand. Next to her statue was one of young Ou-yang Hsiu writing in his sandbox. That's what I should have done. I made a note: remember to build a sandbox next life.

Rejoining Mr. Lu, I told him I had one last stop: the grave of Ou-yang's protégé. Just outside Hsintien, we entered an actual expressway and headed south. The experience of going a hundred kilometers per hour lasted a whole hour. At the exit for Chiahsien, we returned to earth then headed west on Highway 238. Just past the village of Hsuehtien, I saw the sign I was looking for, but it had changed since my last visit. Instead of Three Su Cemetery, it announced Three Su Park. Also, the road was much wider, and paved. While parks and paved roads weren't necessarily a bad thing, they weren't necessarily a good thing either. I reserved my judgment as to what might lie ahead.

The road wound past a low hill named Chuntientai. Atop this hill around 2600 BC, the Yellow Emperor conducted the ceremony that established his dominion, and that of the Han Chinese, over what later became known as China. I considered going for a hike to see what was there, but the day was already half-over, and I still had a long way to go. We continued past fields of cotton and corn until the road ended seven kilometers later at a parking lot that could have held a hundred buses. That was the downside of paved roads. They made getting to places so much easier, and people wanted to go places. They had the time and the money now. And yet, there were only two taxis and not a single bus. I didn't question the will of the gods and accepted their largesse.

My two previous visits, I was able to drive to within a short walk of the gravesite. Now that the place had been upgraded to a recreation area, the new parking lot was much farther away. At least the area around the gravesite hadn't changed. The final 200 meters still led past the same row of ancient cedars and the same series of huge stone figures usually reserved for the approach to an emperor's tomb. Beyond them I bypassed the shrine hall I had visited before and headed for the graves. As the name of the place indicated, there were three of them: three small grass-covered mounds with a stone altar in front of each – the grave of Su Hsun flanked by those of his two sons, Su Tung-p'o and Su Tzu-you.

The Sus are the most celebrated literary family in Chinese history. All three are ranked among the greatest writers of the Sung dynasty. No other family ever achieved such a distinction. I had never read any of the father's works, but I was familiar with those of his sons. In my translation of Lao-tzu's *Taoteching*, I quoted extensively from the younger son's commentary, and I had been reading the older son's poetry ever since I started reading Chinese poetry. And here I was at his grave again. This time, though, I brought something to share.

Since I was the only person there, I took the place over. I set out a cup on each altar then read two of the older son's poems. The first was one of his earliest, "On the River, Looking at Mountains" 江上看山, in which he recorded his impressions of sailing down the Min River:

From our boat I watched mountains race by like horses
herds in the hundreds passing in a flash
those ahead diverging suddenly changing shape
those behind merging running away in fright
looking up I saw a narrow winding trail
and in the mist above someone hiking
I waved from the boat and started to yell
but our sail flew past like a bird heading south

船上看山如走馬，倏忽過去數百群。前山槎枒忽變態，後嶺雜沓如驚奔。
仰看微徑斜繚繞，上有行人高縹緲。舟中舉手欲與言，孤帆南去如飛鳥。

He wrote this in 1059, when he was twenty-two. He and his younger brother were accompanying their father from their home south of Chengtu to Kaifeng, 2,000 kilometers away, to begin their careers as officials. Following their arrival at the Sung capital, their lives would be forever in transit. It wasn't a dangerous time to be at court, not like when Ts'ao Chih and Juan

Chi were in Loyang, but factional disputes and shifting allegiances were an inescapable part of their lives. Along with Ou-yang Hsiu, the Sus were in the Conservative faction and constantly at odds with the Reform faction, led by such fellow poets as Wang An-shih. Despite the relative civility of their disputes, rustication, outright exile, and even imprisonment were common, and both brothers suffered such expressions of disfavor. Hence, they were seldom together once they began their careers.

One occasion came in 1094 toward the end of their lives. The younger brother had been posted to Juchou, west of where I was standing, and the older brother had been ordered into exile, this time to the farthest reaches of the empire, near Vietnam. The brothers spent several days hiking in the countryside around Juchou, and one of the places they visited was the small hill I passed where the Yellow Emperor conducted his ceremony. Standing on top of the hill, the brothers surveyed the landscape to the north and were struck by how similar it looked to the landscape near their home in Szechuan. They decided to buy a piece of land at the foot of the hill to the north, which was called Lotus Mountain, and to make that the family cemetery. That was the last time they were together. Su Tung-p'o died in 1101 on his way back from exile, and his brother died eleven years later.

Despite their constant separation, no two brothers in China's long literary history were closer, and they got together whenever they could. Their favorite time was the full moon of autumn. Watching the moon cross the Milky Way – or Silver River, as the Chinese call it – Su Tung-p'o wrote "Mid-Autumn Moon" 中秋月:

> As evening clouds withdraw a clear cool air floods in
> the Jade Wheel rolls silently across the Silver River
> this night this life has rarely been kind
> where will we see this moon next year

暮雲收盡溢清寒，銀漢無聲轉玉盤。此生此夜不長好，明月明年何處看。

For the brothers it was not next year, or the year after, or the year after that. They wouldn't see each other again for ten years, not until Su Tung-p'o returned from his first exile. One thing becomes clear as one learns more

Left: Graves of Su Tung-p'o (foreground), his father, and his brother

about China's literary heroes: the heart that gave rise to their poetry also gave rise to as much sorrow as joy. It was the curse of the Muse. Connecting one's mouth to one's heart was a recipe for a drink that was often hard to swallow. Judging from the lives of such recent poets as Ai Ch'ing (1910–1996) and Mu Tan (1918–1977), it still is. Before leaving, I read one more poem. It was among Su Tung-p'o's last, "Impromptu" 縱筆:

> Poor Tung-p'o is a sick old man
> his white hair flutters like snow in the wind
> his son mistakenly smiles to see his face so rosy
> I laugh how could he know the red is from the wine

寂寂東坡一病翁，白鬚蕭散滿霜風。小兒誤喜朱顏在，一笑那知是酒紅。

Su died shortly afterward, on his way back from exile. After paying my respects at his grave and the graves of his brother and father, I walked back to Mr. Lu's car, which was over a kilometer away. By the time I got there, it was three o'clock. I had a hotel reservation in Loyang and was looking forward to ending the day early. Normally, I didn't make reservations, but Loyang had lately become a major tourist destination, so I had taken the precaution of making sure I had a room. From Three Su Park, we returned to the highway then followed it thirty kilometers to Juchou.

Juchou was where Su Tung-p'o and his brother said goodbye for the last time. Normally I would have stopped there to see the daughter of a potter I knew. Her father spent twenty years trying to rediscover the secret of the most famous glaze of the Sung dynasty, a glaze called sky-after-rain. It not only looked like the sky after rain, the color changed throughout the day as the light changed. Unfortunately, the emperor's tastes changed, too, and to preserve the secret of the glaze and to prevent anyone else from enjoying what he had enjoyed, he ordered the execution of everyone at the kiln. For nearly a thousand years, no one knew what was in sky-after-rain, until my friend's father finally discovered the secret ingredient: cat's-eye agate. Big shots from all over China bought his cups and bowls with the *ju* glaze, which got its name from the kiln, which got its name from the town, which got its name from the local river.

I didn't have time, though, for sky-after-rain. It was already past four when we pulled up outside the Juchou bus station, and Loyang was still seventy kilometers away. Just as we arrived, a bus bound for Loyang was leaving the station. And it was an express — at least the sign on the front said so. I jumped out and waved it down and asked the driver to wait. I raced back to the taxi, grabbed my backpack, paid Mr. Lu, bade him and his paramour adieu, and climbed aboard. At least I was on a bus, and it was headed where I planned to spend the night. I was hoping "express" meant it would take the expressway. The road gods, though, love a good joke. We bumped along on the old highway. Then it began to rain. And it didn't stop. No sky after rain. By the time we reached Loyang, it was pouring, and we were just in time for rush-hour traffic. Halfway through town I realized we weren't that far from my hotel. I asked the driver to let me off. The bus was going so slow, it wasn't a problem. I put on my backpack, got out my umbrella, and entered the downpour. I dodged traffic and crossed the street and boarded the first bus going my way. It was just before seven when I checked into the Shentu. Finally I was back on schedule, a tired but happy pilgrim looking forward, like Su Tung-p'o, to turning my cheeks rosy.

I woke up in Loyang, the capital of a dozen dynasties. The Lo River, after which the city was named, was just below my window. So were a few early morning risers. They were going through their exercise routines in the riverside park. Loyang was one of my favorite cities. Everything I saw reminded me of some story or poem from the past. It was where Ts'ao Chih and Juan Chi lived, as well as just about every poet of significance for the next 700 years. While I was watching the people in the park, a poem by Wei Ying-wu (737–791) came to mind. The park was there in his day, stretching along the river's grassy banks from the city's West Grove to its East Grove, and my hotel was in the middle, one block from the street that led south from the palace to the river. Wei's title was almost as long as his poem: "Waiting for Lu Sung, Who Writes Saying He Can't Come Because the Day Is Late and He Has No Horse, to Him I Send This Poem in Reply" 期盧嵩枉書稱日暮無馬不赴以詩答.

Such a fine day shouldn't be missed
I hoped you would finally honor my door
South Street is still full of people
and West Grove isn't dark yet
I lean on my staff by the gate in vain
and your cup waits alone in the garden
don't say you lack a conveyance
I know you have an old cart

家期不可失，終願枉衡門。南陌人猶度，西林日未昏。
庭前空倚仗，花裏獨留罇。莫道無來賀，知君有短轅。

It was a deceptively simple poem by a poet wanting nothing more than to share some wine with a friend. It was a sentiment with which I could identify. But it was early morning, not late afternoon. And I had big plans for the day. I wasn't going to try to visit all the poets who had lived in Loyang, only a few for whom the city formed an especially important part of their lives. I put the day's itinerary in my shoulder bag along with the accompanying maps and headed downstairs. I didn't bother with breakfast. I had poets to see.

It was eight when I walked outside. A taxi was waiting in the street, just for me it seemed. I got in and decided not to bargain. I figured I would pay whatever the meter read at the end of the day. The driver's surname was Huang. He was about sixty, and his taxi was a clunker. Normally I avoided clunkers, but we were going to be traveling on a few bad roads – at least at the beginning. Drivers whose taxis were in good condition often refused to go down such roads, or they jacked up their previously agreed upon prices beyond what was reasonable.

Once I outlined my itinerary for the day, Mr. Huang said he didn't have enough gas for all the places I hoped to visit and drove to one of the city's four natural-gas stations. After he pulled up to the pump, he told me to get out and stand clear while his tank was being filled. Passengers weren't allowed to stay inside the car. While I stood watching, I took a photo and was immediately reprimanded by the attendant. Photography, he said, was not allowed – a spark might set off an explosion. I put away my camera and waited. The whole process didn't take much longer than filling up at a regular gas station.

My first destination was a shot in the dark, or two shots in the dark. I had with me two accounts posted online by previous pilgrims in search of the same grave, but they didn't agree as to the location. I decided to begin with the one that advocated Fenghuangshan (Phoenix Mountain), a 300-meter-high east–west ridge about twenty kilometers northeast of Loyang. We headed east out of town on Highway 310, Loyang's main east–west thoroughfare since ancient times. About five kilometers past White Horse Temple, we turned north onto Highway 207. Two kilometers later, Phoenix Mountain rose beyond the farmland to our right, and we began stopping every few hundred meters to ask people walking along the road about possible graves. At least they all agreed, which simplified our quest. Everyone said the only graves on the mountain were up a dirt road that ended just below the summit at a place called Nine Dragon Cemetery. The road was deeply rutted, but the cemetery at the end of it was new, with rows of landscaped mausoleums for cremated remains rather than bones. Mr. Huang parked outside the gate, and I went I search of the caretaker. Once I found him, I told him I was looking for the grave of Meng Chiao (751–814). The online post I was following was by a man who claimed to be a descendant. Although he didn't actually find his ancestor's grave, some villagers had directed him to an area where there were several T'ang-dynasty tombs, and he concluded one of them must have been his ancestor's. The caretaker said he had never heard of any T'ang tombs on the mountain. All the graves were recent. That was disconcerting, but I wasn't about to give up so easily. We drove back down to the foot of the mountain and followed a series of local roads around to the other side, stopping to ask anyone we saw along the road.

Of all the great poets during China's Golden Age of Poetry, Meng Chiao was one of the few who saw himself as a poet rather than someone who happened to write poetry. It was said that he never left his house without writing a poem. If that were true, he must have thrown a lot of poems away, as only 500 have survived. Or maybe he didn't leave his house that often. In any case, all Meng cared about was writing poems. He was a poet's poet. And in Loyang he found himself in poet's heaven.

He came to the Eastern Capital late in life and spent his final eight years here. He grew up a thousand kilometers to the south outside the city of Huchou, where he lived the life of a poet-recluse until he was forty. It was only after his uncle traveled to Ch'ang-an and passed the civil service exams that his mother convinced him to do the same. And so Meng Chiao followed his mother's brother to the Western Capital. The exams, though, were harder than he expected. It was only on his third attempt, at the relatively advanced age of forty-six, that he finally passed. Passing the exams, though, didn't result in anything more than a few minor appointments and the occasional sinecure. His real success came through poetry, and that didn't begin until nine years later, when he moved to Loyang and fell in with a group of poets that included Han Yu, Chia Tao, and Chang Chi, men he had met in Ch'ang-an who had since relocated to the Eastern Capital. It was here that he wrote his best-known poems, including a series he titled "Cold River" 寒溪. This is the second of its nine verses:

> On its way past the shores of Loyang
> where the river flows by Meng Manor
> a boat breaking through new ice
> made a sound like porcelain shattering
> green water turned into green jade
> white waves into white quartz
> everything in this jeweled mirror
> shared equally Heaven's light
> stumbling forward down a steep winding trail
> clutching my staff I heard a bird cry
> as the cold fog slowly lifted

the frozen world remained a blur
I looked ahead and listened in silence
having lost the trail I wandered without aim
hemmed in by thorns on the shore
there are so many words for "sorrow"

洛陽岸邊道，孟氏庄前溪。舟行素冰折，聲作青瑤嘶。
綠水結綠玉，白波生白珪。明明寶鏡中，物物天照齊。
側步下危曲，攀枯聞嬬啼。霜芬稍稍歇，凝景微茫齊。
痴坐直視聽，懇行失踪蹊。岸童劚棘勞，語言多悲凄。

Meng Chiao was clearly indebted to Ts'ao Chih and Juan Chi for the five-syllable line, but he did so much more with the form. In any given line, anything could happen – and *did*. His poems startled with their imagery as well as their subject matter. They also revealed the hardship that dominated his life and inspired his poetry.

After an hour of driving around Phoenix Mountain looking for his grave, I gave up. I decided to give the second account a try. We returned to Highway 207 and drove north again. A few kilometers later, we turned southwest onto Highway 238 and followed it about five kilometers until a group of farmers directed us onto a narrow country lane that led west to the village of Fenghuangtai, or Phoenix Tower. The village was near the Loyang airport on the crest of a low ridge of hills known as Peimang, the most famous hills in China. In ancient times there was a saying: "To live in Hangchou, to be buried on Peimang." Beginning as early as the Neolithic, these hills were chosen for their geomantic properties as the ideal place to be buried. I was hopeful that Meng's friends were guided by the same considerations.

When Meng Chiao died, it seems that every poet in China wrote a poem titled "Grieving for Meng Chiao." Despite his lack of worldly success, he was one of the most admired poets of his day. His friends in Loyang scraped together money to buy a plot and a tombstone, and his friend Han Yu wrote the epitaph through his tears.

I didn't expect to find the tombstone, but I hoped for *something*. We parked in the middle of the village, and I went looking. Fenghuangtai was fairly large, but I must have walked through all of it asking people where I could find Meng Chiao's grave. His name elicited only blank stares. I was surprised. The account read as though I could walk right up to the grave. After an hour, I gave up. But before we drove away, I took out one of Meng's poems and read it into the wind. It was poem 4 in a series of eleven titled "Autumn Reverie" 秋懷:

I feel older and poorer when autumn arrives
my broken-down house doesn't have a door
slivers of moonlight fall on my bed
wind enters my clothes from all sides
my infrequent dreams no longer go far
but at least my weak heart can find its way home
there's not much green left in the vines
coiling and fighting for the vanishing light
my countryside outings are fewer too
I'm sick and I brood and I'm withdrawn
the lives of insects hiding in the grass
mean about as much as mine

秋至老更貧，破屋無門扉。一片月落牀，四壁風入衣。
疎夢不復遠，弱心良易歸。商菰將去綠，繚繞爭餘輝。
野步踏事少，病謀向物違。幽幽草根蟲，生意與我微。

Unlike Ts'ao Chih and Juan Chi, Meng Chiao wasn't bothered by his failure to serve at court, but he was disappointed that the Muse to whom he devoted himself didn't make his life a little easier. I was disappointed, too, that I couldn't join Han Yu and Chia Tao and everyone else who paid their respects at his grave. Ironically, shortly after I returned home from my pilgrimage, I read another account online. It was by two men who came to Fenghuangtai a few weeks before me, also in search of Meng Chiao's grave. They met a village elder who led them to a cornfield not far from the local elementary school. He told them that was where the grave used to be. There was no marker of any kind, not even a bump in the field. Meng Chiao's grave had been reduced to the memory of an old man who pointed in the direction of a cornfield.

As we drove away, my disappointment was somewhat assuaged when I realized I could still offer Meng Chiao some whiskey at my next destination, which was the grave of the man who wrote his epitaph. I felt better. We drove across the same farmland we had earlier, and just after we reached Highway 238 again, we entered an expressway that led north to a bridge that spanned the Yellow River. The river looked pathetic. It was the beginning of September, when the water level should have been near its peak, but the river wasn't more than 500 meters across. The dikes, meanwhile, were three kilometers apart. China's River of Sorrow had finally been tamed, not by dikes but by industrialization. Thousands of factories now sucked it dry before it reached the sea.

We took the first exit after the bridge and headed east toward the town of Mengchou. Five kilometers later, we turned north onto a road built for the sole purpose of leading visitors to the grave of Han Yu (768–824). He was buried here ten years after Meng Chiao died. The road ended a kilometer later. After I paid the entrance fee and walked through the gate, I couldn't help staring in amazement. The place

Statue of Han Yu at his gravesite

was palatial. Surrounding a vast courtyard were several exhibition halls and a huge shrine hall. And in the middle of it all was a statue of Han Yu. Nothing had changed in death for these two men. Meng Chiao's grave had been plowed under by some farmer who decided *what the hell*, while Han Yu was buried in surroundings fit for a king. I followed the long path from the courtyard to the back of the compound. It was a Sunday, and I was the only one there. It was eerie. Apparently, word hadn't gotten around to tour operators. I set out my cups in front of the tomb and poured enough bourbon for the three of us: Han Yu, Meng Chiao, and me.

Han Yu's poetry also distinguished him from Meng Chiao. His poems have a casual, conversational air. They don't appear to have been thought out — though of course they were. Most literary critics say he was one of the two greatest essayists of the T'ang — the other being Liu Tsung-yuan. Poetry for him was just another way of telling a story. And he told great stories. In honor of the season I read the eighth of an eleven-poem series also titled "Autumn Reverie" 秋懷, the same as his friend's:

Leaves spiraled round as they fell to the ground
then hurried on the wind past my door
they seemed to be saying something

chasing each other this way then that
alone in my study as dusk turned to night
I sat not speaking a word
my attendant came in from outside
and blew out the lamp on my desk
he asked how I was but I didn't answer
he brought me food but I didn't eat
then he sat down against the west wall
and read a poem out loud several times
not by someone today
but someone who lived a thousand years ago
whose words still touched my heart
and stirred the old sadness again
I turned and told the boy
to put the book down and go to sleep
your master has something on his mind
and work to do that never ends

卷卷落地葉，　隨風走前軒。　鳴聲若有意，　顛倒相追奔。
空堂黃昏暮，　我坐默不言。　童子自外至，　吹燈當我前。
問我我不應，　饋我我不餐。　退坐西壁下，　讀詩盡數編。
作者非今士，　相去時已千。　其言有感觸，　使我復淒酸。
顧謂汝童子，　置書且安眠。　丈夫屬有念，　事業無窮年。

I'm guessing the boy was reading one of Ch'u Yuan's poems, maybe "The Fisherman," which extolled serving the government when rulers were wise and retiring to the countryside when they weren't. Han Yu wrote this series after he returned to Ch'ang-an from his first exile. Maybe he was thinking of building a hut in the Chungnan Mountains south of the capital. Or maybe he was thinking about the blindness of the emperor and his court and was wondering how to avoid another exile. But Han Yu didn't share Meng Chiao's love of seclusion, so the hut option wasn't likely. He was Confucian through and through. In fact, it was his Confucian rigor that led him to criticize the emperor's excessive devotion to Buddhism, resulting in a second exile. Han Yu, though, was forgiven and called back. Even his enemies admired him.

Another poem I brought with me to read was one many scholars think is his last, the third in a series of three titled "Finally Floating Down the River to the South" 南溪始泛, in which he visits the Chungnan Mountains south of Ch'ang-an and drifts down the Fan River that roared out of the mountains but quieted by the time it flowed past the plateau on which he lived:

> My legs are too feeble to walk
> it was time I ended my visits to court
> a sedan chair of course could carry my frail body
> but how could I give up this sight
> below the escarpment to the south
> having heard about the river and its rocks
> I pushed my boat into their midst
> where the current was clear and wild
> unwilling to trust the waves
> I poled myself through the rapids
> an egret rose as if to guide me
> flying in front a boat-length away
> willow after willow crowded the shore
> pine tree upon pine tree rose from the bank
> the night was gone when I returned home
> who says I wasn't at work

足弱不能步，自宜收朝迹。羸形可輿致，佳觀安事攦。
即此南坂下，久聞有水石。拖舟入其間，溪流正清激。
隨波吾未能，峻瀨乍可刺。鷺起若導吾，前飛數十尺。
亭亭柳帶沙，團團松冠壁。歸時還盡夜，誰謂非事役。

I could imagine the exhilaration Han must have felt. It was as good a way as any to bring one's life to a close: a day on the river. I sprinkled his share of bourbon on his grave. It wasn't river spray, but it was wet. I poured Meng Chiao's share on the grave too then downed mine and returned to Mr. Huang's natural-gas mobile. Instead of heading back the way we came, we followed the main highway ten kilometers east through the town of Mengchou to another expressway that took us south to another bridge that spanned the Yellow River. Five kilometers beyond the river, we exited at a sign for Tu Fu's Old Home. I tried to imagine an exit sign in America for Hart Crane's Old Home, without success.

We pulled into yet another vast, empty parking lot. Like the palatial grounds surrounding Han Yu's tomb, the place where Tu Fu was born and grew up had been developed beyond anything he could have imagined. The

Tu Fu's cave home east of Loyang

local government saw the tourist potential in such a place. I sighed and shrugged at the same time. I'd gotten used to such developments. It was the price a pilgrim paid nowadays, in addition to the no-longer-insignificant entrance fees. At least I got the senior discount. As at Han Yu's tomb, I breezed past the exhibition halls. I lingered in such places when I visited a poet for whom there wasn't much information available, but Tu Fu was China's most celebrated poet. There was *too much* to read. I made my way, instead, to the rear of the grounds, to a courtyard residence and set of caves carved into the loess hillside. This was where Tu Fu spent his youth. The courtyard residence, though, was probably nicer than anything he actually lived in. Until recently, most people in this part of China preferred a loess cave to a house made of bricks. Such caves were cooler in summer and warmer in winter. Tu Fu's faced west, toward the courtyard, and I had no trouble imagining him sitting outside reading until the sun set, then retiring to his earth lodging for the night. He undoubtedly wrote poems during his youth, but the only datable one to survive is "Visiting Fenghsien Temple at Lungmen" 游龍門奉先寺, which recounts a visit to the Lungmen Caves south of Loyang:

I visited the temple before
I stayed there again last night
sounds floated into space from a dark ravine
faint shadows danced in the moonlit woods
I gazed at the stars in a sliver of sky
and shivered beneath my robe all night in the clouds
just before dawn I heard the bell
it made me think as I woke

已從招提遊，更宿招提境。陰壑生虛籟，月林散清影。
天窺象緯逼，雲臥衣裳冷。欲覺聞晨鐘，令人發深省。

He wrote this in 735, at the age of twenty-three. Another poem from his early years was one he wrote in 744 when he met Li Pai for the first time. Li Pai had been banished from Ch'ang-an for his drunken behavior. He was traveling east and searching for a place to cultivate Taoist meditation and alchemy in his continuing quest to join the immortals. Tu Fu, meanwhile, had moved from his loess cave to nearby Loyang. During their brief time together he wrote "For Li Pai" 贈李白:

Two years as a guest in the Eastern Capital
I've experienced its traps and snares
a country boy seeing meat and fish
having never felt full on vegetarian fare
how can I have a smile on my face
when I lack the meagerest of food
sadly I haven't any drugs
the woods have been picked clean of their traces
the noble Master Li from palace gates
has escaped in his quest for seclusion
I too am planning an eastern journey
I'm still hoping to find magic plants

二年客東都，所歷厭機巧。野人對腥膻，蔬食常不飽。

岂無青精飯，使我顏色好。苦乏大藥資，山林迹如掃。
李侯金閨彦，脫身事幽討。亦有梁宋游，方期拾瑤草。

This poem reveals a side of Tu Fu few have mentioned. Drugs. Escape. Seclusion. Immortality. He was young and so impressed by Li Pai: the prospect of following the Taoist path of transforming his mortal body into an immortal one was hard to resist. He joined Li Pai again the following year on Stone Gate Mountain near Confucius's hometown. However, his Confucian training led him to give up that quest in favor of a career. After parting from Li Pai at Stone Gate, he moved to Ch'ang-an and resumed his studies.

Since I planned to meet Tu Fu there as well, I didn't linger. I had two more stops. I headed back toward Loyang and its major tourist attraction, the Lungmen Caves, where every day thousands of people visit the buddhas carved out of the cliffs on the west bank of the Yi River. After exiting the expressway, we entered the eight-lane boulevard that led there, but I had a different destination in mind. Halfway to the caves we turned east onto Pei-hsin Street and followed it for five kilometers until it petered out in Lion Bridge Village. I had been there before and knew what to look for. I asked Mr. Huang to park next to the entrance of a driving school. Since no one was driving, I asked the attendant whether it was okay to walk across to the adjacent walled-off piece of land. He waved me through, and I made for the far wall. On the other side was a two-story cement structure in the middle of an acre of land. The structure was unfinished, and the land was planted with grapes. There was also a small shack for a caretaker and a shed for a guard dog.

My first visit here had been inadvertent. A crew from Tienchin TV was filming me at various sites in China associated with the poet Wei Ying-wu. Wei lived for a number of years in a Buddhist temple in the suburbs of Loyang, and I had asked the local official in charge of cultural relics whether he knew where the old temple was located. The official misunderstood: he thought I was talking about the poet Pai Chu-yi (772–846) – which was, I suppose, a comment on my Chinese – and he led me to this cement structure. It was one of those mistakes that turn out to be fortuitous. I would never have found the place otherwise. This was where Pai Chu-yi lived in retirement. I had already been to the village where he spent his first twelve years. In between childhood and retirement, he spent forty years enjoying a relatively successful career as an official, with the usual ups and downs and periodic banishments. In 824, he retired to this piece of land next to the driving school. It was the sunset of his life – a long and a glorious sunset. Pai wrote some of my favorite poems here, including "Complaining about Losing My Hair" 嗟髮落:

> I complained about losing my hair in the morning
> I complained about losing my hair at night
> once it was gone I complained even more
> but once it was gone wasn't so bad
> no need to wash it or rinse it
> no need to comb it or tie it
> perfectly fine in the sun or rain
> my head with no topknot felt light
> and once I took off my dirt-covered cap
> and untied my dusty hatstrings
> and filled a silver vase with cold water
> and poured it over my crown
> anointing myself with fine oil it seemed
> I suddenly felt cool and refreshed
> now I know why those carefree monks
> avail themselves of a shave

朝亦嗟髮落，暮亦嗟髮落。落盡誠可嗟，盡來亦不惡。
既不勞洗沐，又不煩梳掠。最宜濕暑天，頭輕無髻縛。
脫置垢巾幘，解去塵纓絡。銀瓶貯寒泉，當頂傾一勺。
有如醍醐灌，坐受清涼樂。因悟自在僧，亦資于剃削。

The cement structure that now occupied the place where Pai once anointed himself was a failed attempt to develop the site for tourists. Only one thing had changed since my previous visit: the caretaker had put a chair on the roof, so he could enjoy the sunset. He was gone that day, and I didn't bother trying to scale the wall. The guard dog was on duty.

I returned to the taxi, and we proceeded to where Pai spent his final four years. After eight years at Lion Bridge Village, he moved even farther out of town. We drove back to Lungmen Boulevard then turned south toward Lungmen Caves again. But before we reached the end of the road and one of China's largest parking lots, we turned off and made our way to the east side of the Yi River. I told Mr. Huang to park on the roadside and wait for me, while I headed for the gate that led to my destination. But things had changed – the gate for one thing. There wasn't a gate in the past. And there wasn't an attendant either. The attendant directed me to a ticket office. That was new too. In the past, tourists paid one fee to see the buddhas on the west side of the river and another, much smaller fee to visit the garden that had developed around Pai Chu-yi's grave on the opposite side, which most visitors ignored.

When I told the woman in the ticket office I just wanted to see the garden, she asked for the equivalent of twenty dollars. I repeated that I just wanted to visit the garden. I didn't want to see the buddhas. She said it was now one ticket for everything, and the ticket was 150RMB. I sighed and told her I was over sixty-five and asked for the standard 50 percent discount. I was so used to my status in China that I was surprised when she said the discount didn't apply to foreigners. This was like the old days, when foreigners were charged ten times what locals paid. That practice had largely stopped, but clearly there were holdouts. We argued for several minutes. She wouldn't relent, and I was in one of my stubborn moods. Finally, I walked away. I had no idea what I was going to do, and I was running out of time.

Just then, I noticed a large group of Chinese tourists passing through the

Grave of Pai Chu-yi at Lungmen

gate with their guide. I walked straight into the middle of the group, and the gate attendant didn't notice. I was in, but not completely in. Pai Chu-yi Garden was still a hundred meters down the road. And when I tried to enter, the attendant there asked to see my ticket. While I pretended to look, the group I snuck in with lined up behind me. The attendant saw I wasn't making any progress and the people behind me were growing impatient. He waved me through, and I disappeared up a side trail that led to the grave. I had been there a dozen times, and it didn't take more than a couple of minutes to reach the tomb. It was one of my favorite places, and I knew one of the caretakers, Mr. Cheng. During my last visit, he led me to the back of the garden and showed me a pillar with Pai's injunctions to his descendants. With that in mind, I brought a similar poem he wrote about the same time. After I set out my offering in front of his grave, I read "Crazy Advice to My Nephews" 狂言示諸侄:

The world cheats those who can't read or write
I'm ashamed of my skill with a brush
the world cheats those with no office
I'm ashamed of the posts I have held
so many complaints come with old age
happily I am free of illness
so many attachments come with old age
finally I am done with marriage
nothing affects a mind at peace
nothing affects a body at rest
thus for the past ten years
my body and mind have been idle and free
and surely will be as I become older
my needs amount to so little
a coat keeps me warm in winter
a meal keeps me full all day
and don't say my house is too small
I can only sleep in one room
and why would I want more horses
I can only ride one
people as lucky as me
there might be seven in ten
people as content as me

there isn't one in a hundred
regarding others people see fools
compared to themselves even sages have flaws
I dare not tell this to others
such crazy talk is for nephews

世欺不識字，　我忝攻文筆。　世欺不得官，　我忝居班秩。
人老多病苦，　我今幸無病。　人老多憂累，　我今婚嫁畢。
心安不移轉，　身泰無牽率。　所以十年來，　形神閑且逸。
況當垂老歲，　所要無多物。　一裘暖過冬，　一飯飽中日。
勿言舍宅小，　不過寢一室。　何用鞍馬多，　不能騎兩匹。
如我優幸身，　人中十有七。　如我知足心，　人中百無一。
傍觀愚亦見，　當己賢多失。　不敢論他人，　狂言示諸侄。

While Pai and I were sipping our bourbon, I saw a groundskeeper. I walked over and asked him whether Mr. Cheng was working that day. I'd tried to call him, but he didn't answer. The groundskeeper said Mr. Cheng was taking the day off—and he had upgraded from a landline to a cell phone. Everyone was getting a cell phone. Even I had one. I wrote down the new number for next time and wrapped up my graveside ceremony. I walked back down to the road and out the gate and waved to the woman in the ticket window. It had been a big day, and I was tuckered out. I asked Mr. Huang to take me back to where the day began.

DAY

6

I always look forward to spending two nights in the same hotel. The clothes I wash the first night have plenty of time to dry, and, if need be, I can pack any still damp from the second night – or wear them. So I was caught up in the clean-clothes department. When I checked out of the Shentu and stepped outside the next morning, I looked for Mr. Huang. He had agreed to take me on another excursion – but farther afield. His taxi was there, but someone else was behind the wheel, and a young woman was sitting beside the driver. The man turned out to be Mr. Huang's son, and he had his girlfriend with him. I was surprised. Then I realized the younger Huang was taking his girlfriend for a ride through the countryside and getting paid to do it. The son said his father had something to do that day, which was too bad. He was not as affable as his father.

Another surprise: our first stop wasn't on my itinerary. The son told me his father suggested a spot he doubted I knew about. It was in an alley in the Muslim quarter north of Tungkuan Boulevard. On one side of the alley, there was a brick wall with a stele set in the middle. I got out and inspected the inscription. I was stunned. Mr. Huang was right: I didn't know about this place. This was where Confucius asked Lao-tzu about ritual and music. It was also where Lao-tzu once lived.

Ritual and music were the pillars upon which Confucius based his understanding of the Tao. It was all about harmony. Harmony was the Tao made manifest. When Confucius came to the Chou-dynasty capital, Lao-tzu was in charge of dynastic records, and Confucius visited him at his residence, seeking instruction in the ceremonies of the ancient kings. Lao-tzu was eighty, and Confucius a young man of thirty-five. The year was 516 BC, and they met only this once. Shortly after their meeting, Lao-tzu left Loyang and headed west. Two hundred kilometers later, at the Hankukuan Pass, he wrote down the text known as the *Taoteching* 道德經 then disappeared. Confucius, meanwhile, returned to Chufu, where he developed his teaching of harmony: harmony in deeds, harmony in sounds, and harmony in words. Ritual, music, and poetry.

One thing I have always thought curious is that no one has ever talked about Lao-tzu as a poet. And yet clearly he was. His *Taoteching* is a collection of eighty-one poems and remains the most revered and memorized of all Taoist texts. Take number 40, for example:

The Tao moves the other way
the Tao works through weakness
the things of this world come from something
something comes from nothing

反者道之動，弱者道之用。天下之物生於有，有生於無。

Couldn't be simpler. Yet when it comes to instruction, nothing beats simplicity. Confucius got it, at least the "weakness" part. So did his early followers. They called themselves *ju-chia*, "disciples of humility" — the word *ju* referring to someone small or weak and thus humble. I took a photo of the stele — there was nothing left of Lao-tzu's residence — and raised an early morning toast to

Stele in Loyang where Confucius met Lao-tzu

China's two great sages and to the karmic forces that brought them together, however briefly, 2,500 years ago. I thanked Mr. Huang's son for the chance to thank a poet I had nearly overlooked.

After filling up with enough natural gas for the day, we took the same expressway across the Yellow River as the day before. This time we kept going: fifteen kilometers north, then twenty kilometers east on another expressway — where we encountered a traffic jam in the middle of nowhere — and finally, after exiting at Poaihsien, west on Highway 104. Thirty minutes later, just past the town of Hsuliangchen, where the highway bent north, I asked Huang the Younger to take the next road on the right. There weren't any signs, but I trusted my map. The road was freshly paved, and we followed it for a kilometer or so. When I didn't see what I was looking for, we stopped, and I asked a woman walking along the side of the road. She was dressed as if she were going to a party — or maybe a wedding. She pointed back the way we had come, to a cornfield on the other side of a grove of trees.

Getting past the trees was easy, but I had to struggle through the corn. It was another hot day, and I was wearing a T-shirt. When I looked at my arms afterwards, they were covered with red welts from the corn's razor-sharp leaves. I'd never realized corn leaves could be so dangerous. It was a small price to pay, though. Suddenly, in the middle of the cornfield, I came to a stone retaining wall that encircled a bramble-covered mound. I followed the wall until I came to a tombstone that confirmed this was the grave of Li Shang-yin (813–858).

Li was one of the greatest poets of the T'ang and also one of the most difficult. His language was full of unexpected delights, but it could just as easily be obscure. It suggested a deep interior life, of which his poems only revealed glimpses. His father died when he was nine, and he grew up with his uncle's family in Chengchou. Once he came of age, he never spent more than a few years in any one place. He said he never felt at home. Poetry became his refuge. Of his 600-odd surviving poems, none was more famous than "Gilded Zither" 錦瑟:

> This gilded zither's fifty strings for no apparent reason
> recall my youthful years in every string and bridge
> the morning dream of Master Chuang enchanted by a butterfly
> the springtime love of Emperor Wang spellbound by a cuckoo
> moonlight on the ocean forming tears from pearls
> sunshine on Lantien producing mist from jade

such images have meanings waiting to be found
as I now reflect already they're unclear

錦瑟無端五十弦，一弦一柱思華年。莊生曉夢迷蝴蝶，望帝春心托杜鵑。
滄海月明珠有淚，藍田日暖玉生煙。此情可待成追憶，只是當時已惘然。

His poetry could even mystify him. He loved metaphors and allusions. In this poem, for example, the reader needs to know that zither strings were made of silk until modern times. The instrument was meant to be enjoyed by friends, not by neighbors. Also, this particular kind of zither, known as a *se*, originally had fifty strings, but by Li's time it only had twenty-five. Hence, Li projects himself into the past, when zithers had fifty strings, when the Taoist master Chuang-tzu dreamed he was a butterfly and upon waking wondered whether he was a butterfly dreaming he was Chuang-tzu, and when Emperor Wang was so enchanted by a cuckoo he forgot everything else. As for pearls and jade: pearls were once thought to be the offspring of oysters and moonlight, and the cloudy white jade mined on Mount Lantien, southeast of Ch'ang-an, was highly prized during the T'ang. Chinese commentators have suggested a dozen explanations as to what these images really mean. For me, the language is simply too beautiful to care. The same is true of many of Li's poems. His language was sometimes so exquisite it could mesmerize. Pai Chu-yi admired Li's poetry so much he said he hoped to be reborn as Li's son in his next life.

Li, however, was known first as a writer and only later as a poet. He was hired as a private secretary by several high-ranking officials while still in his twenties. Unfortunately, his career didn't improve even when he passed the exams. His close ties to the two competing cliques at court resulted in nothing but minor posts. He was always on the move. It wasn't until relatively late in his life that he served in a position where he

Grave of Li Shang-yin near Hsuliangchen

actually stayed awhile. In 851, he was asked to go to Tzuchou (modern San-tai) in Szechuan. His job was to serve as a secretary to the official in charge of military affairs in what was the ancient state of Pa. Li spent four years there, his longest stay anywhere since childhood. Of course, he was far from his friends and his children – his wife died just before he left for Szechuan – but he was also far from the court and free from its distractions. It was a produc-tive time for him as a poet. Among the poems he wrote there is "Night Rain, Sent North" 夜雨寄北:

> You ask when I'll return but when doesn't have a date
> the rain tonight in the hills of Pa floods the autumn lakes
> when will we trim candlewicks by the west window again
> and talk about when it rained in the hills of Pa this night

君問歸期未有期, 巴山夜雨漲秋池。何當共剪西窗燭, 卻話巴山夜雨時。

When his patron's assignment to Tzuchou ended in 855, Li followed him back to Ch'ang-an, where he received another nominal post, again with his patron's help. After two years he resigned and moved back to Chengchou. He was ill and spent his last year living quietly just outside the city where he grew up. Commentators think "In Late Winter Living in Seclusion" 幽居冬暮 is the last poem he wrote:

> With their time-ravaged wings
> in the quiet of a country garden
> a rooster shakes snow from a tree at dawn
> a wintering duck guards an ice-covered pond
> the shorter days remind me it's late
> the waning years have found me decrepit
> why has my role in helping the country
> not matched my earlier aspirations

羽翼摧殘日, 郊園寂寞時。曉雞驚樹雪, 寒鶩守冰池。
急景忽云暮, 頹年寖已衰。如何匡國分, 不與夙心期。

Li wanted to be more than a secretary, but he never got the chance. He died at the age of forty-five. His body was brought to this place in the countryside

where his great-grandparents were buried. I had no way of knowing whether their graves were still here as I couldn't see more than a few feet in any direction through the corn. Li also had a grave outside Chengchou. Since it was early in the day, and I was planning to visit that grave as well, I limited the two of us to a single shot of bourbon and made my way back to the taxi.

I showed Mr. Huang's son the map to my next destination, Yuntaishan, the southeasternmost corner of the Taihang Mountains. Although he'd never been there, the place had become a major tourist destination, and the route was clear. Once we returned to the expressway at Poaihsien, we headed northeast. Just past the city of Chiaotso, we exited and followed a new highway through a landscape of stupendous mountain views. We were just about the only vehicle on the road. As we drove along, I envisioned this stretch of road appearing in future car commercials.

As we got closer, I caught glimpses of Yuntaishan. In the past, poets living in or passing through Loyang who wondered what "spectacular" looked like made it a point to come here. Among them was the seventeen-year-old Wang Wei (699–759). During his visit, he wrote one of his earliest known verses, "On the Ninth Day of the Ninth Month Thinking of My Brothers Off in the Eastern Hills" 九月九日憶山東兄弟:

> A stranger alone in a strange land
> thoughts of my family dominate this day
> I imagine my brothers climbing some place high
> wearing dogwood garlands one person short

獨在異鄉為異客，每逢佳節倍思親。遙知兄弟登高處，遍插茱萸少一人。

Climbing hilltops and towers and wearing garlands of bright-red dogwood berries were customs associated with the Double Ninth — the number nine being the perfect male number, as opposed to its female counterpart, the number six. Even though Double Ninth was still a month away, I was looking forward to climbing someplace high.

The reason for my foray wasn't just to visit a mountain the young Wang Wei visited. Yuntaishan was the home of the Seven Sages of the Bamboo Grove, which included Juan Chi. This was the mountain whose sanctuary

Left: Yuntaishan and the Taihang Mountains

they sought whenever life in Loyang became unbearable – or dangerous. On arriving, we pulled into one of the biggest parking lots I had ever seen. Like the lots near the Great Wall, it could have held a thousand buses. And yet, except for three other sedans, it was empty. After we parked, I walked up to the entrance and discovered why.

The trails inside what is now known as Yuntaishan National Park were being repaired. There were a number of dangerous routes along the mountain's cliffs, and the work was being done in preparation for Golden Week, the first week of October, which was still a month away. It was the busiest travel holiday of the year. Inside the administration building, I pleaded with officials, but they were not allowing anyone inside the park, except construction workers. I had to content myself with viewing the mountain from afar.

The area I'd wanted to reach was Paichiayen, the location of the original bamboo grove where Juan Chi and his friends played their zithers and composed their poems. People often got the wrong idea about this group, thinking these seven men drank all the time. They certainly drank, but they did most of their drinking at court, where it kept them out of trouble and made them appear harmless. Here, they did what sages, or would-be sages, did. They meditated and practiced various forms of Taoist yoga. However, they were human would-be sages, as Juan Chi tells us in poem 70 of his *Songs from the Heart* 詠懷:

> We know sorrow because we have feelings
> if we felt no sorrow we would be insensate
> as long as we don't get caught in a net
> or require a thousand-acre estate
> soaring on the wind we touch the sky
> and crimson clouds lit by the sun
> with our cold-ash minds in our dead-tree abodes
> why would we turn toward worldly attractions
> but once we succeed in forgetting our selves
> can we learn to leave our selves in peace

有悲則有情，無悲亦無思。苟非嬰網罟，何必萬里畿。
翔風拂重霄，慶雲招所晞。灰心寄枯宅，曷顧人間姿。
始得忘我難，焉知嘿自遺。

In addition to cultivating forms of meditation that turned their minds into ashes and their bodies into withered trees, they also droned. I had also hoped to climb to a promontory known as Sun Teng's Droning Tower. Sun Teng was a long-haired Taoist hermit who played a one-string zither and who served as the group's mentor in Taoist matters, which, of course, included droning. The bamboo grove and the droning tower, however, were no longer accessible, at least not that day, so I returned to my taxi to consider my options. I suddenly had time on my hands. After looking at the map, I decided to visit Sun Teng's own droning tower. The one on Yuntaishan was named for him, but the tower he built for himself was outside the town of Huihsien, less than an hour's drive away. That was where Juan Chi first met Sun. Juan was so impressed, he wrote a 700-line poetic essay known as "Biography of the Great Man," in which he argued for Taoist anarchism and against the Confucian state, using Sun as his exemplar. Sun, of course, would have winced had anyone called him a "great man." But having spent half his life at court, Juan Chi was accustomed to hyperbole.

We asked directions only twice. Sun's tower was just north of Huihsien, inside Paichuan Park, a park of a hundred springs dominated by a small lake with a zigzagging bridge across the middle. I walked to the north end of the lake then followed a trail up a small hill known as Sumenshan. Ten minutes later, I arrived at the place where Sun droned.

Huihsien had changed since then, but the mountain was still a mountain. The view was expansive, and it would have been a fine place to drone. The tower, though, was gone, and there was now a pavilion on the site. A young couple was sitting in its shade. I didn't infringe on their privacy and restricted myself to taking in the view. Once I caught my breath, I scattered a shot of bourbon into the wind and left.

From Huihsien we headed east, then south, and recrossed the Yellow River. Just north of Chengchou, we turned onto another expressway, one that circled Honan's provincial capital. Traffic slowed to a crawl, and I began to regret adding Sun Teng's tower to my itinerary. I was going to have to cut things short. When we finally reached the expressway's westernmost point, we exited onto Highway 310 and after a kilometer turned south on Shangyin Road. A minute later we parked just outside the second of Li Shang-yin's graves. This one was in the middle of a well-manicured park named in his honor. At the entrance was a relief in stone of Li playing his zither and a calligraphic rendering of his famous poem. Passing the relief, I followed a walkway through the park until I came to a huge boulder. In addition to the poet's name, the boulder included a small portrait outlined in blue. His grave was just behind it. This was quite an upgrade from the cornfield. I poured Li another shot of Stagg and read one of his "Untitled Poems" 無題詩, one that made it into the anthology *Three Hundred Poems of the T'ang* 唐詩三百首:

It's not easy to meet and not easy to part
the east wind can't keep flowers from fading
silkworms spin silk until they die in spring
candles drip tears until their wicks turn to ash
before her sunlit mirror she mourns her graying temples
reciting poems at night she feels the moonlight's chill
the peaks of Penglai aren't so far from here
bluebird I beg you help me to reach her

相見時難別亦難，東風無力百花殘。春蠶到死絲方盡，蠟炬成灰淚始乾。
曉鏡但愁雲鬢改，夜吟應覺月光寒。蓬山此去無多路，青鳥殷勤為探看。

Li was fifteen when he wrote this. While he was living with his uncle's family, he did some traveling. One of the places he visited was the mountain of Yuyangshan, just west of the cornfield outside Hsuliangchen. Li cultivated

Grave of Li Shang-yin near Chengchou

Taoist meditation there, hoping to join the immortals on the mythical island of Penglai. One day, he met a young woman who was doing the same. She was the handmaiden of one of the emperor's daughters. They fell in love, and they were together long enough for her to get pregnant – but not long enough to make plans. She returned to the palace, and Li returned home to his studies. Thus, he called on the bluebird messenger of Taoism's Queen Mother of the West to convey his feelings to his far-off lover. For the second time that day, I poured bourbon on Li's tomb. Unfortunately, I only had time for one poem and one shot. I had a train to catch.

A minute later, we were back on Highway 310, this time heading east toward downtown Chengchou. If I had somehow squeezed another hour out of the day, I would have visited the grave of Liu Yu-hsi (772–842). It was only two kilometers to the west and on the same road. Regrettably, I couldn't visit all the poets I admired. Still, I had a poem ready just in case. As we drove toward the train station, I unrolled the car window and read his "Ode to the Autumn Wind" 秋風引:

Where does the autumn wind come from
rising it sees off the geese
entering courtyard trees at dawn
it wakes a lone traveler first

何處秋風至,　蕭蕭送雁群。　朝來入庭樹,　孤客最先聞。

This lone traveler had a ticket for a train leaving in thirty minutes, and it was rush hour. As we approached the center of the city, it became clear I was in danger of missing my train. Mr. Huang's son said he had never driven in Chengchou before, and he wasn't sure how to get to the train station. When we came to a red light, I paid him, grabbed my bag, and jumped into an empty taxi in the next lane. I told the driver I would pay him double if he got me to the train station in time. Considering the deft maneuvering that ensued, it was clear I made the right decision. Once we reached the station, I ran all the way to the platform. I was still trying to catch my breath as the train pulled out, with me on it. I was headed west again.

Two hours after leaving Chengchou, we stopped in Lingpao. Fifteen kilometers to the north was the Yellow River, and between the river and the town was the defile through the loess plateau known as the Hankukuan Pass.

According to the account by Ssu-ma Ch'ien (d. 86 BC), it was here that Lao-tzu stopped long enough to write down the 5,000 characters that made up his *Taoteching*, the poetic work that begins, "The way that becomes a way / is not the Immortal Way / the name that becomes a name / is not the Immortal Name" 道可道, 非恆道. 名可名, 非恆名. In the time it would have taken for the old sage to write down those lines, we were gone. It was the standard two-minute stop.

The sun set, and an hour later we pulled into Sian, the modern incarnation of Ch'ang-an. It took the train less than three hours to travel the 500 kilometers from Chengchou. I used to consider myself lucky if the bus or train I was on averaged fifty kilometers an hour. I welcomed the change, but like all changes, it came at a price: people, villages, even mountains had to be moved out of the way to make that speed possible. There was also a certain amount of inconvenience for travelers, as the new trains and their elevated tracks required new stations, and the new stations were usually far from the center of town. In the case of Sian, the city's new North Station was fifteen kilometers away, which meant a longer, more expensive taxi ride as well. I almost fell asleep on the way to my hotel. I usually stayed near the Bell Tower in the center of the old part of town. I liked the location, but the ever-increasing traffic and noise, as well as the difficulty in hailing a taxi there, led me to try the Forest City off Tungtachieh. It was on a quiet street called Chrysanthemum Garden, which sounded nice. It was nine thirty by the time I checked in. I didn't even bother washing my clothes. Since I was staying two nights, I figured I would do that the next day and wear my almost-dry backup set in the morning: the orange T-shirt and gray pants, as opposed to the black T-shirt and green pants. Making that decision was all the energy I could muster before slipping off to dreamland.

I woke up in Eternal Peace, Loyang's western counterpart.
Ever since Ch'ang-an was first established as a political center
around 200 BC, if *it* wasn't China's capital, Loyang was. Ch'ang-
an was easier to guard against the periodic invasions of nomads,
which usually came from the northeast, while Loyang was closer
to grain supplies in the Yellow River floodplain. Both cities pros-
pered, but Ch'ang-an prospered more. During the T'ang, it was
home to two million people and one of the great cities of the ancient world. In
904, as the T'ang was winding down, the emperor moved the capital to Loy-
ang one last time and ordered Ch'ang-an destroyed. He didn't want to leave
anything useful behind. What remained barely qualified as a town until a
new wall was built around the central part of the old city in 1370, at the begin-
ning of the Ming dynasty. With the new wall came a new name – Sian, West-
ern Peace, as opposed to Eternal Peace – and a new role. Instead of serving
as the nation's capital, it guarded the country against invasions of tribes to
the northwest, particularly forces allied with Tamerlane.

The invasions never materialized, and Sian remained a provincial back-
water until the first waves of economic development hit the city fifty years
ago. Despite the flood of construction, enough of its past was still visible that I
could imagine some of my favorite poets walking down the very same streets.
I had a copy with me of a map made by a local historian that showed where
poets lived back in the T'ang. Ch'en Tzu-ang and Liu Tsung-yuan, for exam-
ple, lived just south of my hotel. This was where the best jobs were, and poets
were first and foremost would-be officials. Then too, since poetry was one
of the job qualifications, this was also where the best poets were. For some,
though, it was more than a job qualification: it was life and the transcen-
dence of life. After washing the clothes I wore the day before, I reviewed my
itinerary for the day. Five men were on it, five men who transcended death
as well as life.

I needed to get an early start and was out on the street before eight. I
thought that would be early enough, but I was already late. I couldn't find
a taxi. I walked from one street corner to the next. Finally, I saw one stop to
let out its passengers on the other side of the street. I dodged cars and buses
and managed to jump inside before anyone else. I told the driver we were
going to the countryside. I thought that would cheer him up. What driver
wants to spend the day stuck in city traffic? But we *were* stuck in city traffic,

and we were heading the wrong direction. At least it was a beginning. It took forty-five minutes to reach the expressway that ringed the city and another thirty to reach the G70 Expressway that led southeast toward the Chungnan Mountains.

Once we were on the G70, we found ourselves nearly alone. After the congestion of the city, it felt like being weightless. Sian was behind us. A few minutes later, the town of Lantien was behind us as well. A few minutes after that, we were in the mountains, literally, as we began passing through one tunnel after another. It was as if the expressway said, "Out of my way, mountains." Ten kilometers past Lantien, we exited at the village of Wangchuan and switched to the old road, the same road many poets traveled on their way into exile. I had been on it once before, in 1989. Back then there were only a few scattered farms and nothing worth calling a village. Despite the beauty of the Wang River Valley, it was simply too remote, even for farmers. Things had changed. The old road that followed the river upstream was now lined with weekend getaways for the bureaucrats and office workers who served the new rulers of Sian.

After several kilometers, we began asking directions for Paichiaping. It wasn't far, and the third person we asked said it was around the next bend— which it was. Around the next bend we turned left onto a much narrower road, and a minute later we drove through a gate that should have been closed but wasn't. Two hundred meters later, we pulled up just short of the huge ginkgo that led me here. It was planted by Wang Wei in the middle of his Wang River Retreat, a tract of land previously owned by the poet Sung Chih-wen (660–710).

Although his tree was still here, the fenced-in area, where Wang Wei kept deer, was gone. He called it Deer Park, in honor of the place in India where the Buddha gave his first sermon. It was the setting for one of his most famous poems, titled, appropriately, "Deer Park" 鹿柴:

> Deserted mountain no sign of people
> except for the sound of their voices
> as the light comes back through the forest
> it illuminates the green moss again

空山不見人，但聞人語響。返景入深林，復照青苔上。

The mountain was no longer deserted. Sitting on benches near the ginkgo were half a dozen workers taking a smoke break. As I got out and walked over to Wang's tree, they got up and said I shouldn't be there. They all wore blue work uniforms and were employed in a pair of adjacent buildings. The buildings were where the Chinese manufactured warheads for nuclear weapons. The production facilities were moved here in the 1950s when China wasn't getting along with Russia and decided to decentralize some of its more sensitive military operations. I thought by now they would surely have moved somewhere else. That I could simply stumble into such a place was admittedly absurd.

The first time I visited the Wang River, in 1989, I was also looking for Wang Wei's old estate, but I went looking in the adjacent valley instead. After several hours in the moun-

Ginkgo planted by Wang Wei at his Wang River Estate

tains, I was hiking back down with my photographer friend Steve Johnson, when we were arrested by military police and taken to Sian for interrogation. Fortunately, we saw them before they saw us: Steve was able to tuck his film into a sock and put new film in his camera for the authorities to expose later. We were saved on that occasion by our obvious stupidity. Later, a friend who analyzes satellite photos for the CIA pointed out that the peculiar apparatus along a stream in one of Steve's photos was a high-capacity heat sink used to reduce temperatures involved in the manufacture of such things as warheads. This confirmed what I overheard that day from the military police. They didn't know I spoke Chinese, and I did nothing to disabuse them of that impression.

At least the workers left me alone. Their break was over, and they returned to the huge metal buildings that were connected to the mountain. Even though the tree was backlit, I took a few photos with my two cameras, a new digital one and an older one loaded with black-and-white slide film. I thought about continuing into the valley. That was where Wang Wei's home was located and also Luyuan (Deer Park) Temple, which replaced it. I decided not to press my luck. I returned to my taxi, and we drove back to the gate.

But we didn't quite make it out. Three men ran out of the building next to the gate, motioning for us to stop. One of them ordered a guard to close the gate and even to padlock it. Then they began questioning my driver. I got out and asked what was wrong, as if I didn't know. When the officer in charge asked me what I was doing there, I told him, in Chinese this time, that I had come to pay my respects to Wang Wei. Not only was the ginkgo he planted still there, so was his grave, in a manner of speaking, somewhere underneath the abandoned brick buildings of the old Hsiangyang Munitions Factory, now dwarfed by the new metal ones next to them.

When the officer asked me whether I had taken any photographs, I told him I had, of the ginkgo and the sign that said the tree was planted by Wang Wei. I told him I was writing a book about my visits to the graves and homes of China's most famous poets of the past and hoped to include a photo of Wang Wei's tree. He conferred with the other officers then made a call on his cell phone. After he was finished, he told me to give him my camera. I reached into my arm bag and gave him the digital one. He turned it on and reviewed my recent photos. One by one, he deleted all those I had just taken, except the photo of the sign. That surprised me, that he left any photos at all. Then he handed it back. As I put the camera into my arm bag, he said the area was off-limits to everyone, to Chinese as well as foreigners. I apologized for my ignorance. But before getting into the taxi, I asked him if he could take a picture of the tree *for* me, without including any buildings in the background. He conferred with his fellow officers again but then reiterated that the area was off-limits. No photos. I told him I had seen a photo of the tree online, but that didn't sway him. It was clearly time to leave. I thanked him, and he told the guard to unlock the gate.

We retraced our route to the expressway. But as we approached the entrance, I told the driver to keep to the road we were on, which followed the river downstream. After a kilometer or two, I asked him to pull over. I wanted to share some bourbon with Wang Wei. The driver was only too happy to stop. The incident at the weapons factory had left him visibly shaken. I walked down to where the river made a wide bend before it entered a gorge. Once I found a suitable spot, I set out a cup for Wang Wei and one for his friend Pei Ti and another for the river. I sat on a boulder and watched the water ripple over the rocks and tried to recall the images of Wang Wei's famous Wang River Scroll—he was as famous for his paintings as he was for

Left: Wang River gorge

his poetry. Among the twenty poems both he and Pei Ti added to the scenes that made up the scroll was Wang Wei's "Deer Park." Another poem on the scroll was Wang's "Bamboo Retreat" 竹里館:

Sitting alone amid dense bamboo
playing my zither and droning
deep in the forest no one else knows
until the bright moon looks down

獨坐幽篁裏, 彈琴復長嘯。 深林人不知, 明月來相照。

Like Juan Chi, Wang Wei was both a musician and a cultivator of spiritual arts. He, too, could drone. But unlike Juan Chi, he served at the highest level of government and even rose to the post of deputy prime minister. His heart, though, was in the mountains. He called himself Layman Vimalakirti, after the interlocutor of the Buddhist sutra of the same name Whenever he wasn't needed in the capital, this was where he came to meditate, to drone, to play music, to paint, to hike, or to do nothing at all. It must have been hard for him to go back to town. Clearly, he found the river as entrancing as I did. To remind the river of its old friend, I read Wang Wei's "On Leaving My Wang River Retreat" 別輞川別業:

With reluctance I left in my horse-drawn carriage
sadly the tree moss is now behind me
I could bear leaving the blue mountains
but the green water wasn't so easy

依遲動車馬, 惆悵出松蘿。 忍別青山去, 其如綠水何。

After finishing what Wang and Pei didn't, I emptied the remaining cup into the river. By the time I returned to the taxi, the driver was his old self. The events at the weapons factory, I imagined, were going to be the center of conversation at dinner that night. Hopefully, everyone would find it funny.

A few minutes later, we exited the gorge and turned west onto Highway 107, which soon merged with Highway 108. I wondered who thought up these country highways. They were paved, far wider than they needed to be, and almost completely devoid of traffic. Such pleasant roads in China were rare, especially roads that seemed to have no other purpose than to skirt mountains – in this case, mountains that rose like a wall out of the windblown loess that had been accumulating there for the past million years.

These were the Chungnan Mountains I hiked into to find the hermits who formed the basis of my book *Road to Heaven*. The book wasn't exactly a best seller in America, but the Chinese translation sold over 200,000 copies. The Chinese hold hermits in the highest esteem. The recluse has always been an important part of their culture. The same year my book appeared in Chinese, the Buddhists in Sian formed an association to help the men and women who cultivated solitude in these mountains. Since the association was headquartered just down the road at Hsingchiao Temple, I decided to say hello.

About seven kilometers past the village of Yinchen, I asked the driver to turn right and follow a narrow road that led up a dirt hillside. As we pulled into the small parking lot at the end of the road, a man came out of one of the buildings and waved. He was in charge of taking care of the temple's bookstore. A few years earlier it was through his efforts that I met the person who purchased Wei Ying-wu's tombstone from a pair of grave robbers. But that is another story.

This time he said to wait there. A minute later, the hermit association's deputy director appeared. He was a layman, not a monk. His Buddhist name was Hsin-yi. After exchanging introductions, he led me to his office, and, over several cups of tea, he brought me up-to-date about the goings-on in the mountains. Some hermits had moved down, others had moved up, and a few had died. I was sad to hear about the deaths – not for the people who died, but for me, that I wouldn't be seeing them again. They were the happiest people I had ever met. Nothing is quite so liberating as choosing to live on next to nothing, and doing it. Of course, such a way of life isn't for everyone, and there is always the question of that first winter.

Hsin-yi also updated me on the documentary being filmed in the mountains by Emei Film Studios. I had helped introduce the head of the studio to some of the hermits I knew and was relieved to learn that the filming was being done with care and respect. As a parting gift, Hsin-yi gave me the cup I had just emptied. It had a lovely celadon glaze, and on its underside were the characters for the Chungnan Mountains. He put the cup in a protective box to ensure it got back to America in one piece, which it did. Every time I use it, which is almost every day, I think of my friends in the mountains and the long and venerable tradition of doing nothing, of which I, too, am a practitioner. Every day I try to do a little less. Doing nothing, though, is still a ways off. In poem 181 of his *Mountain Poems,* Stonehouse makes it sound so simple:

> Letting go means letting everything go
> buddhahood has to go too
> each thought becomes a demon
> each word invites more trouble
> survive instead on what karma brings
> pass your days in freedom
> make the Dharma for your practice
> lead your ox to the mill

放下全放下，佛也莫要做。動念即成魔，開口便招禍。
飲啄但隨緣，只麼閒閒過。執法去修行，牽牛來拽磨。

Words are easy. My ox has a mind of its own.

On my way out, I stopped at the stupa that contained the remains of the monk Hsuan-tsang (602–664). He was one of China's greatest translators and one of my heroes. Naturally, he didn't get any bourbon, just the standard three bows.

From Highway 108 we soon turned onto Highway 104, which led north toward Sian. After five kilometers, I told the driver to stop so I could ask directions. It took a few tries, but I finally found someone who knew which road led to Chupo Village on the adjacent Shaoling Plateau. I had read a story on the Internet by a descendant of the T'ang writer and poet Liu Tsung-yuan (773–819) who determined that his ancestor's grave lay between the villages of Chupo and West Yangwanpo underneath a field of winter wheat. He didn't say how he had determined the spot, and he didn't mention a tombstone or any other surface remains. Still, since he was lobbying authorities to mark the site, I wanted to see whether he had been successful.

Liu Tsung-yuan and Han Yu were the two greatest essayists of the T'ang. However, unlike Han Yu, Liu was not as well known for his poetry. That changed when he was banished in 805 because of his support for a reformist faction at court. Poetry has always been much better than prose for expressing, and for transcending, suffering, which was what happened in Liu's case, as is evident in his "River Snow" 江雪:

A thousand mountains and not a bird flying
ten thousand trails and not a single footprint
an old man in his raincoat in a solitary boat
fishes alone in the freezing river snow

千山鳥飛絕，萬徑人蹤滅。孤舟蓑笠翁，獨釣寒江雪。

This was written during Liu's banishment to Yungchou in southern Hunan province. It was born of loneliness, and yet it transcended loneliness. Over the centuries this poem has inspired more paintings than any poem ever written in China. Who hasn't seen such a painting? After ten years in Yungchou, Liu was recalled to the capital. But two months later he was banished again. This time he was sent even farther, to Liuchou, just north of Vietnam. During his time there, he sent poems to several friends who had likewise been banished to other out-of-the-way places in South China. All were members of the wrong faction at court. One such poem is "Climbing Liuchou Tower, Sent to the Magistrates of Chang, Ting, Feng, and Lien Counties" 登柳州城樓寄漳汀封連:

The city tower here borders wilderness
my cares are as endless as the ocean sky
a sudden wind churns the lotus-filled water
a downpour beats against the vine-covered wall
ridgetop trees block distant views
the river's bends are as tortuous as my thoughts
since coming to this land of tattooed tribes
we share a realm beyond the reach of letters

城上高樓接大荒，海天愁思正茫茫。惊風亂颭芙蓉水，密雨斜侵薜荔墻。
嶺樹重遮千里目，江流曲似九回腸。共來百越文身地，猶自音書滯一鄉。

Liu and his fellow exiles were sent 1,500 kilometers from the capital. Such an "assignment" was tantamount to a death sentence. Liu managed to survive four years among the tattooed tribes before he succumbed to one of the region's tropical diseases. There is still a grave in Liuchou that contains his clothes. His body, though, was brought back to Ch'ang-an and buried on the Shaoling Plateau somewhere near Chupo Village.

From the highway, we followed a narrow paved road up a rather steep slope to the top of the plateau and soon found our way to the village. It was about a kilometer northwest of the huge brick stupas built to contain the remains of the founders of the Huayen school of Chinese Buddhism. The stupas dated back to the early T'ang, and their environs would have been an auspicious place to be buried. I walked around the village for an hour and asked anyone who looked curious whether they knew anything about a Liu Tsung-yuan grave. All I got were shrugs. I finally gave up. Either the local authorities didn't think the site worth investing in or they didn't think Liu Tsung-yuan's descendant had found the right place. I kept the bourbon in my bag and headed back the way we came.

As we reached the edge of the plateau, I asked the driver to stop. I wanted to survey the floodplain to the west while I still had a good view. The plain was the work of the Fan River and was home at one time or another to many of the great poets of the T'ang. Tu Fu, Pai Chu-yi, Li Shang-yin, and Tu Mu all lived there. Although I wasn't aware of a specific site associated with any of them, it was instructive to see the network of gullies the river had carved out between floods and to reflect on all the poems written on its banks.

It wasn't a long reflection. There were three more poets on the day's itinerary. Returning to the highway, we headed north again. Two kilometers later, I asked the driver to turn onto another side road. This one led to a shrine first built 800 years ago for Tu Fu. Tu Fu lived in this area for more than a dozen years when he was trying to pass the civil service exams. The exact location of his residence is unknown, but he identified himself with both the river and the plateau. Sometimes he called himself the Old Man of Fan River and sometimes the Bumpkin of Shaoling. I'm guessing the choice had something to do with fluctuations in his income. It was cheaper to live closer to the river, but it was less secure.

Like so many of the places I had been visiting, his shrine was deserted, which suited me fine. It was a nice place to walk around and featured the standard courtyard-style brick home whose wings contained exhibits outlining the poet's life. Among the exhibits was the earliest-known portrait of the poet, which showed him looking very official-like. I had seen copies before, so I wasn't surprised. But one exhibit that did take me by surprise was a stele of the only surviving example of Tu Fu's calligraphy. It was a poem. Unfortunately, too much of it was missing or illegible. The date, though, was clear:

the second year of the Chienyuan reign period, or 759. Later that same year, Tu Fu left Ch'ang-an and never returned.

Although I gave up on the poem, I lingered over the calligraphy. It expressed a relaxed freedom not usually associated with Tu Fu. Li Pai, yes, not Tu Fu. I had often felt that sort of freedom in his poems. Seeing it in his calligraphy was even more revealing. He was hardly wild and crazy, but he enjoyed an outing as much as anyone. While he was studying for the exams, one of his favorite places for getting away from the books was a reservoir on the Fan River floodplain less than two kilometers west of his shrine. During one such excursion, he wrote a pair of poems titled "Encountering Rain at Changpa Reservoir One Evening While Enjoying a Cool Breeze with Some Rich Young Men and Their Singsong Girls" 陪諸貴公子丈八沟攜妓納涼際遇雨:

Sunset is just right for boating
a light breeze stirs a few waves
boaters pause by the dense bamboo
breathing the cool lotus-flower air
the young men add ice to their drinks
the girls prepare lotus-root slices
clouds overhead turn dark
surely the rain will bring poems

落日放船好，輕風生浪遲。竹深留客處，荷淨納涼時。
公子調冰水，佳人雪藕絲。片雲頭上黑，應是雨催詩。

Rain arrives and drenches the mats
wind beats against the prow
the girls from the south wring out their red skirts
the girls from the north lament their mascara
even with the boat tied to a willow
the awning still lifts in the spray
the road home looks desolate now
on a fall day in May at the lake

雨來沾席上，風急打船頭。越女紅裙濕，燕姬翠黛愁。
纜侵堤柳繫，慢卷浪花浮。歸路翻蕭颯，陂塘五月秋。

Ah, life in the capital. It certainly could be pleasant. Poets didn't always have to suffer to write good poems.

Since I didn't find anything else at the shrine worth lingering over, we returned to the highway, but only briefly. Just before the highway intersected with Changan Road, I asked the driver to turn onto yet another side road. This one was even narrower and led uphill to the village of Huangtzupo. This was where Han Yu used to live. In fact, the northern part of the village that once looked out over ancient Ch'ang-an was still called Han Manor. Again I was searching for something that had long since vanished. Twelve hundred years ago, the view would have included most of the capital and scenes like the one in a poem Han wrote to fellow poet Chang Chi, "Early Spring – for Supernumerary Chang of the Water Bureau." In later collections the title was shortened to "Spring Rain" 春雨:

> The streets of Heaven glisten in light rain
> I see grass in the distance but not nearby
> this is truly the best time of spring
> the sight of misty willows veiling the royal city

天街小雨潤如酥，草色遙看近卻無。最是一年春好處，絕勝煙柳滿皇都。

By Heaven, Han was referring to Ch'ang-an, where he spent his twenties studying for the civil service exams, his thirties coming and going, and his fifties in a series of high-level posts. His forties were spent mostly in Loyang with Meng Chiao, Chang Chi, and Chia Tao. It was also while living in Ch'ang-an that he wrote his famous memorial complaining about the emperor's excessively reverential attitude toward what was said to be the Buddha's finger bone. For his lèse-majesté, he was banished to Chaoyang on the distant southeast coast. On his way there, passing through the Chinling (aka Chungnan) Mountains, he wrote this poem to his nephew, Han Hsiang, who accompanied him as far as the pass – and who later became one of Taoism's Eight Immortals – "For My Nephew Hsiang on My Demotion and Arrival at Lankuan Pass" 左遷之藍關示姪孫湘:

> I submitted a memorial to the palace at dawn
> I was bound for Chaoyang by dusk a thousand miles away

hoping to rid the court of its mistaken ways
I dared in my senility to begrudge my final years
Chinling clouds now obscure the way back home
Lankuan snow still blocks the path ahead
there must be a reason you've come this far
no doubt to retrieve my bones from some infested river

一封朝奏九重天，夕貶潮州路八千。欲為聖朝除弊事，肯將衰朽惜殘年。
雲橫秦嶺家何在，雪擁藍關馬不前。知汝遠來應有意，好收吾骨瘴江邊。

It was a bone joke, and I'm guessing the emperor didn't laugh. Two years later his successor relented, recalling Han to the capital and appointing him to a series of senior posts. However, the poet's health never recovered from his banishment, and he died three years after his return.

Having taken in the view, such as it was, I directed the driver back down to the highway then asked him to turn right on Changan Road. We followed it along the northern edge of the Shaoling Plateau more than ten kilometers, until it finally ended at Highway 113, whereupon we turned southeast, toward Yinchen and the mountains. When we came to the village of Tunghsiang, I started asking farmers the way to West Ssuma Village. The third farmer pointed us south down a newly paved road. Two kilometers later, we were there.

It wasn't much of a village, maybe 200 meters on a side. I approached an old man sitting on a stool repairing his mattock and smoking what looked like a hand-rolled cigar. I asked him whether he knew where Tu Mu (803–852) was buried. I always enjoyed asking questions like that, where someone lived or died or wrote a poem over a thousand years ago. Being an optimist, I always expected a positive response, even when it didn't seem likely. In this case, the old man nodded and led me behind the cluster of one-story brick houses that made up the village. As we walked along, I looked at his cigar again. It was a single tobacco leaf, not tobacco held together by another leaf wrapped around it. Several other villagers joined us in the field. They were smoking the same kind of cigars. Tobacco must have been one of their crops. After walking a hundred meters or so through fields of beans then eggplant then corn and finally onions, the old man stopped and pointed to a pit at the edge of a recently harvested field. He said that was where the grave used to be. Some officials came there in the 1970s and took away whatever it was they dug up. The pit was all that remained, and it was full of trash.

Tu Mu's gravesite at West Ssuma Village

Tu Mu was one of the few major poets of the T'ang who was born and raised in Ch'ang-an. However, once he passed the civil service exams and received his first appointment, he spent most of his life elsewhere. As he was getting ready to leave Ch'ang-an to take up his final post, he wrote "Climbing Leyou Plateau Before Leaving for Wuhsing" 將赴吳興登樂遊原：

> The times might be peaceful but not for me
> I envy the freedom of clouds and the stillness of monks
> about to take my banner to the shores of the Yangtze
> from Leyou Plateau I look toward Chaoling

清時有味是無能，閑愛孤雲靜愛僧。欲把一麾江海去，樂遊原上望昭陵。

Wuhsing was over a thousand kilometers away, just north of Hangchou. And Chaoling was the name of the tomb of the founder of the T'ang dynasty, Emperor T'ai-tsung. It was about eighty kilometers northwest of Leyou Plateau and would have been visible as a bump on the horizon. When Tu Mu wrote this poem, it was not a peaceful time – his first line is facetious. His last line refers to the beginning of the dynasty. T'ai-tsung was known as an astute judge of men, and Tu Mu regrets not having benefited from serving a similar ruler. He remained disappointed in that regard, and died three years later, shortly after returning from Wuhsing.

I filled a cup with bourbon and took a sip, then I poured the rest into the pit, and read his most famous poem aloud. It was titled "Purification Day" 清明. In Confucius's time, people celebrated this day by bathing in a river. By Tu Mu's time, it had become a day for visiting the graves of ancestors. When he wrote this poem, Tu Mu was nowhere near his ancestors' graves. He was traveling along a road near the Yangtze river town of Kueichih:

> Purification Day and the rain keeps falling
> traveling on foot I feel like I might collapse
> I ask a herdboy if he knows where there's a tavern
> he points in the distance to Apricot Flower Village

清明時節雨紛紛，路上行人欲斷魂。借問酒家何處有，牧童遙指杏花村。

The farmers standing there smoking their cigars all knew the poem by heart and joined me. They had probably memorized it in elementary school. I poured another cup and offered it to the old man who led me there. He took a sip, and his eyes widened. He handed it back and took another drag on his cigar. He said something to his fellow farmers, and they all laughed. It was dialect, and I didn't understand. I refilled the cup, took one more sip, and poured what remained into the trash-filled pit that was once Tu Mu's grave. Apricot Flower Village was, and still is, famous for its white lightning. No doubt, it resuscitated Tu Mu that day. If his spirit had been around the day I was there, I have no doubt the Stagg would have done the same. I thanked the old man, and we all walked back to the village.

As I headed back to the city, I realized the road went past the very loess plateau Tu Mu climbed before heading to his final assignment. According to a road sign, it was now home to the Leyou Golf Club. There is simply no way to anticipate life's little jokes.

I asked the driver to drop me off at Sian's South Gate. I paid him double the metered fare for what must have been a difficult day, and climbed the steps that led to the gate's ancient parapet. I looked out over the southern part of the city. Beyond the twenty-first-century skyline, I could see the vague outline of the Chungnan Mountains. I set out my three little cups on the ledge and filled them with the rest of the bourbon in my flask. Then I lifted them one at a time in the direction of the mountains and toasted all the poets who had lived there. After taking a sip from each, I read Wang Wei's "Sent from the Mountains to My Younger Brothers and Sisters" 山中寄諸弟妹:

These mountains are full of Dharma friends
we meditate and chant in a world apart
if you look for us from the city wall
all you will see are clouds

山中多法侶，禪誦自為群。城郭遙相望，唯應見白雲。

While I was taking in the view, a dozen Russian girls joined me on the wall. They were a dance troupe and arrived with a TV crew to film a promotional video. I stayed long enough to watch their rendition of the cancan then strolled back to my hotel. It wasn't often that I had time on my hands before the sun went down. After a seafood gumbo at the restaurant next to the hotel, I washed my clothes and was in bed by eight. Next to a hot bath, going to bed early was my favorite travel luxury. I was asleep in minutes.

The next thing I knew, I was sipping coffee as the sun rose. Every day was a good day, but this one was going to be even better. I was going to be spending it with Wei Ying-wu (737–791). I had translated more poems by Cold Mountain and Stonehouse, but their poems were rarely autobiographical. They wrote about the mountains on which they lived and also about the no-mountains on which they lived. They didn't reveal much about themselves. Wei Ying-wu's poems were about Wei Ying-wu. I felt a kinship with him I didn't feel with the other poets I admired.

For a change, I didn't have to look for a taxi. Before parting from my driver the previous day I'd asked him whether he was up for a repeat. I promised him it would be trauma-free – at least I had every expectation it would. When I checked out of the Forest City, he was waiting. I tossed my bag in back and sat in front. His name was Mr. Ma. For some reason, I didn't look at the ID on his dashboard the previous day and never bothered asking his name. I was distracted, I guess, by maps and side roads, not to mention the Wang Wei episode.

We began by driving to the traffic circle at the Bell Tower then headed south. Ten kilometers later, we turned west onto Weichu North Street. I began looking down the alleys on my side of the street. In the middle of the second or third block – it wasn't clear what constituted a block – I saw what I was looking for: an alley that went uphill. Mr. Ma parked, and I went to investigate.

I walked up the alley about 200 meters then worked my way up an adjacent alley until I came to a small shrine. I climbed the steps and read the inscription that recorded the shrine's most recent renovation. Several locals who had followed me up the alley also followed me up the steps. One of the older men said that when he was a boy the land occupied by the shrine included the entire hill for half a dozen blocks in all directions. It was called Laoyehtzu, or Old Man Shrine. The twin doors were padlocked, but through the crack where they met I could see a statue of the earth god – Laoyeh being a name by which he is also known. A protector of places, he protected Wei District, named for Wei Ying-wu's ancestors. That's why I was here. The hill was part of his ancestor's estate. When I asked the man how to get to the top, he directed me down a side alley that led east. I followed it to a set of steps that disappeared beneath a tangle of vines just below the summit. Beneath the vegetation was the former location of Duke Wei's reading terrace. It was

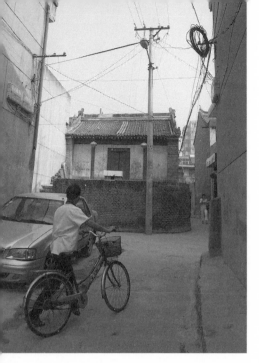

Looking for the reading terrace of
Wei Ying-wu's ancestor

once sufficiently famous that travelers noted it in their journals. There wasn't any sign, but it was the only elevated place in the district, so this had to be it.

The duke's name was Wei Hsiung (d. 578). He was Wei Ying-wu's hero. Rather than bow and stand in attendance at court, he chose to spend his time playing his zither and reading books, which he did on this hill. Instead of being ostracized by those in power for his disdain of their ceremonial lives, he was held in the highest esteem. People regarded him as someone above the fray. They called him the Carefree Duke.

During the T'ang, the Wei clan was one of the most powerful in the empire. Somewhere along the way, his branch must have committed an unforgivable indiscretion of some kind. His poems mention his father and grandfather only in reference to an unnamed unfortunate event. Still, given his lineage, Wei was asked to join Emperor Hsuan-tsung's personal guard when he was only fifteen. Even though his family wasn't doing that well, his position allowed him to lead an indulgent, dissolute life — following his emperor's example. Meeting a fellow guardsmen years later, in the aftermath of the An Lu-shan Rebellion, Wei thought back to their time together in "Entertaining Adjutant Li" 燕李錄事：

When we were fifteen we both served at court
we climbed the red steps through incense at dawn
we toured the Han Garden in bloom
and bathed on Lishan in the snow
but the Immortal has flown and isn't expected back
his advisers are scattered assuming they're alive
meeting you today as I think about the past
one cup makes me happy the next one sad

與君十五侍皇闈，曉拂爐煙上赤墀。花開漢苑經過處，雪下驪山沐浴時。
近臣零落今猶在，仙駕飄颻不可期。此日相逢思舊日，一杯成喜亦成悲。

Eventually Wei realized the path he was on was a dead end, and he switched his allegiance from the emperor – the Immortal in the poem – to his ancestor. I offered his hero an early morning shot of Stagg and sprinkled it on the tangled vines and broken bricks that covered the place where the duke spent his carefree days and nights. I'm sure there were still people surnamed Wei in the district, but it would have taken forever to track them down. And it wouldn't have mattered. The area around the reading terrace wasn't where Wei Ying-wu lived. He was born and raised about ten kilometers to the southeast, somewhere between Han Yu's estate at the northern edge of the Shaoling Plateau and Tu Mu's grave at the southern edge. The place had a name, Choukueili Village, but no one knows exactly where it was. The location of his grave also remains a mystery. A few years ago his tombstone was unearthed by grave robbers, but they sold it without revealing where they found it.

Since I couldn't visit Wei's home or his grave, I decided to visit two places where he lived, where he experienced the saddest and the happiest times of his life. I began with the saddest time and the town of Huhsien, thirty kilometers west of Sian. When Wei Ying-wu got married, the light went on in his life. When his wife died twenty years later, he was devastated. One of Wei's friends was the mayor of Ch'ang-an and arranged for him to be assigned as magistrate of Huhsien, thinking it would be a better place to recover than the capital. Shortly after Wei arrived there, he wrote "Call of the Cuckoo" 子規啼:

Dew drips from tall trees on a clear summer night
in the hills to the south a cuckoo calls
the widow next door comforts her child
I turn in bed and wait for first light

高林滴露夏夜清，南山子規啼一聲。鄰家孀婦抱兒泣，我獨展轉何時明。

A few blocks from his ancestor's reading terrace, we entered the expressway that encircled Sian, then turned onto an expressway that led southeast. Thirty minutes later, we took the Huhsien exit and drove through the town. Two kilometers west of its old bell tower – I was surprised it was still there – we crossed a bridge. We took the next road on the right and two minutes later parked outside the fence surrounding Meipo Reservoir. This was where Wei came to be alone. It was the sort of place people nowadays visited only on weekends. Other than the caretaker and my driver, I was the only one there. There were a few duck-billed paddleboats along the shore, but no one was paddling. I walked along the trail that circled the reservoir then settled on a bench. It was ten o'clock and steam was rising from the water in the sunlight. I read Wei's "Letting My Eyes Roam at Meipo Reservoir While Serving as Magistrate of Huhsien" 任鄠令渼陂遊眺:

> White water surges along the embankment
> mist swirls in a sunny sky
> green is taking over the trees
> there's jade on a thousand mountains
> fish are swimming up to the surface
> lotuses aren't thick yet
> I come here to be alone with my thoughts
> I regret lacking social skills

野水灧長塘，煙花亂晴日。氤蘊綠樹多，蒼翠千山出。
游魚時可見，新荷尚未密。屢往心獨閒，恨無理人術。

Near my bench was a bridge to a small island in the middle of the reservoir – probably the result of dredging the mud that accumulated over the centuries. I walked across to inspect an abandoned villa that dated back to the Ming dynasty. While I was investigating its vine-covered archways and walls, I woke two guard dogs, a Newfoundland and a Doberman. The dogs were chained, but their barking ended my excursion.

I returned to the car and asked Mr. Ma to take me to the mountains. When Wei Ying-wu was living in Huhsien, he befriended a number of hermits. One of them was a Taoist who wrote to Wei about the tiger that frequented his garden. Wei responded with "In Reply to Taoist Master Tung-lin" 答東林道士:

> How many peaks are you west of Tzuke
> in your thatched hut this snowy night beside those tiger tracks
> if I knew where you were in that distant darkness
> I would follow your evening bell all the way up the mountain

紫閣西邊第幾峯，茅齋夜雪虎行蹤。遙看黛色知何處，欲出山門尋暮鐘。

Tzuke, or Purple Pavilion, is the highest peak in the section of the Chungnan Mountains southeast of Huhsien and was my next destination. It took twenty minutes to reach Highway 108, the same road I took the day before which ran along the base of the mountains, and another twenty to find the road that went up the right gorge, the one known as Tzukeyu (Purple Pavilion Gorge). As we started up the gorge, I could see the peak in the distance. The drivable section, though, only lasted a kilometer and ended at a small café that catered to weekend hikers. I left Mr. Ma there and started walking. He was happy. So was I. I was in the mountains. Walking along a rutted dirt road, though, felt strange. I would have preferred a trail.

The rutted road became somewhat more bearable when it dipped down to follow the stream. The water was so clear, I wouldn't have been able to distinguish it from the streambed if not for the occasional ripple. After about an hour, I came to the former site of Paolin Temple. This was, more or less, my destination. In honor of the peak at the end of the gorge, it was also called Tzuke Temple. Most of the major poets of the T'ang wrote about their visits here. The temple, though, was gone, and workers were putting up a steel structure that looked as if it, too, would soon be catering to weekend hikers.

Just past the worksite there was a side trail leading to Chingte Stupa. Just as I was about to head up, a farmer came walking down. He had been looking for wild plants and had a bunch of them in a bag. After he satisfied himself that I wasn't lost, we chatted. I asked him whether any hermits were living in the area, anyone who cultivated the Tao. He said there were, but they had moved deeper into the mountains, beyond Tzuke Peak, beyond the range of weekend hikers. I thanked him and started up the trail. Along the way I noticed several huts across the gorge. Apparently, not everyone had moved beyond the peak.

The reason I was hiking up the trail was to pay my respects once again to Hsuan-tsang, the monk whose translations of Buddhist texts had inspired my own efforts at

Chingte Pagoda in Purple Pavilion Gorge

rendering sutras into English. It was recently discovered that part of his cremated remains were placed inside the stupa at the end of the trail. It only took ten minutes to get there, but they were an exhausting ten minutes. I arrived so out of breath I had to sit down in the middle of the path pilgrims had worn around the stupa and lean against its protective railing. I thought I might have a better view of Purple Pavilion from here, but there was too much vegetation and too much haze.

Once I stopped panting, I got up and made three circumambulations of the stupa and bowed once more to the monk who traveled all the way to India and back just to satisfy his quest for knowledge. My own journey suddenly seemed so pedestrian. It was just a pilgrimage. I turned my attention back to the poet who led me here.

Like most of China's great poets, Wei Ying-wu was torn between a career of service to the state and a life of personal cultivation. I read another poem he wrote to the same Taoist hermit, who couldn't have lived more than a hoot and a holler from the stupa. The title alone took most of the breath I'd regained: "Shu-chien, Layman Tung-lin of Tzuke, Sends Me Pine Pollen Balls, Which I Am Glad to Receive – Though They Are Not Meant to Be Eaten by People in the World of Dust. I Respond with a Poem Instead of a Letter" 紫閣東林居士叔緘賜松英丸捧對忻喜蓋非塵侶之所當服輒獻詩代啟.

From five-needle pines in beryl-blue gorges
gathered in the clouds along with the dew
you made your magic pills after summoning the immortals
thinking of benighted friends you sent some down to me
fasting before an altar today I finally ate them
suddenly the stench of mundane life seems wrong
gazing at your cloud-wrapped peak I send this back in thanks
the brass seal at my waist tugs against my heart

碧澗蒼松五粒稀， 侵雲采去露沾衣。 夜啟群山合靈藥， 朝思俗侶寂將歸。
道場齋戒今初服， 人事葷羶已覺非。 一望嵐峯拜還使， 腰間銅印與心違。

Despite the attraction of the mountains, Wei stayed at his post in Huhsien until his three-year assignment ended. When it did, he headed back toward Ch'ang-an. It was time for me to head there myself. On my way to the car, though, I met a young monk walking up the road, scouting sites for a hut. He said there were more than a dozen monks and nuns living farther up the gorge, and he was hoping to join them before winter. When I told him what the farmer told me, he said I asked the wrong question. I'd asked whether anyone in the mountains was cultivating the Tao. The monk said I should have asked whether anyone was cultivating the Dharma. In the past, asking about the Tao always worked. I was glad to hear there were still people cultivating, no matter what it was they were cultivating. Vegetables would have been fine too. I wished him luck and continued down the road.

When I finally reached Mr. Ma, I told him I had one more stop, and showed him my map. We began by taking the highway back the way we had come. The roadside was lined with farmers selling grapes. Mr. Ma stopped and bought a bunch, and he offered me some. They were so huge, juicy, and sweet, they distracted me from the road: we missed our turnoff and had to double back. When we finally found County Road 213, we turned north and drove for ten kilometers, until the road intersected with Highway 105, the same road Wei Ying-wu would have taken when he left Huhsien for the capital. We followed him east. Then, just after we crossed the Feng River, we turned off the highway and took the first road on our right. It ran along an irrigation ditch and ended two kilometers later at a set of sluice gates. The Feng River was the major source of water for the farms and factories west of Sian. It was also where Wei Ying-wu stopped after he left Huhsien. He never reached Ch'ang-an.

I began walking along the poplar-lined embankment and stopped to talk to two boys who were fishing with bamboo poles – no reels, just poles with lines tied to hooks. They already had half a dozen carp swimming in a bucket. They said they were going to sell them to a restaurant in the next village. Young Huck Finns with a plan. I also stopped to talk to an old man who was watching his goats eat their way along the river. That was one of the advantages of growing old: you got to watch goats.

I must have walked a kilometer or more. I wanted to get a sense of the river along which Wei Ying-wu spent his happiest days. After his term in Huhsien ended, he received another appointment east of Ch'ang-an. He turned it down and chose, instead, to live as a farmer. Right here where I was walking, on the east shore of the Feng, Wei finally lived the life he had been drawn to ever since his wife died, if not before. Fortunately, he wasn't dependent on what he grew. He still received rental income from tenants who worked the land around the family estate on the Shaoling Plateau, so he didn't starve.

As a young man, Wei had been inspired by his ancestor Wei Hsiung. As he grew older, the poet T'ao Yuan-ming (365–427) replaced the Carefree Duke atop Wei's pantheon. T'ao had also given up his career as an official and

Boys fishing on the Feng River

retired to the countryside, where he tended chrysanthemums and enjoyed the company of farmers. The four years Wei Ying-wu spent in similar circumstances along the Feng River were not only his happiest years, they were also his most productive. He summed up his new life in a poem to a friend in the capital, "In Reply to Gentleman-in-Attendance Ch'ang Tang" 答暢校書當:

> I just happened to quit my post
> and end up in the countryside
> where the rising sun lights thatch huts
> and gardens and groves support simple folk
> though I'd agree I'm without means
> my wine cup is rarely empty
> I delight in ripening grain
> and sigh at the work of creation
> in step with villagers dawn to dusk
> there's nothing they do I don't
> I cut bamboo along the stream to the south

and return at night to the Feng's east shore
I retired because of incompetence
it wasn't to follow a higher path
I read your essay of jade and gold
its beautiful lines lit up my face
day after day I've wanted to reply
that was in spring and now it's winter

偶然棄官去，投跡在田中。日出照茅屋，園林養愚蒙。
雖云無一資，罇酌會不空。且忻百谷成，仰嘆造化功。
出入與民伍，作事靡不同。時代南澗竹，夜還灃水東。
貧寒自成退，豈為高人蹤。覽君金玉篇，彩色發我容。
日月欲為報，方春已徂冬。

Despite Wei's obvious contentment, his sense of responsibility was irrepressible. He couldn't resist the call to serve at court once more — but even then he kept thinking back to his years on the Feng. I found a spot where there were some boulders along the shore, just right for setting out my standard three-cup offering. After I poured part of each cup into the river, I drank the rest. My day was just about over. The cicadas were throbbing but sounded tired. It had been a long, hot summer. I was tired too, and I probably should have poured more of the whiskey into the river. At nearly 143 proof, it didn't take more than a few sips to do what whiskey does so well.

When I returned to the car, I asked Mr. Ma to take me to the train station. An hour later, he dropped me off three blocks short of there. He said he was afraid of the police near the station. I'm guessing he had unpaid tickets or an expired license. It didn't matter — I had time. Again I paid him double the meter and thanked him for indulging my excursions. I put on my pack and trudged down the street and through the chaos that invariably swirled outside the entrance to every train station in China: the migrant workforce waiting for a job or a train to somewhere else. Once inside, I opted for the "tearoom." The extra 10RMB meant I could avoid the mob that formed when it was time to punch tickets, which happened fifteen minutes before a train was scheduled to depart. People in the tearoom also had a shorter route to the platforms. Plus there were benches — and free tea.

As I took a seat, a man across from me stood up and walked over and took the seat next to mine. "I know you," he said. "I have your book, the one about hermits." He was a retired English teacher and wanted to practice with a native speaker. I was tired and didn't hold up my part of the conversation very well, but at least he got a chance to practice his English.

Thirty minutes later, my train was called, and I got up to leave. The man reached into his bag and handed me a small box of Wutzu green tea, grown on the south side of the Chungnan Mountains. The box he gave me was part of a much larger one he was taking to his relatives. I thanked him and a few minutes later collapsed in the train's air-conditioned comfort. It left Sian at six o'clock sharp. Ninety minutes later, I got off in Paochi, 180 kilometers to the west.

Paochi wasn't my final destination. I still had a connecting train to catch. But I saw that as an advantage. After my day in the mountains, I needed a shower. Since my next train wasn't due for two and a half hours, I rented a room at a cheap hotel across the street from the station. The room came not only with a bathroom but also with a computer and an air-conditioner. I turned on the aircon, checked my e-mail, and took a shower. I even washed my clothes, which I then wrapped in the two towels that came with the room and stepped on them to get out as much water as possible. Then I hung them in front of the aircon and lay on a bed whose sheets were as tight as the bed I made every morning in the army. It was such a relief to lie down, I actually nodded off and was glad I remembered to set my alarm. When it went off, my clothes were still damp but dry enough to wear. I walked outside feeling refreshed. Twenty minutes later, I boarded the ten o'clock express to Li Pai's hometown, or at least one of his hometowns. He had four. He was Li Pai.

In the old days, the T'ang-dynasty days, the trek from Paochi to Szechuan across the Chinling Range was one of the most formidable in China. Li Pai wrote: "Traveling the road to Shu is harder than climbing to Heaven" 蜀道之難, 難于上青天. Shu is the old name for the westernmost part of Szechuan. The road was long, and it was dangerous. In many places, it turned into kilometer-long sections of peg-supported planks edged against sheer cliffs. I was grateful for trains, especially trains with berths.

Mine was bound for Chengtu, the capital of Szechuan, but I was getting off two hours early. As the darkness gave way to another day, I was the first person in my compartment to awake. I sat up in bed and gazed out the window. The landscape had changed. The endless flat fields of corn, soybeans, and cotton I had been seeing for the past eight days in the Yellow River watershed had been replaced by terraces of rice, hillsides of bamboo, and waterways crowded with lotuses. I could almost smell the flowers. Szechuan forms the westernmost part of the Yangtze watershed, and it rains a lot. Szechuan is why the Yangtze carries more water than any river in the world. About the time my compartment companions began to stir, I put on my shoes, grabbed my pack, and walked down the corridor as the train pulled into the town of Chiangyou. It was just after nine.

In the past, travelers who made it through the Chinling Range either continued overland to Chengtu or switched to boats in Chiangyou then sailed down the Fuchiang River. The Fuchiang flowed southeast into the Chialing, which flowed into the Yangtze at Chungching. Chiangyou was a fine place for a merchant to set up shop. With the advent of railways and expressways, that has changed. Nowadays the town's fame and at least part of its economy rested on its claim as the hometown of Li Pai.

Li Pai, though, wasn't born here. The consensus among scholars is that the Poetry Sage was born in 701, in Kyrgyzstan, to a Chinese merchant father and a Turkic-speaking mother – presumably a member of one of the ethnic minorities along that part of the Silk Road. Sometime after the boy's birth, the merchant returned to his home west of Paochi, to which his ancestors had been banished centuries earlier for some undisclosed offense. Then in 705, for reasons we are left to imagine, the father "escaped" over the same mountains I had just slept through and settled his family on the Fujiang River just south of Chiangyou. I thought I would begin with the family homestead.

Statue of Li Pai at his old home in Chinglien Village

Walking out of the station, I was disappointed to see so few taxis. There wasn't even a queue. A queue meant all I had to do was climb inside, announce my destination, and the meter dropped. No queue meant negotiations, and I've never been very good at negotiations. Since both places I wanted to visit were outside the city, and at least one of them was beyond the range of public transportation, I had no leverage. I offered one of the drivers 100RMB, which he promptly dismissed. Before I could make a new offer, another driver interjected that he would do it for 150. That was good enough for me. I threw my bag in the back and sat in front. He was my kind of driver, one with a lead foot. We zoomed out of the city on the old Chengtu highway. Twenty minutes later, just after entering the town of Chinglien (Blue Lotus), we turned onto a newly paved road and followed it to the entrance of Lunghsi Villa. Lunghsi was the name of the area in Kansu province where Li Pai's father was from, where Li Pai lived between the ages of one and five.

As I got out of the taxi, I didn't know what to think. The local authorities were right in step with the times – if not a step or two ahead – namely, the all-out, no-holds-barred development of *anything* with tourist potential. And what had more potential than Li Pai's old home? I arrived in the wake of a massive construction project. The place was immense. Just inside the entrance, I walked across a stone-lined plaza the size of a soccer field. On the far side were steps leading to a pagoda at the top of a hill. I looked at the map printed on my entry ticket and decided to bypass the pagoda. Instead I followed the steps that led to a rebuilt version of the family "villa."

Its courtyards and galleries looked pleasant enough, but I limited myself to the dioramas inside that showed Li Pai growing up, learning to use a sword, and writing his first poems – none of which have survived. One of the dioramas showed Li Pai and his sister grinding ink with wellwater and practicing calligraphy. I wondered whether his sister wrote poems. If she did, they haven't survived either. After viewing the dioramas, I walked behind the family compound and stopped at her grave. The inscription next to her tomb said she married a local man and spent her whole life here. Despite the fact that she left no poems, I offered her some bourbon anyway and asked her to share it with her brother.

I walked back to the entrance feeling somewhat disappointed. I always seem to be looking for something I never find. I had hoped to learn something about Li Pai's parents, something other than the standard story about how his mother dreamed she was impregnated by Venus (T'ai-pai in Chinese) and named her son after the star (Pai was short for T'ai-pai). There was nothing about his father, who remains a mystery. Even his name, Li K'o, was not necessarily his real name. The word *k'o* means "traveler" or "guest," and it was often used by men who were living in exile or incognito. Scholars have suggested different theories: he was a wanted man, a knight-errant, a recluse, or a merchant whose business dealings required him to be on the road or in hiding from creditors. Once he settled his family in Chinglien, he seems to have disappeared. Li Pai never mentions him.

In his father's apparent absence, Li Pai became the man of the house. By the time he was twenty, he had fought duels and killed men. It was about the same time that people began praising his poetry. This marked the beginning of the Li Pai legend, a legend of many parts. When he was thirty, he wrote "On Being Asked Who I Am by Commandant Kashyapa of Huchou" 答湖州迦葉司馬問白是何人：

I'm the Blue Lotus Recluse I'm the Banished Immortal
for thirty years my fame has been limited to wineshops

Earth god shrine on the trail to Li Pai's reading terrace

if the Commandant of Huchou must know
I'm the reincarnation of Golden Grain Buddha

青蓮居士謫仙人，酒肆藏名三十春。湖州司馬何須問，金粟如來是後身。

In this poem Li Pai likens himself to a recluse, to an immortal, to an exile, to a drunkard, and finally to the buddha whose later reincarnations included Vimalakirti Bodhisattva. He also changes the identity of his questioner to Kashyapa, the First Patriarch of Zen. But the poem wasn't just a joke. It reflects Li Pai's progression, from studying the Confucian classics at home to cultivating the Taoist arts of immortality, to becoming known for his drinking as much as his poetry, to being banished from court, and to living among Buddhist monks, which he did off and on from the time he was an adolescent until his death. Li Pai was known for his playfulness and for the deftness with which he displayed an erudition that never seemed like erudition. No doubt, such skill began at home and at the local Confucian academy. But the training that truly separated him from others began when he left home at fifteen and moved to the top of Kuangshan, toward which I next turned my attention.

We returned to Chiangyou then drove west on Highway 302 for seven kilometers. Just after the highway tollbooth, we turned north onto a narrow road that led into the countryside. After about three kilometers, we crossed a river then started up Kuangshan, or Little Kuangshan, as it's also known. Big Kuangshan is farther north. When the driver reached the saddle between the mountain's two peaks, he pulled into a dirt parking lot. It was big enough for five or six cars, but ours was the only one there. The driver had been to Kuangshan before and knew where the trail to the top began. After he locked my bag in the trunk, we started up. I was surprised that he joined me. He said he had never been to the top and this was as good a time as any. I welcomed the company.

The trail was steep and didn't get a lot of foot traffic. We saw only one person along the way, an old man coming down who said he walked up every day. I nodded. I don't know what I would do without my daily walk. I live on top of a hill and walk down to the beach when the tides aren't too high then along the shore and back up the hill from the other side. It's maybe a two-mile walk and takes about forty-five minutes. Considering all my bad habits, it's often the only good thing I do every day to be worthy of another day in this body. Just before the summit, we came to a small trailside shrine to the local earth god. I stopped and offered him a libation in thanks for taking such good care of the young Li Pai. A few minutes later we were at the top, and I was completely out of breath.

In light of the massive development at Li Pai's home, I didn't know what to expect. Fortunately, the summit was beyond the reach of bulldozers. I could see why Li Pai chose this location. It was flat and would have been perfect for martial arts exercises. At the far end of the summit, there was a new shrine hall where Li Pai's reading terrace once stood. At some point droning towers were replaced by reading terraces among China's intelligentsia. Droning, I'm guessing, didn't do as much for a person's résumé or help with passing the exams. Still, it's not surprising that so many of China's great poets had some sort of elevated place where they could be closer to celestial and atmospheric influences. I'm thinking tree houses might be something Western poets might want to look into. Li Pai's reading terrace, whatever it had been when he was here, was now simply a shrine hall without much of anything inside. Outside, there were also a few memorial steles scattered about the summit and a small building for the caretaker, and that was it. I felt relieved to find so little. I was pooped.

Outside the caretaker's was a table with a large kettle of water for visitors. My throat was so parched, I poured myself three glasses one after the other. According to the caretaker, the water came from a spring just behind the shrine hall. I walked around back and poured a shot of bourbon into the spring in thanks. Afterward, I walked back to the archway that welcomed me and the driver to the summit and took in the view. Li Pai spent his days where I was standing but his nights down below at the foot of the mountain, at Taming Temple. The temple was gone, but its name was still on the map I'd downloaded from the Internet.

When I turned to look in the opposite direction, all I could see were trees. I was hoping to see the mountain to the north that was the scene of the earliest Li Pai poem we have, "Visiting the Taoist Master of Taitienshan and Finding Him Gone" 訪戴天山道士不遇:

> Amid barking dogs and flowing water
> and peach blossoms heavy with rain
> I could see deer through the trees
> but the stream drowned out the noon bell
> between the wild bamboo and blue clouds

a cascade hung from jade peaks
no one knows where he went
resting against one pine then another I sighed

犬吠水聲中，桃花帶雨濃。樹深時見鹿，溪午不聞鐘。
野竹分青靄，飛泉掛碧峯。無人知所去，愁倚兩三松。

He wrote this when he was about twenty after trying to pay a social call on a recluse who lived on the mountain I couldn't see. It wasn't in the earliest collections of his poems and was only added after it was found carved on two steles at his reading terrace. Clearly, Li Pai did a bit of rambling in the Chiangyou area. Home base, though, was here, with days on top of this small, forested mountain and nights at the Buddhist temple below. After ten years of reading texts and practicing meditation and swordsmanship, he decided it was time to go forth into the world. He commemorated his departure with "Leaving Kuangshan" 別匡山:

Its dawn-lit peaks are a painting of serrated jade
my doorway is graced by the shadows of windblown vines
when I hiked its trails I took a dog along
when I returned at dusk I brought back firewood
below Gibbon Howling Tree travelers scan the clouds
in Departed Crane Pond monks wash their bowls
don't think I've lost my love of transcendence
I'm off with books and sword to serve an enlightened age

曉峯如畫碧參差，藤影風搖拂檻垂。野徑來多將犬伴，人間歸晚帶樵隨。
看雲客倚啼猿樹，洗鉢僧臨失鶴池。莫怪無心戀清境，已將書劍許明時。

This was another poem that didn't make it into the earliest collections. It was discovered on a stele at Taming Temple — where the poem's tree and pond were also located. It reveals better than any biographical account the sort of person Li Pai was when young and his intense sense of purpose. Of course, the world was not as welcoming as he had hoped. The slightest inquiry would have revealed that he wasn't fully Han Chinese and thus ineligible to serve as a regular official. The only post he ever held at court was as a translator of Turkic dialects, and that only briefly. So much for the enlightened age toward which he traveled.

I followed him down the mountain and returned to the train station. I had a "hard seat" (think proletariat) ticket on the 12:30 to Chengtu, and the driver got me there with twenty minutes to spare. I expressed my gratitude with an extra fifty. While waiting on the platform for the train, I wondered about Li Pai's life in and around this town. The only member of his family with whom he seemed to have had a close relationship was his sister. I'm guessing that when he thought about his family, he thought more about the family he didn't have. What happened to his father? What happened to his mother? And why, once he left the Chiangyou area, did he never return? He certainly wasn't averse to travel, and it's not as if he forgot the way home. Years later, he woke up one night and wrote one of the most famous poems in the Chinese language – the one poem my wife taught our son when he was a child – "Thoughts on a Quiet Night" 靜夜思:

At the foot of my bed the light is so bright
it looks like a layer of frost
lifting my head I gaze at the moon
lying back down I think of home

牀前明月光，疑是地上霜。舉頭望明月，低頭思故鄉。

Li Pai could never hide his heart. That was why everyone loved him. He rode his heart into the heavens with such seeming ease. But it was also his heart that kept him tied to this world in which he never quite fit.

The train was only ten minutes late. As I queued up to board my car in the hard-seat section – all that was available when I bought my ticket – the stationmaster saw me and led me to the conductor. He asked her to upgrade me to the soft-sleeper section, which she did. She found me a lower berth where, for an additional 30RMB, I stretched out in comfort on fresh bedding. It was such an unexpected pleasure, I fell asleep. Two hours later, I arrived in Chengtu.

Of all the major cities in China, Chengtu was the only one whose name hadn't changed in over 2,000 years. It means something like "true capital" and was first given to the city around 400 BC. But even before that, it was already the center of power in the region as early as 1200 BC, which was when it became the capital of the ancient state of Shu. In addition to its location at the intersection of several major trade routes, it was situated on the western edge of one of China's richest agricultural regions, the Szechuan Basin.

Separated, and thus protected, by the Chinling Range to the north, the Yangtze Gorges to the east, the Tibetan Plateau to the west, and more mountains to the south, Szechuan developed in relative isolation from the rest of China. Although migrations of Han Chinese eventually overwhelmed the other ethnic groups and brought Szechuan into the orbit of what we now call China, its cultural diversity persists. Of course, that diversity is being eroded by the monoculture of modernization, as it is everywhere these days, but people in Szechuan still stand out. They take their time. This is especially true of Chengtu, where there are more teahouses than in any other Chinese city, and more Taoists too. The city is the headquarters of the Tienshih (Celestial Masters) school, China's largest lay sect, and the nearby Chingcheng Mountains are home to hundreds of Taoist monks and nuns belonging to the monastic Chuanchen (Complete Truth) sect. The teahouses and the Taoists, though, would have to wait for another time. I was here for the city's poets and checked into the Tienchenlou Hotel on Chinghua Road. Just down the street was one of the entrances to the eighty-acre park that surrounded Tu Fu's Thatch Cottage.

Tu Fu left Ch'ang-an with his family in 759 in the wake of the An Lu-shan Rebellion, and arrived in Chengtu the following year. He arrived without a job or money but not without prospects. The magistrate was an old friend, the poet Pei Ti — the same Pei Ti who co-authored the poems that accompanied Wang Wei's Wang River Scroll. Pei Ti helped finance construction of a modest residence for his friend. If any years of Tu Fu's life could be called idyllic, they were the years he spent in and around the true capital.

Since there was still light in the sky, I dropped my bag in my room and hurried to the nearest park entrance. During my taxi ride from the train station, I phoned my Australian friend Martin Merz. Marty and I first met in Taiwan in 1973 when we "served" together in the Austrian Army during the filming of the Chinese movie *Boxer Rebellion*. When the director wasn't marshaling our ranks for the periodic charge through the smoke of canon fire, we chatted about Chinese stuff in a barren field made to look like a battlefield. Marty had since moved to Hong Kong, where he earned his living exporting shoes. You're probably wearing a pair of Marty's shoes right now, or know someone who is. He also translated modern Chinese novels in his spare time and enjoyed the occasional foray into the Middle Kingdom to expand his knowledge and experience. Since the poets of Chengtu qualified as foray-worthy, we'd arranged to visit them together.

It was just after four o'clock when I reached the park. The sunshine I had enjoyed in Chiangyou was gone. It was gloomy, and the light was fading. The park was due to close in an hour. Another exchange of phone calls brought Marty and me together just outside Tu Fu's cottage. The cottage had been fixed up over the centuries, but it had retained its rustic appearance. The roof was still thatch. A stone tablet dug up during a recent renovation confirmed this was where Tu Fu lived, right next to the same Huanhua (Flower Washing) Creek. I could see Tu Fu sitting in the courtyard waiting for inspiration while his wife cooked dinner and his children played beside the stream. Among the poems he wrote after moving into his new home was "Choosing a Residence" 卜居:

> At the west end of Huanhua Creek
> my benefactor chose a quiet tree-lined bank
> knowing beyond city walls my worries would fade
> and a traveler's cares would dissolve in still waters
> dragonflies by the score flit here and there
> two mandarin ducks take turns diving
> if a whim should take me a thousand miles east
> aboard my little boat I could reach Shanyin

Tu Fu's Thatch Cottage in Chengtu

浣花溪水水西頭，主人為卜林塘幽。已知出郭少塵事，更有澄江銷客愁。
無數蜻蜓齊上下，一雙鸂鶒對沈浮。東行萬里堪乘興，須向山陰上小舟。

Shanyin is an old name for Shaohsing, a thousand miles to the east. Tu Fu was hoping for a whim with momentum, one that might carry him down the little stream next to his cottage all the way to the Yangtze and beyond, to Whimsyland. Living here on Flower Washing Creek, he let his mind wander. It was one of the most productive periods of his life. Of his nearly 1,500 surviving poems, 240 were written in Chengtu. One of my favorites is "River Village" 江村:

A clear stream winds around the whole village
in the middle of summer life here is quiet
swallows come and go above the rafters
seagulls meet and mate on the current
my wife draws a chessboard on a piece of paper
my children bend needles into fishhooks
as long as friends keep sharing their salary rice
what more does this poor body need

清江一曲抱村流，長夏江村事事幽。自去自來堂上燕，相親相近水中鷗。
老妻畫紙為棋局，稚子敲針作釣鉤。多病所須唯藥物，微軀此外更何求。

Although he had a place to live, Tu Fu had no income and relied on friends such as Pei Ti. Officials were paid in units of grain they could use as food or convert to currency. When his friend Yen Wu became military governor of the province in 763, he gave Tu Fu a sinecure, and his life improved. But Yen died two years later, and his successor was not so helpful. Tu Fu decided it was time to follow his earlier whim. He sailed down the Min River to the Yangtze, then followed its waters east. During the subsequent journey in his "tall boat"—one with a mast and sail—he wrote "Recording My Thoughts While Traveling at Night" 旅夜書懷:

A shore of thin reeds in light wind
a tall boat alone at night

stars hang over a barren land
the moon rises out of the Yangtze
how could writing ever lead to fame
I quit my post due to illness and age
drifting along what am I like
a solitary gull between Heaven and Earth

細草微風岸，危檣獨夜舟。星垂平野闊，月湧大江流。
名豈文章著，官應老病休。飄飄何所以，天地一沙鷗。

As Tu Fu sailed off, I emptied a shot of bourbon into the stream to help speed him on his way, then Martin and I made for the exit. But on the way we stopped at the park's bookstore, where each of us bought a three-volume string-bound selection of Tu Fu's poems printed in woodblock style with big type. A fine companion for old age, I thought. This was how poems were meant to be read: big type, lots of space, room to let the eye and the mind roam, an ink-black landscape appearing out of the mist then disappearing into the mind transformed.

This was going to be an easy day, a day in town with no buses, or trains, or countryside excursions, so I took my time getting started. While I drank my coffee in bed for a change, I read over my notes for my day with Hsueh T'ao (781–831). Hsueh was the first woman whose poetry was ranked alongside the great male poets of her day – her day being the height of China's Golden Age of Poetry. She was born in Ch'ang-an, where her father was serving as a minor official, and she was still a child when he was transferred to Chengtu. He died prior to leaving for his next assignment, and Hsueh and her mother remained here. Before he died, her father had encouraged his daughter's literary talent. She could write poems at the age of eight, and it later became her métier. How she and her mother supported themselves without her father's salary is a mystery, but when Hsueh was sixteen she joined the guild of courtesans and entertainers and began life as a singsong girl.

The guild supplied women to private dinners and get-togethers convened by those who could afford something more than food and wine. Some women, no doubt, worked as prostitutes, but most were hired for their theatrical, musical, or literary talents. In Hsueh's case, her talent for poetry made her a sought-after entertainer, and she became friends with many of the great men of the time – not only men who passed through Chengtu but also those who had never met her and who wrote to her after reading poems she shared with her clients. In ancient China anyone holding office was required to write poems, and to do so extempore. Thus, there was a great appreciation for good poetry, especially among officials. For one such admirer, Hsueh wrote "Seeing Off a Friend" 送友人:

> There's frost on the reeds tonight in this riverine world
> the mountains look dreary in the cold moonlight
> who says the miles between us begin this very night
> my goodbye dream goes with you beyond the farthest passes

水國蒹葭夜有霜，月寒山色共蒼蒼。誰言千里自今夕，離夢杳如關塞長。

The image of waterside reeds in autumn, with their white plumes in bloom, was a symbol of separation that went back to the Book of Poetry. This also impressed her clients. She was as well read as they were.

At some point Hsueh saw those passes firsthand. She was banished from Chengtu for some unspecified offense involving a high official. From her border post, she sent two poems to her patron, Governor Wei Kao, titled "Thoughts on Being Exiled to the Frontier, for Lord Wei" 罰赴邊有懷上韋相公. This is the second:

I heard life was harsh near the Wall
now that I'm here I know
having chosen a song from your court
to sing to these borderland boys

聞道邊城苦，而今到始知。卻將門下曲，唱與隴頭兒。

Her place of exile was the Tibetan outpost of Sungchou, 200 kilometers to the north. Living conditions were hardly what Hsueh was used to. However, she was not without connections, and one of them, perhaps the governor, arranged for her return to Chengtu before a year had passed.

In addition to officials in high places, her friends included such famous poets of the day as Chang Chi, Tu Mu, Pai Chu-yi, and Yuan Chen. Some scholars have wondered whether Hsueh and Yuan were lovers. There is, however, no evidence for this, other than what can be read into the letters and poems the two exchanged expressing admiration for each other's work. In "Sending Some Old Poems to Yuan Wei-chih" 寄舊詩與元微之, Hsueh addresses Yuan by his sobriquet, Wei-chih:

Poets all have their own voice and cadence
a light languid style is all that I know
on moonlit nights extolling the paleness of flowers
on misty mornings praising the suppleness of willows
I've kept my greenest jade in a hidden place
I've expressed myself instead in notebooks of crimson
too old now to sort through them all
I'm sending you these to show to your son

詩篇調態人皆有，細膩風光我獨知。月下詠花憐暗澹，雨朝題柳為欹垂。
長教碧玉藏深處，總向紅箋寫自隨。老大不能收拾得，與君開似教男兒。

Of course the poems were for Yuan and not his son, but it would have been too bold to say so.

Hsueh's combination of charm and poetic art was such that she eventually became the governor's official hostess, charged with entertaining his important guests. It was a duty at which she excelled. The governor was so impressed he sent a memorial to the emperor asking him to appoint Hsueh editor of the imperial library, an honorary post reserved for men of the highest literary promise. Alas, the appointment was denied because of her gender. However, Hsueh has been addressed ever since by the title she would have held, Editress Hsueh. Being the recipient of such praise, she began to reconsider her status, as in "A Dog Free of Its Master" 犬離主:

> Five years she passed through his crimson gates
> because she knew his mind she earned his love
> having recently snapped at a favorite guest
> she sleeps no more on his red silk carpets

出入朱門四五年，為知人意得人憐。近緣咬着親知客，不得紅絲毯上眠。

Hsueh tired of having to entertain whoever showed up at the governor's residence and chafed at the ambiguity of her position and, thus, her treatment. Having accumulated sufficient funds, she quit as the governor's hostess and became an independent entertainer. She bought a house at Paihuatan, on the Chinchiang River, not far downstream from the tributary along which Tu Fu once lived.

Hsueh also became famous for her handmade "notebooks of crimson," which were prized by those who wanted something special in which to record their compositions. I've always thought she bought her house at Paihuatan because that section of the Chinchiang was known for its paper makers. I suspect that might have been where she and her mother worked to make ends meet when she was a child, and why she was so good at making notebooks.

Unfortunately, the tapestry I wish I could weave of her life consists of too many threads that lead nowhere. We know, for example, that she became a Taoist priest, but we know nothing about her practice. All we know is what can be found in the poems and accounts left behind by friends and admirers, and in her own poems, which doesn't go much beyond what I've written here. After she died, someone published an edition of her poems called the *Chinchiangchi* (Brocade River Collection). It contained 450 verses. However, the last known copy of that edition disappeared 700 years ago. Today fewer than a hundred poems are all that remain of her work.

In addition to losing her poems, we have also lost her biography. The year after Hsueh's death, Tuan Wen-ch'ang became governor of the province for the second time. Having known Hsueh ten years earlier during his previous assignment there, he wrote an account of her life as an epitaph and had it carved on the back of her tombstone. The whereabouts of the tombstone and her grave, however, are unknown. It was thinking about such things that finally got me out of bed.

After meeting up with Marty again, we drove off in a taxi to find Hsueh's long-lost grave. I had read the accounts of people who had visited her tomb over the centuries and had concluded, as had a number of scholars, that she was buried in the southeast section of the city. The only records that gave the exact location were two editions of the *Huayang Gazetteer* published during the Ch'ing dynasty. Both stated that her grave was located in a place called Hsuehchiahsiang (Hsueh Family Alley). Although local historians hadn't been able to find this place, odd as it may seem, I came across this very name while I was studying a detailed map of the city online. It was, of course, in the southeast part of the city, and that was where Marty and I headed.

From the city center, we followed Yitu Road east into the outskirts. Just past Yitu's intersection with Highway G4201, we turned south onto Lungcheng Road. Six hundred meters later, we turned east again onto a divided road. It was so new, there were no road signs. The driver called it Tamien Middle Road, named for the nearby village of Tamien. After another six hundred meters, we pulled over. According to my map and Marty's GPS, we were there.

We got out and looked for someone to ask. A man with a hoe pointed us down a slope to the middle of a huge tract of farmland surrounded by an equally huge housing development. Soon there were a dozen people following us as we labored across vine-covered piles of rubble and dirt. To my surprise everyone seemed to know the name of the place: Hsuehchiahsiang. Why hadn't local historians located it? Stuck in the libraries, I guess. Somewhere in this vast landscape was Hsueh T'ao's grave, and it was about to be

Looking for Hsueh T'ao's grave

bulldozed. I was hoping peach trees would give it away, as her grave was known for them. But there were no trees, peach or otherwise, just a vast expanse of farmland and rubble and shacks about to be cleared for high-rise apartment buildings.

It turned out that the people following us were all surnamed Hsueh. Their clan hall, they said, had been bulldozed three months earlier, and they were being forced to move. The whole site, which I estimated at a hundred acres or more, was due to be leveled in another three months. The man with the hoe led me and Marty to the earliest extant grave. It was only 200 years old, but under the circumstances, it seemed a good enough place to share a libation with Hsueh via a kinsman. After pouring out the standard three cups, I decided that instead of reading one of Hsueh's poems, I would honor her with a work by a foreign admirer, an American poet named William Hollis, whose "Poem-Chanting Tower" begins:

> I can not imagine the years
> when generals sat smiling at your song
> or scholars came a great distance
> to ask a favor

years later
when it was no longer necessary
for you to rise in the middle of the night
to comfort an official
dropped by the latest turn of government
I stood watching
from the shadow of an arbor
as you sat in the sun
and brushed poems
on slips of bright paper

and I was there
when young poets brought scrolls
with small perfect poems
though I was not among the pretty ones
who played golden lutes
but a gray one
with breath too short to finish a line

when you came close and listened
the very air trembled
and lilies burst open
with a shudder
and flooded the garden with perfume
as rich and haunting as the musk
in the scarf you wound about my shoulders

I keep it still
in a box with these poems
that were for you

when all the world was a landscape
fading from the scroll that hung in a corner
lit only by the turning of the stars

The poem continued, but I thought that was enough. Hopefully, Hsueh got the message that she was loved and admired, even among barbarians in the land where, according to an ancient Chinese myth, the sun rests at night. After sprinkling some whiskey on the grave of the Hsueh clan intermediary, and drinking what I didn't sprinkle, I said goodbye to the dozen or so Hsuehs who had gathered and who seemed to enjoy my little ceremony for their ancestor.

We asked the driver to take us back to the center of town. It was nearly noon, and Marty and I had a lunch date with Ho Shih-p'ing, the head of Emei Film Studios. Mr. Ho was making a documentary, about the hermits in the Chungnan Mountains south of Sian, for which I served as a consultant. After a far too sumptuous lunch, his assistant showed us some of the footage, which was impressive. Emei was one of China's largest film studios, and I was concerned about that. I had urged Mr. Ho to keep the crew down to three. He had gone me one better with a crew of two. Often they just set up a camera, he said, and left it running for hours at a time. Judging from the foot-

Hsueh T'ao's Poem-Chanting Tower in Chengtu

age, they had gained the trust of their subjects and were being careful not to intrude unnecessarily upon their lives, which is the art of documentary filmmaking.

After an hour of viewing footage, Marty and I left for one last stop, Wang-chianglou, or River Viewing Tower. At some point the people of Chengtu, or at least their government, decided to honor Hsueh with her own residence, much like Tu Fu's Thatch Cottage. Over the years, she lived in several places in and around the city, one of them being the house that she actually owned. The local government decided on a place farther downstream from her original Paihuatan residence, but one that was still on the Chinchiang.

In a matter of minutes, we were walking through a thirty-acre park laid out in her honor. It included everything a Hsueh T'ao aficionado might want: a memorial hall, an exhibition hall that included her famous red notebooks, a well whose water could be used for paper making, a fake grave where people could light incense or pour a libation, and finally, at the far end of the park, a multistoried pavilion called Yinshihlou (Poem-Chanting Tower), the tower after which her American admirer titled his poem.

Marty and I strolled through one bamboo grove after another. There were dozens of varieties: some as thin as a pencil, some as thick as a thigh, some as short as an asparagus, some as tall as a palm tree, and, of course, yellow and black and striped and every shade of green. Our entry ticket said there were over 200 varieties. Hsueh T'ao loved bamboo. She once traveled from Chengtu down the Min River all the way to where it merged with the Chinsha to become the Yangtze. She had heard that a shrine to Lord Bamboo was there, and she wanted to pay her respects.

One day a thousand years before Hsueh visited the place, a woman washing clothes beside the river heard what sounded like crying coming from inside a section of bamboo floating past. She reached out and grabbed it. When she split open the bamboo, she found a baby boy. She took the child home and raised him as her own, and the child grew up to become the King of Yehlang and known as Lord Bamboo. This was the story behind Hsueh T'ao's "Written at the Shrine to Lord Bamboo" 題竹郎廟:

Ancient trees stand before the shrine to Lord Bamboo
the lower the sun sinks the greener the hills become
somewhere in this riverside village someone is playing a flute
every note from a song honoring Lord Bamboo

竹郎廟前多古木，夕陽沈沈山更綠。何處江村有笛聲，聲聲盡是迎郎曲。

The sun went down on us, too, ending what had to be the easiest of days on the pilgrim trail. I should have planned more such days.

I followed the sun around the world in my sleep. As it rose, so did I, just after six. This was going to be a long day, hence I didn't linger. An hour after I rose, I was aboard the first bus of the day bound for Santai, 150 kilometers northeast of Chengtu. The bus took the old route, north to Teyang, then east over the mountains, and finally down into the basin on the other side. Not long into the journey, I put on my reverberation-reducing knit hat and leaned my head against the window. I was only half-awake and thought why be half-awake when I could be not-awake.

About the time we began winding through the mountains, I opened my eyes again. The old highway was barely wide enough for two lanes, and as we wound our way up and over and down the mountains, our bus often needed more than its share of the road, especially around curves. At least it was scenic: sunbathed hillsides of fir and bamboo, and fog-filled valleys with the occasional small farm. I also noticed a lot of beehive boxes – where would we be without bees? In places where the road straightened out, farmers were selling pomelos, the grandmother of the citrus family. I liked pomelos because I could eat one section at a time without getting juice all over my hands and beard. I made a note: buy a pomelo for the next bus ride.

Once we descended into the basin, the forests were replaced by rice fields. It was the end of the growing season, and farmers were harvesting their rice, drying it in their courtyards, or burning piles of rice straw in their fields. It was work that involved every family member who wasn't off in a factory – in other words, the very old and the very young.

Three hours after leaving Chengtu, we finally pulled into Santai, or Tzuchou, as it was called when Li Shang-yin served here. It was just after ten. I was here to visit Tu Fu again. After stowing my bag at the bus station, I took a taxi to the city's Tzuchou Park. The park included another thatch cottage built in Tu Fu's honor. Despite having settled in Chengtu in 760, Tu Fu was forced to take refuge in Tzuchou in the summer of 762. He was seeing off a friend north of Chengtu when a rebellion broke out in the city. Chengtu was called West River District at that time, and Tzuchou East River District, as the two cities served as the major administrative centers for the adjacent Min River and Fuchiang River watersheds. Since returning to Chengtu was impossible, he sought refuge in Tzuchou. Once more, with the help of a local official, he was able to land on his feet, which he made clear in "For Yen Pieh-chia: A Song on Meeting" 相逢歌贈嚴二別駕:

Traveling to East River District
every ten steps I looked back
in the desolation and chaos of Chengtu
was my Huanhua Creek hut still there
and who was this hero of Tzuchou
long known for his service to the city
taking my arm entertaining me with wine
drunken swordplay and dragon-like roars
dusting off my cap and feeding my donkey
while his silk-robed servants brought food
and candle-covered plates radiating light
as midnight neared we moved closer
when I knocked on your gate at sunset
who would have guessed at this sudden concurrence
my endless worries rendered inconsequential
such happiness rare in this lifetime
with a truly noble soul and unfettered spirit
the cares of constant travel are dispelled
viewing these times from afar is depressing
experiencing them firsthand is equally troubling
I don't regret meeting you so late in life
for someone like you I'd have to search among the ancients

我行入東川，十步一回首。
成都亂罷氣蕭颯，浣花草堂亦何有。梓中豪俊大者誰，本州從事知名久。
把臂開罇飲我酒，酒酣繫劍蛟龍吼。烏帽拂塵青驄粟，紫衣將炙緋衣走。
銅盤燒蠟光吐日，夜如何其初促膝。黃昏始扣主人門，誰謂俄頃膠在漆。
萬事盡付形骸外，百年未見歡娛畢。神傾意豁真佳士，久客多夏今愈疾。
高視乾坤又可愁，一軀交態同悠悠。垂老遇君未恨晚，似君須向古人求。

Tu Fu spent twenty months in and around Santai and wrote more than 140 poems during that time. His house was in front of what is now Santai High School's Run Run Shaw Science & Technology Building, near the city's East Gate. Although his house disappeared centuries ago, a Ming-dynasty official decided to honor Tu Fu's memory by building a replica on Oxhead Mountain (Niutoushan). It was a kilometer west of Tu Fu's original residence on a mountain he often visited.

Statue of Tu Fu on Oxhead Mountain

The mountain was really just a hill. After the taxi dropped me off at the foot of the south side, it took me only five minutes to follow the circuitous path that led to a set of tile-roofed buildings at the summit. As I walked through the archway into the main courtyard, my eyes were drawn to the building at the far end. It announced itself as the History of Poetry Hall. What a wonderful prospect! I was looking forward to finding out more about Tu Fu's life in Santai, but now I was going to learn about the history of poetry as well. Alas, the doors were locked, and the person with the key was gone. It was one of the unfortunate limitations of bureaucracies everywhere. Certain responsibilities and powers are not shared, especially when a key is involved.

Since the history of poetry was not happening, I continued through the grounds and strolled past half a dozen picture-taking spots. I finally stopped at Oriole Pavilion, which was built to commemorate Tu Fu's "Climbing to Oxhead Mountain Temple" 上牛頭山寺:

I couldn't stop thinking about mountains
step after step on my way up Oxhead
no longer held back by restraints
I was finally wandering without a plan
in the quiet of a flower-scented temple in spring
in the seclusion of a bamboo-veiled pond
where is that oriole singing
it hasn't stopped the whole time

青山意不盡，袞袞上牛頭。無復能拘礙，真成浪出游。
花濃春寺靜，竹細野池幽。何處鶯啼切，移時獨未休。

The park occupied the entire summit and was designed in light of the various poems Tu Fu wrote about his visits here. Next to the pavilion was the bamboo-veiled pond, and standing on a rock in the pond was a statue of the poet looking for that oriole. If an oriole were singing, I wouldn't have heard it. Niutoushan was in the middle of the city. I could hardly hear the cicadas over the horns. Next to Getting Drunk Alone Pavilion, I poured a shot of bourbon into the pond for Tu Fu, had an early morning shot myself, and checked Santai off the day's itinerary.

Instead of returning the way I came, I availed myself of the steps that led straight down the north side of the hill. They ended at the city's main traffic intersection and the source of all the honking. From there I took a pedicab to the bus station. My Santai excursion lasted only an hour and gave me hope that I might make it to Anyueh by nightfall. But first Shehung. After reclaiming my bag, I discovered that the next bus to Shehung didn't leave for another hour. Normally, that would have been okay, but not that day. I went back outside and walked over to one of the waiting taxis. I told the driver where I wanted to go, and he agreed to take me there for 120RMB. It was such a low fare I knew it would rise by the time we reached Shehung, but I figured I would deal with that then. I was glad to shorten the day.

From Santai, we headed southeast on Highway 205, which more or less followed the Fuchiang River. Traffic was minimal, and the road was paved. It wound through a landscape of forested hills and small farming villages and included an occasional view of the river. Halfway to Shehung, just after the road began paralleling the river, we turned off.

I had two stops to make on the way to Shehung, and the first was the modest ridge of Chinhuashan, which rose between the road and the river.

Statue of Ch'en Tzu-ang on Chinhuashan

There was a parking lot at the base of the mountain, but for an extra 15RMB we were able to drive to the top. As the road neared the north end of the summit, I asked the driver to stop. I saw the sign I was looking for. On the other side of the road was the reading terrace of Ch'en Tzu-ang (658–701). I got out and walked across the road and entered a series of new buildings surrounded by a long, red wall.

Ch'en was the first major poet of the T'ang, and it was good to see him getting some respect. He was born just down the highway, in Shehung, to a father of wealth and prestige who inherited his fortune from his father. Rather than concern himself with adding to the family estate, Ch'en's father devoted himself instead to local philanthropy, meditation, and alchemy. The father's ideals rubbed off on his son. As a youth, Ch'en envisioned himself as a knight-errant, righting wrongs, much as Li Pai did at the same age. And like Li, Ch'en eventually traded his sword for books. Which he did here on this ridge, across the river from where his father cultivated the path to immortality.

Ch'en's ancestors must have performed some noteworthy service for the royal family. When Ch'en turned twenty-one, he traveled to Ch'ang-an and was allowed to enroll in the Imperial Academy, a singular honor restricted to the nobility and to friends of the court. The academy's 500 students were supposed to enroll between the ages of fourteen and nineteen. Anyone older had to have a connection in order to arrange the necessary dispensation, as was the case with Wei Ying-wu, who enrolled at the advanced age of twenty-three. Ch'en also decided to forgo the academy's six-year course of studies. He registered for the exams after only two years. Although Ch'en impressed several high-ranking officials in the capital with his learning and his abilities, he failed the exams. His connections didn't help. Humiliated, he returned home and built a reading terrace, on Chinhuashan, where he could study without distractions. Five decades later, Li Pai did the same thing, just upriver. However, Li Pai spent ten years in relative seclusion, whereas Ch'en Tzu-ang spent only a fraction of that. He was a man in a hurry.

The current incarnation of Ch'en's place of study was just for show. It was a memorial hall, like Li Pai's. But unlike Li Pai's, there was a very nice alabaster statue inside, and the galleries along the outside walls were covered with Ch'en's poems written out by the leading calligraphers of the present era. There were also gardens and a pavilion that looked across the river toward the mountain where Ch'en's father built his hermitage. Despite Ch'en's fame during the T'ang, he was the least known of its great poets, and I was hoping for something more. I had yet to come across a good commentary to his poems. But there were no commentaries for sale or even copies of his poems. I walked out to the road and followed it along the ridge another 200 meters to the Taoist complex at the south end of the summit. It was named Chinhua Observatory after the mountain.

Despite its location on a mountain being groomed by the local authorities for its tourist potential, it was still a functioning monastery. There were eighteen priests in residence, all members of the Chuanchen sect. One of the younger priests told me it was a good place to practice and that they didn't get many visitors, except on weekends. He was quick to add that it was the visitors who provided the donations that made their life here possible and that it was a good thing the authorities were investing in the mountain. The authorities couldn't have said it better. It was Saturday, though, and I saw only half a dozen people on the entire ridge. We didn't fill too many rice bowls that day — my own largesse being limited to 10RMB worth of incense I lit in Ch'en Tzu-ang's honor.

One of the poems Ch'en wrote here was "Climbing Chinhua Observatory on a Spring Day" 春日登金華觀. Taoist temples were often called *kuan* (observatories), because those who built them tried to include a tower of some kind from which to observe celestial phenomena as well as the surrounding world. Taoists thought that the heavens operated according to the same principles as the body. Hence, anyone who wanted to join such immortals as Master Red Pine in the Cinnabar Hills needed to study celestial phenomena to better understand what was going on internally. It made sense. There is only one Tao, and the skies are usually clearer than the energy centers and pathways in the body. Here is Ch'en's poem:

From this ancient jade terrace of the immortals
the Cinnabar Hills aren't so far away
the mountains and rivers are all clouds and sunshine
the towers and pavilions are veiled in mist
by a thousand-year-old dancing-crane tree
on a hundred-foot-long rainbow-arched bridge
I met Master Red Pine again
he invited me to join him on the road to Heaven

白玉仙臺古，　丹丘別望遙。　山川亂雲日，　樓榭入烟霄。
鶴舞千年樹，　虹飛百尺橋。　還逢赤松子，　天路坐相邀。

Ch'en was having one of his more transcendent days. There was a stone tablet behind the monastery marking the original spot of the reading terrace where he composed this and other poems. Although Ch'en's studies clearly included Taoist texts, he remained focused on the exams and the Confucian classics. After two years, he decided he was ready to try again.

The capital, meanwhile, had been moved from Ch'ang-an to Loyang, so that was where he traveled in 684. This time, he passed. Passing, of course, did not guarantee a position. Many successful candidates waited years for an appointment. Ch'en, characteristically, was not content to wait. He dared to submit a memorial to the throne regarding the burial of the recently deceased emperor. He suggested that a lavish funeral would impose too great a burden on the public. His memorial was rejected, but the empress dowager, the wife of the deceased emperor, was impressed by the artful way he presented his arguments. She ordered him to continue writing on topics of concern. She appointed him "proofreader" at the imperial library and personally handed him a roll of paper and a brush to use in his work. He put them to good use. His prose style became the envy of every great writer of the T'ang. Men such as Han Yu and Liu Tsung-yuan modeled their work after Ch'en's.

In addition to his memorials, Ch'en also began writing poetry. In this, too, he went his own way. He rejected the ornamental, fantasized poetry of his day in favor of simpler, more realistic verse — his poem about meeting Red Pine being a youthful exception. Chinese literary critics have called him the founder of realism. That might be going a bit far, but it suggests the nature of his importance as a poet. Among the poems for which he is best known is a series of thirty-eight he called "Kanyu" 感遇, or "Impressions," which were similar in style and conception to Juan Chi's eighty-two *Songs from the Heart*. Ch'en wrote poem 35 in 686 when he was sent to report on the military campaign against nomadic tribes in Inner Mongolia. Although he was only there a few months, it was long enough for him to ride to Ting-ling Pass, climb to Chanyu Terrace, and criticize the court's border policies:

The son of a noble family
I've admired great men all my life
to serve my country in a time of need
I drew my sword and left the backwoods
to Tingling Pass I rode in the west
to Chanyu Terrace I climbed in the north
from the heights gazing into the distance
I couldn't stop thinking of the past
who says we never forget our failures
we've trampled them into the dust

本為貴公子，平生實愛才。感時思報國，拔劍起蒿萊。
西馳丁零塞，北上單于臺。登山見千里，懷古心悠哉。
誰言未忘禍，磨滅成塵埃。

The Chinese have a saying: Enjoy success, but don't forget failure. Ch'en couldn't repress his disapproval of a court oblivious to repeating its mistakes. When he returned to Loyang, he put the same sentiments in his memorials, but to no avail. In addition to criticizing what he felt were the court's misguided border policies, he also began submitting memorials arguing against the execution of court officials and members of the royal family. Such memorials likewise fell on deaf ears.

One memorial that didn't came in response to the empress dowager's request for suggestions on how to regulate the universe's primeval energy. The empress dowager saw herself as some sort of celestial figure sent to bring order to the world. Her likeness can still be seen south of Loyang in the face of the huge statue of Vairocana Buddha, before whom millions of people take each other's photographs every year. She looks so benign, but a crueler monarch would be hard to find.

In response to her request, Ch'en suggested she set up a Mingtang, or Hall of Light, where she could harmonize such energy through the performance of certain ceremonies. Such a hall had been called for a thousand years earlier in the Book of Rites, where it was described as a simple structure made of thatch. The empress dowager was not interested in thatch. She ordered a monumental tower built of wood and tile. Ironically, during my visit to Loyang a week earlier, I noticed a new steel and cement version of the Hall of Light rising once again. After a thirteen-century hiatus, it was going up on the original spot, just a few blocks from my hotel. Once again, it was going to be monumental.

It should have been obvious to Ch'en why the empress dowager was so receptive to his suggestion about the Mingtang and so dismissive of his advice concerning her imprisonment and execution of court officials and members of the royal family. She was a megalomaniac. Finally, in 690, having killed or silenced anyone who might have objected, she ascended the throne as China's first and only female ruler, Empress Wu Ts'e-t'ien.

Fortunately for Ch'en, he left the capital a few months later. His stepmother died, and he returned home for the traditional period of mourning. He spent the next two years in the mountains near his old reading terrace. This time, instead of studying Confucian texts, he focused on Taoist meditation and alchemy. Poem 5 of his "Impressions" gives a good sense of what was on his mind:

Merchants take pride in cleverness and knowledge
concerning the Tao they're benighted
exerting themselves to outdo each other
blind to where their bodies end up
unaware of the seeker of truth and mystery
who sees the world as in a crystal vase

who leaves Heaven and Earth far behind
who rides into the infinite transformed

市人矜巧智，於道若童蒙。傾奪相夸侈，不知身所終。
謁見玄真子，觀世玉壺中。宵然遺天地，乘化入無窮。

Despite his Taoist cultivation, Ch'en didn't ride off into the infinite. Once the period of mourning ended, he returned to the capital only to discover things had gotten worse. Unhappy with the situation at court, Ch'en began studying the *Book of Changes*. But studying change doesn't keep it from happening. He was accused of an unspecified impropriety and imprisoned for more than a year. Upon his release he thanked the empress for her compassion and volunteered to join the army in repulsing Khitan invaders from the northern plains. His sense of righteousness was irrepressible.

From Loyang he traveled north and joined the imperial forces in Youchou (Beijing), where one of the empress's nephews held command. It didn't take long for Ch'en's patriotic enthusiasm to wilt before the reality of nepotistic incompetence. Ch'en openly criticized the nephew's strategy. Disappointed on seeing the fate of the country in such hands, he wrote his most famous poem, "Climbing Youchou Tower" 登幽州臺歌:

I don't see the ancients who came before me
I don't see those yet to come
facing the endlessness of Heaven and Earth
I am so overcome I cry

前不見古人，後不見來者。念天地之悠悠，獨愴然而涕下。

The empress's nephew countered by assigning Ch'en clerical duties, thus silencing him. Ch'en took refuge in poetry and waited for the war to end. When it did, four years later, Ch'en returned to the capital, but nothing had changed. In 699 he asked for permission to return home to care for his invalid father. He sensed he would not be coming back and wrote his final memorials, attempting to rectify the court's policies regarding his home province. As usual, such memorials went unheeded.

Ch'en's reunion with his father was brief. His father died soon after he arrived. Later that same year, Ch'en was imprisoned and tortured on trumped-up charges brought by a local official on the orders of another of the empress's nephews. Ch'en didn't survive the ordeal and was buried south of his reading terrace, at the foot of Tutsuoshan. It was a bitter end for a man who was so talented and so ardently hopeful that he could make his world a better place. His grave was my next stop, and I showed my driver a map of the area where it was reportedly located. Looking at the roads we were going to have to take, he shook his head. I decided to head off the inevitable and told him not to worry, I would increase his fee accordingly. That seemed to do the trick, and back down the mountain we went.

We continued south on the highway through the village that had grown up around the foot of Chinhuashan. Just past the last building, we turned east and drove across a bridge that spanned the Fuchiang. On the other side, we turned south again and began winding our way through the country-side. Eventually the paved road turned to dirt, and after several kilometers of slow going we entered the village of Lungpao. At the far end of the village there was a paved road leading up a hill to a Buddhist temple. Thinking that might be Tutsuoshan, we followed the road and parked outside the temple. It turned out to be a nunnery, and the nuns were just finishing lunch. I declined their invitation to join them and told them I was looking for Ch'en Tzu-ang's grave. A laywoman said the grave was at the foot of the mountain and she would be happy to show me, as she was going back down anyway. She called the mountain Lungpaoshan, not Tutsuoshan. Maybe that was just a local variant. In any case, when we reached the bottom, she directed me back toward the village. Less than a minute later, she pointed to a wall on the right. She said the grave was on the other side of the wall, across from the village elementary school.

I got out and walked over to the entrance and discovered the gate was pad-locked and the wall too high to climb. When the laywoman saw me looking perplexed, she pointed out a place where the adjacent wall wasn't so high. Sure enough, I was able to stand on some rubble and ease myself over. On the other side, I found myself next to one of the most unusual graves I had ever seen. It was about two meters high and ten meters long, a huge weed-covered casket of stone. According to an inscription near the front, the area around the tomb was renovated in 1999. If true, it didn't look as though anyone had visited since then. I cleared off a spot on the altar in front of the grave and set out my three cups. Unlike most T'ang poets, Ch'en didn't write about drink-ing. I'm guessing he preferred herbal elixirs. Bourbon, though, was all I had.

In the summer of 762, six decades after Ch'en died, Tu Fu traveled north from Chengtu to say goodbye to a friend. In honor of their parting, Tu Fu wrote "Seeing Off Commissioner Li of Tzuchou on His Way to Assume Office" 送梓州李使君之任. At the end of the poem, Tu Fu wrote: "Master Ch'en died from ill-will / the land of Shu is still filled with grief / when you pass through Shehung / please weep for him on my behalf" 遇害陳公殞, 于今蜀道憐. 君行射洪縣, 為我一潸然. Later that same winter, unable to return to Chengtu, Tu Fu visited Chinhuashan and shed his own tears at Ch'en Tzu-ang's reading terrace. I don't know whether he ever visited the grave.

While Ch'en was wondering what to do with the elixir from Kentucky, I walked through the overgrown grounds of what must once have been a rather large memorial park. There were remains of balustrades and pavilions and stone lions and small bridges on either side of a walkway stretching more than a hundred meters to the east. Clearly, Ch'en had his admirers. But other than me, the only visitors that day were cicadas, frogs, and swallows. I walked back to his grave and read him the second of his "Impressions," in which he likened himself to one of the more fragrant plants of the forest:

> Eupatorium grows in spring and summer
> its foliage so wonderfully green
> in the seclusion of deserted woods
> from purple stems emerge red buds
> slowly the days grow shorter
> softly the autumn wind rises
> as seasonal flowers bend and fall
> what becomes of their sweet intent

蘭若生春夏, 芊蔚何青青。 幽獨空林色, 朱蕤冒紫莖。
遲遲白日晚, 嫋嫋秋風生。 歲華盡搖落, 芳意竟何成。

I scattered a cup of elixir on Ch'en's tombstone on Tu Fu's behalf and one on his stone casket on my behalf and drank the third. Then I eased myself back over the wall and out to the road and my taxi. Twenty minutes later, we were at the Shehung bus station. I gave the driver 200RMB, thinking an extra eighty was about right for the sortie to Ch'en's grave. But he didn't look happy, and I try to leave people happy. Another fifty did the trick. Apparently, the road gods approved. A minute after walking into the station, I was on a bus. Anyueh was my final destination, but there were no direct buses. I had to transfer in Suining.

Grave of Ch'en Tzu-ang

During my forty-five-minute layover there, I stashed my bag in the luggage depository and looked for a China Mobile office. I needed to add minutes to my cell phone. I never travel in China without one anymore, though I barely know how to use it. Reporters have laughed during interviews to see me fumbling with its buttons. I had to go to three China Mobile offices before I found someone able to take care of my simple request. The phone system remains a mystery to me. Back at the station, I reclaimed my bag and actually remembered to buy a pomelo. One hour and one pomelo later, thanks to the driver's preference for expressways, we arrived in Anyueh. When I checked into the Anyueh Hotel, it was just before six. From sunrise to sunset, I had neither heard nor spoken a discouraging word.

The reason I spent the night in Anyueh was because of Chia Tao (779–833). He wrote one of my favorite poems, "Looking for a Recluse and Finding Him Gone" 尋隱者不遇:

Below the pines I ask the boy
he says his master has gone to find herbs
he's somewhere on this mountain
but the clouds are too thick to know where

松下問童子，言師采藥去。隻在此山中，雲深不知處。

So simple, so artless. It's a poem everyone in China knows by heart. Of course, looking for people, namely poets, was the purpose of my pilgrimage. Now it was Chia Tao's turn, and Anyueh was where he was buried. But it wasn't where he was born. He was born near Choukoutien, within walking distance of Peking Man Cave. His parents were sufficiently poor that they gave their son to the monks of nearby Wuhsiang Temple to raise. His uncle's family did the same with their son. Most likely the two boys weren't yet in their teens.

When they were finally ordained at the age of nineteen, Chia Tao received the Buddhist name Wu-pen (No Talent), and his cousin the name Wu-k'o (No Ability). It was the abbot's little joke based on the Buddhist teaching of negating arbitrary distinctions: "No eye, no ear, no nose, no tongue, no body and no mind" 無眼耳鼻身意, to quote the *Heart Sutra*. Hence the name of the temple, which meant "No Form." One advantage of giving one's child to a monastery or nunnery to raise was the guarantee of an education. In order to chant the texts that were part of every ceremony, monks and nuns needed to be able to read. In addition to sutras and mantras, the boys' studies would have included poetry. After all, most sutras included verse passages, and some were entirely in verse. Although we don't have any of their early work, Chia Tao and his cousin were recognized as prodigies, and both became known for their poetry during their lifetimes.

Chia Tao's life as a poet began when he accompanied his abbot to Loyang and Ch'ang-an when he was twenty-two. It was a brief trip, yet somehow Chia Tao managed to meet Meng Chiao, Han Yu, Yao Ho, and Chang Chi, four of the most famous poets of the time. Chia Tao was so inspired, he began corresponding with these men and even visited them several times in Loyang.

In 810, at the age of thirty-two, he left No-Form Temple for the last time and traveled to Ch'ang-an. He stayed at Chinglung (Blue Dragon) Monastery, but he didn't stay long. He decided to return to lay life and found a place to live next door to his friend Chang Chi, which was ironic, considering Chang's open distaste for anything Buddhist or Taoist. Like Han Yu, Chang was a Confucian through and through, though he wasn't as bold as Han Yu in voicing his antidevotional sentiments at court.

Like Li Pai, Chia Tao saw himself as a knight-errant, but one whose weapon was language, as he makes clear in "The Swordsman" 劍客, a poem he wrote not long after taking off his robes:

> I've polished this sword for ten years
> its icy blade has never been used
> I'm showing it to you today
> in case you know of injustice

十年磨一劍，霜刃未曾試。今日把示君，誰有不平事。

His fellow poets loved his innocence, his aspiration, and especially his poetry. Four years later, Han Yu wrote this poem titled simply "For Chia Tao" 贈賈島:

> When Meng Chiao died and was buried on Peimang
> the sun and moon and stars felt forlorn
> worried the art of words might disappear
> Heaven gave the world Chia Tao

孟郊死葬北邙山，日月星辰頓覺閒。天恐文章渾斷絕，再生賈島在人間。

Even though Chia Tao was soon recognized as one of the major poets of the day, poetry paid nothing. He still needed to earn a living. One of the advantages of being a monk was free food and lodging. As a layman, he had to find a new means of support, which he did by tutoring and occasional secretarial work. He also began studying for the exams that he hoped would lead to a career as an official. His first attempts ended in failure, and were it not for the friends he made, in particular his fellow poet Yao Ho, he would not have survived.

According to one early account of his life, Chia Tao finally passed the exams in 822. However, no job prospects materialized, and he continued to rely on his friends. He spent several years living on Yao Ho's country estate northeast of Ch'ang-an and somehow he managed to get married. Then came the Sweet Dew Incident.

For years the court had been controlled by a clique of eunuchs. At the end of 835, the emperor tried to wrest control by plotting their assassination. The scheme — named for an auspicious form of heavenly moisture found on a pomegranate tree outside the palace, where assassins waited to ambush the eunuchs — was exposed, and thousands of officials, including their families, died. The retributions that ensued destabilized the government for years. Chia Tao was caught up in the aftermath and accused of slander, though whether it involved a eunuch or emperor isn't known. He would have been executed had it not been for the intercession of Ling-hu Ch'u, a former chancellor who had maintained control of the executive branch both during and after the Sweet Dew Incident.

Despite his noninvolvement in the plot, Chia Tao had to be punished for whatever it was he said or wrote, and in the summer of 837 he was given his first official "assignment." He was sent to serve as an assistant to the magistrate of Changchiang in Szechuan. So off he went across the Chinling Range, the same range I crossed at night on my way to Li Pai's hometown. En route, before he reached Tzuchou (Santai), let alone Changchiang (Suining), he sent back this poem to the man who saved him from execution, "Written on the Road to Changchiang" 作赴長江道中：

Hurrying staff in hand to a mountain inn
I asked a traveler about Tzuchou
and how to reach Changchiang
all he could do was sigh

策杖馳山驛，逢人問梓州。長江那可到，行客替生愁。

Although Ling-hu Ch'u was ill and would die later that year, he sent Chia Tao a poem in reply, written out by his personal secretary, the poet Li

Shang-yin. Ling-hu was thoughtful enough to include a set of warm clothes, so Chia Tao arrived in Changchiang at least ready for winter. After serving there for three years, he was transferred to Anyueh, to assist that town's magistrate. As in Changchiang, Chia Tao didn't have much to do and spent his time hiking in the hills and enjoying the sights, a few of which he lists in "Climbing South Tower on a Summer Night" 夏夜登南樓:

> Having seen the Yuehyang and the Summer Woods
> I climbed the chilly tower by the river with the moon
> the year's first firefly announced the fall
> now where I wonder might Enlightenment be

水岸寒樓帶月躋， 夏林初見岳陽溪。 一點新螢報秋信， 不知何處是菩提。

The scenic sights of the Yuehyang River and the Summer Woods lay west of town, as did the twenty-three carved-out caves and 500 stone buddhas of Puti (Enlightenment) Temple. Chia Tao liked puns.

Three years later Chia Tao died in Anyueh, just after being elevated to become the town's magistrate. Somehow he had managed to reach the age of sixty-five, which was remarkable considering his lifelong poverty. His wife survived him and arranged for his burial on Anchuanshan, a small hill a kilometer or so southwest of town.

After my morning coffee, I checked out then looked for a taxi, which took a while. Anyueh was not a taxi town. The one that finally stopped already had another fare inside. The driver motioned me in anyway. Once the driver had delivered the other man to his destination, it was my turn. We drove out of town on Wainan Street, which was the old highway and which was missing half its pavement. Thankfully, we didn't have far to go. I had been there before and remembered the way. From South Gate Bridge, where South Tower once stood before it was destroyed during China's Great Leap Backward, we drove exactly 1.3 kilometers.

I told the driver to park next to several brick buildings where trucks were being repaired and rebar was being pounded for use in cement forms. There was a trail between two of the buildings that led west past fields of corn and sweet potatoes and groves of lemon trees — the Anyueh area was famous for its lemons. I followed the trail into the hills about 200 meters then switched to another trail that led up the south slope of Anchuanshan. After less than a hundred meters, I reached the gravesite and was welcomed by the same

German shepherd who had greeted me on my previous visit. He was kept chained to a post during the day to protect the site from grave robbers and started barking as I approached. When I reached out my hand, he stopped. He must have been terribly lonely, chained there all day. It was a cruel fate. Any grave robber worthy of the title could simply visit the place at night. At least the local authorities were making an effort. They had also erected a cement roof over several steles and historical markers. I passed them by and started up the steps to the grave. They were completely overgrown. I'm guessing the local officials sent someone here once a year, with a machete, around Grave Sweeping Day in early April. I was here in September, and it was only with effort that I made it to the tomb. There was barely enough room to stand among the vines and wild bamboo.

Judging from his poetry, Chia Tao wasn't a big drinker, if he drank at all. I suppose it was his monastic training. I poured him a shot anyway, and myself one as well, then read him "Sick Cicada" 病蟬. In China, the cicada has long been a symbol of rebirth, because it sheds its skin when it comes out of the earth in early summer. Relatives often put jade ones in the mouths of the deceased with that in mind. I put this poem in Chia Tao's:

Chia Tao's overgrown grave

Sick cicada unable to fly
you crawled onto my hand
with your broken wings still trembling
and your mournful song so shrill
with dew clinging to your belly
and dust clouding your eyes
and the orioles and hawks above
still longing to end your life

病蟬飛不得，向我掌中行。折翼猶能薄，酸吟尚極清。
露華凝在腹，塵點誤侵睛。黃雀並鳶鳥，俱懷害爾情。

I hope Chia Tao appreciated the last of the Stagg. I thought that the bottle I brought from America would last fifteen days, through the first half of my journey. I probably should have brought something I didn't like so much. Next up was an eighteen-year-old Willett. It was 98 proof, as opposed to the Stagg's 142.6. Being far easier to drink, I could foresee a logistics problem down the road. But that was down the road. I savored the last of the Stagg and scattered Chia Tao's share on the dew-covered vines and bamboo that had overwhelmed his grave. Then I read him another poem, but not one of his – "Mourning My Cousin Tao" 吊從兄島 by Wu-k'o, with whom Chia Tao had grown up:

You sighed every day in obscurity
a lofty lone peak of a man
your poetry eclipsed a generation
yet your life ended in disgrace
did they make a new edition of your poems in Shu
are the funerals in Pa any different
here in Ch'ang-an reading your old scrolls
I wish we could meet but how

盡日嘆沈淪，孤高碣石人。詩名從蓋代。謫宦竟終身。
蜀集重編否，巴儀薄葬新。青門臨舊卷，欲見永無因。

I patted Chia Tao's guardian goodbye and returned to the taxi. Twenty minutes later I was on the 8:30 bus to Suining, or Changchiang as it was called in Chia Tao's day.

When he first arrived in Changchiang in 837, he couldn't have been too happy. Still, getting away from the political turmoil of the capital and ending up in a small provincial town was not such a bad thing. Chia Tao liked the place so much, he titled his collected poems after it: *Changchiangchi* (The Changchiang Collection). Here is one he wrote upon ending another day at the office, "Written in Changchiang" 題長江:

> The talking and reasoning have ceased
> at sunset the office is deserted
> as the watchman locks up for the night
> a snake slithers into the ancient paulownia
> after a fresh rain in Changchiang
> beneath the stars and the moon
> if this exile could leave
> he would float all the way to the Yen

言心俱好靜，廨署落暉空。歸吏封宵鑰，行蛇入古桐。
長江新雨後，明月眾星中。若任遷人去，西浮與剡通。

The Yen River was 2,000 kilometers east of where Chia Tao was serving. It was south of Shaohsing and famous for providing the background for a story about Wang Tzu-you, who one snowy night followed an impulse to visit a friend who lived upriver. After a night of rowing, just as Wang approached the place where his friend lived, he stopped, turned around, and rowed home. When someone later asked why, he said he went upriver because he was inspired to do so, and when the inspiration faded, he saw no reason to continue. The story was recorded in *New Tales of the World* (*Shihshuo Hsinyu*). Shao-hsing and its Yen River was the T'ang-dynasty escape to which no one could actually escape. Currents changed. So did whims and inspirations. Reaching the Yen didn't mean getting there. Also worth noting, the royal paulownia in the courtyard where Chia Tao served was cut down in anger by a previous official. It was just a stump when he was there. As for the snake, commentators say its appearance accentuates how deserted and quiet the place was and how precarious Chia Tao's position. He was lucky to find refuge wherever he could, even in a stump.

Of the poems he wrote during his rambles around Changchiang, quite a few mention Mingyuehshan (Bright Moon Mountain), where he became friends with a number of recluses, including Tu Ku-ch'ung. Chia Tao, of course, was famous for his poems about recluses and was once a monk himself. Even in exile, though, he remained on the Confucian side of the "to serve or not to serve" conundrum, as is evident in "On Mingyuehshan Thinking about Tu Ku-ch'ung" 明月山懷獨孤崇:

There's a bright moon forever in my eyes
there's a bright moon forever in my heart
in my heart and in my eyes
for what then do I go in search
I long to see the bright-moon man
beneath the shade of early summer
I imagine him sighing at the thought
whether in my urban joys I forgot the quiet woods
but I grew up near the Northern Peak
my hatred for the eastern tribes is deep
I wish the bones of the earth would shrink
and I didn't have to wait for Heaven's grace
I thirst of course for seclusion's fruit
but attacks by others I cannot bear
the bells on our sacred peaks they say
now ring from weed-covered towers
I would rather march behind our noble lord
before walking in the fragrant woods again

明月長在目，明月長在心。在心復在目，何得稀去尋。
試望明月人，孟夏樹蔽岑。想彼嘆此懷，樂喧忘幽林。
鄉本北岳外，悔恨東夷深。願縮地脈還，豈待天恩臨。
非不渴隱秀，卻嫌他事侵。或云岳樓鐘，來繞草堂吟。
當從令尹後，再往步佰林。

We see something in this poem that reveals Chia Tao in a different light. While Buddhists are known for their cultivation of compassion, such cultivation doesn't take place in a vacuum. Every practitioner has a different karmic background. Chia Tao clearly did not feel much compassion for the Khitans who ravaged the area where he grew up. In this poem, Chia Tao makes it clear he would rather forego seclusion and even the fruit of enlightenment in favor of beating back the barbarians, or at least guarding the country against further incursions. Although the Khitans were not active in his home area at the time he wrote this poem, they were certainly active in his memory. Fortunately, Heaven never graced Chia Tao with such an assignment, and he was able to spend his final years visiting his friends on Mingyuehshan and writing poems about those who did not, like him, have a job in town.

Once I arrived in Suining, I stashed my bag at the train station and hired one of the two available taxis. I wanted to go to Changchiangpa (Changchiang Embankment), the location of Mingyuehshan. To make sure the driver understood, I showed him my Internet map. The village was about twenty kilometers to the north, on the west bank of the Fuchiang River, the same river that flowed past Li Pai's home and Ch'en Tzu-ang's as well. The driver nodded in recognition and said he would do it for 150RMB or so. Of course, whenever a driver said, "or so," it meant more than "just a tad." As usual, I wasn't in a position to negotiate.

We headed out of town on good old Highway 205, the highway that followed the Fuchiang all the way from Li Pai's hometown. After about fifteen kilometers, just past the village Chikou, we turned onto a local road, a *very* local road, that cut eastward across farmland. After four or five kilometers, the road ended at the village of Changchiangpa. The farmers were harvesting peanuts and sesame, and in front of every house stood piles of one or the other. I had never seen sesame in its natural state. Its galaxies of black seeds were inside pods attached to meter-long stalks, and piles of stalks filled the village square and surrounded the village's sacred tree. The only building without any piles in front was also the only building with a tile facade. It turned out to be the Chia Tao shrine I was looking for. Until a few years ago, it was the only Chia Tao shrine in China. There is now another very nice one in North China near the town where he was born, the town ravaged by the Khitans. The shrine at Changchiangpa, though, dated back to just after he died. It had been destroyed and rebuilt many times, and I was happy to see its condition was on the upswing.

My driver parked between the piles of sesame, and I approached the shrine. When I tried the door, it was locked, so I walked over to a dry goods store where some men were playing cards. I asked whether anyone there had the key. One of them did, a Mr. Hu, Hu Chien-yin. I had to wait until they finished their game, which was a card version of mahjong. A few minutes later, Mr. Hu unlocked the shrine for me. Chia Tao was inside, sitting behind an altar. He was flanked on one side by the king of a Taoist heaven and on the

Chia Tao's shrine at Changchiangpa

other by the Taoist deity who bestows children. I set out my three-cup offering. This time, it was the Willet. Two superb bourbons in the same day. Too bad Chia Tao didn't drink. I presumed that was not true of the gods.

While I was waiting for the whiskey to reach the appropriate heaven, I asked Mr. Hu about the shrine. He said it was built in 2007. The original shrine had been on the slope behind the village, but it was gone. Mr. Hu didn't explain why, but I could guess. Everyone from the surrounding area now came to the new one to light incense, which they did on new and full moons and during festivals. Chia Tao had become the local deity. I smiled at the thought. Nobody lit incense at the graves of the eunuchs and officials who banished him here.

During his time in Changchiang, Chia Tao often gathered with his friends to watch the moon at a place called Wanyuehting (Moon Play Pavilion). Since Chia Tao described it as being on top of Mingyuehshan, I asked Mr.

Hu whether it was farther up the slope past the shrine's former location. Mr. Hu shook his head and offered to show me where it used to be. Instead of taking me behind the village, he led me in the opposite direction, out into the fields. Mr. Hu said the pavilion had been washed away in a flood, but he knew where it used to be. I followed him south along a cart path past fields where sweet potatoes and corn had recently been harvested. After about 200 meters, he turned west and worked his way through a field of corn still taking in a few more days of September sun. After another 150 meters, he stopped. This was where Chia Tao's Wanyueh Pavilion once stood. But the ground was flat in every direction. Seeing my puzzlement, he explained that the flood that had destroyed the pavilion had also leveled the top of the hill. Bright Moon Hill was a hill no more.

Having shown me what he could, Mr. Hu continued south through the fields to his home to have lunch. After watching him disappear down the embankment of the Fuchiang, I headed back to the village. Mr. Hu's card-playing friends had followed us out to the fields, and on the way back one of them stopped to show me some tile shards from the old pavilion. Apparently, the flood wasn't that long ago. Back at the shrine, I finished what was left of my offering then reclaimed my seat in the taxi.

After we rejoined Highway 205 we turned south and followed the road back to Suining. As we drove through the edge of town, I saw a temple on a hill, and the driver confirmed that it was Kuangte Temple. Chia Tao often visited the temple and its monks, especially the abbot, Master Yuan, with whom he exchanged a number of poems. Master Yuan's teacher was Tsung-mi (780–841), a famous Zen master of their day and also a patriarch of the Huayen school of Buddhism. Chia Tao met Tsung-mi when he was living in Ch'ang-an, and they became close friends. A few months after Chia Tao left Changchiang for Anyueh, Master Yuan sent word to him that Tsung-mi had died. Chia Tao sent back "Crying for Zen Master Tsung-mi" 哭宗密禪師:

Up a trail for birds to that snow-covered ridge
who goes to meditate since the master died
does his bookstand gather dust in his absence
do the trees look different from before
does his stupa hum with the pines
are his footprints still visible beside the stream
and does the tiger that listened to him chant
ever come to visit his fallen-down hut

鳥道雪岑巔，師亡誰去禪。几塵增減後，樹色改生前。
層塔當松吹，殘蹤傍野泉。唯嗟聽經虎，時到壞庵邊。

My train was due to leave in little more than an hour. Still, I couldn't resist taking a look at the temple Chia Tao once frequented. We drove up the hill to the entrance and parked in a lot that had room for a hundred taxis. It was a Sunday, but there were no other cars. The driver saw my surprise and told me that people only came here on holidays. Clearly the temple was expecting something more than holiday visitors, as someone had invested a lot of money in restoring it. I hurried through the gate and up the steps to a series of shrine halls. The place was enormous. I wasn't expecting anything so extensive or extravagant. I was out of time even before I began and limited myself to reading an inscription at the base of a very tall stupa. It contained the remains of a T'ang-dynasty monk, but not those of Master Yuan. I hurried back down the steps to the taxi and made it to the train station with fifteen minutes to spare. When the driver finally revealed what he meant by "150 or so," I wasn't surprised. He asked for 300. It was ridiculous, but I paid it. He was happy, and so was I. It had been a good day. And it continued. The train was on time.

As it pulled away from the platform, I found my berth in the hard-sleeper section – the train didn't have the soft variety. It was a lower berth, always hard to pass up when it wasn't occupied, and someone was unable to resist. Once the person left to claim another berth, I lay down, relieved to be aboard and horizontal. When the conductress came by to check my ticket, I asked whether the train had air-conditioning – it was hot, and I was perspiring. I was being sarcastic and felt like I was putting a note in a bottle. A few minutes later, cool air began blowing through the vents. I sighed and wondered what would happen if the Chinese ever started complaining about such things. I didn't wonder long. I stretched out and watched the countryside slip by and soon fell asleep. Traveling by train was such a pleasure and the pleasure lasted until nine o'clock, when I got off in Wanchou. Wanchou was as close as trains got to the western end of the Yangtze Gorges.

Outside the station, I climbed into a motorized rickshaw and headed into town. Fifteen minutes and 15RMB later, I got out in front of the Nanpu Hotel, a hotel I chose for its proximity to the bus station that I would be starting out from the next morning. On my way into the lobby, I walked past five prostitutes standing outside the entrance. It was 9:15, and their workday was just beginning. After a hot bath, mine ended.

I woke to the sound of riverboat horns, muffled by the morning fog on the Yangtze. Wan-chou is where most of the hotel-sized boats begin or end their tours of the Three Gorges. I wasn't interested in a tour, but I did want to get to where the Gorges began, and that meant another bus ride.

When I walked outside the hotel, the ladies of the night were gone. The street was deserted, and the pavement was wet from an early morning rain. I walked two blocks to the bus station and twenty minutes later watched Wanchou disappear out the bus window. I was on the seven o'clock express to Fengchieh, which was at the western end of the Gorges. It used to take five hours to get there from Wanchou on the old highway that wound up and around the mountains. The express took the new highway that went *through* the mountains. It arrived in half the time. Once again I was looking for Tu Fu.

At the beginning of 765, Tu Fu's sabbatical in Chengtu finally came to an end. His patron died, and the military leaders there began a rebellion against the central government. Tu Fu sailed with his family down the Min River, to where it joined the Chinsha to become the Yangtze, then continued downstream to Fengchieh, or Kueichou, as it was called. Slowed by illness, he didn't reach Kueichou until early summer of the following year, but when he did, he was blessed with good fortune. His friend Po Mao-lin had become governor of the region and provided Tu Fu with a sinecure as his secretary. He also presented the poet with a seven-acre orchard of orange trees and arranged for him to rent a house near the orchard. Once again, Tu Fu was saved. Times, though, were not good. Most of the men in Kueichou were off fighting the rebels, and the women who stayed behind weren't much better off than the men. Shortly after Tu Fu arrived, he recorded his impressions in "Ballad of the Firewood Carriers" 負薪行:

Unmarried women in Kueichou are gray-haired
forty or fifty and still without husbands
who can afford a wife in such times
resentment and sighs fill their lives
men stay home here and women get jobs
men guard the doorways while women seek work
nine out of ten gather firewood

and try to survive on their earnings
even middle-aged they wear braids
wildflowers sweet herbs and hairpins of silver
or they work in the market or scale heights
or risk their lives in a salt mine
makeup and jewelry can't hide their tears
life is hard below the cliffs without land or warm clothes
but don't think Wushan women are ugly
Chao-chun after all was from here

夔州處女髮半華，四十五十無夫家。更遭扣亂嫁不售，一生抱恨長咨嗟。
土風坐男使女立，男當門戶女出入。十有八九負薪歸，賣薪得錢應供給。
至老雙鬟只垂頸，野花山葉銀釵幷。筋力登危集市門，死生射利兼鹽井。
面妝首飾雜啼痕，地褊衣寒困石根。若道巫山女粗丑，何得此有昭君村。

Wang Chao-chun was one of China's great beauties and was born near the middle of the Gorges. Since the Gorges' most famous peak was Wushan, just east of Kueichou, its name was often applied to the entire area. Hence, Kueichou women were also referred to as Wushan women as they are here. Witnessing such human hardship was nothing new for Tu Fu. What *was* new was the landscape. It inspired Tu Fu to write more poems than he did anywhere else.

Before I could visit the source of his inspiration, however, I needed to arrange transportation to my next stop. While I was planning this trip back in America, I had tried without success to find out how to proceed from Fengchieh through the Gorges in a single afternoon. The cruise ships took at least a full day, if not two. Fortunately, a Chinese friend came up with the name and phone number of a travel agent in Fengchieh. So I called Ms. Huang, and she assured me that I could, indeed, do what I planned. She told me to call her when I got close, which I did. She said she was going to be busy that day, but her husband, Mr. Ch'en, wasn't. He met me as I walked out of the Fengchieh bus station and led me down the street to the boat terminal, where for 230RMB I was able to buy a ticket on the two o'clock *k'uai-t'ing* – the last express boat of the day. It was so easy. My concerns were for naught. With the question of my ongoing transportation solved, Mr. Ch'en arranged for my local transport as well. Five minutes later, a driver arrived and for 200RMB agreed to take me to the three places where Tu Fu once lived. The road (and the river) gods were smiling on me that day.

View of Wushan and the entrance to Chutang Gorge

I thanked Mr. Ch'en and began my excursion. It was ten o'clock, which gave me four hours. I began with Paiticheng (White Emperor Fortress). It was less than fifteen kilometers east of town, and the road was perfect. Fifteen minutes later, we pulled into a huge parking lot. I should have guessed from the road. But once again, the lot was empty. I got out and walked over to the entrance. The fee was rather steep: 120RMB or twenty bucks. Fortunately, the senior discount for those seventy and over was in effect, even for foreigners, and that day sixty-eight was close enough.

Paiticheng was originally a small peninsula that jutted into the Yangtze from the river's north shore, and it had a great view of the entrance to Chutang Gorge, the first of the Three Gorges for those sailing downstream. For thousands of years, it functioned primarily as a military fortification to prevent enemies from entering Szechuan by boat. It was, however, a peninsula no more. The rising waters of the Yangtze, due to the Three Gorges Dam, had created a small island, which was now connected to the shore by a very long pedestrian bridge. I hadn't noticed the wind before, but walking across I had to zip up my parka.

I was there on a Monday in early September. Once again I was practically alone at a major tourist site. Where *was* everyone? I concluded it was just a matter of timing. Paiticheng was doubtlessly wall-to-wall tourists whenever boats stopped at Fengchieh. I must have arrived between boats. I counted my blessings. Despite having the place pretty much to myself, time was limited. I passed up the shrine halls at the island's summit. I chose instead the new cement walkway that circled the island about fifty meters above the water level. Either the authorities were planning for floods or the Dam was going to be impounding more water. The only sounds I heard above the wind were those of crickets and doves. I was also joined by a passel of sparrows and what must have been the last butterflies of the year. Summer was over, but word hadn't reached everyone.

As I walked around the island, the view got better. No wonder Tu Fu was inspired. From the east side of Paiticheng, I had a perfect view of Chutang Gorge and the distant peak of Wushan. It was one of the most famous views in China. People saw it every time they used a 10RMB note. It was also the view Tu Fu saw every day when he first arrived, as this side of the island was where he lived. Being at the western end of the Gorges, he called his house his Western Study. His study was now underwater. A replacement had been carved out of the rocks near the summit, but I had no interest in visiting it. While standing above where he once lived, buffeted by the wind, I read a poem he addressed to a friend upriver, with whom he had spent the previous winter, "Waiting in Vain for the Third Time for the Magistrate of Tachang to Join Me for the Night at My Western Study" 西閣三度期大昌嚴明府同宿不到:

> I asked if you could come for the night
> I was hoping to talk of important things
> night after night my zither case is empty
> morning after morning my notebooks are full
> a frost-covered bell interrupts the silence
> I rise and snuff out the candles
> ducks waking down by the river
> wing to wing slowly fly away

問子能來宿，今疑索故要。匣琴虛夜夜，手板自朝朝。
金吼霜鐘徹，花催蠟炬銷。早鳧江檻底，雙影漫飄飄。

Below me on the river was a dock, and several boats were tied up. For a fee, visitors could go out onto the river for an even better view. It was too windy for me, and I contented myself with watching two huge tour boats enter the gorge. The name *chu-t'ang* means "bellows." At only eight kilometers, Chutang was the shortest of the Gorges. It was also the narrowest and by far the windiest. But no one on board seemed to mind. Hundreds of people lined the railings of both boats taking pictures of what was a stupendous scene.

What was so remarkable about Tu Fu's stay in Kueichou was that during those two years he wrote 440 of his 1,500 surviving poems. The poems poured forth, and I had hoped to visit the places from which they poured. Unfortunately, the Three Gorges Dam had raised the river's water level 175 meters (500 feet). The places where he and everyone else once lived were now home to fishes.

Despite this sad state of affairs, I was not without recourse. A Taiwanese scholar who specialized in Chinese literature came to Fengchieh before the Dam was completed and made a detailed study of the locations where Tu Fu lived. His name is Chien Chin-sung. In addition to making repeated visits to the area, Professor Chien went through all the poems Tu Fu wrote while he lived here as well as poems written by others who visited him or his former dwellings after he was gone. He also went through the local gazetteers and historical records to cross-reference and confirm the names of mountains, rivers, and villages mentioned in Tu Fu's poems – names, it turns out, that had changed quite a bit over the years. By comparing all this information and by eliminating erroneous suppositions, he was able to triangulate the locations of the two huts where Tu Fu wrote most of his Kueichou poems. Professor Chien was a man after my own heart: all that effort to locate the places where poems were written 1,300 years ago. In this case, it involved 30 percent of the extant poems of one of the world's greatest poets. I felt honored that such information had fallen into my hands – which happened in a Taiwan bookstore the year before.

After recrossing the pedestrian bridge, I showed my driver the map from Professor Chien's book, 杜甫夔州詩現地研究 (Research on the Actual Locations of Tu Fu's Kueichou Poems). We began with Tutiling Ridge, where Tu Fu's Nanghsi (Nang West) Hut was located. According to Professor Chien, it was on the southwest slope of a ridge that led down to the Tsaotang River in what was now Section One of Huanhua Village, a village named after the stream beside which Tu Fu lived in Chengtu.

We were there in minutes, and from the edge of the road, I scanned the slope below. There used to be a brick factory somewhere down there, but it disappeared about the time the Dam was finished, as did a lot of things – and people. The hillside was now covered by dozens of terraced farm plots and a few small hovels masquerading as farmhouses. I worked my way downhill but stopped short of going all the way to where the Tsaotang – formerly the Nang River – joined the Yangtze. Somewhere below where the rivers met was Tu Fu's Nang West Hut and his orange grove.

Although Tu Fu rented the hut, the land was a gift from the governor, and the money he made from the harvest, along with the stipend he received for simply being who he was, more than covered his expenses for food and rent as long as he was in Kueichou. A few of the farmers were still growing oranges, but most of the slope and the land down along the river were devoted to vegetables. Among the hundreds of poems Tu Fu wrote here was a series of five he titled "Written in Late Spring at Our Newly Rented Nang West Thatch Hut" 暮春題瀼西新賃草屋. In the background are Chinese blackbirds, which are known to sing as many as 130 different songs:

A traveler in the Gorges I keep sighing
encountering late spring yet again
I wish the blackbirds would be quiet
how long can these flowers last
diaphanous clouds in deserted valleys
fading sunlight on surging waves
I wonder if the war will ever end
but that isn't what hurts my heart

久嗟三峽客，再與暮春期。百舌欲無語，繁花能幾時。
谷虛雲氣薄，波亂日華遲。戰伐何由定，哀傷不在茲。

The fighting had been going on for a dozen years, ever since the An Lushan Rebellion erupted in 755. What weighed on Tu Fu's heart, though, wasn't the war. It was the thought of spending another spring apart from relatives and friends in Loyang and Ch'ang-an, and he was running out of springs.

I hiked back up to the road, and we continued on to Tu Fu's second hut, the one he called his Tuntung (East Tun) Hut. We followed the same road down to the Tsaotang (Thatch Hut) River then crossed Thatch Hut Bridge – gestures to Tu Fu by the authorities in charge of naming things. On the other side we continued uphill about 300 meters. The second place to which Professor Chien directed me was Section Two of Pachen Village.

A man standing in front of the house where we parked verified we had the right location. The man was also kind enough to point out the trail that led down along an adjacent dirt ridge for several hundred meters to a place identified by Professor Chien as Huangchuehshu. Planted with orange trees, it overlooked the intersection of the Tsaotang River on the right and the Shihma River on the left. In the fall of 767, Tu Fu turned over his Nang West residence to a friend in need of lodging and moved here. He recorded the event in a series of four poems titled "Moving from My Nang West Bramble Gate to My East Tun Thatch Cottage" 自瀼西荊扉且移居東屯茅屋. This is the second:

> Nang West or East Tun
> I'm still on the same clear river
> from one thatch hut I moved to another
> I wasn't attached to the rice fields
> being close to a market had its advantage
> there aren't any trails through these woods
> when people visit this decrepit old man
> invariably they get lost

東屯復瀼西，一鍾住清溪。來往皆茅屋，淹留未稻畦。
市喧宜近利，林僻此無蹊。若訪衰翁語，須令剩客迷。

Tu Fu's East Tun Hut was twice as far from town as his Nang West Hut. Although the place saw fewer visitors, it saw more poems. He could have established his reputation on the creative yield from this one brief residence alone. Standing at the edge of the ridge overlooking the place where he lived, I thought this was as good a spot as any for the usual oblation. Hopefully, I didn't kill the orange tree whose roots I used as an intermediary.

After hiking back up to the road, I talked with the man who owned the orange trees. He had lived there all his life and said the place I was looking for was farther down the ridge and now underwater. He said before the Dam was built there were a number of ancient *huang-chueh* trees (*Ficus virens*) above the river. Hence, the name of the place: Huangchuehshu. He estimated they

View of where Tu Fu's East Tun Hut was located

were now fifty meters below the water level. The trees were so big, he said, it took the outstretched arms of several people to encircle one of them. The *huang-chueh* was a relative of the banyan and was often used in that part of China to honor sites of historical or communal importance, and the site of Tu Fu's former house would have qualified. I thought about all those branches waving in the current where so many poems were written. It wasn't simply the landscape that inspired Tu Fu's poems. It was also his life coming to an end, and he felt it.

I thanked the farmer and told the driver to take me back to Fengchieh. I had a boat to catch. Once again, there was hardly another car on the road, and the driver clearly enjoyed making sure I got back in time. I arrived at the terminal with half an hour to spare — just enough time for a bowl of noodles.

At quarter to two, I entered the terminal and walked down several hundred steps to a hydrofoil that was tied to the dock. It was long and sleek with plexiglass windows on all sides. There were about twenty passengers already on board and room for another hundred. At exactly two o'clock the captain honked the horn twice then shoved off.

Once again, I was following in Tu Fu's wake. Before he left, he gave his orchard to a landless acquaintance, commemorating the occasion with "About to Leave for Wu Gorge, I Give My Seven-Acre Nang West Orchard and Garden to Elder Brother Ch'ing of the South" 將別巫峽贈南卿兄瀼西果園四十畝:

Moss and bamboo are easy to love
but duckweed has no fixed home
my children have grown up on the road
I've left so many huts and orchards behind
facing all these pink blossoms
to which brocade can't compare
with my boat set to leave for the Gorges
I walked through my garden and wanted to pick up a hoe
but at the end of the first month when orioles chatter
finally it's my time to fly
plum trees beside the snow-covered fence in full bloom
willows by the viewpoint pavilion just budding
I'm giving all this to Old Mister Ch'ing
expressing my unrestrained joy in a song
I'll be spending my last years downriver
with fisherman or woodcutter neighbors

苔竹素所好，萍蓬無定居。遠遊長兒子，幾地別林盧。
雜蕊紅相對，他時錦不如。具舟將出峽，巡圃念攜鋤。
正月喧鶯末，茲辰放鷁初。雪籬梅可折，風榭柳微舒。
托贈卿家有，因歌野興疏。殘生逗江漢，何處狎樵漁。

As we turned into the river, I couldn't help think of Tu Fu's friend Li Pai. In 759, eight years before Tu Fu wrote his poem, Li Pai traveled upstream from Chiangling all the way through the Gorges on his way into exile in Yunnan. Just past Paiticheng, word reached Li Pai that he had been reprieved. He turned his boat around and sailed back to Chiangling, which was a thousand *li* (600 kilometers) downriver, and wrote "Early Departure from Paiticheng" 早發白帝城:

Leaving Paiti early amid dawn-colored clouds
a thousand *li* back to Chiangling in a day
on both shores the constant howling of gibbons
in the wake of my sanpan ten thousand peaks

朝辭白帝彩雲間，千里江陵一日還。兩岸猿聲啼不住，輕舟已過萬重山。

I wouldn't have heard gibbon howls above the whine of the hydrofoil's engines as we, too, left ten thousand peaks in our wake. It was awe-inspiring to watch them pass by. The captain said he averaged sixty kilometers an hour and made no stops. This was not the scenic tour. The goal was to reach the other end of the Gorges as quickly as possible. There was a video screen at the front of the cabin, and it kept those passengers who didn't fall asleep entertained with a pair of Hong Kong movies.

Near the back of the boat there was a small poop deck, where three or four people could stand outside and smoke. Despite the higher water level, the Gorges were still spectacular, and I took several how-could-I-not photos. However, the sight of so much swirling flotsam, veritable galaxies of garbage, drove me back inside. The Yangtze was an open sewer. It was also the biggest highway in China, and the captain acted as if he were driving a bus. He honked his horn every time he approached a barge from the rear and again as he left it in his spray.

Although the captain said he wasn't making any stops, he got a phone call asking him to pick up eighty construction workers at a place called Patung. They were going to the big city of Yichang for two nights of R&R and were wearing their big-city best. Finally, three and a half hours after leaving Paiticheng, we arrived at the Taiping River Docks, where passengers whose boats weren't going through the Dam's locks disembarked.

Three Gorges Express

We had arrived, but we weren't yet on shore. We still had to walk through three tour boats that had docked earlier. It was an odd system, but it eliminated the need for a long pier with room for each boat. When we finally walked through the last of the three boats and onto the pier, there were several hundred steps — meant to allow for changes in the river's water level — between us and the terminal. There was also a cable car, and the 2RMB it cost to ride was worth it. At least I didn't enter the terminal out of breath. Inside, I was met by the usual gaggle of taxi touts. I ignored them and walked out to the parking lot hoping to find something less annoying, but there wasn't anything else. One by one the buses and taxis left, except one taxi with whose driver I finally made peace. Twenty minutes later, I arrived in Tzukuei.

It should have been called New Tzukuei. The original Tzukuei was underwater thirty kilometers upstream on the other side of the river. That was, more or less, where I was hoping to spend the night. I just didn't know how I was going to get there. The Dam had changed everything. The taxi driver let me out at the town's Fenghuangshan Bus Station. It was only six o'clock, but the doors were already locked. Most bus stations in China were open until midnight, if not later. There was always a bus going somewhere or coming from somewhere — but not in New Tzukuei.

Since I had to wait until the following morning, I checked into the Fulin Hotel next door. The town was new, but the hotel already looked old. My room, though, was clean, and at 158RMB I couldn't complain. Next up was finding a place to eat. There weren't a lot of choices. I opted for one that advertised "country cooking." It turned out the owner was from the hometown of the beautiful Wang Chao-chun, which wasn't far from where I wanted to go, which was Lepingli. He said there were two buses a day, but not every day. All I could do was trust that the next day would be the right day.

Back in my room, the prospect of a hot bath never materialized. A lukewarm shower had to do. At least I was able to wash my clothes. I hadn't been able to do that for three days, and they needed it, as did I. Before I went to sleep I opened the window for some air. I had a view of the bus station parking lot below and, beyond it, the muddy Yangtze that I hoped I would be crossing in the morning. Taking in the view, I suddenly realized the air was fresher and lighter than the air at the other end of the Gorges. It was so quiet I could hear crickets. In the Gorges, people went to bed early. There was nothing else to do.

I forgot to set my alarm, but there was no need. The fog-horns woke me up. The boats that had tied up for the night weren't waiting for the fog to clear. When I looked out my window, I couldn't see them, but I could hear the chug of their engines. I could also hear people yelling in the bus station parking lot. It was time to go.

As I walked out of the hotel I still couldn't see the river. The shore was only 200 meters down the street, but the street disappeared before it got there. When I entered the bus station, passengers were already boarding one of the buses. Just in case it was the bus to Lepingli, I hurried to the ticket window.

When I told the ticket agent where I wanted to go, she said there were two buses to Lepingli, one at 9:30 and one at 2:30. I was hoping to get an earlier start, but it didn't look like I had a choice. I told her I would take the 9:30. One disappointment, though, wasn't enough. She said the 9:30 wouldn't be running that day: there was a problem with the engine. I suppose she could have told me that before she said there were two buses, but it didn't matter. I needed a new plan. No way was I going to wait until 2:30. While I considered my options, I went over to the snack counter. I figured it might be a long day and bought enough peanuts to last until dinner. When I told the saleswoman my plight, the road gods once again came to my aid. She said there was a 7:40 bus going upriver and that I could get off at Ssuchichiao (Four Seasons Bridge), take the ferry across the Yangtze to the north shore, then hire a taxi to take me to Lepingli. She said a bus also left for Lepingli every morning at eight o'clock from Maoping near the Three Gorges Dam. Those were my options. Since Maoping was in the opposite direction, I decided in favor of the 7:40. The sooner, the better. If something went haywire, I could wait for the bus from Maoping to catch up to me, assuming it was taking the same route – and assuming it was running that day.

The snack counter also operated as the luggage depository, so I gave the woman my bag and told her I would be back before she closed at five. At least I hoped I would. The 7:40 left right on time. An hour later, after a memorable, white-knuckle mountain drive, it dropped me off at Four Seasons Bridge. Just beyond the bridge, there was a metal awning where people could shelter in the rain, and next to the awning there was a man on a motorcycle. I asked him how to get to the ferry. He said it was three kilometers down a side road, and for 5RMB he would take me. He kick-started his motorbike, I threw my leg over the rear seat, and off we roared.

A minute or so later he pulled up to the ferry landing – no way was it three kilometers. There were two boats waiting on the Yangtze's south shore: a small passenger/motorbike ferry that left on the hour and a car ferry that crossed the river four times a day. I was just in time for the nine o'clock passenger ferry. I paid the captain 10RMB and climbed aboard. I noticed that the boat had two engines and asked why. He said all ferries were required to have a backup. The authorities didn't want any accidents near the Dam or the adjacent locks. When I told him where I was hoping to go, he said I should have been wearing more clothes, that it would be much colder in the mountains. Up to that point, the weather had been so warm I hadn't considered the possibility. I looked forward to the chill.

Ten minutes later, we were met on the other side by a dozen men with motorcycles and three-wheelers. They wanted 3RMB to take people uphill to the township of Chuyuanchen half a kilometer away. I was hoping for something enclosed, like a car. Lepingli was thirty kilometers away, and I didn't look forward to going that far on the back of a motorcycle or bouncing around in a carryall on who-knows-what kind of road. I didn't see any taxis, but there *was* one very old van. I told the driver where I wanted to go, and he said he would take me there and back for 200RMB. I was amazed at how easily my transportation dilemma was solved.

The driver's name was Yu Hsien-k'ai, and I didn't need to show him my map. He knew the way, which was a relief, because for the next ninety minutes it was just us and the fog on a road of endless curves that wound up and down and around a series of mountains. I quickly lost all sense of direction, not that it mattered. Just about the time the fog lifted, we turned onto a side road and headed into the valley of Lepingli. I had thought surely the flood of tourism would have reached it by now, but it looked just as it did when I first visited twenty years ago. As we drove down the mountain then through the village, I *did* see something new: two hostels catering to overnight visitors. There was also a large sign showing trails to various sights. Tourism had arrived, but barely. Beyond the village, we drove across a bridge to the base of a promontory. Perched above us was a shrine to Ch'u Yuan. That was why I was here. Lepingli was where Ch'u Yuan (343–278 BC) was born. That was about all anyone knew about his early life. At some point he traveled east to Ying, the capital of the state of Ch'u, and he rose to become an adviser to its ruler, King Huai. Alas, the king was vain and easily flattered, and he was seduced by the empty promises of the neighboring state of Ch'in, which eventually absorbed Ch'u in its quest to conquer and unify what later became known as China.

Ch'u Yuan's forthright counsel resulted in his banishment and also in one of the great poems in the Chinese language, "Lisao" 離騷 (Encountering Sorrow). It recapitulated the poet's effort to warn his king and his subsequent attempt to transcend the corrupt world in which he found himself. Naming names would have been impolitic, so he used the names of plants to represent people and their virtues. Of its forty-six eight-line stanzas, I've translated four as well as the poem's final quatrain to give a sense of its style and its progression:

Blessed with an abundance of inner beauty
to which I added acquired skills
I donned angelica and lovage
I twined autumn orchids into a belt
swiftly I traveled as if I were late
fearful my time here was brief
I gathered wild gardenias in the morning
in the evening I collected marsh sedge   (couplets 5–8)

紛吾既有此內美兮，又重之以修能。扈江離與辟芷兮，紉秋蘭以為佩。
汩余若將不及兮，恐年歲之不吾與。朝搴阰之木蘭兮，夕攬洲之宿莽。

Amid illicit pleasures of partisan cliques
on darkened paths fraught with danger
I wouldn't care if I died
as long as my lord's chariot stays safe
I urged him this way then that
on the mighty way of ancient kings
but sweet flag saw not my heart
deceived by slander he spurned me   (couplets 17–20)

惟夫黨人之偷樂兮，路幽昧以險隘。豈余身之憚殃兮，恐皇輿之敗績。
忽奔走以先後兮，及前王之踵武。荃不察余之中情兮，反信讒而齌怒。

Turning away I let my eyes roam
thinking to visit the four quarters

I adorned my belt with flowers
whose fragrance grew ever stronger
everyone finds joy in something
my constant is a love of beauty
facing dismemberment I still wouldn't change
how could I forsake my heart (couplets 62–65)

忽反顧以游目兮，將往觀乎四荒。佩繽紛其繁飾兮，芳菲菲其彌章。
民生各有所樂兮，余獨好修以為常。雖體解吾猶未變兮，豈余心之可懲。

In this age of chaos and change
how can I remain any longer
orchid and iris have lost their fragrance
sweet flag and cymbidium are mere grasses
where are the sweet-smelling plants of the past
all I see now is wormwood
what other reason could there be
than the death of the love of beauty (couplets 154–159)

時繽紛其變易兮，又何可以淹留。蘭芷變而不芳兮，荃蕙化而為茅。
何昔日之芳草兮，今直為此蕭艾也。豈其有他故兮，莫好修之害也。

Alas in this land where none understands me
why should its ancient capital concern me
since no one is able to govern with beauty
I shall go where P'eng Hsien dwells (couplets 186–187)

已矣哉，國無人莫我知兮，又何懷乎故都。既莫足與為美政兮，
吾將從彭咸之所居。

P'eng Hsien was an ancient official who drowned himself to protest his ruler's blindness and incompetence, and Ch'u Yuan would later follow his example.

Reading "Encountering Sorrow," it's easy to see where poets such as Ts'ao Chih got their inspiration. Ch'u Yuan introduced poetry to transcendence – or maybe it was the other way around. In any case, he was both the instigator of and the medium for the spirits that made his poetic flights possible. Beautiful and sustained, they mark the first truly memorable use of the

Ch'u Yuan shrine at Leplingli

Chinese language in poetry. The rhythm, the cadence, and the language are exquisite. Wang Wei once said he never traveled anywhere without a copy of Ch'u Yuan's poems. I doubt anyone said that about the Book of Poetry. Ever since I discovered Ch'u Yuan's poems, I, too, have kept them close at hand.

The shrine hall built in his honor looked the same. On my first visit, I reached Lepingli by taking a bus up a side gorge from Old Tzukuei, walking across a suspension bridge, then hiking five kilometers. On that occasion, I walked up the dirt trail that led from the bridge to the shrine. This time I was in a van, and we followed the road. It was deeply rutted and walking up the trail would have been faster, but Mr. Yu was committed to driving it. The road ended at the back of the hall. I got out and walked to the rear entrance and banged on the door. No one answered. Nearby several men were sitting on stumps outside a farmhouse. I walked over and asked them where the care-taker was. They said he was in a hospital in Yichang, and he had the only key.

I felt deflated. I had come all the way to Lepingli to see him. He was in charge not only of the shrine hall but also of the local poetry society, which consisted of village farmers. They and their predecessors have been writing poems for over 500 years. It's called the Saotan Shihshe, or Saotan Poetry Society, after Ch'u Yuan's "Lisao." It's the oldest poetry society in China.

The caretaker was Hsu Cheng-tuan, whom I first met in December 1992, when I was collecting material for a series of radio programs about the Yangtze Gorges. I was amazed at the beauty of Lepingli and also that Ch'u Yuan was still such an important part of the lives of the local people. When I explained why I was there this time, one of the farmers told me where Mr. Hsu was convalescing and even his hospital room number. Suddenly I started feeling better about my chances of seeing him again.

After Mr. Yu turned his van around, we drove down the hill, through the village, and up the slope to the road that brought us there. I asked Mr. Yu to stop at the sign for Chaomienching, or Face-Reflecting Well, then I got out and followed a flight of stone steps down to a spring. Ch'u Yuan used the spring's water as a mirror to see his faults and to wash them away. I poured some bourbon into his magic mirror and read a poem by Li Sheng-liang, a member of the Saotan Poetry Society. Someone had carved his "Chaomien-ching" 照面井 on a rock beside the spring:

Its ability to reflect the face is unique
in every ripple are countless poems
don't speak of West Lake or Lingyin Temple
the Pool of Heaven pales before the Master's water

扦堪照面獨稱奇, 一股清流萬古詩。莫道西湖靈隱寺, 大夫遺水勝瑤池。

The poets of Lepingli had been doing some traveling, or at least some reading. Mr. Li's poem refers to Hangchou's West Lake, to the small stream in front of Hangchou's Lingyin Temple, and to the pond of the legendary Queen Mother of the West in Central Asia. I dipped my hands into the spring, washed my face, and for a moment felt fault-free. Drying my face with my bandanna, I looked at the hillside directly across the valley from the spring. That was where Ch'u Yuan lived. In 1992 one of the farmers told me that if anyone except the owner of the property ate the grain grown there, they got

Right: Face-Reflecting Well at Lepingli

diarrhea. It was an odd bit of arcanum that had stuck with me for over twenty years. I never tested the claim.

I walked back up to the road and asked Mr. Yu to take me back to the ferry. I wanted to get to the hospital in Yichang before the sun went down. The return trip was much faster. It was mostly downhill. We reached the river at 12:40, and I reckoned I was just in time for the one o'clock ferry. But there wasn't a one o'clock ferry. Mr. Yu said the ferry captain took a break for lunch, and the next ferry was at two. Since I had an hour to kill, I visited the local Internet hole-in-the-wall. But when I learned that the server was down that day, I came up with Plan B. I asked Mr. Yu whether there was any way to call the ferryboat captain and ask him to make a special trip, just for me. I was feeling extravagant. Mr. Yu took out his cell phone and made the call. It was that easy. The captain said he would do it for 50RMB.

Twenty minutes later, I was back on the south side of the river. When I didn't see the motorcycle driver who ferried passengers to and from the highway I asked the captain whether he knew when the man would be back down. The captain pulled out his cell phone and called him. A few minutes later, I was on the highway waiting for a bus. For such an out-of-the-way place, things happened fast at Four Seasons Bridge. Five minutes later, I flagged down a passing minivan heading to Tzukuei. And five minutes after

Yangtze ferry at Four Seasons Bridge

retrieving my bag at the bus station, I was on a bus bound for Yichang. An hour after that, I checked into the city's Innca Hotel. The road gods were in an especially good mood that day, for which I was grateful.

After dropping my bag in my room, I went back outside and asked a taxi driver to take me to the city's Central Hospital. Traffic in Yichang had gotten much worse since the Dam. The hospital was only four kilometers away, but getting there took nearly an hour. Dam traffic, I mused. It was almost five when I arrived. The hospital was huge, occupying an entire hillside. It took me another half hour to track down the right building.

When I finally walked into what I hoped was the right room, I was surprised. It was a private room. Mr. Hsu waved for me to sit down on the chair next to his bed. He was expecting me. Someone from the village had called ahead. His wife was there, too. After the introductions, he asked her to go get dinner. When she'd gone, he leaned over to tell me he had lung cancer and that the doctors gave him six months to a year – and he didn't want his wife to know. I'm guessing she already did. I'm also guessing he smoked. Pretty much every man of his generation smoked. If he didn't when he was young, he must have started when he was in prison. It gave people something to do.

Mr. Hsu was born in Lepingli in 1928, which made him eighty-four. His parents were farmers, and they wanted at least one of their children to have an education. He was the one they chose, and he eventually became a teacher in the village school. An education, though, had its drawbacks. In 1957 he was convicted of counterrevolutionary activity and wasn't released until 1977 when the Cultural Revolution was declared over. When he returned to Lepingli, he wasn't young anymore, but he wasn't old either. He still wanted to do something – which was to rebuild the village's Ch'u Yuan shrine. He set aside money every month from his teacher's pension and managed to amass 26,000RMB, which he used to fix up the old shrine hall and to have all of Ch'u Yuan's poetry carved onto stone tablets so that everyone could see what someone born and raised in Lepingli could do. He also helped resurrect the Saotan Poetry Society, which had been forced to disband during the Cultural Revolution. When I first visited him at the shrine hall twenty years earlier, he had shown me a set of volumes dating back to the Ming dynasty, which included thousands of poems written by society members across the past five centuries. There were over fifty members when I first met him, but now there were only a dozen. He said there were people wanting to join who weren't accepted, because they couldn't write old-style poems. All they wanted to write about was sex, he said. Mr. Hsu admitted that even current members weren't that active any more and some showed up only a few times a year.

The one day everyone showed up was the anniversary of Ch'u Yuan's death, observed on the fifth day of the fifth moon, which was Poets Day in China.

While we were chatting, Mr. Hsu's wife returned with two cold beers and told him dinner was on the way. Half an hour later their two sons arrived with takeout. There was a small table in the corner of the room that fit onto the bed. The sons lifted it into place, and Mrs. Hsu spread everything out. We gathered around the bed and shared a memorable meal. During the conversation, I learned that it was one of the sons who had put me up for the night twenty years ago. Mr. Hsu also said it was his sons who were paying for the private room, which cost 150RMB a day. He was clearly proud of them. About the time we finished dinner, a nurse came in with medications. I took that as my cue to leave. As I got up, I asked Mr. Hsu if he would send me some of his poems and handed him a name card with my address. He said he would. Even though he could barely walk, he got out of bed and escorted me to the elevator.

Two months later, I received a chapbook that he and three other society members had published. It was titled *Saotan Lienyungchi* (Collection of Saotan Couplets). He'd also included several dozen handwritten poems not published in the book. The anthology began with a poem of his from 1987, ten years after his release from prison, "This Corn Sprout" 這株玉米苗:

> This corn sprout
> sucks rain and dew with all its might
> fights over fertilizer
> its color so green
> its stalk so tall
> in autumn when harvest time comes
> it produces no corn
> just a big puffball

> 这株玉米苗，使劲吮吸雨露，争夺肥料。
> 他颜色分外绿，苗株格外高。
> 到了秋收季节，不结玉米，但生一個灰包。

It was a farmer poem, and I wish he had written more farmer poems. The chapbook was full of the glories of liberation and advances under the banner of the Communist Party. Twenty years of prison had left their mark. Here is one he titled "Mourning My Elder Brother Hsu Cheng-jung" 吊徐正容兄:

He toiled and suffered his entire life
as a teacher and as a soldier
marching north and south he fought rebels
summer and winter he taught children
he studied the classics when he retired
he worked in his garden when he had time
he volunteered to fix the bridge and the road
he put others first and deserves a medal

碌碌忙忙苦一生，半從教育半從軍。闐南闐北殲殘匪，御署御寒課幼群。
老退居家攻子史，休閒園藝樂辛勤。修橋補路舒心事，舍己為人可樹勳。

The bridge Hsu's brother repaired was the bridge I drove across at the foot of the promontory on which Ch'u Yuan's shrine was located. It was named Volunteer Bridge in his honor, which was, I thought, better than a medal. Among the poems Hsu wrote out by hand was "Consolation" 自慰:

Despite the unsurpassed reputation
a teacher's duties are heavy and endless
late at night correcting papers under lamplight
passing on knowledge all day at the blackboard
it's easy to mislead while leading
and hard to sleep through the night
the pay can't compare to that of others
but when a student succeeds I'm consoled

無上榮譽至頂巔，教師任重不停鞭。深更備改燈光下，盡日傳幫講桌前。
誘導真難防誤導，睡眠總是不安眠。酬金莫與他人比，學子成材亦慰然。

Hsu's poems, unlike Ch'u Yuan's, would have been at home in the Book of Poetry. They were old at heart and ancient in style: poems by a farmer who learned how to hitch his thoughts and feelings to the buckboard of poetry. Hopefully, I'll have a chance to join his sons at some future meeting of the Saotan Poetry Society. Maybe I'll even write a poem myself.

Whenever I rose to the surface during the night I heard the rain. It never stopped. My hotel was only a few blocks from where the Yangtze sluiced over Yichang's Kechoupa Dam – not to be confused with the Three Gorges Dam fifty kilometers upstream. Over the course of the year, the Yangtze carried more water than any river in the world, and the water had to come from somewhere. When I got up the next morning, it was *still* raining. The only people outside – and there weren't many – hid beneath ponchos and umbrellas. After the usual morning coffee, I slipped galoshes onto my canvas shoes. It was the first time I needed them, and I was glad I had remembered to bring them.

My plans for the day were unusually modest: two nearby destinations and an afternoon train ride. First up was Sanyoutung, or Three Travelers Cave. As soon as I walked outside, a taxi appeared. I didn't question the road gods' largesse and got in. I asked the driver to take me to the cave. It was ten kilometers north of town at the eastern end of Hsilinghsia, the easternmost of the Three Gorges. Due to the rain, there was almost no traffic, and I was there in minutes.

The cave was inside a large mountainside park on the Yangtze's north shore, and there was a bit of walking required – walking in the rain. Before entering, I stopped at a small store that catered to visitors and bought an umbrella. Thus equipped, I proceeded to the entrance and paid the admission fee. I noticed on the price list that there was an optional fee for a boat excursion on the river. If it hadn't been raining so hard, I might have indulged. Walking, though, seemed like enough of an adventure.

From the entrance, I followed a trail of stone steps downhill. They were so slippery, I had to walk sideways and clutch the iron chain along the cliff. The chain was lined with thousands of locks previous visitors had attached to memorialize their visits. At one point, I passed a record of Pai Chu-yi's visit carved on a stele. He came here in 819 with his brother Hsing-chien and his (and Hsueh T'ao's) friend Yuan Chen. They were the three travelers after whom the cave was named.

A bit farther down, I came to the cave. It was much bigger than I had expected, over twenty meters across, at least that deep, and nearly ten meters high. It was divided into several chambers by a number of natural pillars. Their presence made me feel better about walking under the cave's roof. Leaning against the walls were dozens of stone tablets, left by visitors over the centuries, and the walls themselves were covered with inscriptions carved by pilgrims. Too many of the characters, though, had been worn away, and I made no attempt to read what remained. At the back of the cave were statues of the three travelers. Pai Chu-yi, of course, was the star. In 815 he was exiled to Chiuchiang, 700 kilometers downriver. Four years later he was traveling to his next post in Szechuan and stopped in Yichang with his brother. They were joined by Yuan Chen, who had been rusticated to the next town downriver from Yichang.

    Although it wasn't close to noon, given the rain and the cold, I figured we could all use a shot of whiskey. As the fragrance wafted its way to Traveler Heaven, I read a poem Pai Chu-yi wrote to his brother later that year, after he had been rehabilitated and both brothers had returned to Ch'ang-an, "For Hsing-chien, While Drinking" 對酒示行簡:

> Today after one cup of wine
> I feel so wonderfully happy
> a happiness that comes from inside
> others aren't likely to know

Three Travelers Cave

only a pair of brothers
forever suffering apart
then this spring from the Gorges of Pa
after ten thousand miles we came home safe
home to our two sisters
of marriageable age but unmarried
whose weddings we recently concluded
to good and trustworthy men
my concerns for them have been dispelled
as if a sword had cut through a harness
I feel so light and unrestrained
I want to leap into the sky
whenever I feel the weight of life's burdens
even eating meat I feel hungry
now that my heart is set free
I could grow fat on water
Hsing-chien drain your cup
then put it down and listen
I don't worry when we're far from home
and I don't mind our pay is so little
I only care that you and I
never part again this life

今旦一罇酒，歡暢何怡怡。此樂從中來，他人安得知。
兄弟唯二人，遠別恆苦悲。今春自巴峽，萬里平安歸。
復有雙幼妹，笄年未結褵。昨日嫁娶畢，良人皆可依。
憂念兩消釋，如刀斷羈縻。身輕心無系，忽欲凌空飛。
人生苟有累，食肉常如饑。我心既無苦，飲水亦可肥。
行簡勸爾酒，停杯聽我辭。不嘆鄉國遠，不嫌官祿微。
但願我與爾，終老不相離。

That was why there were so many locks on that chain along the cliff. The people who came to pay their respects hoped the locks would rust through before they would have to part from their loved ones. Reading through the works of China's poets of the past, one can't help noticing how many titles begin with the words *sung* (seeing off) or *pieh* (parting from) or *chi* (sent to). As if being an official weren't stressful enough, it meant frequent separation.

The Pai brothers and their friend Yuan Chen weren't the only trio whose visit to the cave was imbued with such sentiments. Three members of the Su family came here in 1059: Su Hsun and his sons, Su Tung-p'o and Su Tzu-you. Earlier that year, Su Hsun returned with his sons to their home south of Chengtu to bury his wife. On their way back to the Sung capital of Kaifeng, they stopped in Yichang, and they also visited this cave. Like the Pai brothers, the Sus were known for their affinity. Two years later, when Su Tung-p'o left Kaifeng to begin his career at a town 800 kilometers to the west, he parted from his brother for the first time. Su Tzu-you accompanied his older brother as far as the west gate of Chengchou, and Su Tung-p'o commemorated the occasion with "Poem Composed on Horseback and Sent to Tzu-you after Parting at the West Gate of Chengchou on the Nineteenth Day of the Eleventh Month" 辛丑十一月十九日既與子由別於鄭州西門之外馬上賦詩一篇寄之：

Why do I feel drunk without drinking
my heart is following your saddle home
your thoughts are already with our father
but how shall I deal with this loneliness of mine
climbing above the ramparts between us
all I see is your bobbing black hat
the weather is so cold and your robe so thin
and you're riding that nag beneath a waning moon
"On the road people sing at home they're happy"
offered my attendant seeing me so sad
of course I know life is full of partings
what bothers me is how fast it's passing
remember when we faced that sputtering lamp
listening to the wind that rain-filled night
that is something I know you won't forget
don't fall in love with a government career

不飲胡為醉兀兀，　此心已逐歸鞍發。　歸人猶自念庭闈，　今我何以慰寂寞。
登高回首坡隴隔，　但見烏帽出復沒。　苦寒念爾衣裳薄，　獨騎瘦馬踏殘月。
路人行歌居人樂，　僮僕怪我苦淒惻。　亦知人生要有別，　但恐歲月去飄忽。
寒燈相對記疇昔，　夜雨何時聽蕭瑟。　君知此意不可忘，　慎勿苦愛高官職。

Su Tung-p'o was referring to the night the two brothers read Wei Ying-wu's "For Ch'uan-chen and Yuan-ch'ang" 示全真元常, in which Wei complained about having to endure so many years apart from his nephews. Reading Wei's poem, the two Sus resolved to retire from office as early as possible, and spend their remaining years together reading and writing poetry. Such simple pleasures. Such a noble, yet modest, goal. Yet neither brother succeeded. Nor did Wei Ying-wu. The Pais and the Sus served as officials, and were always being assigned or banished somewhere away from their loved ones. They never stopped traveling, not until it was too late to make good on such resolutions. Their separations were the source of so much heartbreak, I felt embarrassed offering them so little whiskey.

After collecting the cups and finishing what remained, I continued along the path. Since going up looked safer than going down, I followed a side trail to a pavilion above the cave, an unusual three-tiered structure called Chih-hsiting. Carved on a stele at the base was an account of its construction written in 1037 by Ou-yang Hsiu. From the upper level, there was a view of Hsiling Gorge, and I suppose it might have functioned as a naval lookout. Its name, though, meant "happy arrival pavilion" and referred to the relief boatmen and travelers felt upon successfully navigating the Gorges. Had the pavilion another tier or two, I might have been able to look in the opposite direction and see the place where the clear water of the Lower Lao joined the muddy Yangtze on the Yichang side of the mountain. During his first visit, Ou-yang Hsiu had the same thought. Unlike me, he acted on his thought, as he tells us in "The Lower Lao River" 下牢溪:

> I could hear a river in the next valley over
> crossing the ridge I found it
> its transparent current its submerged white boulders
> the silent shadows of a myriad peaks
> rock cliffs lined with unfading flowers
> and impossibly lush jade-green cedars
> how could I focus on the rippling water
> looking down then up at the swirling clouds

隔谷聞溪聲，尋溪度橫嶺。清流涵白石，靜見千峰影。
巖花無時歇，翠柏郁何整。安能戀潺湲，俯仰弄雲景。

Unlike the Pais and the Sus, Ou-yang wasn't just passing through. He had been banished to Yichang. Serving at court was like crossing a minefield. Being banished, though, had its advantages. Such an out-of-the-way place was relatively stress-free, and Ou-yang spent many of his days wandering in the nearby mountains instead of dodging vendettas at court. During his two years in Yichang, the Lower Lao became one of his favorite haunts. Here is another poem he wrote about it, "The Lower Lao Ford" 下牢津:

> The Lower Lao flows on and on
> ancient guardian of serrated ridges
> as I entered the gorge the river turned
> around each bend the mountains multiplied
> white birds flew from white sandy shores
> dark dreams merged with dark peaks
> a banished official first passing this place
> expresses his grief with the songs of Ch'u

依依下牢口，古戍郁嵯峨。入峽江漸曲，轉灘山更多。
白沙飛白鳥，青障合青夢。遷客初經此，愁詞作楚歌。

The banished Ou-yang Hsiu looks back in this poem to the banished Ch'u Yuan and recalls Ch'u Yuan's poetic anguish at being slandered by rivals and dismissed by his sovereign. He must have wondered whether it was the curse of all those who served. That damn job again. It was the inevitable consequence of connecting one's mouth (or brush) with one's heart. As Ou-yang notes in the last line, every banished official who came here could quote Ch'u Yuan's "Encountering Sorrow." In the penultimate line, though, he suggests that it would only be a matter of time before those officials would no longer have to rely on Ch'u Yuan for their expressions of grief.

From the pavilion, paths led every which way. All the steps were equally slippery, and I decided I had seen enough. I followed those that led, I hoped, to the exit. It took a while to find, but the noise from a group of tourists coming through the gate helped guide me there. Out on the road, I boarded the next bus back to town, then made my way on foot to Ou-yang Hsiu Park, which was at the west end of Hsiling First Road, just past my hotel.

If there was one poet associated with Yichang it was Ou-yang Hsiu, and I thought the park might include a memorial hall. He made such an impression

Ou-yang Hsiu and last couplet of his poem "In Reply to Yuan-chen"

during his stay that he became the town's de facto poet laureate. Literary critics say his writing changed while he was here, from "critical idealism" to "constructive realism." Despite being highfalutin literary terms, they actually mean something when viewed through the lens of his poetry. An example I had with me was "Old Tile Inkstone" 古瓦硯:

A tile made of clay is a poor lowly thing
but it works just fine with a brush and some ink
everything has its use
whether elevated or base
gold is certainly precious
and jade invariably hard
but using either to make ink
can't compare to a broken tile
of course it's a lowly thing
but its value is hard to deny
and not just a piece of rubble
since ancient times people too

磚瓦賤微物，得厠筆墨間。於物用有宜，不計丑與妍。
金非不為寶，玉豈不為堅。用之以發墨，不及瓦礫頑。
乃知物雖賤，當用價難攀。豈惟瓦礫爾，用人從古難。

Ou-yang Hsiu became one of the great poets and essayists of the Sung. However, his family was poor, and he was largely self-taught. At the beginning of his career, his better-educated colleagues disdained him. He was only thirty when he wrote this poem, but it's clear he saw himself as being just as capable in expressing coherent views on good government, which begins with making one's ink. Since ancient times, the Chinese produced their ink by grinding a stick made of soot and glue on a flat surface, and adding drops of water as needed. Slate was the preferred surface, but any port in a storm — even a broken roof tile like Ou-yang Hsiu would do.

My expectation of a memorial hall at the park was mistaken. It was simply an open plaza with a single humongous rock from which Ou-yang Hsiu's head and upper torso protruded. Carved along one side of the rock was the last couplet of another Yichang poem, "In Reply to Yuan-chen" 對答元珍 (a different Yuan-chen than Pai Chu-yi's and Hsueh T'ao's friend of the same name). Here is the entire poem:

Spring it seems hasn't reached this edge of heaven
the Second Month in this rustic town and nothing is blooming
a few oranges still hang from snow-bent branches
roused by winter thunder bamboo shoots are stirring
I heard migrating geese last night and thought about home
the illness I've had since New Year has infected everything alive
having once been a guest in the gardens of Loyang
why should I complain if the flowers here are late

春風疑不到天涯，二月山城未見花。殘雪壓枝猶有桔，凍雷驚笋欲抽芽。
夜聞歸雁生鄉思，病入新年感物華。曾是洛陽花下客，野芳雖晚不須嗟。

Loyang was the location of Ou-yang's first assignment. It was only a few years earlier, and the memory was fresh. It was a much more refined place to serve. Still, he made the best of his banishment to the boondocks, and he left such an impression on the people that they named the local Confucian academy for him. Situated on a hill at the east end of Hsiling First Road, it was called Liuyi Shuyuan, or One of Six Academy — in honor of Ou-yang's nickname, Layman One of Six. When people asked him to explain the name, he listed his six favorite things: a library of books, a collection of ancient seals, a zither, a chess set, a jug of wine, and a body that wasn't yet dead. He was one of his six favorite things. The old academy was blown to smithereens during World War II, and the hill on which it stood is now a memorial park for the town's war dead. Old One of Six was moved down the street closer to the river. I poured None of Six a shot of Willett and sprinkled it on his stone head, then I poured one for myself and called my visit to Yichang good.

I walked back to my hotel, checked out, then took a taxi to Yichang's new East Station. Since my train originated in Yichang, it was already waiting. As I boarded, I was welcomed by "Cherry Pink and Apple-Blossom White" coming over the loudspeakers. It had been forty years since I had heard that song. I couldn't resist mamboing up the aisle to my seat. The people boarding behind me must have thought I was out of my mind, or off my medication. I threw my bag on the rack overhead and sat next to the window. The music was on a loop and continued playing as the train pulled out.

Forty years earlier, when I was living in New York and working on a PhD in anthropology at Columbia, during the summer break I flew to Stockholm to marry a Swedish girl who changed her mind, but not until after I arrived. Since the dates of my plane ticket were fixed, and I couldn't afford another one, I filled the summer with Swedish-language lessons and ballroom dance. All summer long I danced to Pérez Prado. "¡Viva el mambo!" I said to my non-existent seatmates. Then I leaned my head against the window and stretched my legs out onto the empty seat across from me and watched the countryside go by. At some point, I slept.

Three hours later, I disembarked in Hsiangyang and checked into the stately and extravagant Chuanhui Hotel in the old part of town. After depositing my bag in my mirrored, gold-filigreed room, I walked back outside and looked for a place to eat. It started to drizzle. Down the street, I saw a white sheet with a red cross in the middle of a doorway. It was a welcome sight. Beyond the sheet was a man, his wife, and two massage tables. The wife was blind, but the man was partially sighted and told me to lie down. My back thanked me. I keep forgetting how important a good massage is for a traveler. An hour later, I remembered. I'm sure I had dinner, but the memory of it was overwhelmed by others.

I woke up in Hsiangyang, where Meng Hao-jan (689–740) used to wake up. The rain was gone, and sunshine was streaming through the window. Meng's "Spring Dawn" 春曉 came streaming in, too:

Sleeping in spring oblivious of dawn
everywhere I hear birds
after the wind and rain last night
I wonder how many petals fell

春眠不覺曉，處處聞啼鳥。夜來風雨聲，花落知多少。

It's one of the best-known poems in the Chinese language and a personal favorite. People who write about Chinese poetry have always marveled at the sheer loveliness and joy of the poem. The loveliness I understood, not the joy. What I felt was heartbreak: one of the most beautiful scenes of the year outside, and Meng Hao-jan couldn't get out of bed. The thought enervated my usual optimism. I knew, for example, that there was no petal-covered world waiting for me outside. It was autumn. Still, whether petals or leaves, it was time to see what Meng left behind.

When I finally ventured forth, I could feel the wind moving ever so slightly. Some people were wearing light jackets in anticipation of more wind. I considered their optimism reckless and stuck with a T-shirt. I'm glad I did. It didn't take long until I was perspiring. I went looking for Meng's grave in a park just outside the city wall.

Hsiang-yang was one of the few cities in China whose ancient walls and moat were intact. The park was only a few blocks from my hotel, and, per-spiration aside, it was a lovely place for a walk. The loveliness, though, didn't help. I doomed my search with the fictitious memory of having seen a map showing Meng's grave located in the park's moat-side recreation area, whose length and breadth I searched: past the carousel and the Ferris wheel, past half a dozen pavilions, past the MiG-15, all in vain. I asked anyone who looked like a daily visitor or a park employee. They all shook their heads. I even asked a group of old men sitting on benches listening to their caged thrushes sing.

I considered asking the thrushes. I used to speak thrush. Back in 1978, not long after I moved to the farming village of Bamboo Lake, on a mountain north of Taipei, a thrush showed up at my bedroom window one morning and started calling and wouldn't stop until I called back. The next day it returned, and again it wouldn't stop until I called back. This went on for months. Then one day it showed up with two fledglings and proceeded to introduce the young birds to our morning ritual. It became a family affair. And it continued like that for six years, until the landlord raised my rent and I moved to another farmhouse farther up the mountain. I never saw that thrush family again. I saw other thrushes, but they never answered. Different dialect, I guess. Seeing the thrushes in the park clinging to the bars of their cages, I sighed and walked on.

Having exhausted the possibilities in the park, I tried the embankment along the Han River, which formed the city's northern border. I also walked up and down the street east of the moat. No luck there, either. After an hour, I returned to the hotel and went online. There was nothing about a Meng Hao-jan grave *in* the city, but I *did* find something about a grave thirty kilometers southwest, at a place called Tengfenglin. However, it was clearly part of a tourist development, and I dismissed it out of hand. Several websites, though, mentioned a grave on Lumenshan. That was where Meng lived and studied between the ages of fifteen and twenty-five, just as Li Pai and Ch'en Tzu-ang had done on mountains near their homes. It seemed a likely spot, so I ventured forth once more. To this day, I still don't know where I got that mental image of a little box on a Hsiangyang map with the words "Meng Hao-jan Grave." I wish it would go away.

I got into the first taxi that pulled up at the hotel entrance and headed for the mountain. Lumenshan was fifteen kilometers by crow but thirty by car. First we had to cross from Hsiangyang into Fancheng on the north side of the Han River. Then we had to drive through a disaster of city planning, stop to fill up with natural gas, and finally cross the Tangpai River just upstream from where it joined the Han. Highway 218 was waiting on the other side and took us across the floodplain formed by the junction of the two rivers.

As we sped along, the driver said the government planned to level most of Fancheng. They were going to rebuild it from scratch on the floodplain. He said they were calling the soon-to-be city Hsiangchou District. As he pronounced the name, he shook his head. His apartment was in the area about to be leveled, and the authorities were refusing to pay market value. He said it had taken him and his wife over ten years to save enough to buy the apartment, and the government was offering twenty fen on the RMB. All he could do was sigh, and I sighed with him. It was my second sigh of the day, and the day was still young.

After less than three kilometers, we turned off Highway 218 onto another paved road and followed it for ten kilometers. The driver said we wouldn't want to be on that road in another week or so. The rice that covered the flood-plain was about to be harvested, and the farmers would be using the road to dry their grain. I counted my blessings – no petal-covered ground, but at least no rice-covered road. As we continued south, half a dozen hills came into view. The closest turned out to be Lumenshan. We turned off at the foot of the mountain, and I paid the admission fee. This was happening every-where in China. Mountains were becoming recreation areas and forest pre-serves. While it was good news for hikers and tourists, it was bad news for hermits. I tried to imagine a hermit lobby, without success.

We followed the road that led up the mountain a few hundred meters, then I asked the driver to stop. I saw a turnoff to something that claimed to be the Meng Hao-jan Memorial Hall. That sounded promising. In addition to commemorating famous people, such places were often sources of informa-tion and publications available only locally. I told the driver to take the side road. It ended less than 200 meters later at a group of traditional-style build-ings. They were new and looked imposing. Someone had spent a lot of money on Meng Hao-jan. When I got out of the taxi to investigate, a man appeared from a doorway and told us to go away. All he would say was that the person who owned the land had hired a contractor to build the buildings but couldn't come up with the money to pay for the work. The place was closed until he did. It was just as well. I was looking for Meng's grave, and it wasn't there.

We returned to the main road and continued another 300 meters to Lumen Temple. It dated back to the first century, when Buddhism first arrived in China, and its buildings once covered most of the mountain What remained wouldn't have covered an acre – wars, revolutions, and the chang-ing times had taken their toll. I entered the front courtyard and had a brief conversation with the abbot. When I told him I had heard that Meng Hao-jan was buried nearby, he said that was true. He then led me back outside the front gate and directed me up the road. The grave, he said, was a mere hun-dred meters away, then added that it wasn't the real grave: it contained only the poet's clothes. I walked up the road to see for myself. It was just a small mound with a simple tombstone flanked by two stone tablets, each with a poem carved onto its surface. Even though this wasn't where Meng was bur-ied, I poured out three cups of bourbon for his clothes. While the fumes were wafting their way to Robe and Hat Heaven, I walked behind the mound to see what else I might find.

I saw a path off to the side and followed it fifty meters up a pine-shaded slope to a brick building dedicated to P'ang Te-kung. P'ang was a mountain recluse of the third century. And he wasn't your average recluse. People came from all over China to seek his advice. He was a sage. He was also Meng Hao-jan's hero, and Meng built his hut near where P'ang once lived. Although the young Meng returned to Hsiangyang on occasion, this was where he came back to at night. He described one such late return in his "Coming Back to Lumen at Night Song" 夜歸鹿門歌:

> The peal of a temple bell as day turns to dusk
> the noise of the Yuliang Ferry as it struggles across
> people walking along the shore to their villages by the river
> me taking a boat too returning to Lumenshan
> the Lumen moon lighting treetops above the clouds
> me suddenly arriving at Master P'ang's hut
> on a long lonesome trail past pine-guarded cliffs
> only a recluse would take

山寺鐘鳴晝已昏，漁梁渡頭爭渡喧。人隨沙岸向江村，余亦乘舟歸鹿門。
鹿門月照開煙樹，忽到龐公棲隱處。嚴扉松徑長寂寥，唯有幽人往來去。

My friend Gary Flint once retraced Meng's route between the city and the temple and posted photos on his website, Mountainsongs.net. They're still there as of this writing. Gary was another pilgrim. However, instead of a taxi, he hired a boat and floated down the Han past the ten-kilometer-long Yuliang sandbar until he was as close as he could get to Lumenshan. Then he disembarked and hiked to the temple, which he said was an hour from the shore. Presumably, that was what Meng's song was for. The location of the shore, no doubt, had changed, but at night the path would have seemed long and lonely.

I returned to the grave to collect my cups and read the two poems on either side of the tombstone. The characters were barely legible, but the poems were short. One of them was by Wang Wei, "Crying for Meng Hao-jan" 哭孟浩然:

> I can't see the person I knew
> the waters of the Han keep flowing east
> describe for me my Hsiangyang friend
> Tsaichou's barren landscape

故人不可見，漢水日東流。借問襄陽老，江山空蔡州。

Tsaichou was the name of a small sandbar in the Han River south of Hsiang-yang. It was later washed away in a flood, and people have wondered why Wang mentioned it in his poem and how it was connected with Meng. I wondered about that myself. Wonderment, though, never prevented people from admiring Wang's poem.

Although Meng and Wang never spent much time together, they were the closest of friends. They were also linked artistically. Literary critics called them the two greatest landscape poets of the T'ang. When they weren't writing about mountains, they were writing about rivers. Unlike Wang, Meng never served as an official. By the time he traveled to Ch'ang-an to take the exams, he was forty. It was then that he and Wang became friends. When Meng failed the exams, he returned home and never traveled to the capital again. However, the two men maintained a lifelong correspondence, and when Meng died, Wang was heartbroken.

On the other side of Meng's tomb was a poem by another friend: Li Pai's "For Meng Hao-jan" 贈孟浩然：

I love Master Meng
known to the world for his carefree ways
a young man disdaining the regalia of office
an old man resting among clouds and pines
drunk beneath the moon on the wine of sages
smitten by flowers he serves no lord
I can no longer think of mountains as high
I bow in vain to the fragrance of his virtue

吾愛孟夫子，風流天下聞。紅顏棄軒冕，白首臥松雲。
醉月頻中聖，迷花不事君。高山安可仰，徒此揖清芬。

Li bowed in vain because he was passing through Hsiangyang and hoping to meet Meng, but Meng wasn't there. He was traveling. Thirteen hundred years later, he still wasn't there. I bowed, too, finished what was left of the whiskey, and returned to my taxi.

From Lumenshan, we retraced our route through the soon-to-be-harvested floodplain and the soon-to-be-leveled urban blight of Fancheng then recrossed the Han River into Hsiangyang. I asked the driver to take me back to my hotel long enough for me to check out. I wanted to find the place where Meng lived when he wasn't living on Lumenshan. In his poems, Meng Hao-jan said his home was outside the city wall just south of the Hsiang River. He called it his South of the River Garden, which he longs for, while far from home, in "Thoughts When Cold Comes Early" 早寒有懷：

> Leaves are falling and geese are flying south
> the north wind has turned the Yangtze River cold
> my home is where the Hsiang's waters wind
> at the other end of the clouds over Ch'u
> I've exhausted my hometown tears this trip
> watching the horizon for a single sail
> unsure of the ferry who can I ask
> at dusk all I see is an endless sea

木落雁南渡，北風江上寒。我家襄水曲，遙隔楚雲端。
鄉淚客中盡，孤帆天際看。迷津欲有問，平海夕漫漫。

After a decade on Lumenshan, Meng spent the next ten years traveling in the lower reaches of the Yangtze, where the river was so wide he couldn't see the far shore. The Yangtze watershed east of the Gorges was synonymous with the state of Ch'u, which once conquered all the land between the Gorges and the sea. Hence, Meng was at the eastern end of Ch'u, and his home was at the western end, a stone's throw south of the Hsiang.

From the hotel, we drove through the city's South Gate then immediately turned west onto Highway 207. After a kilometer or so, we pulled over, and I got out to see what was left of the river after which the town was named. I sighed my third sigh of the day. Meng said he often set sail just beyond his gate. And boats traveled the Hsiang well into the middle of the last century. But due to urban development, the Hsiang had been reduced to something about as wide as an irrigation ditch. Nowadays it was called South Ditch (Nanchu), which was what it was, and a stagnant one at that. So much for the Hsiang.

As for Meng's residence, scholars have suggested different locations. The arguments that made the most sense to me — based on what Meng saw from his home and recorded in his poems — put the site near the northwest foot of Hsienshan in the fields behind Hospital 364, approximately a kilometer southeast of the city's South Gate. Shengfeng Road, on the other side of the highway, led us there. It was paved, and we followed it past the hospital, until we had to choose left or right. Right led to Chingshan, left to Hsienshan. Since Hsienshan was Meng's favorite mountain, I chose left, which meant slow-going on a narrow dirt road. We eventually came out behind the hospital in an area of vegetable fields surrounded by mud-brick houses. It would have been a twenty-minute walk or five minutes by horse — just about right, I reck-oned, for someone coming home after a night in town. Even though it was at the edge of a city, it still seemed bucolic. I had no trouble imagining Meng's "Scenes at My South of the River Garden Sent to the Esteemed Mister Chiao" 澗南園既事貽皎上人:

> My humble hut is beyond the outer wall
> my property consists of nothing but farmland
> surrounded by woods and brambles
> beyond the noise of the city
> I fish from the bank of the river to the north
> woodcutter songs reach my study from the south
> my books are about the life of seclusion
> I look for people who don't talk to talk with

弊盧在郭外，素產唯田園。左右林野曠，不聞朝市喧。
釣竿垂北澗，樵唱入南軒。書取幽棲事，將尋靜者論。

I got back in the taxi and asked the driver to go a bit farther. I wasn't look-ing for anything special, just trying to get a better idea of the lay of the land. We followed the dirt road uphill another four or five hundred meters, until we suddenly came out into a vast, deserted clearing. It looked so odd — the vastness, the desertedness so close to a city. I asked the driver to stop. He got out, too. When I asked him what this place was for, he pointed at his head with his hand in the shape of a gun and then pulled the trigger. He said this was where people were executed during the Cultural Revolution. The only structure was a small cement tower about five meters high, presumably where the officer in charge stood when he gave the order to shoot his fellow citizens. It was an eerie and yet such a pastoral setting. Walking up the tow-er's stairs to the top, I felt disembodied. The place was so quiet, as soon as a thought arose, it died. When I finally got tired of dead thoughts, I turned and looked toward the city. Its ancient wall was about two kilometers away.

I figured the execution ground would have been a bit too far for Meng if he was coming home late, especially the last uphill part, but not too far for people in town to hear the gunfire.

We returned to the highway and to the city's South Gate, then continued east another two or three kilometers. Just before the highway passed under a railroad bridge, I asked the driver to stop. I was looking for a monument. The citizens of Hsiangyang put it up 1,700 years ago, to honor a man named Yang Hu. Yang governed the region and used Hsiangyang as his base. He was a benevolent governor and also the primary strategist of the man who founded the Western Chin dynasty (265–316). The plans he made eventually succeeded, but he died before they did. In gratitude, the emperor had the report of victory read at the stele the people of Hsiangyang had erected at the foot of Hsienshan, in his memory. The site they chose was where Yang often came to drink. Meng Hao-jan also visited the stele, and memorialized the occasion with "Hiking on Hsienshan with Friends" 與諸子登峴山:

> Our lives are marked by transience
> our comings and goings forming past and present
> this landscape has its noteworthy sights
> to which we hiked to see once more
> when the water level drops the fish traps appear

Former execution ground outside Hsiangyang

during the winter the marshlands expand
the monument to Master Yang is still here
reading the words I keep wiping my tears

人事有代謝，往來成古今。江山留勝跡，我輩復登臨。
水落魚樑淺，天寒夢澤深。羊公碑尚在，讀罷淚沾襟。

It wasn't just Meng's own transience that gave rise to his tears. It was the world's, too. Depending on the season, Meng could see the Han River shrinking or expanding. And standing here, he couldn't help thinking of the time Yang Hu came to that very spot one night with his friends and lamented that he had come like others before him who had since disappeared and that he would be followed by others thinking the same thought. And Yang was right. In honor of Meng's poem, the people of Hsiangyang renamed the stele Falling Tears Monument. They built a shrine and conducted a ceremony here every year. At least they did until modern times. The only structure that remained was an abandoned shack next to the railroad embankment. Only by accident did I spot the stone tablet. It was sticking out of the embankment, surrounded by garbage. Carved onto its surface I could see "Falling Tears Monument." On behalf of Yang and Meng, the citizens of Hsiangyang, and all my fellow transient beings, I poured a shot of whiskey on the tablet. I decided it was better than tears.

Afterward we followed the road east then south. On the way back from Lumenshan, I had called the local cultural affairs office for information about Meng's grave. The official I spoke with verified that the grave at the temple contained only clothes. He said the real grave was somewhere on the south side of Hsienshan. It had been destroyed during the Sung dynasty, and the tombstone was taken to Kuyin Temple for safekeeping. When I asked about the grave at Tengfenglin, the tourist development thirty kilometers southwest of Hsiangyang, he said it was just a memorial grave. That was all he knew.

Kuyin, or Chingkung Temple, as it was called in the T'ang, was at the south foot of Hsienshan. It was one of Meng's favorite haunts. I'd heard about it before. The Buddhist translator Tao-an (312–385) lived and taught there. When I asked the driver whether he had heard of it, he shook his head. But I had never let not knowing where something was stop me from looking for it. I figured we would continue south and see what turned up. After another kilometer or so, I spotted a Buddhist temple overlooking the river and asked the driver to stop. I followed a foot trail across a pile of rubble to the front steps of the temple, which was called Kuanyin Pavilion. I walked behind two shrine halls to the edge of the river. I could see Lumenshan and its neighboring peaks in the distance.

On my way back past the shrine halls, I met the abbot and asked him whether he knew anything about Meng Hao-jan's grave or Kuyin Temple. He didn't. He talked about his plans instead. As with many Buddhist temples in China nowadays, the plans were grandiose. Since the land between the highway and the river was limited, the abbot wanted to build a skywalk across the highway and a series of shrine halls at the base of a nearby pyramid-shaped hill known as Tienchushan. It all looked impressive in the architectural drawing on his wall, but I have never been able to understand why monks want to live in palaces. I know the excuse:

Ancient ginkgo and former site of Kuyin Temple at the foot of Hsienshan

"It's for the faithful." It's an old excuse and one that has worked for millennia, and not only in China. I thanked the abbot and returned to my taxi.

I decided I had gone far enough. I asked the driver to turn around. I still wanted to visit the sunny side of Hsienshan. As we backtracked about 200 meters, I saw a side road that led toward the mountain. Most of the pavement was gone, but the driver was game. After a few hundred meters, we came to a padlocked gate. I got out and discovered the padlock was just hung there to look like it was locked. I undid the chain and pushed the gate open. We drove on for another kilometer until the road ended at a quarry. Between the quarry and the mountain was a cluster of abandoned, two-story brick buildings covered with vines. I walked over to investigate, and my driver followed me. He told me to be careful. He said he had heard of this place. It was the prison used during the Cultural Revolution. Judging from the number of cells, it must have held a thousand inmates. The authorities, no doubt, found it convenient. The execution ground was just across the ridge.

As I exited one of the weed-choked buildings, I saw an ancient ginkgo off to the side and walked over for a closer look. Near its base was a stone bearing the name Kuyin Temple. That was what I was looking for. Another hundred meters away, I saw another ginkgo. They would have been on either side of the temple's entrance, assuming it faced east, toward the river. That was the standard arrangement at temple entrances: facing south or east and flanked by a pair of trees, sometimes cedars, sometimes locusts, but usually ginkgos. The temple itself was long gone, and Meng's tombstone was probably buried somewhere nearby in the detritus of the centuries. I poured a shot of bourbon onto the tree's roots. I figured Meng would get the message.

I also poured myself a shot and considered once again the last line of Wang Wei's poem. It finally hit me. Meng Hao-jan's grave wasn't on Hsienshan. It was a few hundred meters away on the sandbar that had since disappeared. It was only natural that Wang Wei knew where his friend was buried — on "Tsaichou's barren landscape," as he put it. It explained why Meng's tombstone had been moved to the temple: the grave was destroyed *not* by warfare or grave robbers but by the Han River. It all made perfect sense. I thanked the Willett family and their eighteen-year-old elixir for helping lay this mystery to rest. Having seen what I could of Meng Hao-jan's world, I asked the driver to take me to the city's new East Station, on the doomed Fancheng side of the river. I had a ticket for the 3:41 to Anlu.

As my train pulled out, more or less on time, I concluded that it had been a good day after all. My optimism was restored. I let Li Pai's "On Hsienshan Thinking of the Past" 峴山懷古 transport me:

> I climbed Hsien Summit in search of the past
> from the heights I gazed on Hsiangyang
> the sky was so clear I could see the far peaks
> the river was so low sandbars appeared
> I imagined river maidens fingering pearls
> and I recalled drunk Magistrate Shan
> my sighs gave rise to thoughts about autumn
> while the pine trees sang in the evening wind

> 訪古登峴首，憑高眺襄中。天清遠峰出，水落寒沙空。
> 弄珠見游女，醉酒懷山公。感嘆發秋興，長松鳴夜風。

It was Li Pai's turn to sigh, as he thought about Hsiangyang's river goddesses and its forever-drunk former magistrate, Shan Chien. They were all gone. So was the man Li Pai and I had come to see. Out the train window, the world looked ready for harvesting. It was autumn, again. Two and a half hours later, I got off with Li Pai in Anlu.

Several years ago, the city of Chiangyou sued the city of Anlu for advertising itself as Li Pai's hometown. Chiangyou was where Li Pai lived between the ages of five and twenty-five, which is normally when people form links to a place. However, once Li Pai left Chiangyou, he never returned. He sailed down the Yangtze and through the Gorges and wandered around the river's middle reaches for two years. Then in 728 – Li was twenty-seven – he married a woman from Anlu and lived there (or nearby) for the next ten years. Those, too, were important years in Li Pai's life. The authorities of Anlu naturally agreed, and to promote tourism they began touting their city as Li Pai's hometown. Thus began the legal wrangling. Eventually, China's State Administration for Industry and Commerce was asked to adjudicate the matter, and declared that Anlu's claim did not involve copyright infringement. It was free to call itself Li Pai's hometown, as was Chiangyou. This didn't settle the matter, though. Not long after the ruling, a town in Kyrgyzstan added its name to the list of Li Pai Hometowns, as it was Li Pai's birthplace, and so did a city in Kansu province, Li Pai's home until he turned five. Everyone wanted a piece of Li Pai. If Li Pai weren't already dead, he would have laughed himself to death. But Anlu's tourism promotion worked. How could I pass up another Li Pai hometown?

It was, however, going to be a quick visit. My plan to spend an entire day was significantly altered by a plea from my friend Andy Ferguson. Andy supported himself in part by leading groups of Western Buddhists to Zen sites in China, and he was scheduled to guide a twenty-person tour that began the next day in Kuangchou. After months of planning, life conspired against him, and he couldn't come to China. We had worked together before on similar tours, so he asked me to take his place and made me an offer I couldn't refuse. I reasoned my poet friends would still be there the next time I came to China. There was, however, one place near Anlu I thought I could squeeze in before Kuangchou, and getting an early start was essential.

I was standing outside the Anlu Guesthouse at 7:30 and flagged down the first taxi I saw. I asked the driver to take me to Paichaoshan. That was where Li Pai made his home during nine of the ten years he lived in the Anlu area. As we headed out of town, I asked the driver whether she had been to Shoushan, where Li Pai spent his first year. I wondered whether there were any traces of his brief stay. She said she had been to Shoushan, but she hadn't heard of anything connected with Li Pai. It was Paichaoshan or nothing, which made me feel better.

Road construction rendered the route a mystery. My driver changed direction five times before she hit the old highway. Shortly afterward, I saw the telltale brown-and-white road sign that indicated a site of historical or scenic importance ahead. The mountain was off to our left, and so was Li Pai. He was standing on top. He was completely white and shimmered in the early morning sun. He was over fifty meters high and bigger than any Mao statue I had seen. Anlu had gone all out — or at least its investors had. They clearly expected a big return. There *was* money in poetry after all — just not for poets.

The road we turned onto was another example of their expectations. It was wide enough for ten cars and led through what used to be the village of Pishan. *Pi-shan* means "jade mountain," and it was one of the mountain's two names, the other being Paichaoshan (white omen mountain). The original village was gone, and so were the villagers. In its place, a new T'ang-dynasty-style village was under construction. Anlu was not about to be outdone by Li Pai's other hometowns, even if it meant leveling the place where Li Pai had lived.

Considering that Li Pai's wife was the granddaughter of a former prime minister, one would have expected him to move to the capital after the wedding and begin knocking on the doors of the rich and powerful. Not long after Li Pai moved to Pishan, someone asked just that question: why would such a young, talented, and suddenly well-connected person choose to live on a mountain? Li Pai wrote one of his most famous poems in response, "Conversation in the Mountains" 山中問答:

> You ask why I settled on Jade Mountain
> I smile and don't answer my heart is at peace
> the peach blossoms in the stream disappear into the distance
> there's another world beyond the world of man

問余何意棲碧山, 笑而不答心自閑。桃花流水窅然去, 別有天地非人間。

Li Pai was referring to the story "Peach Blossom Spring," by T'ao Yuan-ming, about tracing peach petals upstream and discovering their source in a hidden valley where for centuries people had lived untouched by war or famine. The last line of Li Pai's poem was one of John Blofeld's favorites. John was a fellow translator and partly to blame for me writing this book. In fact,

I doubt whether I would have ever written any books if he hadn't taken me under his wing thirty years ago, hadn't encouraged me to translate not merely a selection of Cold Mountain's poems but all of them, and hadn't forced me to accept the notion that when you translate a poem you have to make a poem. I can still see the Chinese characters of the first part of Li Pai's last line on John's front gate in Bangkok: "There's another world" 別有天地.

After driving through the nonexistent-but-soon-to-be-ancient village of Pishan, we continued uphill on a long paved road to yet another mammoth parking lot. Ours was the only car there. Maybe I was early: it wasn't quite eight o'clock. I got out and read the sign at the ticket window. Hours were from six to six – a gesture to the early-morning exercise crowd, I presumed – and yet there was no one on the business side of the window. I walked around to the back of the building and knocked on a door. It opened, and the man inside said the place was still under construction. He waved for me to go ahead. There was no charge.

With entrance formalities out of the way, I walked back and told my driver I would return around ten. We hadn't discussed a fee, but I figured a hundred for the round-trip and another hundred for waiting would be about right – not that my calculations mattered. I had gotten used to accepting whatever fees drivers came up with, within reason. I then headed for the huge memorial hall beyond the gate.

Anlu already had a Li Pai Memorial Hall before the court battle over the hometown issue began. Judging from photos I had seen online, it looked like it was worth visiting. If nothing else, it enjoyed a lovely setting overlooking the Fuho River, which flowed past the city. But it was closed, and its contents were in storage until the new hall on Paichaoshan was finished. The new hall was, as the man in the ticket office said, still under construction. I poked my head inside anyway. It looked chandelier-fancy, but it was just a big, unfinished shell, and I had a mountain to see.

Li Pai had two residences at Paichaoshan. Shortly after moving there, his wife gave birth to a daughter, and he had a house built at the foot of the mountain in the village of Pishan to provide a more comfortable place for his family. He also built a hermitage for himself just below the western edge of the summit – I'm guessing he preferred sunsets to sunrises, which was understandable considering his fondness for spirits.

The reason he came here was to continue the Taoist studies and practices he had begun outside his earlier hometown. Over the centuries certain mountains in China were considered efficacious for spiritual cultivation, while others were simply . . . mountains. Hence, Li Pai wasn't alone, and he became friends with many of his fellow recluses. It's worth noting that just because such men and women chose to live in relative seclusion didn't mean they were ascetics. Take, for example, Li Pai's "Drinking with a Recluse in the Mountains" 山中與幽人對酌:

> The two of us drinking and wildflowers blooming
> one cup another cup and still one more
> I'm drunk and need to sleep and you're about to go
> tomorrow if you come again don't forget your zither

兩人對酌山花開, 一杯一杯復一杯。我醉欲眠卿且去, 明朝有意抱琴來。

Life in the mountains could be far more refined than life in town, if only because there were fewer distractions. You could take your time. Walking up the road, I was glad to see that the mountain hadn't been devastated by quarrying or logging. It would have been a fine place for a hut if it weren't about to become a major tourist site. As I continued uphill, the road disappeared around the mountain's north side. I kept to the trail that went more or less straight up the east side. After some accelerated hiking, I came to a shack that catered to the needs of visitors, and I had a need. I was thirsty. While I stopped to catch my breath, I had a cold Hochicheng "health drink." It was so good I had a second. The man who worked there said the mountain had opened for tourism two years ago, but construction was still going on, and the formal opening wasn't scheduled until November. I was two months early. When I asked where the road went, he said it ended on the west side of the mountain at a hotel that was also under construction. I was glad I stuck with the trail. As I prepared to leave, he told me to take it easy, to slow down. He said he saw me coming and thought I was walking too fast. I didn't try to explain and continued on at the same relentless pace as before.

The trail consisted of several thousand stone steps and brief stretches of cement, with donkey tracks in the cement parts, and it passed through stands of pines, cedars, and locusts. The locusts were especially memorable. They were in bloom and smelled like sweet Indian incense. Even though it was September, the cicadas were still singing.

The trail eventually led to a saddle, where there was another shack with more cold drinks for sale. I enjoyed another Hochicheng then switched to the trail that led along the mountain's north–south ridge. Even though the

Statue of Li Pai on Paichaoshan

air was fresh and pleasantly cool, I was sweating from the hike up and had to stop every few minutes to wring out the bandanna I kept tied around my forehead. I was glad I wasn't climbing the mountain in summer. Considering Li Pai's "Summer Day in the Mountains" 夏日山中, I think he felt the same:

> Too tired to wave my white feather fan
> hatless in the dark green woods
> I hung my cap on a granite cliff
> exposing my crown to a soft pine breeze

懶搖白羽扇，裸袒青林中。脫巾掛石壁，露頂灑松風。

To be without headgear of some kind in ancient China was looked down upon by members of the educated class – even in the mountains. The fact that Li Pai wrote this poem suggests the high standards expected of someone of his status. It also suggests his disdain for them.

Paichaoshan was primarily a Taoist mountain, and the ridge trail I took led past several Taoist temples. Among Li Pai's heroes was a man named Hung Yai, who cultivated the Tao in the mountains west of Chengtu not far from his other hometown. Hung Yai was famous for his ability to ride clouds. It was said he eventually rode them all the way to the Isle of Immortals, off the coast of Shantung. Li Pai came to Paichaoshan hoping to achieve similar results. One day he was reminded of his earlier aspiration and wrote "As the Sun Sets in the Mountains, Suddenly I Have a Longing" 日夕山中忽然有懷:

> Having slept in the mountains forever
> the clouds are the mountains' friends
> the deeper the mountains the better the clouds
> playing all day until sunset
> the moon rises from the peaks beyond my study
> a spring washes the rocks below the steps
> it's here that my mind becomes clear
> the truth doesn't come from somewhere else
> flying squirrels chatter in the cassia trees in fall
> the wind dies and everything is silent
> I keep thinking about Hung Yai's skill
> I would visit him if he weren't across the sea

what's taking my cloud carriage so long
leaning on my armrest I can only sigh

久臥青山雲，遂為青山客。山深雲更好，賞弄終日夕。
月街樓間峰，泉漱階下石。素心自此得，真趣非外惜。
鼯啼桂方秋，風滅籟歸寂。緬思洪崖術，欲往滄海隔。
雲車來何遲，撫几空嘆息。

A cloud carriage would have been welcome, indeed. As I labored up the trail, I came to Patriarch's Hall, which honored Chen Wu. He was the resident deity of the martial arts center of Wutangshan in the western part of the province. All the temples on Paichaoshan were its subtemples, places where Wutangshan sent its priests once they had trained there long enough. Although the priests at Patriarch's Hall were sent to look after the buildings and collect donations, they said it was a great place to practice when tourists weren't there—and, of course, that included me. Opposite the entrance was

a weather-beaten ginkgo. It must have been over a thousand years old but looked as if it would be lucky to see another spring. Then again, this was just the sort of tree the Taoist sage Chuang-tzu said lived the longest. Thinking about that made me feel better. I was beginning to feel like an old ginkgo.

As I continued along the ridge, I came to another shrine hall. This one honored Taoism's Three Purities that marked the progression of Taoist practice: the transformations of this earthly body into energy, then essence, and finally spirit. I talked briefly with a Taoist priest inside, lit some incense, and caught my breath. I had hoped to continue past the huge looming statue of Li Pai to his former residence near Peach Blossom Cliff, but I was out of time. I chose, instead, a trail back to the saddle via the shady western flank of the mountain. It was refreshingly cool and led past a number of inscriptions carved into the cliffs. It also led past Paiyun

Ancient ginkgo on Paichaoshan

Spring. The spring, I decided, was the perfect place to share some bourbon. The authorities had erected a wooden railing to keep people like me out of the spring. But since no one else was there, I eased myself over and poured in one cup, another cup, and still one more, thus conveying greetings to Li Pai and his fellow hermits from the ancients of Kentucky who discovered how to transform corn into spirits.

Once again, I didn't linger. I had to be in Kuangchou that evening, and Kuangchou was over a thousand kilometers away. I followed the trail back to the saddle then started down the same stone steps. It was a relief to be going down instead of up, and when I came to the cement sections, I skipped. I wondered whether Li Pai or his hermit friends ever skipped. It was definitely the best way to go downhill on a relatively flat surface. When I slowed down for the steps, I noticed things I hadn't noticed coming up, such as tiny green-and-white-striped fruits on thorn-covered vines that turned yellow as they matured — a member of the nightshade family, I guessed. In the hands of a Taoist adept, they probably served as an ingredient in an elixir. I also noticed black and turquoise butterflies still behaving as though it were summer. As I reached the final stretch of steps, the cicadas sounded tired and sang in spurts rather than in the steady drone I had heard earlier. Their year was just about over — as was my day, at least the Paichaoshan part. After nine years on the mountain, Li Pai, too, ended his stay. But before he did, he had this advice for another would-be recluse, "To Attendant Liu Wan, Sent from Peach Blossom Cliff on Anlu's Paichaoshan" 安陸白兆山桃花巖寄劉侍御綰:

I've lived in the clouds thirty years
I love the freedom and I love the immortals
their island home might be far off
but a shy crane heart can soar
since coming to Peach Blossom Cliff
I've slept below a cloud-filled window
been befriended by hermits on the neighboring ridge
and shared the springs with gibbons
I've even climbed the jade-green scarps
to the top of distant Lofushan
whose twin peaks guard the Eastern Ravine
and whose ridge spans the Western Heaven
the dense woods make escaping the sun easy
but the narrow cliffs make it hard to see the moon

wild plants constantly transform the landscape
hanging vines sway in the mists every spring
I built a stone hut to be apart
and cleared some steep land for the seclusion
my reason for living on this mountain
was to be free of worldly ties
now that you've left the court behind
don't go back for the next thousand years

雲臥三十年，好閒復愛仙。蓬壺雖冥絕，鷰鶴心悠然。
歸來桃花巖，得憩雲窗眠。對嶺人共語，飲潭猿相連。
時昇翠微上，邀若羅浮巔。兩岑抱東壑，一嶂橫西天。
樹雜日易隱，崖傾月難圓。芳草換野色，飛蘿搖春煙。
入遠構石室，選幽開上田。獨此林下意，杳無區中緣。
永辭霜臺客，千戴方來旋。

Li Pai's "thirty years" was an exaggeration. He was in his midthirties when he wrote this poem. "Twenty" would have been about right. In any case, the poem did a good job of describing the highlights of his mountain home, the mountain home I had to leave far too soon.

When I finally returned to the taxi, I told the driver to take me back to town, which she did, in a matter of minutes. She dropped me off at the bus station, and I gave her 200RMB without bothering to ask how much she wanted. She smiled and told me she was going to spend the rest of the day playing mahjong. I wished her luck.

I was just in time for the eleven o'clock bus to Wuhan, the capital of Hupei province. Before it left, though, there was a negotiation regarding the route. The driver turned around and yelled that if no one was getting off before Wuhan, and if those of us on board could come up with 100RMB for the road tolls, he'd take the expressway. It was the first time I had heard of passengers being given the choice, and I immediately offered to pay the entire amount. Unfortunately, several passengers weren't going as far as Wuhan, so I settled in for what turned out to be an incredibly slow, four-hour drive to go less than a hundred kilometers. What the hell. I still made the 3:30 bullet train and was in Kuangchou before eight. The rest of my pilgrimage would have to wait.

When I interrupted my journey it was Friday, September 14, 2012. By the time the stars realigned, it was Saturday, March 9, 2013. After a four-hour train ride from Beijing, I exited the same Wuhan station I'd entered

Boulder marking the former site of Yellow Crane Tower

six months earlier and took a taxi to the Crown Hotel. After checking in and dropping my bag in my room, I went outside and flagged down another taxi. I asked the driver to take me to Yellow Crane Tower. There were still a few hours left in the day, and I wasn't quite done with Li Pai.

Having missed Meng Hao-jan in Hsiangyang, Li Pai heard Meng was planning to travel down the Yangtze to Kuangling (or Yangchou) and sent a letter suggesting they meet in Wuhan, which they did in 730 – whereupon Li Pai wrote "At Yellow Crane Tower Seeing Meng Hao-jan Off to Kuangling" 黃鶴樓送孟浩然之廣陵:

At Yellow Crane Tower I said goodbye to a friend
in the flowered mists of March he left for Yangchou
as the outline of his sail merged with the sky
all I saw was the Yangtze flowing past the edge of Heaven

故人西辭黃鶴樓，煙花三月下揚州。孤帆遠影碧空盡，惟見長江天際流。

The driver let me out below the steps that led to the latest version of the tower. It was made of cement and steel, an impressive fifty-meter-high edifice. It was as high as the statue of Li Pai on Paichaoshan. The name came from a crane that landed here 2,000 years ago and carried a Taoist immortal to paradise. This, though, wasn't where Li Pai wrote his poem. The original tower was located just below the Yangtze Bridge, the first bridge built across the Yangtze. It was a kilometer away, and there was, I had heard, a boulder that marked the spot. After taking in the tower's latest incarnation, I walked back down to the road and followed the sidewalk to the bridge.

At the first archway a uniformed guard stood at attention, heroically trying not to succumb to the exhaust fumes of the cars and buses. Just past where he was standing, I took an elevator to the base of the bridge. The boulder was easy to spot. It was in the middle of the esplanade that bordered the river. It was all that remained of the original tower, where Li Pai and Meng Hao-jan said goodbye, and also where Li came twenty-eight years later after his release from prison. He'd been implicated in a revolt led by the emperor's brother. Although he was freed, his punishment wasn't over. The emperor banished him to the remote hill-tribe outpost of Yehlang, south of Changsha. When Li Pai stopped in Wuhan on his way, he heard someone playing the tune "Plum Blossoms Falling" and wrote "On Yellow Crane Tower Hearing a Flute" 黃鶴樓聞笛:

Going into exile on my way to Changsha
looking toward Ch'ang-an I don't see my home
from Yellow Crane Tower I hear a jade flute
plum blossoms fall in this city in summer

一為遷客去長沙，西望長安不見家。黃鶴樓中吹玉笛，江城五月落梅花。

When I first read this poem, I thought it curious that Li Pai would think of his home as being in Ch'ang-an, where he had stayed only briefly and from which he was banished. Did we have yet another contender for the title of Li Pai's Hometown? But thinking about it more, I realized Anlu was in the direction of Ch'ang-an. So maybe this was just further evidence in its favor. Earlier, while I was walking toward the place where this poem was written, I wondered whether someone might have planted a plum tree. It was an odd thought, but it was not misplaced. Someone had, and it was in bloom. I was always gratified when others thought about such things and acted on their thoughts. I inhaled the tree's perfume then walked over to the railing next to the river and poured a shot of whiskey onto the rocks below. The next time it rained, I mused, the river surely would carry my modest offering to where Li Pai drowned while trying to embrace the moon — or so people say. It was a happy thought, and it followed me back to the hotel, where I went to sleep knowing I would finally be turning a new page on my itinerary.

Su Tung-p'o (1037–1101) was next. Not only was he one of China's best-known poets, he was also one of its most admired essayists and calligraphers. But such admiration meant nothing at court. What had a greater bearing on the course of his life was his opposition to the economic reforms of Wang An-shih, which resulted in a series of exiles. The first of these was to the Yangtze river town of Huangchou. An early morning train ride from Wuhan transported me to Echou, across the river from Su's place of exile. Since I needed to make an early departure from the same station the next day, I decided to stay on the Echou side of the river and checked in at the Changcheng Garden Hotel.

DAY

18

It was just after ten in the morning. For once, I had an entire day and the briefest of agendas. While I was drinking coffee and reviewing material about Su's life, there was a knock on the door. It was a maid, and she had a basket of fruit: bananas, pears, grapes, and cherry tomatoes. I thought she had the wrong room. She said, "Welcome to Echou." The fruit was for me. After she placed it on the tea table and left, I just looked at it. I couldn't bring myself to disturb the arrangement.

I left it sitting there and walked out to the street. I waved down a taxi and asked the driver to take me to Huangchou, or Huangkang as it's called nowadays. Su first came here in 1080, and it was here, shortly after his arrival, that he started using the name Tung-p'o, meaning "east slope." Up until then, he was simply Su Shih. My first destination was the Su Tung-p'o Memorial Hall. After crossing the Yangtze, the driver dropped me off at a park that surrounded Huangkang's Yi-ai Lake. He told me to follow the stone walkway to the east side of the park. 300 meters later, I was there. The memorial hall was new and had that elegant Sung-dynasty look: the walls were white and the roofs black. The exhibits inside were new as well and a welcome change from the usual glass cases. Someone must have taken a course in museum management, one that emphasized dioramas and audiovisual displays.

As I walked into the main hall, I heard Teng Li-chun (1953–1995) singing "I Only Hope as Long as We Live" 但願人長久. It was her rendition of Su Tung-p'o's "Water Tune Song" 水調歌頭, a poem to his brother:

> How many moons do we have
> lifting my cup I ask the sky

in the palaces above I wonder
what year it is tonight
I considered riding the wind
but feared those towers of jade
too high and cold for me
and dancing in those icy shadows
no match for here on earth

As it rolls past painted gates
and silk-curtained windows below
and lights those not asleep
I shouldn't bear it ill will
but why is it always full when we part
we have our goodbyes and reunions
the moon too waxes and wanes
nothing has ever stayed whole
I only hope as long as we live
Ch'ang-o bridges the miles between us

明月幾時有，把酒問青天。不知天上宮闕，今夕是何年。
我欲乘風歸去，又恐瓊樓玉宇，高處不勝寒。
起舞弄清影，何似在人間。

轉朱閣，低綺戶，照無眠。不應有恨，何事長向別時圓。
人有悲歡離合，月有陰晴圓缺，此事古難全。
但願人長久，千里共嬋娟。

Ch'ang-o lived in a palace on the moon and dispensed pills that made mortals immortal. In Huangkang, Teng Li-chun had taken her place. Teng was from Taiwan, but she was just as popular on the Mainland in the 1980s, despite Beijing's refusal to allow her music to be sold openly – it was considered too bourgeois. Still, there was a saying in China in those days: "Teng Hsiao-p'ing rules the day, Teng Li-chun rules the night." A lot had changed in thirty years – and a lot hadn't changed.

Teng's voice faded as I made my way past a remarkably heroic statue of Su and through a series of galleries. The first consisted of photos of all the places around China where Su had lived. There were also photos of his and his brother's graves and a photo of one grave that surprised me. I had visited the grave before and even conducted a ceremony there on a friend's behalf. It was the grave of Su's wife, Wang Chao-yun (1062–1096). Su bought her out of indentured servitude when she was twelve, and she became his lifelong companion. She died in Huichou, not far from Hong Kong, during Su's final exile. Su said she died chanting the poem that ended the *Diamond Sutra*:

> All created things
> are like a dream an illusion a bubble
> a shadow a dewdrop or lightning
> view them all like this

一切有為法，如夢幻泡影。如露亦如電，應作如是觀。

Her devotion to the Dharma had a great effect on her husband. It was during his stay in Huangchou that Su took up meditation and the study of Buddhist sutras such as the *Diamond,* the *Vimalakirti,* even the *Lankavatara.*

The next gallery consisted of dioramas depicting scenes from Su's life in exile. My favorite was one of Su and his wife going over their budget trying to figure out how to get by on his meager salary. It was an activity I knew too well. There were also plasticized examples of the culinary skills he developed and the dishes named for him: Tungpo Fish, Tungpo Pork, Tungpo Tofu, Tungpo Chowder, even Tungpo Cookies. On a wall was a scroll, by the fourteenth-century calligrapher Hsien Yu-shu. It was a poem Su wrote about a tree near his house, and about the arrival of spring. It was titled "Crabapple" 海堂:

> The wafting east wind and rays of sublime light
> as the moon crossed the porch perfume filled the air
> worried the night was late and flowers about to sleep
> I held up a candle to see her red dress

東風裊裊泛崇光，香霧空濛月轉廊。隻恐夜深花睡去，故燒高燭照紅妝。

The only other person in the hall was a caretaker, who knitted the entire time. That was what caretakers did in the old days. Nowadays they sent text messages, but not in Huangkang. Suddenly a group of VIPs arrived, and a memorial hall official appeared out of nowhere to give them a guided tour.

It was a whirlwind tour and was over in minutes. Clearly lunch was next on their agenda. I lingered over the dioramas. They were done so well. There was also one of Su playing his zither and, on the wall behind him, his "Zither Poem" 琴詩:

> You say a zither's sound comes from its strings
> why then doesn't it play in its case
> or you say the sound comes from the fingers
> but why are your fingertips silent

若言弦上有琴聲，放在匣中何不鳴。若言聲在指頭上，何不於君指上聽。

Best of all was a model of the city during the Sung dynasty with all the sites inside and outside the walls marked where Su lived and wrote. The city had changed, but the old walls were, for the most part, intact. The final exhibit was an interactive display. I reached out and pulled on a pair of oars. Suddenly I was on the Yangtze rowing past Red Cliff. There was even a recording of oars dipping into the river. How could I resist? My next stop was the cliff.

I exited the hall and walked through the park. But before I reached the place where the taxi driver had dropped me off, I stopped. There was a huge stone edifice inscribed with Su's "Red Cliff Odes" and a relief of Su out on the river. In my singular focus to reach the memorial hall, I had overlooked it. After reacquainting myself with the odes, I read his "Cold Food Day Rain" 寒食雨 on an adjacent stone slab:

> Since I arrived in Huangchou
> I've spent three Cold Food days
> I've tried every year to hold on to spring
> but spring's departure can't be delayed
> this year the rain was heavy as well
> the past two months have seemed like fall
> from my bed I can smell crabapple flowers
> their red and white mud-spattered petals
> for taking things away surreptitiously

Left: Statue of Su Tung-p'o at his memorial hall in Huangkang

Relief of Su Tung-p'o composing his two "Red Cliff Odes"

> nothing outdoes the night
> like when a young man becomes ill
> and recovers to find his hair white

自我來黃州，已過三寒食。年年欲惜春，春去不容惜。
今年又苦雨，兩月秋蕭瑟。臥聞海堂花，泥污臙脂雪。
闇中偷負去，夜半真有力。何殊病少年，病起頭已白。

The celebration of Cold Food Day in early April goes back to a story about a king who insisted a hermit come down from his mountain and visit him at court. When the hermit refused, the king instructed his henchmen to force the hermit down by setting fire to the mountain. The hermit still refused and was burned to death. Afterwards, the king was so disconsolate he ordered a three-day ban on fires. The actual origin of Cold Food Day probably had more to do with the rite of purification celebrated on the third day of the third lunar month that preceded the annual visit to ancestors' graves. Cold Food Day was really about death and renewal, and in the last couplet we see Su confronting his own mortality. This was his Buddhist period.

After reading the poems inscribed in stone, I turned my attention to finding a ride to Red Cliff. Huangkang wasn't much of a taxi town. All I saw were buses and private cars. I could have taken a bus, but place-names on a bus-stop sign are always a mystery in a new town. So I waited. Finally after nearly half an hour, a cab pulled up to deliver three more visitors to the park. I told the driver where I wanted to go, and we were there in minutes.

I was expecting something different. The cliff was just outside the city's ancient West Wall, as it had always been, but it no longer overlooked the Yangtze. It was now behind a dike near the far end of a park. There was also a pond between the cliff and the dike. Apparently, the pond was designed to make the cliff feel better about being landlocked and twenty meters shorter, which was my estimate of the difference between the water levels of the pond and the river. Although Red Cliff had lost some of its height, it was still a cliff, and I walked over for a closer look.

This was where Su Tung-p'o rowed out into the Yangtze one night in 1082, with several friends and a jug of wine, and wrote two of his most famous poems. In the first, he lamented the impermanence of the ever-flowing river and the ever-changing moon, then laughed in praise of their inexhaustible presence. In the second, he fell asleep drunk only to wake and look in vain for the crane that flew above him in his dream and transformed itself into a Taoist immortal. Su was also a student of Taoism, especially its alchemical side.

When I reached a spot that faced the cliff, I set my three cups on a rock near the shore. This time I filled them with rye. It was another grain that didn't reach China until modern times. Representing this hardiest of cereals was 128-proof Thomas H. Handy. I felt confident Su would appreciate the transformative effect, not to mention the taste. While I was taking in the view, it started to rain. At first I thought it was the pond's minnows rising to the surface. But how could the pond have that many minnows? While I watched, a Su Tung-p'o poem titled "Fish" 魚 came to mind:

> I released some minnows at the lake
> newly hatched and unafraid
> once they learn about hooks
> I'll never see them again

湖上移魚子，出生不畏人。自從識鉤餌，欲見更無因。

Sipping my share of the rain and rye, I changed my mind about Red Cliff. At first I didn't like it being separated from the river, but the place grew on me. At the far end of the pond was a stand of last year's lotuses, desiccated and bent over, waiting to collapse into the mud and make way for new ones.

Red Cliff

Along the bank, willow catkins were just beginning to turn green. And in the distance, I heard firecrackers announcing another transition in life. I could envision more odes being written here. As I sprinkled the last of the rye into the pond and thanked Su for all the poems, a large fish did a belly flop. "You're welcome," I said.

I was glad I remembered to bring my umbrella. It took a while for another taxi to show up. When one finally did, I wondered why anyone would visit the park in the rain. Someone like me, I guess. Before the people getting out could change their minds, I got in and asked the driver to take me to the intersection of Shengli Street and Payi Road. The intersection marked the highest point in the old part of town. It took only a few minutes to get there, but in that brief amount of time, the rain thankfully stopped. I got out and started walking down Payi Road looking for an opening between the buildings on the west side of the street. Local historians had concluded the house Su called Hsuehtang (Snow Hall) and the farm he called Tungpo (East Slope) were in that area. I could see a number of large, ancient-looking trees rising behind the buildings, but I couldn't find a way to reach them — no alleys, no lanes, just one building after another. The size of these trees in the center of town – the city's largest department store was on the east side of the street – suggested they were being preserved for something other than firewood. When it started to rain again, I turned my attention to Su's other dwellings. I took out my umbrella and headed downhill along Chingchuan-hu Road.

The road was the current incarnation of the path Su walked every day between his field and his first home, which he called Linkaoting (Overlook Pavilion). From its doorway he could look out onto the Yangtze – thus the name. Coming home late one night, he wrote this poem to the tune of "Lin-chiang-hsien" and titled it, appropriately, "Returning to Linkao at Night" 夜歸臨皋:

> Drank tonight at East Slope sobered up then drank again
> it was after midnight when I finally made it home
> the houseboy was asleep and snoring like thunder
> I knocked on the gate but nobody answered
> leaning on my cane I listened to the river
>
> Long have I regretted this life I don't control
> will I ever stop running errands
> with night about to end and a light wind on the water
> I'm leaving in my sanpan
> to spend my last years on the river

夜飲東坡醒復醉，歸來仿佛三更。家童鼻息已雷鳴。
敲門都不應，倚杖聽江聲。

長恨此身非我有，何時忘却營營。夜闌風靜縠紋平。
小舟從此逝，江海寄餘生。

The last two lines gave rise to the rumor that Su had fled his place of exile. When the local magistrate heard the poem, he actually checked on Su's whereabouts. When the emperor heard the story, he laughed – but he didn't shorten Su's term of exile.

The path between Su's field and his Linkao home led past kilns, which was how the street got its name: Blue Tile Lake Road. That hadn't changed. The shops along Chingchuanhu Road still specialized in ceramic tile. Su's Linkao house was somewhere off to the river side of the road. Once again, I saw only storefronts and apartment buildings. Every time I stopped to ask someone, all I received were shrugs.

Another of Su's favorite haunts was Tinghui Temple. It was farther down the street and also on the river side. Su stayed there briefly when he first came to Huangchou while the Linkao house was being readied. Even after he moved uphill to his Snow Hall residence, he often went there to talk with the monks. This was, after all, the beginning of his study of Buddhism. Among the poems he wrote there was "Written While Staying at Huangchou's Tinghui Temple" 黃州定惠院寓居作 composed to the tune "Pu-suan-tzu" 卜算子:

A waning moon hung from a leafless paulownia
the dripping had stopped and people were finally still
I noticed a recluse who arrived here alone
resembling more or less a solitary swan
startled he looked around
annoyed no one paid him any heed
he wouldn't land where the branches were bare
but the sandbars were cold and lonely

缺月掛疏桐，漏斷人初靜。時見幽人獨往來，縹緲孤鴻影。
驚起却回頭，有恨無人省。揀盡寒枝不肯棲，寂寞沙洲冷。

The dripping is that of a water clock. And the paulownia is the only tree on which a phoenix will land. In this case, the tree was leafless and its branches exposed to hunters and predators, but spending the night on a sandbar wasn't much of an option. The tradition at most monasteries was that any visiting monk or nun could stay for up to three nights if there was room. Apparently the only room for this sorry recluse was the leafless branch of a paulownia. As I looked down the alley where local historians claimed the temple once stood, all I saw was a neon sign for the Tinghui Hotel. Paulownia Hotel would have also worked.

I continued down Chingchuanhu Road until it ended at what remained of Blue Tile Lake then followed another road west. It led to my final destination of the day, Ankuo Temple. I was surprised to see the temple still standing—an actual place where Su Tung-p'o spent time. There were two new shrine halls, and the temple's Ming-dynasty stone pagoda was still standing. But it was no longer a place of religious practice, except for funerals. It was now part of a park that offered rides. I tried to imagine monks sitting inside the spinning teacups. I had hoped to find a bathhouse to better imagine Su's "Bathing at Ankuo Temple" 安國寺浴:

> The older I get the lazier I become
> I don't think about a bath until I'm dirty
> but even receding hair that falls short of my ears
> still needs a monthly washing
> this hillside town burns so much charcoal
> the smoke obscures the sunlight
> the dirt doesn't stay on me long
> suddenly I'm free of restraints
> I sit in a robe beneath a pavilion
> and untie my hair behind the bamboo
> my troubles and worries vanish
> lying on a bed I feel fine
> but how can I forget when washing my body
> to wash my reputation too
> returning home in silence I don't say much
> this is a matter that requires more thought

老來百事懶，身垢猶念浴。衰髮不到耳，尚煩月一沐。
山城足薪炭，煙霧蒙湯谷。塵垢能幾何，儵然脫羈梏。
披衣坐小閣，散髮臨修竹。心困萬緣空，身安一床足。
豈惟忘淨穢，兼以洗榮辱。默歸毋多談，此理觀要熟。

Until quite recently all Chinese cities had bathhouses where you could wash and also enjoy a massage and a nap. Thinking about the bathing and the napping drove me back out to the street, where I got lucky. I caught a taxi going my way, back to Echou. Ten minutes later, I was in my room. It wasn't two o'clock, and I was done for the day. My room didn't have a bathtub, so I had to content myself with a shower. Still, a shower followed by a nap was a rare gift on the pilgrim trail. I accepted it with gratitude. Afterward, I ate all the fruit the maid brought that morning, including the cherry tomatoes.

DAY

19

I was glad the second part of my journey began with an easy day. The next day, namely this one, was going to be a long one, which necessitated an early start. I had arranged for a taxi to pick me up at the hotel at 5:45, for a train that left at 6:25. The taxi was on time, which was a good beginning.

The new Echou station to which the driver delivered me far too quickly wasn't quite finished. I felt like I was walking into a blimp hanger. It was vast, empty, and cold. The temperature had dropped during the night into the low 40s. I joined a dozen other early morning travelers rubbing their hands and moving their feet to stay warm. Thankfully, the train was only twenty minutes late. Before I knew it, I was back where I had begun the previous day, at Wuhan's old Wuchang Station. It was 7:45, and I needed to catch an 8:45 train leaving from Wuhan's new bullet train station, fifteen kilometers away on the other side of rush-hour traffic. When it was my turn in the taxi queue, I conveyed to the driver the need for speed. He assured me he would get there with time to spare. I braced myself. But the driver knew every alley and lane in the city and wove in and out of a dozen of them. I arrived fifteen minutes early and expressed my gratitude with a picture of Lhasa's Potala Palace on the back of a 50RMB note.

By nine o'clock, Wuhan was a memory. Flashing by outside were bamboo-covered hills and flooded rice fields interspersed with fruit trees and rapeseed in bloom. Spring was thinking about summer. Such sights, though, didn't last long. We were going 300 kilometers per hour. The train didn't bother going around hills — it went through them. Forty minutes later I disembarked in Yuehyang along with five other passengers. Everyone else was bound for the provincial capitals of Changsha and Kuangchou. Had it been a thousand years ago, they would have been on their way into exile. Now, I'm guessing, they were on their way to get rich.

As I exited the station, I turned my attention to local transportation. It was going to be the key to the next two days of cross-country galivanting. There were three taxis to choose from, and I chose the newest one. The driver said it was only a month old. I felt like I had been upgraded. While we headed into town, I told the driver I wanted to hire him (and his vehicle) for two days. I outlined my itinerary, and he made a phone call to ask the company that owned the taxi. A few minutes later, he got a callback and quoted a price of 2,400RMB. It sounded fair, and I agreed. However, he had a prior commitment for the next day and said he would have to find another driver for me while I was doing whatever it was I was going to do in Yuehyang.

What I was going to do was visit Yuehyang Tower, which was no surprise. It was the city's most famous sight. Thirty minutes later, we were there. The tower was on the east shore of Tungting Lake and enclosed by a park. The driver told me he would be waiting there when I was done and would arrange for another driver in the meantime.

From the entrance, it was a five-minute walk to the tower. The building had been rebuilt in the 1980s with a series of roofs that looked as if they were about to lift the structure off the ground. I walked up the stairs to the second-floor balcony and took in the view. The tower overlooked the northern section of the lake, where its waters merged with those of the Yangtze another kilometer to the north. I had visited the lake on several occasions, and it looked different each time. Over the millennia, it served the purpose of flood control in the Yangtze's middle reaches and varied in size from 3,000 square kilometers in winter to 20,000 in summer, when it swelled to become China's second largest freshwater lake. In winter the water level dropped below three meters. People could ride bicycles to some of the islands. This was mid-March, and spring rains had raised the water level. Barges carrying sand and gravel were chugging past on their way to the Yangtze, and in the distance I could see a tour boat bound for Chunshan Island, home of one of China's most famous green teas and the graves of two sisters who were the lake's resident spirits. Their suicide by drowning 4,500 years ago gave the lake an allure many have found hard to resist.

The view from the balcony was why the tower existed. Eighteen hundred years ago it was built as an observation platform for naval maneuvers. It had been rebuilt many times since then — each time in a different form. Its current manifestation was meant to look as it did during the T'ang. I imagined myself standing next to Tu Fu, who stood there in 768, only two years before he died, and wrote "Climbing Yuehyang Tower" 登岳陽樓:

> I heard long ago about Tungting Lake
> here I am climbing Yuehyang Tower
> where Wu and Ch'u divide south from east
> where yin and yang drift day and night
> of family and friends I have no news
> old and sick all I have is a boat

warhorses block the passes to the north
leaning against the railing I can't stop sobbing

昔聞洞庭水，今上岳陽樓。吳楚東南拆，乾坤日夜浮。
親朋無一字，老病有孤舟。戎馬關山北，凭軒涕泗流。

The ancient kingdom of Wu controlled the lower reaches of the Yangtze to the east, while the kingdom of Ch'u controlled the river's middle reaches, including the watersheds of the Yuan and Hsiang to the south, which provided the lake with most of its water. Unable to return to his home in the north, Tu Fu left Yuehyang and sailed up the Hsiang at the invitation of a friend. However, a mutiny among government forces in Changsha, and his deteriorating health, compelled him to return to the lake, whereupon he sailed up the Milo River to seek help from another friend.

Having seen what I came to see, I headed for the Milo. At the park entrance, my driver was waiting. He introduced me to his replacement and to a new twist on hiring a car and driver. We all had to drive back to the company's headquarters to fill out a form, and I had to pay half the agreed-upon fare. Then we had to drive to police headquarters to register my passport in order to take the car out of their jurisdiction. It took some time, but compared to the bureaucratic hassles of the past, it was pleasantly routine. It was just past noon when the second driver and I finally headed south on Highway 201.

As we approached the 31km marker, we turned west on a paved road that skirted the north side of the Milo River floodplain. I had been there before and always enjoyed the drive. The Milo wandered around quite a bit before it reached Tungting Lake, and its floodplain was dotted with sheep and cattle. They did such a good job grazing that the grass looked like it had been mowed. After a few kilometers we left the floodplain and drove through a series of fir-covered hills that were just as pleasant. Finally, about six kilometers after leaving the highway, we came down to the river at Chutzu Village. Just before the road ended at the local ferry, we turned onto a side road that led upstream to a forested hill and the shrine built in honor of Ch'u Yuan, who heard the call of those two sisters who drowned in the nearby lake into which the Milo flowed. When we reached the shrine I saw that the doors were closed. I was puzzled. Then I realized it was Monday. That had never mattered in the past. Now apparently it did. The caretakers were taking the day off, as were their colleagues at museums and memorial halls around the world. After checking the side doors and pounding on them for good measure, I walked back down the road to a pavilion that looked out on the section of the river where Ch'u Yuan committed suicide.

After leaving his hometown in the Gorges, Ch'u Yuan lived in the Ch'u capital of Ying, not far downstream from Yichang. Eventually, he rose to become a senior adviser to the king, but he was too forthright for his own good. He suffered from the poet's curse. When he tried to warn the king about the intentions of the neighboring kingdom of Ch'in, he was slandered by jealous rivals and banished to the watery confines of Tungting Lake. One day a fisherman met him wandering south of the Milo where the Hsiang joined the lake. The account of their meeting has been handed down ever since in a poem attributed ironically to Ch'u Yuan, "The Fisherman" 漁夫:

When Ch'u Yuan was banished
he wandered along rivers
he sang on their banks
weak and forlorn
until a fisherman asked
aren't you the Lord of the Gorges
what fate has brought you to this
Ch'u Yuan answered
the world is muddy
I alone am clean
everyone is drunk
I alone am sober
and so they sent me away
the fisherman said
a sage isn't bothered by others
he can change with the times
if the world is muddy
splash in the mire
if everyone is drunk
drink up the dregs
why get banished
for deep thought and purpose
Ch'u Yuan said he had heard
when you wash your hair
you should dust off your hat
when you take a bath

you should shake out your robe
why should I let something so pure
be ruined and wronged by others
I would rather jump into the Hsiang
and be buried in a fish's gut
than let something so white
be stained by common dirt
the fisherman smiled
and rowed away singing
"When the river is clear
I wash my hat
when the river is muddy
I wash my feet"
and once gone he was heard from no more

屈原既放，遊於江潭，行吟澤畔，顏色憔悴形容枯槁。
漁父見而問之曰，子非三閭大夫與，何故至於斯。
屈原曰，舉世皆濁，我獨清，眾人皆醉，我獨醒，是以見放。
漁夫曰，聖人不凝滯於物，而能與世推移。世人皆濁，
　何不淈其泥而揚其波。眾人皆醉，何不餔其糟而歠其醨。何故深思高舉，
　自令放。
屈原曰，吾聞之，新沐者，必彈冠，新浴者，必振衣。
安能以身之察察，受物之汶汶者乎。寧赴湘流，葬於江魚之腹中。
安能以皓皓之白，而蒙世俗之塵埃乎。漁夫莞爾而笑，鼓枻而去乃歌曰，
滄浪之水清兮，可以濯吾纓。
滄浪之水濁兮，可以濯吾足。遂去不復與言。

Washing one's hat was a metaphor for preparing to serve at court when times were good, while washing one's feet was a metaphor for retiring to the countryside when times were bad. Such was the dialectic of the Confucian career. Ch'u Yuan ignored the fisherman and took his own advice. He jumped into the Milo and drowned. Ever since then, the Chinese have honored his memory by racing dragon-shaped boats to reach his body before the river dragons do. In English this is known as Dragon Boat Festival. In Chinese, it's Tuanwuchieh, the Festival of the Midday Sun, celebrated on the fifth day of the fifth month, within a week of the summer solstice. It's one of China's oldest festivals and has been associated with Ch'u Yuan for over 2,000 years. Nowadays it's also celebrated as Poets Day.

After returning to the taxi, I asked the driver to take me to the ferry. I wanted to share some rye with Ch'u Yuan. He was China's first great poet. His use of language was breathtaking. His poems sang. Reading them made me want to dance, although not in public, and I wanted to thank him for putting his heart into words. Standing on the shore just downstream from where he drowned, I read his last poem. It was later appended to the end of "Huai-sha" 懷沙 (Embracing the Sand), one of nine poems in his "Chiuchang" 九章 (Nine Declarations) series:

The Yuan and the Hsiang are in flood
their separate currents surge
dark is the road and long
uncertain and endless the path
clinging to what I love and cherish
I find myself with no peer
the true judge of horses is gone
how shall a great steed be known
the life of every person
each has its proper place
with resolute heart and high purpose
what then should I fear
and yet the pain and grief I suffer
give rise to constant sighs
in this corrupt world where no one understands me
I can't speak of my heart to others
since death can't be avoided
let me be free of attachments
you virtuous ones of the past
it's you whom I now follow

浩浩沅湘，分流汩兮，修路幽蔽，道遠忽兮。
懷質抱清，獨無匹兮。伯樂既沒，驥焉程兮。
萬民之生，各有所錯兮。定心廣志，余何所畏懼兮。
曾傷爰哀，永歎喟兮。世溷濁莫吾知，人心不可謂兮。
知死不可讓，願勿愛兮。明告君子，吾將以為類兮。

Once I had stunned a few fish with my offering, we headed uphill back the way we came. In the middle of the village, under an awning, a man

Ch'u Yuan's Grave Number Six

was making a dragon boat. I decided to take a closer look. The man said he was making boats for the annual races, which were still three months away. He had already finished half a dozen and had orders for a dozen more. Everyone, he said, wanted a dragon boat from the village where dragon-boat racing began. He made his boats from the fir trees that grew on the hillsides we'd passed earlier. We passed them again.

When we reached the highway, we turned north, backtracking to the 30km marker. There was a sign announcing that Pute Temple was only eight kilometers away, with an arrow pointing east. We followed the arrow. The road kept forking, and there were no more arrows, but everyone we stopped to ask knew the way. The temple was an old Taoist shrine, but when we pulled up, it wasn't old anymore. It had been completely rebuilt and with shrine halls for different deities — something for everyone. It was far too ostentatious for such an impoverished area, but I wasn't there to see the temple anyway and followed a path next to the main shrine hall that led to one of Ch'u Yuan's graves.

Between the ferry at Chutzu Village and Pute Temple, he had twelve graves. The first time I visited the shrine above the ferry, the curator told me that no one knew which was the real one, and that was the idea. The proliferation of graves was intended to confound grave robbers. He said archaeologists had dug into some of them, and their contents dated back to Ch'u Yuan's time. Years earlier, I'd visited Number Twelve by the railroad tracks. This time I limited myself to Number Four near Pute Temple then Five and Six near Hsiwang Elementary School, a kilometer west of the temple. While I was walking around Six my foot caught on a vine, and I fell flat on my face. That was the sign I was waiting for. I got out my flask and offered Ch'u Yuan another shot of rye.

Three Ch'u Yuan graves, I decided, were enough for the day. I still had another poet's tomb to visit. We retraced our way to Highway 201 then headed south once more. Eight kilometers later, we turned east on Highway 308 and followed Tu Fu up the Milo. After being forced by illness and a local rebellion back to Tungting Lake, he sailed up the Milo toward Pingchiang where another friend had offered him shelter. Tu Fu was fifty-eight, and "Escaping Trouble" 逃難 is one of his last poems:

A white-haired old man in my fifties
I've fled north and south away from trouble
this feeble body wrapped in thin clothing
always on the move and never warm
beset by illness and failing health
the world all mud and ashes
for ten thousand miles on Earth or in Heaven
I haven't found a place I belong
my wife and children are still with me
whenever I see them I sigh
my hometown is a wasteland of weeds
all my neighbors have scattered
I don't see a road leading back
I've cried out my eyes on the Hsiang

五十頭白翁，　南北逃世難。　疏布纏枯骨，　奔走苦不暖。
已衰病方入，　四海一塗炭。　乾坤萬里內，　莫見容身畔。
妻孥複隨我，　回首共悲歎。　故國莽丘墟，　鄰里各分散。
歸路從此迷，　涕盡湘江岸。

As we drove along, I saw men in barges dredging sand from the river and others along the banks who appeared to be panning for gold. When I asked my driver what they were doing, he confirmed the gold theory, adding that the authorities had ordered them to stop. There they were, though, looking for something that glittered. Up ahead was a turnoff to Pingchiang, where Tu Fu's friend served as magistrate, but we kept going. A few kilometers later, we turned south onto a narrow paved road that led into the countryside. A sign on the highway said Tu Fu's grave was four kilometers away. He never reached Pingchiang. His son and the friend whose help he sought buried Tu Fu at a place called Hsiaotien (Little Field). When I first heard the name, I thought it was Little Heaven, as the Chinese words for "field" and "heaven" are homophones. I preferred Little Heaven.

I had hoped to reach Little Heaven earlier in the day. The sun was already low in the sky and children were walking home along the road. They were coming from the elementary school, and I wondered whether the grave and

the shrine that enclosed it would be open. A few minutes later, we pulled off the road into the meadow that served as the shrine's parking lot. Walking toward the building, I had a sinking feeling. The door was closed. I gave it a push and could feel it was barred from inside. I thought maybe it was closed because of Monday – Museum Monday. But that wasn't why. When I looked at the sign next to the door, it said it was open every day from eight until four. It was ten after four. Out of habit, I banged on the door anyway. As I was about to bang again, the door opened.

Things had changed since my first visit. I was with my friends Finn Wilcox and Steve Johnson, and we arrived in a carryall pulled by a tractor— there was no paved road then. The shrine had been turned into an elementary school. As we pulled up outside the entrance, the principal came out to see what a tractor was doing there. We waved, and he waved back. When we explained the purpose of our visit, he led us in. There was a portrait of Tu Fu off to one side, but over the entryway in the place of honor were portraits of Marx, Lenin, Mao, and Stalin. The portrait of Stalin was especially noteworthy, as it was 1991. Mao had denounced the Russian version of Communism thirty years earlier. Apparently, word traveled slowly in the Hunan countryside.

On that first trip, we followed the principal along several corridors and past the third- and fourth-grade classrooms. Finally, he unlocked a gate that led to a weed-filled, walled-in enclosure. At the back was Tu Fu's grass-covered grave mound surrounded by a stone wall. In front was a tablet with his name on it. Among the weeds, we spotted a marijuana plant in flower but made no attempt to harvest its buds. While we were standing there, the whole school gathered to watch us. Our presence was too disruptive to maintain order in the classrooms. We paid our respects as best we could, then thanked the principal and returned to our tractor. As we pulled away, half the school chased us. Several children even managed to grab hold of the railing of the carryall and climb inside. As we passed their houses, one by one they jumped off then stood waving until we were out of sight. They were going home for lunch.

The portraits of the heroes of the revolution were now gone. So were the students. It was Tu Fu's shrine again. A new elementary school had been built next door. Although the caretaker said the place was closed, I pleaded with her that I had come a long way and would only need a few minutes.

Tu Fu's grave at Little Heaven

I just wanted to pay my respects. She relented and let me in, and I passed through the same corridors as before and came out in front of Tu Fu's grave again. I poured my three-cup offering and waited for the whiskey's fragrance to spread across Little Heaven. While I was waiting, I read "A Guest Arrives" 客至, which Tu Fu wrote in Chengtu when he lived in his thatch hut between two bends of Huanhua Creek – one of the few happy periods of his life:

On the river in spring north and south of my house
it's only the seagulls that come every day
I've never swept the flower-lined path for a guest
but for you I've left the gate open
with no foodstalls nearby our fare here is simple
the wineshops are depressing and only sell dregs
if you don't mind drinking with my neighbor
I'll call across the fence and we can finish what's left

舍南舍北皆春水，但見群鷗日日來。花徑不曾緣客掃，蓬門今始為君開。
盤飧市遠無兼味，樽酒家貧隻舊醅。肯與鄰翁相對飲，隔籬呼取盡餘杯。

I sat for half an hour on the bench next to his grave. Good neighbors have always been hard to come by, and a neighbor with whiskey to share even harder. I'm certain Tu Fu would have written more poems if he had had something better to drink – not that he didn't write enough. Finally, the caretaker found me and said she had to go home and fix dinner. I thanked her for letting me spend some time with Tu Fu and sprinkled what remained of the rye on his grave. When I got back to the taxi, I showed the driver the map of where I wanted to spend the night. It was over a hundred kilometers to the south, and we didn't get there until after seven. It had been, as I knew it would be, a long day, but I had no complaints.

I began the day in the town of Shangli. I was surprised to find a good hotel in such a modest-sized town. I drove through once on my way back from the Zen monastery where Linchi (Rinzai) Zen began. Back then I didn't see a single building above two stories. Thirteen years later, I was having breakfast in the splendor of the Shangli International. My driver was impressed, too, and went back for thirds. He was in his early twenties and was a decent driver. He indulged all my directions and misdirections, which is all I ask of any driver. I felt bad pulling him away from the buffet, but we really had to get going.

The hotel was on Highway 319, the highway we followed into town the night before. Another kilometer or so down the same road, we turned onto Highway 312. Seventy-five minutes of rolling hills later, we arrived in Tanpuchen. I had originally hoped to spend the night here, but I was pleased we didn't make it this far. It was more of an overgrown village than a town and certainly didn't have any hotels the likes of the Shangli International. As we drove through, I asked the driver to stop. I got out and asked two shopkeepers directions to the next poet I hoped to visit. Since their directions agreed, that was all the assurance I needed.

As we exited Tanpuchen, we looked for a side road on the left. Both shopkeepers had said to turn there. But neither of us saw anything that looked like a road — just houses and village stores, and the dirt lanes between them — so we kept going. After about two kilometers, I concluded we had gone too far. We backtracked and asked a group of women waiting for a bus. They pointed to a lane between two houses we'd passed earlier. It looked like a dirt driveway to the back of someone's property, but it turned out there was pavement under the dirt, and it continued past the houses.

We followed it for 200 meters until the road forked. We chose left, but after a kilometer it was clear we had chosen wrong. We returned to the fork and took the road on the right. After 300 meters, I saw what I was looking for: a building that didn't belong. Its exterior was tiled, and there were pillars supporting the eaves. It announced itself as the Hsieh Ling-yun Memorial Hall.

Hsieh Ling-yun (385–433) was one of the two most celebrated poets of the fifth century, the other being T'ao Yuan-ming. Literary critics considered him a founder of the Mountains and Rivers school, which isn't far from the truth. He opened up new territory in the poetic landscape. Of course, Chinese poets had written about the world beyond city walls long before Hsieh, but they wrote about it at arm's length or simply imagined it. Hsieh didn't *imagine* mountains and rivers, nor did he observe them from afar. He spent more time *in* them than out of them. He is even credited with inventing a kind of hiking shoe with removable cleats that could be adjusted depending on whether one was going uphill or downhill. For Hsieh, the world outside city walls held the promise of freedom – freedom from a society in which he felt constrained, and freedom to cultivate a life of the spirit.

Although Hsieh belonged to one of the wealthiest families of his day, he had little interest in fame or fortune. Thanks to the wisdom of an uncle, Hsieh grew up in a Buddhist monastery, where he even learned enough Sanskrit to assist in translation projects. He also made friends with Taoist priests and hermits. As he came of age, he felt he had more in common with them than he did with fellow members of the ruling elite. Among the poems he wrote at his home in the mountains is "While Irrigating Newly Planted Trees in the Orchard South of the Fields" 田南樹園激流植援:

> Hermits share mountains with woodsmen
> but go there for a different reason
> and differ in more than that
> they heal themselves in their terraced gardens
> gardens that ward off confusion
> with a purity and openness to distant winds
> I chose a hill leaning north for my hut
> a river to the south for my view
> water from a brook instead of a well
> for a windbreak I planted hibiscus
> my doorway is hidden behind trees
> the windows look out on mountains
> I zigzag my way down to the fields
> and gaze in the distance at towering peaks
> reducing desires means less work
> something in which few succeed
> I made a path for fellow recluses
> I keep hoping friends will visit
> pleasures I know are hard to ignore
> but I wish I could share these wonders

> 樵隱俱在山，由來事不同。不同非一事，養痾丘園中。
> 中園屏氛染，清曠招遠風。卜室倚北阜，啓扉面南江。

激澗代汲井，插槿當列墉。群木既羅戶，眾山亦當窗。
靡迤趨下田，迢遞瞰高峰。寡欲不期勞，即事罕人功。
唯開蔣生徑，永懷求羊蹤。賞心不可忘，妙善冀能同。

There is a downside to freedom. It is often accompanied by loneliness. Hsieh felt himself drawn back to the society he tried to escape. As much as he loved his life in the mountains, he was too rich and too well connected for his own good. Being the scion of the two most prominent families of his day, the Hsiehs and the Wangs, he was expected to serve at court in Nanking. And he did. His fondness for mountains, though, engendered a noticeable aloofness. Also, he had a strong sense of loyalty and continued to speak highly of members of the ruling family of the Eastern Chin (317–419), even after that dynasty had been replaced by the Liu Sung (420–478). Naturally, he suffered the consequences – a series of banishments, and eventually execution.

His first rustication was to the coastal town of Yungchia. It was basically a slap on the wrist and gave him the opportunity to spend more time in the mountains. But he missed his old home. After less than a year, he resigned, feigning illness, and retired to the family estate east of Hangchou and south of Shangyu. The estate was huge, occupying most of two counties, and it included some spectacular scenery. This was where he wrote his book-length "Ode to Mountain Life" 山居賦.

Even in seclusion Hsieh got into trouble. He had already annoyed the wrong people at court, and when the local governor accused him of usurping public lands, he was banished again. This time he was sent much farther away, to Linchuan in Kiangsi province. Fortunately, there were lots of mountains in Kiangsi, and not long after he arrived, he visited the peaks named for the Taoist immortal Hua-tzu Ch'i. In addition to the Dharma, Hsieh cultivated Taoist yoga and alchemy, and he admired those who had taken to the mountains in the past to transform their mortal bodies into immortal ones. But while he admired their quest, he was not smitten by it, as he makes clear in "Going Up Huatzu Ridge via the Third Valley of Ma Creek" 入華子岡是麻源第三谷:

> Truly the Southland is ruled by heat
> sweet olive illuminates the mountains in winter
> copper ridges shimmer in emerald streams
> rock ledges are washed by vermilion springs
> for worthies in search of seclusion

or those who would build a retreat
the trails are dangerous beyond measure
impossible paths that transit the sky
as I climbed the highest peak
I felt like a soaring cloud
but I found no sign of immortals
the Cinnabar Hills were an empty trap
of diagrams and texts there were none
no inscriptions passed down in stone
no trace of a hundred generations
of a thousand years nothing remained
and yet I was bent on transcendence
on bathing in the moonlight and splashing in the streams
it provided a brief indulgence
but not like it did for the ancients

南州實炎德， 桂樹凌寒山。 銅陵映碧澗， 石磴瀉紅泉。
既枉隱淪客， 亦棲肥遁賢。 險徑無測度， 天路非術阡。
遂登群峰首， 邈若升雲煙。 羽人絕仿佛， 丹丘徒空筌。
圖牒複磨滅， 碑版誰聞傳。 莫辨百世後， 安知千戴前。
且伸獨往意， 乘月弄潺湲。 恆充俄頃用， 豈為古今然。

Although Hsieh admired those who went into the mountains in search of spiritual transformation, he was realistic in assessing their attainments. Still, he never failed to enjoy a good hike, and he opened up trails that others have followed, in both mountains and poetry. Sixteen hundred years later, the citizens of Tanpu Township still remember him, and I was here to see in what fashion.

The memorial hall was new, but it was locked and deserted. There was a farmhouse about fifty meters away, so I walked over to see whether anyone was home. As I approached the farmhouse door, a woman came out holding a set of keys. She said she was in charge of the hall. I followed her to the hall's side door, where she proceeded to try the different keys on her key ring. There must have been over thirty, and that was about how many it took for her to find the right one. Finally, one clicked, and she pushed the door open.

The building turned out to be a single, very large hall with a roofless atrium in the middle to let in sunlight. The atrium also let in rain, hence the cement floor below it was a foot lower than the floor along the sides. When it rained, the water made a pond until gutters drained it outside. On either side of the hall, the walls were lined with newspaper accounts of Hsieh's life and of other places in China that honored him in one way or another. I was surprised to read that there was a memorial hall all the way down the coast in Wenchou, not far from the scene of his first rustication in Yungchia. As I approached the rear, it became clear that this wasn't really a memorial hall. It was a clan hall, a place for members of the Hsieh clan to hold funerals and memorial services. There was an altar, and it was lined with rows of tablets of deceased members. I'm guessing the Hsieh clan thought using a revered ancestor's name to raise funds was better than just calling it a clan hall.

As for the hall's existence here in the first place, it turned out that the county of which Tanpu was part had been given to Hsieh's grandfather, Hsieh Hsuan, as a fief in thanks for his service to the country. Hsieh's grandfather was instrumental in defending the Eastern Chin dynasty from invading forces from the north. When he died, the fief was passed to his grandson. And when Hsieh Ling-yun died, the local people asked for his body. The burial site was my next destination.

I thanked the caretaker and decided to save my whiskey for the grave, assuming I found it. We returned to the highway and continued east, toward Wantsai. As before, the road was good and the countryside pleasant. The water in the stream beside the road was even clear. The sight of clear water, other than in mountains, was becoming increasingly rare in China. Thirty minutes later, we arrived in Wantsai. I felt as if we arrived a few years too soon, or a few years too late. The town was an urban disaster. If there was a plan, it wasn't evident. I could only imagine what people from the countryside thought when they came to look for work or to shop for a refrigerator or a television. Maybe I was wrong. Maybe they admired the chaos as a welcome change from the humdrum. I tried to stay focused on my search for Highway 323 out of town. We finally found it across from the bus station and followed it north.

Hsieh Ling-yun's grave, according to everything I had read, was two kilometers north of town, near the village of Lichuan. It sounded easy. But whoever measured the distance needed to check their odometer. We drove four kilometers before we saw a turnoff for Lichuan. As we drove through the village we stopped every few hundred meters to ask people walking along the road and the owners of the few village shops about Hsieh's grave. Shrugs all around. Finally, I tried the elementary school, thinking surely one of the teachers would know, and one of them did. He directed us back the way we had come. It was another kilometer or so farther along the highway then

New grave of Hsieh Ling-yun outside Wantsai—the old one is behind this.

down a side road on the right. He said the side road was opposite a cement factory. Sure enough, just past the cement factory, there was a narrow dirt lane between two country stores. Over the lane was a metal archway with the words Fir Tree Pavilion and New Immigrant Village of Lichuan. I learned later that the villagers, 7,000 of them, were moved here from Chekiang province over fifty years ago when a dam turned the Hsinan River into Thousand Island Lake.

I was puzzled by the sign, though, as it didn't say anything about Hsieh Ling-yun. Also, the road was deeply rutted. Five hundred meters later, it thankfully ended at a cluster of farmhouses. I got out and approached a woman sitting on a stool outside her doorway, weaving a basket. I asked her where I could find Hsieh Ling-yun's grave. She pointed past a stand of bamboo and across a sea of rice stubble and told me to follow the cement path that crossed the fields until I came to a set of steps. The grave was at the top of the steps. Unfortunately, there was more than one set of steps, and I followed the wrong ones. I wandered around for a while then came back down and asked a farmer turning the soil. His field was less than a hundred meters from the right set of steps, and thanks to his help I found the grave.

It looked as though the same funds that paid for the new memorial hall also paid for a new grave. There were still traces of bunting and plastic flowers from the previous year's grave-sweeping ceremony. I walked behind the new facade and found a Ch'ing-dynasty tombstone in front of the actual grave mound. Although it was barely legible, it confirmed that this was where Hsieh's body was brought following his execution. A year after Hsieh was exiled to Linchuan, his enemies at court had him arrested. When he resisted, they had him banished even farther from the capital. He was sent to Kuangchou, where less than a year later he was executed for sedition. In his last poem, "Facing the End" 臨終, as recorded in the *Kuang-hung-ming-chi,* he compared himself to four others in the past who had also supported the ruling family of a dynasty that had been replaced:

> Nothing remains of Kung Sheng
> Li Yeh was put to death
> Lord Hsi's noble ways were suppressed
> Master Huo's life span was cut short
> an evergreen looks stately after a frost
> a mushroom trembles in a gale
> the unexpected can't be avoided
> whether sooner or later isn't worth a sigh
> I regret my gentleman's resolve
> didn't grant me an end in the cliffs
> having borne this pain long enough
> I take refuge before the Buddha
> I only hope next life
> friends and foes will know me better

龔勝無遺生，　李業有窮盡。　嵇叟理既迫，　霍子命已殞。
萋萋後霜柏，　納納衝風菌。　邂逅竟無時，　修短非所愍。
恨我君子志，　不得巖上泯。　送心正覺前，　斯痛久已忍。
唯願乘來生，　怨親同心朕。

Although Hsieh's body didn't make it to the cliffs, where it did end up, on a hill surrounded by bamboo and fir trees, was rather nice. All I could hear were the birds and the distant whack of the farmer's mattock turning soil in the rice fields below. I poured Hsieh some rye from the immortals of Kentucky and offered him my condolences and also my congratulations. A longer life is always preferable, but too few live the life they hope to, long or short. I loved his poems and so did more people than he could ever have imagined.

I walked back to the car and told the driver it was time to head for our final destination, a hundred kilometers to the north, outside the town of Hsiushui. It didn't look far on the map, but I wasn't about to try to reach it via the more direct, yet tortuous, mountain road that formed the traditional route. We returned to Wantsai instead and took a road that connected to another road that connected to another road that connected to an expressway. It took a while to reach, but once we were on it, we flew. It wasn't simply the nature of the road. Long sections were elevated above the valleys. I felt like a wild goose following spring north. It helped, too, that there were hardly any other cars. The mountains we drove past were once home to some of China's most famous Zen masters: Ma-tsu, Pai-chang, Huang-po, and Tung-shan. They looked imaginary, as if painted by someone just learning to paint. Their slopes were covered by monocultures of bamboo or fir, and no mixture of the two. The landscape waved as we passed.

We came back to earth at the Hsiushui exit. Just before we reached the bridge that spanned the Hsiushui River, I asked the driver to pull over. The building on the right was a memorial hall for Huang T'ing-chien (1045–1105). It was perched above the river and looked out on the mountains that surrounded Hsiushui on all sides. It was a lovely setting. As I walked along the corridor outside the hall, I stopped to read one of Huang's poems carved on a stone tablet. Every Chinese schoolchild knew it by heart, at least until the Communist period. "Writing about Echou's South Tower" 鄂州南樓書事:

Mountain light meets water light everywhere I look
from the tower railing I smell miles of water lilies
the soft wind and bright moon without any help from Man
together from the south bring us something cool

四顧山光接水光，憑欄十里芰荷香。清風明月無人管，并作南來一味凉。

Besides being one of the great poets of the Sung, Huang was even more renowned for his calligraphy. A scroll of his was recently sold at an auction in Beijing for US$64 million. Inside the hall were copies of copies. Looking at Huang's calligraphy, I never knew from character to character what he was going to do next. He was eccentric. The same was true of his poetry. He used lines of irregular lengths and moved his caesuras around to create different rhythms. Since he was from Hsiushui, and Hsiushui was in Kiangsi province, literary critics called him the founder of the Kiangsi school of poetry, whose members included many prominent poets of his day as well as the day after, poets such as Lu You and Fan Ch'eng-ta, both of whom I planned to visit in the days ahead.

Although officials were required to write poetry, excelling at poetry never meant much in terms of a career. Like his mentor, Su Tung-p'o, Huang was on the wrong side of the economic reform movement led by their fellow poet Wang An-shih. And like Su, Huang was banished on multiple occasions, his banishment to the empire's distant southwest, being the one from which he did not return alive. His body, though, was brought back and buried near his home in the countryside west of Hsiushui, and that was where I headed next.

From the memorial hall, we retraced our route and after a kilometer turned west onto another highway. Seven kilometers later, we turned north and crossed the Hsiushui River. A sign for Shuangching Village pointed us east. After a kilometer or two, another sign sent us north over some hills and down into a valley of rice fields and tea-covered hillsides. A few minutes later, we were there.

I was surprised. In the middle of the village square was a ten-meter-high statue of Huang. Considering its size, it was quite well done. But where, I wondered, did the village get the money for something like this? Behind the

Statue of Huang T'ing-chien at Shuangching Village

黄 庭 堅

statue was an unfinished memorial hall so big it must have cost more than all the land in the valley was worth. Clearly, this was not a village undertaking. The cultural affairs officials in Hsiushui and beyond must have come up with the plan and the financing. Shuangching wasn't much of a village, but it was on its way to becoming much more than a village.

I took some photographs while the shock wore off then remembered why I was there and started walking down the street that led to Huang's grave. It was lunchtime, though, and a group of village children spotted me. They surrounded me and insisted I visit their school. The teachers hadn't come back from lunch, and the place was theirs. The corridors were lined with copies of Huang's poems, and at the children's insistence I read several aloud, while they chimed along. I was impressed that a country school put poems rather than party pronouncements on its walls, and that the children memorized them. Huang's poetry, like his calligraphy, was full of the unexpected. And he took great delight in observing the minutest details of the world around him. The children's favorite, which they insisted I read with them, accompanied one of his paintings, "Ant and Butterfly Picture" 蟻蝶圖:

A pair of butterflies happily flutters by
suddenly their lives end in a silken web
a column of ants hauls their wings away
returning in glory to the ash-tree world

胡蝶雙飛得意，偶然畢命網羅。群蟻爭數墜翼，策勳歸去南柯。

The poem refers to the story of a man who fell asleep at the foot of an ash tree then dreamed he became governor of a kingdom of ants inside the tree. In time he married the ant king's daughter. But after twenty years of his new life's twists and turns, he woke to find he had been sleeping for less than an hour. Such, he concluded, was the brief and illusory nature of life.

The children then led me over to another set of poems and began chanting them. I was stunned. The calligraphy was that of Huang T'ing-chien, but the poems weren't his. They were Han-shan's (251, 234, and part of 235). The reason I was stunned wasn't because of the poems, which I had translated thirty years earlier. I was stunned because I had seen the original. It was a national treasure worth hundreds of millions of dollars. When I told my calligraphy teacher one day I was working on translations of Han-shan's poems, he surprised me at our next class by unrolling this very scroll at his home.

Children chanting Han-shan poems at village school

He was the curator of the National Palace Musuem's calligraphy and painting collection and had simply brought it home for the day, as his home was right next to the museum. I couldn't help laughing. The children laughed too. I couldn't think of anything more to say except to thank them for guiding me through their school's poetry gallery. I returned to the village's one and only street and resumed my progress toward the far end.

Compared to my morning quest, Huang's grave was a piece of cake. As I exited the village, an old lady steered me down a side road to a walled compound. Inside the compound was another statue of Huang, this one life-size, and his pebble-encrusted tomb. As I set out my usual offering on the altar, I noticed that just beyond the compound someone had built a teahouse. It looked inviting, but I didn't have time for tea. Whiskey would have to do.

Where Huang died was one of the emperor's favorite places to send people he didn't like. Few officials survived long among the hill tribes that inhabited the southwest fringes of the empire. Huang took solace in painting and poetry and the occasional visitor. Just before he died, his older brother, Yuan-ming, and another friend from Hsiushui came to spend the Lunar New Year with him. Huang wrote one of his last poems after he saw them off. He titled it "Parting from Yuan-ming in Yiyang – Using the Character *Shang* (Wine Cup) for the Rhyme" 宜陽別元明－用觴字韻：

May you both enjoy eighty and snow-covered temples
and jugs of wine brewed by your fellow immortals
the pines must be bigger at Moonlight Bend
and surely Remembrance Hall is desolate and overgrown
in a wind-and-rain-filled forest an oriole searches for a friend
in a sky of endless clouds a wild goose breaks formation
sleepless after parting I listen to the gnawing of mice
it isn't the spring tea that stirs my withered heart

霜鬚八十期同老，酌我仙人九醞觴。明月灣頭松老大，永思堂下草荒涼。
千林風雨鶯求友，萬里雲天雁斷行。別夜不眠聽鼠嚙，非關春茗攪枯腸。

Moonlight Bend was a section of the Hsiushui River not far from Huang's grave and also the location of the Huang family shrine. Remembrance Hall, inside the shrine, was where the Huangs conducted memorial services every year. The shrine and its hall were still there, and I would have included them in my visit if there was an extra hour in the day, and if I didn't have a bus to catch.

After paying my respects, I drank what Huang and his two visitors left and collected the cups. When I got back to the taxi, standing next to the car was another man. He said he worked at the local office of cultural affairs. The fact that a small country village had its own cultural affairs office was a testament to the plans afoot. He asked whether we could give him a ride to Hsiushui. I saw no harm in that and told him he could sit in back. By his conversation on the way into town, he impressed me as a sleazy character, but I didn't say anything. Thirty minutes later, the driver dropped me off at Hsiushui's new long-distance bus station. I paid him the balance I owed for the two days and gave him a 700RMB tip. It was a lot of money, but he earned it. As I waved goodbye, the man from the cultural affairs office began talking to him about something. I went inside to buy a ticket on the next bus to Chiuchiang.

Several days later, I got a phone call from the taxi's original driver – the man who picked me up at the Yuehyang train station. He said the young driver who replaced him never returned to Yuehyang. I cringed. I imagined him being scammed out of the money and too embarrassed to go home. He was a fine driver who thoroughly enjoyed the places we visited. He took pictures of everything with his cell phone and sent them to his girlfriend. One never knows when one's life is about to go haywire.

As for me, I just missed the two o'clock bus. I had to wait for the three o'clock, which was the last bus of the day to Chiuchiang, where I hoped to spend the night. While I was waiting, I took out my copy of Huang T'ing-chien's poems. It opened to "Leaving Fenning at Night, for Tu Chien-sou" 夜發分寧寄杜澗叟:

> The song of "Yang Pass" and the river flowing east
> lanterns on Chingyang Mountain and this little boat
> and me I'm as drunk as I have ever been
> the moon on the rippling river sighs on my behalf

陽關一曲水東流，燈火涯陽一釣舟。我自只如常日醉，滿川風月替人愁。

Fenning is an old name for Hsiushui, Chingyang a mountain just east of town, and "Yang Pass" a reference to Wang Wei's "Seeing Off Yuan Er on a Mission to Anhsi" 松元二使安西, which Wang wrote while seeing off a friend about to leave for the Silk Road:

> Morning rain dampens the dust in Weicheng
> new willow catkins have turned the inn green
> drink one more cup of wine my friend
> west of Yang Pass there's no one you know

渭城朝雨悒輕塵，客舍青青柳色新。勸君更盡一杯酒，西出陽關無故人。

Wang Wei's poem became so famous it was turned into a popular tune. Someone must have been singing it as Huang said goodbye, as he floated down the Hsiushui toward his next assignment, at the mercy of the court. Huang T'ing-chien wasn't a philosopher, but a poem can say things better than an essay. For Huang, the whole world was full of light, and not just moonlight. I put his poems away and boarded the last bus to Chiuchiang.

I woke up just after five. If there's one thing I've always been good at it's sleeping. This time, though, I couldn't find my way back to dreamland and decided I may as well get up. I made some coffee, opened the curtains, and looked out into the darkness. The Yangtze was outside my window less than a hundred meters away, and ships were already on the move. I could hear the chug of their engines and the reverberation of their horns in the predawn fog. I was in Chiuchiang, which means "nine rivers" and refers to nine tributaries that flow into the Yangtze within a few miles of each other. It was also the name of my hotel. The first two I tried the night before, the White Deer and the Chevalier, turned out to be shuttered. I found it hard to believe, as I had stayed at both several times, though not lately. My taxi driver said most of the hotels near the river had shut down since the center of town had moved to the new train station. I didn't realize Chiuchiang had a train station. That's how out of touch I was. Fortunately, the driver knew of a riverside hotel still open, the Chiuchiang Grand. It wasn't grand at all, but from my room I had a panoramic view of the fog-shrouded river. That was why I liked to stay in the old part of town. Next to the window there was a tea table and an armchair. Sipping my coffee and watching the sky brighten, I was happy with the driver's choice. Two hours later, he picked me up in front of the hotel, and I began another day.

The early morning fog by then had been replaced by rain. It was going to be one of those galoshes and umbrella days. At least I had a taxi. The driver's surname was Mr. Hsu. He was one in a long line of Hsus who had driven me around China. I must have a karmic connection with the clan. We began by following the road along the dike. About a kilometer east of the Chiuchiang Grand – I just had to say the name one more time – was my first stop: Hsunyang Tower.

Hsunyang is an old name for Chiuchiang, and the tower is its oldest landmark. Wei Ying-wu came here in 785 to assume his post as magistrate soon after it was built. One of the first poems he wrote after arriving from his previous assignment in Chuchou (aka Yungyang) was "Climbing the City Tower, To My Cousins in the Capital and My Nephews in Huainan" 登郡樓寄京師諸季淮南子弟:

I just left my post in Yungyang
and here I am in Hsunyang Tower

a cold rain spatters the balcony railing
the sheer parapets jut out above the Yangtze
I've heard wild geese every night since arriving
I keep recalling our autumn goodbyes
the wine in this cup is useless
diluted by so many cares

始罷永陽守，復臥潯陽樓。懸檻飄寒雨，危堞侵江流。
迨茲聞雁夜，重憶別離秋。徒有盈樽酒，鎮此百端憂。

Chiuchiang is one of a series of posts to which Wei was rusticated, and there was nothing like exile to inspire poems. Considering Wei's association with the tower, I was surprised to be greeted inside by murals and porcelain statues of the heroes of *The Water Margin,* the Ming-dynasty novel that gave rise to the martial arts genre. Having not read the book, I didn't realize its main hero wrote his poem of rebellion under this very roof. It wasn't much of a poem, as poems of rebellion rarely are — overwhelmed by anger. I kept climbing the steps, until I reached the third and final floor, which also served as a café. It was just after eight, and it was a cold, miserable day. Except for the ticket seller at the entrance, no other staff members had arrived, neither had any other visitors. I walked out onto the narrow balcony and watched boats going up and down the river and a few umbrellas bob along the walkway in the riverside park below.

Wei Ying-wu wasn't the only poet associated with the tower. Pai Chu-yi was also banished to Chiuchiang and served as the town's assistant magistrate from 815 to 818. Among the poems he wrote during his stay was "Written at Hsunyang Tower" 題潯陽樓:

I've always loved T'ao Yuan-ming
his thoughts are so lofty and profound
and Wei Ying-wu astounds me
his poetic sense is so clear and serene
now that I've climbed this tower
I finally know what they saw
the bottom of the Yangtze in winter
the color of Lushan changing with the sky

the moon late at night on the Pen
the mist at noon on Incense Burner Peak
the pure radiance and ethereal air
that nourished their writing night and day
lacking alas the talent of either
how could I rank alongside
standing here writing these lines
I've shamed both the mountain and the river

常愛陶彭澤，文思何高玄。又怪韋江州，詩情亦清閑。
今朝登此樓，有以知其然。大江寒見底，匡山青倚天。
深夜溢浦月，平旦鑪峰煙。清輝與靈氣，日夕供文篇。
我無二人才，孰為來其間。因高偶成句，俯仰愧江山。

The view from the tower hadn't changed, at least not its broad strokes. The Yangtze was still flowing a stone's throw to the north, and Lushan still rose as invisible and enigmatic as ever ten kilometers to the south. The Pen, though, was gone. It used to flow next to the road we followed to the tower. When T'ao and Wei and Pai lived here, the mouth of the Pen formed the old harbor. That was the reason there was a town here in the first place. It was the most important of the nine rivers. But it was no longer where it used to be. Sometime during the last century, the Pen was sluiced off to the west before it reached Chiuchiang. City land was too valuable to waste on a river. Incense Burner Peak, though, was still there. Mountains were not so easily moved. At least I assumed it was there. Lushan was shrouded by the mist. I was hoping the mountain's famous peak would show itself, but I couldn't wait. A few minutes of cold rain on the balcony were enough.

From the tower, we continued east along the dike. Just past the new bridge that spanned the Yangtze and that was largely responsible for Chiuchiang's recent transformation into a much, much bigger city, we stopped at another structure. It was called Pipa Pavilion and built to commemorate Pai Chu-yi's association with Chiuchiang, or Chiangchou, as it was called in his day. During his three-year exile, he wrote over 300 poems, including what was probably his most famous, "Pipa Ballad." I got out to see what was inside, but the pavilion was closed. The renovation work wasn't finished. There were piles of building materials everywhere, and the rain was getting heavier. I got back into the taxi and consoled myself. This wasn't where the original pavilion stood anyway. The original pavilion was across the road from where I spent the night. That was where Pai Chu-yi met the woman whose playing on a pipa, or Chinese lute, inspired the eighty-eight-line poem that ended: "sitting in this boat which of us shed more tears / the deputy magistrate's robe is soaked" 座中泣下誰最多．江州司馬青衫濕. The pavilion was moved to its present location in the Ch'ing dynasty, but I don't know why, and there was no one to ask. Even the construction workers were taking the day off. Since I had seen all I wanted to see in Chiuchiang, we turned around and headed west out of town.

The road we took passed by the northern foot of Lushan then skirted the mountain's western flank. A few determined farmers were turning over the soil in anticipation of warmer weather. They were shrouded in dark raincoats and contrasted sharply with the irrepressibly yellow rapeseed they'd planted the previous fall. After passing through a few small villages, the road joined Highway 105. Just after it did, we turned onto a side road and headed toward the mountain. A minute later, we passed Hsilin Nunnery. Another minute later, the road ended at Tunglin Monastery. Tunglin is where the practice of Pure Land Buddhism began back in the fifth century, which involved the chanting of "Omitofo," the phonetic transcription of the name of Amitabha Buddha, in hopes of being reborn in that buddha's Western Paradise. Buddhists have since incorporated the name into their daily lexicon. Anytime something good happens, they say "Omitofo" to remind themselves that it is just an illusion. And anytime something bad happens, they also say "Omitofo" to remind themselves that it, too, is just an illusion.

I had been to the monastery many times and knew the abbot, but this time I stayed in the car, while Mr. Hsu went inside the front gate to ask directions. I had planned to follow the old trail that began at the temple and led to the top of Lushan. That was the path everyone took in the old days, before there was a road. It was a three- or four-hour hike, but the place I wanted to visit was only an hour away. It was where Pai Chu-yi built his hut, which was the sort of thing a deputy magistrate could do. Job, what job? Given the rainy weather, I was counting on there being an alternative, a logging road perhaps, that would make my visit easier. I was in luck. Mr. Hsu returned with news that there was, indeed, such a road, and it led almost all the way to the hut.

In a letter to his friend Yuan Chen, Pai said he had built his hut in the loveliest place he had ever seen, and he hoped to never leave. Of course, he did leave – he was transferred farther up the Yangtze. I had met him earlier, along with his brother and Yuan Chen, at Three Travelers Cave in Yichang.

Over the centuries his hut below Incense Burner Peak had been rebuilt many times, and its most recent incarnation, according to what I had read online, was only a few years old.

From the monastery, we followed a cement road up Lushan's fog-shrouded western slope, passing a hillside of magnolias just beginning to bloom. I thought surely we would see locals along the road, and could ask directions as we got closer, but we didn't see anyone. After taking a few wrong turns and retracing our way back to the beginning, we finally saw a farmer. He knew the way and directed Mr. Hsu up a series of ever-worsening "roads" until we could go no farther. I got out and told Mr. Hsu I would be back in an hour, but he didn't want me walking up the mountain alone. He locked the taxi and joined me. Ten minutes later, we came to a hut where a man was repairing a thatched roof. It turned out he sold tickets to that section of the mountain. It was strange, encountering a box office in such a remote place. Apparently the investor who financed the rebuilding of Pai's hut convinced the authorities to grant him a concession. I paid the 20RMB admission for the two of us, and the man pointed toward a huge boulder on which someone had carved the words "Peach Blossom Stream" 桃花溪. He said the trail led along the stream. The hut was only 300 meters away, which was good news. Up the trail we went.

The mountain's tiny native camellias were in bloom, and even Mr. Hsu paused to take photographs with his cell phone. Their white petals covered the path. It was a lovely scene, but the trail wasn't much of a trail. It was more of a *suggestion* and necessitated constant clambering over boulders. The ticket seller was right about the distance, though. After less than ten minutes, we reached an archway, and beyond it several rustic-looking structures appeared out of the mist. One was a replica of Pai Chu-yi's thatch hut. Although the structures were only a few years old, they were already falling apart, which gave them a patina of authenticity. In addition to the hut, there was a pavilion and a spring-fed pond, and the whole place was surrounded by hillsides of tea.

Written on a wall next to the pavilion was Pai's "Mountain Home" 山居, to which he added these introductory remarks: "Below Incense Burner Peak, I chose a place on the mountain to live. Once my thatch hut was finished, I wrote this on the east wall" 香爐峰下新卜山居草堂初成壁題東壁:

My new hut is three spans and five beams wide
with a stone floor and cassia pillars and woven bamboo walls
the roof facing the sun keeps it warm in winter

the door greeting the wind keeps it cool in summer
a cascading spring makes patterns on the steps
rubbing against the windows bamboos lean helter-skelter
next year I'll add an east wing
and paint Meng Kuang's portrait on the dividing screen

五架三間新草堂，石階桂柱竹編墻。南檐納日冬天暖，北戶迎風夏月涼。
灑砌飛泉才有點，拂窗斜竹不成行。來春更茸東廂屋，紙閣蘆簾著孟光。

Meng Kuang was the wife of a recluse who accompanied her husband into seclusion. Pai was unable to convince his wife to do the same and had to make do with a painting on the screen meant to separate what would normally be the women's quarters.

After poking around the hut and the pavilion, I walked over to the spring that fed the pond. It was the perfect place to set out some whiskey. While the aroma spread across the pond, I walked out to a clearing to look for the peak. It finally appeared but not clearly enough to photograph. Then it disappeared and didn't show itself again. It was just as shy with Pai Chu-yi. To encourage its reappearance, I read Pai's "Singing Alone in the Mountains" 山中獨吟:

Everyone has a weakness
couplets and quatrains are mine
I've let a thousand attachments go
but I can't get rid of this fault
whenever I see a beautiful scene
or meet a kinsman or friend
I sing a few lines as loud as I can
as if possessed by a spirit
since becoming a guest of the Yangtze
I've spent half my time on this mountain
composing new poems
or hiking East Ridge
inching across sheer cliffs
or clinging to cassia branches
I wake the whole mountain with my singing
gibbons and birds come to look
afraid of the world's ridicule
I chose a place without people

人各有一癖，我癖在章句。萬緣皆已消，此病獨未去。
每逢美風景，或對好親故。高聲詠一篇，恍若與神遇。
自為江上客，半在山中住。有時新詩成，獨上東巖路。
身倚白石崖，手攀青桂樹。狂吟驚林壑，猿鳥皆窺覷。
恐為世所嗤，故就無人處。

Halfway through "Singing Alone," Mr. Hsu joined me, to my delight. He had memorized the poem in elementary school, and somehow the memory had survived the Cultural Revolution.

I walked back to the pond, poured one of the cups into the water, and scattered the contents of another on the rocks where the spring emerged. I downed the third cup myself. Considering the cold, I should have downed all three, but I needed a clear head to clamber back down along the stream to the road. Back in the taxi I asked Mr. Hsu to measure the distance downhill to the monastery. It turned out to be 2.7 kilometers from where we parked the car, which would make the hut about 3.5. My recommendation to future pilgrims would be to visit in March when the magnolias and wild camellias are in bloom.

Once again, I passed the monastery and nunnery by. I didn't have time for monks or nuns. I had a date with my favorite poet, T'ao Yuan-ming (365–427). We returned to the highway and backtracked to the turnoff for Shaho, T'ao's hometown and the location of China's one and only T'ao Yuan-ming Memorial Hall. The town was only three kilometers from the highway, but between it and the highway, Shaho had been replaced as county seat by a completely new town – a combination of government buildings and high-tech factories. Mr. Hsu hadn't been to the area since the construction and had to ask directions three times before he found Chaisang Road, which ran through the center of the old part of town. Finally, at the foot of a small hill, he turned onto Yuanming Road and followed it uphill to the memorial hall.

When I first visited, more than twenty years ago, there was just a single, small building. It was still there, but it was now one of half a dozen buildings. And the buildings were surrounded by ponds and pavilions and gardens. As I walked down the path that led through the newly landscaped grounds, I peeked into several of the new buildings, the ones devoted to calligraphy and painting. T'ao Yuan-ming inspired countless landscape paintings. A favorite theme was a recluse in a small hut surrounded by mountain wilderness, which was odd, as T'ao Yuan-ming, unlike Pai Chu-yi, never lived in the mountains. He preferred a village at the foot of a mountain. There were also paintings of the poet drinking with friends, which was closer to the truth, and paintings of the fabled land T'ao described in his story "Peach Blossom Spring."

Approaching the old memorial hall, I encountered a tour group leaving. The woman guiding the group said the place was closing for lunch in ten minutes and advised me to hurry. Not much had changed, other than the addition of a wall map showing the places around Lushan where T'ao Yuan-ming had lived, complete with photographs. His ancestors served as high-ranking officials at the court of the Eastern Chin dynasty (317–419) in Nanking, and he was expected to do the same. However, by the time he came of age his family connections were insufficient to earn him anything other than a few minor posts within a day's ride of his old home. Finally, while serving as aide-de-camp to the military commander of the region east of Chiuchiang, he resigned and retired to a piece of farmland he had previously purchased near the southern foot of Lushan. It was there that he wrote most of his finest poems, including a series of thirteen titled "On Reading the Book of Mountains and Waters" 讀山海經, the first of which begins:

> The first month of summer all the plants are tall
> the trees around my house are dense
> birds are glad to have a place to roost
> I love this refuge of mine too
> having finished the plowing and planting
> I've returned to my books again
> such a remote lane doesn't see many ruts
> it tends to deter even the carts of friends
> I enjoy a cup of spring wine
> and vegetables fresh from the garden
> the lightest of rains comes from the east
> and with it a welcome breeze
> I skimmed the Tale of King Mu
> and I glanced at the pictures in Mountains and Waters
> having surveyed the whole world
> how can I not be happy

孟夏草木長，遠屋樹扶疏。眾鳥欣有託，吾亦愛吾盧。

既耕亦已種，時還讀我書。窮巷隔深轍，頗迴故人車。
歡然酌春酒，摘我園中蔬。微雨從東來，好風與之俱。
汎覽周王傳，流觀山海圖。俯仰終宇宙，不樂復何如。

The Tale of King Mu recounted the excursions of a king of the Chou dynasty (r. 1001–947 BC), who made it his mission to visit the four quarters of the known world. And Mountains and Waters was a first millennium BC account of the geography of China, mythic and real. From his refuge, T'ao thus surveyed the universe and considered himself a lucky man. If one virtue distinguished him from all other poets, it was his sense of contentment. Lao-tzu would have loved him.

I caught up with the guide as she was waving goodbye to the tour group. When I told her I was hoping to visit T'ao Yuan-ming's grave, she pointed to some steps and said his grave was at the top of the hill. I was hoping that she would tell me the grave was now accessible. Instead she pointed to a replacement grave, one built as part of the park that now surrounded the memorial hall. I wanted to visit the real grave. I had tried twice before, in 1991 and again in 2005. It was on a military base, and I was turned away both times. She said that was where the real grave was, but it was *still* closed to the public.

I walked up the steps to the fake grave anyway, but I wasn't sufficiently enthused to get out the whiskey. After a few minutes of reading inscriptions, I returned to Mr. Hsu's taxi and told him I was done. Back we drove through Shaho, or Chaisang, as it was once known. I wanted to visit the place where T'ao Yuan-ming turned living in the countryside into a literary genre, as in his "Reply to Liu of Chaisang" 酬劉柴桑:

> Few people visit such a poor place
> sometimes I forget about the seasons
> until falling leaves cover the yard
> and sadly I realize it's autumn
> even with sunflowers lighting the north window
> and grain nodding in the field to the south
> still I can't feel happy
> not knowing if I'll have another year
> I tell my wife to bring the children
> it's a perfect day for a hike

窮居寡人用，時忘四運周。閒庭多落葉，慨然知已秋。

新葵郁北牖，嘉穟養南疇。今我不為樂，知有來歲不。
命室携童弱，良日登遠游。

Few poets were so adept at making something sound so idyllic and yet at the same time so realistic.

There was still mist in the air, and I wasn't up for another hike. But T'ao Yuan-ming's old home wasn't in the mountains. It was at the foot of Lushan. We headed south 15 kilometers on the old highway, until it intersected with Highway 212. Off to the left was the biggest standing buddha statue in the world. It was hard to miss, the Tunglin Buddha, named after the monastery that had orchestrated its construction. When I first met the monastery's abbot, Master Kuo-yi, he had told me about his plans to build the statue. I found them hard to believe. But there it was: forty-eight meters of steel and cement covered with forty-eight tons of gold leaf. The price tag was one billion renminbi, or US$160 million, all of it paid for by donations. The statue was of Amitabha, the buddha who welcomes devotees to the Pure Land of the Western Paradise, where it is far easier to become enlightened than in this world of constant distraction. I've never been a big fan of monumental art, religious or secular, especially with so many impoverished people living in the lands where such art appeared, but like any tourist I got out to look. In the first chapter of the *Vimalakirti Sutra,* Shakyamuni addressed one of his followers: "Ratnakara, bodhisattvas who wish to reach the Pure Land should purify their minds. As their minds become pure, the world in which they practice becomes pure." Admittedly, it was far easier to build a statue than to purify the mind.

I got back into Mr. Hsu's taxi, and we turned west onto Highway 212. Three kilometers later, we pulled over to the side of the road at Wenchuan Village. Wenchuan means "hot spring." In 1991, the only building not made of mud bricks was an old-age home. When I visited again fourteen years later, it was still a mud-brick village. And in one of the houses, T'ao Yuan-ming's last lineal male descendant had died only the week before. From his yard, I could see the small mountain just south of the village that inspired the fifth of T'ao's twenty "Drinking Poems" 飲酒：

I built my hut beside a path
but I hear neither cart nor horse
you ask how can this be
when the mind travels so does the place

picking chrysanthemums by the eastern fence
I lose myself in the southern hills
the mountain air the sunset light
birds flying home together
in this there is a truth
I'd explain if I could remember the words

結盧在人境，而無車馬喧。問君何能爾，心遠地自偏。
采菊東籬下，悠然見南山。山氣日夕佳，飛鳥相與還。
此中有真意，欲辨已忘言。

Since my last visit, the village and its mud houses had been bulldozed and replaced by hot-spring hotels, apartment buildings, and stores selling bathing suits. Even the trees T'ao planted were gone, as was his little bridge. It was all too depressing. I directed Mr. Hsu instead to the front gate of the five-star Lushan Tianti Holiday Resort, on the other side of the highway. Mr. Hsu was hesitant to drive past the gate guard, but I waved at the guard and told Mr. Hsu to keep going. Just before we reached the main part of the resort, I told Mr. Hsu to pull over. I got out and asked him to wait for me. But Mr. Hsu was up for another adventure. He locked his taxi and followed me up a dirt trail.

A minute later, I introduced him to Drunkard's Rock, where T'ao Yuan-ming met with his friends, and where he was inspired to write his famous story about Peach Blossom Spring and a hidden land lost in time. The entrance to the fabled land was just up the stream. The huge rock on which T'ao and his friends liked to sit and drink was about as big as Pai Chu-yi's hut. We climbed to the top, and I showed Mr. Hsu the account Chu Hsi (1130–1200) left of his visit.

Chu was one of the great neo-Confucians of the Sung dynasty. The characters he had carved into the rock were mostly worn away, but Chu Hsi's name was still visible. Mr. Hsu stared in disbelief and kept shaking his head. He wondered out loud why this rock wasn't in a museum. I was glad it wasn't. Given its size, I didn't think it was going anywhere anytime soon. We sat down and watched the water flow past. It was a lovely spot, and the morning rain had given way to afternoon sunshine. In a poem, Jim Harrison once asked, "How long can I stare at the river?" As we did just that, it kept

Right: T'ao Yuan-ming's Drunkard's Rock

changing into different rivers then back into one river then into no river at all. I'm guessing we lasted ten minutes. After helping Mr. Hsu down from the boulder, I paused beside the stream long enough to pour in a shot of rye. It wasn't peach petals, but it, too, was from another world.

We returned to the highway and backtracked west. Between the 1575 and 1576 road markers, I told Mr. Hsu to turn onto a side road that led toward the mountain. I had been on the road twice before, each time to no avail. I hoped something had changed. A hundred meters later, I realized it hadn't. There was a sign warning us that we were entering a restricted area. Mr. Hsu slowed down, but I told him to keep going. Less than a kilometer later, the road ended at the gate of a naval munitions depository.

After we parked, I walked over to the gate and told the guard I wanted to visit T'ao Yuan-ming's grave. The guard was clearly surprised that I was there, that I was speaking Chinese, and that I was asking to enter the base. He went inside the guardhouse and telephoned whoever was in charge. Two minutes later, several officers arrived in a jeep, and with them more guards. They wanted to know what I was doing there. Didn't I see the warning sign? I told them I was traveling around China paying my respects to their country's greatest poets, and T'ao Yuan-ming was my favorite. How could I not love the man who wrote "Retiring to Live on a Farm" 歸園田居?

I was socially awkward when I was young
I preferred hills and mountains instead
unwittingly I fell into the world of red dust
I was trapped for thirty years
but a bird on a tether longs for the woods
and a fish from the ocean recalls the old depths
after clearing some land well south of town
I retired to farm and lead a simple life
my property includes more than three acres
my thatch hut is maybe nine mats wide
elms and willows shade the garden in back
peach trees and plum trees spread across the front
the nearest village is off in the haze
smoke hangs above the earthen walls
in a distant lane I hear a dog bark
a rooster crows from a mulberry tree

there's no dirt or trash in my yard
my house is empty but filled with peace
no longer imprisoned in a cage
I'm back again and I'm free

少無適俗韻，性本愛丘山。誤落塵網中，一去三十年。
羈鳥戀舊林，池魚思故淵。開荒南野際，守拙歸園田。
方宅十餘畝，草屋八九間。榆柳蔭後園，桃李羅堂前。
曖曖遠人村，依依墟里煙。狗吠深巷中，雞鳴桑樹巔。
戶庭無塵雜，虛室有餘閑。久在樊籠裏，復得返自然。

How could I not visit the grave of such a man? The officers, though, were adamant. No one was allowed on the base without written permission from higher headquarters, whatever and wherever that was. I continued to press my case, but they weren't about to let me in. They also refused my request that they use my camera to photograph the grave. Finally they told me to leave. I was out of options, but not out of ideas. I went back to the taxi and retrieved a paper cup Mr. Hsu had given me earlier that day when he shared some tea. I filled it with a couple shots of rye and asked the officer doing most of the talking if he would pour the contents on the grave for me. His name tag read Captain Fan Shan-feng. Shan-feng means "mountain peak," which I thought auspicious. Captain Fan was so surprised by my request, he couldn't help himself. He took the cup. He even offered to take a photo and e-mail it to me. I knew that was unlikely, and if it was sent, I never received it. Photo or not, I felt confident the whiskey reached the man who gave living a simpler life a voice that still sets people free.

As I turned to leave, Captain Fan said even Chinese weren't allowed on the base and that next time I should arrange for official permission before entering a restricted area. Oddly enough, several months later I received an e-mail from a Chinese friend who went there with the same goal. She said they didn't let her on the base, either. They said a foreigner had come there earlier and was also turned away. So she didn't feel so bad. Neither did I. Success, failure, what does it matter? It's all about the effort.

Having fulfilled all my missions for the day, I asked Mr. Hsu to drive me to the bus station in the nearby town of Te-an. He turned out to be more than a taxi driver that day. He was a fellow pilgrim. I thanked him, and he thanked me. As I walked inside the station, I was just in time for the three o'clock express to Nanchang, the capital of Kiangsi province. Nanchang, however, wasn't my final destination. As soon as I arrived there, I took a taxi to another bus station and caught the next bus to Linchuan. It was, unfortunately, a local, and I didn't get there until seven o'clock. By the time I checked into the Linchuan Hotel, I was exhausted. I don't remember eating dinner, but I do remember washing my clothes and taking a bath and lying in bed reading this poem Wei Ying-wu wrote about his hero titled "In Imitation of T'ao P'eng-ts'e" 效陶彭澤. Pengtse was where T'ao Yuan-ming was serving when he quit for good, and it became one of his nicknames.

When other plants bow to the frost
chrysanthemums alone show their beauty
this is the nature of things
there's no changing the seasons
I sprinkle their petals in homemade wine
at sunset I sit down with farmers
under thatched eaves all of us drunk
life is about more than plenty

霜露悴百草，時菊獨妍華。物性有如此，寒暑其奈何。
掇英泛濁醪，日入會田家。盡醉茅簷下，一生豈在多。

Omitofo.

I was up again before dawn, but feeling surprisingly refreshed. The hot bath and nine p.m. bedtime probably had something to do with that. Once again I was drinking coffee before the sun was up. I was on the second cup when the outside world finally appeared. I could see it wasn't raining. So that was good. It was overcast, but the streets were dry. Since my first destination of the day was just down the street and didn't open its doors until nine, I spent a rare morning catching up on e-mail. I even checked in on Spring Training. I've tried my best to follow Lao-tzu's teaching of being "one with success and one with failure" (*Taoteching*: 23). As a fan of the Seattle Mariners, I had perfected the second part. I could only wonder what the first part was like. I thought maybe this would be the year. It wasn't.

Just before nine I finally left the sanctuary of my room and proceeded to the Wang An-shih Memorial Hall, five blocks away. Admission was free, and half a dozen people were already in the garden doing their *ch'i-kung* exercises. I entered the memorial hall and found myself alone with Wang.

Wang An-shih (1021–1086) was born forty kilometers to the northeast in the town of Tunghsiang, but because his father was an official and often away on assignments, Wang spent most of his childhood at his mother's home in what is now Chenghu Village, halfway between Tunghsiang and Linchuan. Linchuan, though, was the area's administrative center and claimed Wang as its own. Touring the exhibits, I was pleased to see his poems printed in characters big enough for aging eyes. I took particular interest in his poems about where he grew up, such as "Wutang" 烏塘 (Black Pond), a pond near his mother's house:

> Green water lapped against the Black Pond embankment
> people walking past had something in their hands
> I asked if they had found any sign of spring
> "West of Chekang Hill the magnolias are like snow"

烏塘渺渺綠平堤，提上行人各有攜。試問春風何處好，辛夷如雪柘岡西。

Chekang Hill was east of his mother's village. Wang liked it so much he built his study hall on top, much as Li Pai and Ch'en Tzu-ang did on mountains near their hometowns. Growing up as a teenager in semi-seclusion,

Wang became an eccentric early on, careless about his dress and manners. His hero was another eccentric, the recluse Han-shan (Cold Mountain). Among Wang's surviving poems is a series of twenty titled "In Imitation of Han-shan" 擬寒山拾得. This is number 7:

I've read ten thousand books
and plumbed the truths beneath the sky
those who know know themselves
no one trusts a fool
rare are the idle followers of the Way
who escape the hooks of this world
who realize what is important
doesn't come from somewhere outside

我讀萬卷書，識盡天下理。智者渠自知，愚者誰信你。
奇哉閑道人，跳出三句里。獨悟自根本，不從他處起。

While Wang admired idle followers of the Way, he himself was hardly an idler. After his father died, he passed the civil service exams at the age of twenty-three and served in a number of provincial posts, primarily along the Yangtze. He didn't let his views about the hooks of the world prevent him from helping those under his care. Wherever he served, people praised him for his hard work and intelligence. And once he got his chance, he rose quickly at court to become one of the emperor's favorites.

Given his responsibilities, both in the provinces and later at court, Wang rarely returned home. On one such occasion, he wrote "Stopping to Drink at My Cousin's" 過外弟飲 — Wang's cousin's house was between his mother's house near Chekang Hill and Black Rock Hill (Wushihkang).

One day I'm facing wine at my cousin's
then six years of dust and waves
how many more times on this Black Rock Hill road
will I come to see you before we've grown old

一自君家把酒杯，六年波浪與塵埃。不知烏石岡邊路，至老相尋得幾回。

Not many people give Wang credit for the simple artistry of his short poems. He wasn't as clever as Su Tung-p'o or Ou-yang Hsiu. His poetry was more like Pai Chu-yi's: plain and straightforward. He didn't try to impress. He did, however, impress people with his prose. He was considered one of the great essayists of the Sung and the equal of both Ou-yang and Su.

Wang's politics also distinguished him. After becoming prime minister, he implemented the most far-reaching and controversial economic policies ever attempted in China. Mao was a big fan, as was Chou En-lai. Their accolades were prominently displayed on the exhibition hall walls. Having witnessed firsthand the poverty of farmers, Wang resolved to do something to help them. His plan involved loaning them money in spring at 20 percent interest, instead of the usual 60 percent, and having them repay the loans in autumn. His reforms also involved loans to small businesses and even went so far as to require a balanced state budget. Such measures, however, were opposed by those with something to lose, namely, wealthy merchants, moneylenders, the landed gentry, the entrenched supporters of these groups at court, and those who simply preferred the traditional way of doing things. In the face of such opposition, his reforms didn't last. They were swept aside soon after he retired.

When Wang finally left the capital of Kaifeng for good, instead of returning to his old home near Linchuan, he traveled down the Grand Canal as far as Nanking and built a house at the foot of Chungshan (Bell Mountain). Nanking's location near the intersection of the canal and the Yangtze was especially convenient. There was no reason to go home anyway. Both his parents had died. Over the years Wang made many friends, and they all came to visit. Even political opponents, such as Su Tung-p'o, came to share a few cups of wine. Once Wang had resigned himself to being resigned, he spent the last decade of his life enjoying his garden, talking with the monks on Chungshan, and writing poems such as "Nap" 午枕:

While I napped on my wavy-lined mat by the flowers
the sun cast reflections on the curtain hooks
a curious bird called me back from the most tenuous of dreams
to the most agreeable of cares involving the mountain across the stream

午枕花前簟欲流， 日催紅影上簾鉤。 窺人鳥喚悠颺夢， 隔水山供宛轉愁。

Next to a bath, my favorite event of the day is a nap. The more I learn about Wang An-shih, the more I admire him. But the exhibits at the memorial hall only whetted my appetite. When Wang died, he was buried in his garden at the foot of Chungshan. However, sometime during the next two centuries his grave disappeared. No one knew what happened to his remains – until recently. What happened was my next destination.

I checked out of the hotel and went to look for a taxi. Once I found a driver amenable to what I had in mind, I left Linchuan via the bridge that spanned the Fuchiang River then turned southeast onto Highway 316. The road paralleled the river, and we followed it twenty kilometers. Just past the town of Huwan, we turned north onto County Road 946. Eleven kilometers later, just past the village of Liuli, we turned west onto County Road 633, and followed it another eight kilometers across a countryside of farmland and low, rolling hills. I was surprised at the number of earth god shrines and wondered whether the gods that guarded the land smiled on the farmers here or whether they simply demanded more from them. At the village of Huangyuan, shortly after we turned onto County Road 664, the paved portion of the morning's journey ended, and we started working our way south on a road that alternated between dirt and gravel.

When the ruts became too deep, the driver pulled over, and I walked the last 200 meters to the village of Yuehtang. The reason I went to so much trouble to get here – and the reason I've left these bread crumbs for others to follow – is that several years ago some researchers came across the records of the clan to which Wang An-shih belonged, and the records revealed what historians had wondered about for centuries: what had happened to Wang's remains? What happened is that they had been reburied on a hillside next to this village.

Yuehtang wasn't big as villages go, but it was old. I walked past several locusts that must have been planted a thousand years ago. Although all the houses were made of mud bricks, there were two huge stone archways in the middle of the village. The wording on one proclaimed it "The Ancient Home of Lord Ching." Lord Ching was a title the emperor bestowed posthumously on Wang An-shih. On the other archway were the words "The Ancestral Line of Chinling." Chinling was another name for Nanking – and another name by which Wang was known, as it was where he retired and where he died. This village of mud-brick houses had simply grown up around the clan's graveyard. Centuries of villagers had served as its guardians.

After wandering around the village, I walked over to the edge of a pond. To the north were terraced rice fields, and beyond the fields was pyramid-

Wang An-shih gravesite at Yuehtang Village

shaped Fengshan (Phoenix Mountain). According to the villagers I spoke with, the old graveyard used to occupy the foot and lower slopes of the mountain. The fengshui was great. But whatever graves had once been there were gone. The Wang clan had a feud with another clan, and during the Ming dynasty, not long after Wang An-shih's remains were reinterred here, a member of the opposing clan became head of the Ministry of Rites and ordered the entire Wang clan graveyard destroyed. This only came to light recently when a stele recording the event was dug up in the village.

I walked across the fields past an ox enjoying the end of its winter vacation. It had already busted up a few fields, but the real work of spring planting was still a month away. I saw a farmer in the distance repairing an irrigation ditch and walked over and asked him about the location of Taoyuanko (Peach Spring Hollow). According to the most detailed account in one of the clan records, that was where Wang An-shih's body was reburied when it was moved from Nanking. The farmer pointed at the mountain, and I hiked halfway up. But I didn't see anything that looked like a "hollow." All I saw were fields of last year's rice stubble and hillsides of fir trees and bamboo. I could have walked right past the grave for all I knew. I had to accept that this was as close as I was going to get. At least Wang's remains were here to stay, wherever they were.

Since there were no signs of a tomb, I walked back to the pond, which was built by one of Wang's cousins and was shaped like a half-moon. Hence, the village's name, which means "moon pond." It looked like the appropriate place for my usual ceremony, so I sat down on a rock at the edge of the pond and set out my cups. While I waited for the spirits to show up, I thumbed through a book of Wang's poems.

I stopped at the poem he wrote for his daughter. She was born in 1047, the year he arrived in Ningpo to assume his post as that city's magistrate. He was only twenty-seven, and it was while in Ningpo – or Yin, as it was then known – that he first implemented the policies that later formed the basis of his economic reforms. The farmers in his district were overjoyed, but any happiness Wang felt was overcome by grief for his daughter, who died the following year. He buried her beyond Ningpo's south moat, on a small hill he often visited on his days off. Two years later, the night before he left Ningpo for his next assignment, he rowed beyond the moat and the adjacent water-way to the hill one last time. I read "Parting from My Yin Daughter" 別鄞女 back to him:

> I've only lived thirty years and already I feel old
> wherever I look I'm beset by sorrow
> I've come in this little boat to say goodbye tonight
> here where the shores of life and death divide us

行年三十已衰翁，滿眼憂傷只自攻。今夜扁舟來訣汝，死生從此各西東。

I poured Wang's share of rye into Moon Pond and drank what was left. Wang rowed back the way he came, and I returned to the taxi.

From Yuehtang, it was only ten kilometers north as the crow flew to the location of Wang's old study hall. The magnolias, I reckoned, would have turned the place white by then. But at the memorial hall in Linchuan, I read that the hill on which Wang's hall once stood had been swallowed by a new reservoir. Besides, there was no road that paralleled the crow's flight path. It would have taken another hour or so to get there – an hour I didn't have.

We retraced our way back to Highway 316 instead and stopped for lunch in Huwan. Normally, once I set out in the morning, I kept going until night-fall. However, I could tell my driver didn't share my relentlessness. We ordered three of my favorites: scrambled eggs with tomatoes, eggplant with scallions and ground pork, and spinach with lots of garlic. Given my plans for the rest of the day, I wasn't sure whether I'd be eating dinner that night. So at least the day's big meal was out of the way. Before we continued, I also stopped at a pharmacy. I felt a sore throat coming on and bought some erythromycin. Usually, I would drink it to death, but I needed to save the whiskey for the poets.

From Huwan, we headed east on 316 again. Next on my list was Hsin Ch'i-chi (1140–1207), the great lyric poet of the Sung dynasty, rivaled in that genre only by Li Ch'ing-chao. They were both from Chinan, and I had visited their homes and memorial halls on Day 2 of this pilgrimage. Not long after the Jurchens conquered North China, both Li and Hsin fled south and eventually joined the displaced Sung court in Hangchou. In Hsin's case, the heroic nature of his military exploits gained him entrée to the world of émigré officials and southern gentry. However, his outspoken advocacy of policies aimed at recapturing the lost lands of the North were not well received by a court set on appeasement. As a result, he was relegated to a series of minor posts. In 1181, after twenty years of frustration, he retired to the town of Shangjao and spent the next fifteen years there, years he felt he should have been doing something more useful. One of the poems he wrote in Shangjao is "Late Spring" 暮春, sung to the tune "Man-chiang-hung" 滿江紅 (The Whole River Is Red):

> Living south of the Yangtze
> once again I have spent
> Cold Food and Grave Sweeping Days
> on flower-covered paths
> amid gusts of wind and rain
> a scattered profusion
> of red petals sinking in the stream
> shade taking over the garden
> every year I have seen
> coral trees stripped of their blossoms
> utterly sapped of strength
>
> In the stillness of the courtyard
> I think of you in vain
> unable to express

the depth of my despair
I fear the gossiping birds
already know the news
where is your silken letter
of its brocade lines I see no trace
and don't bother asking
I can't bear to climb towers
the countryside here is so green

家住江南，又過了，清明寒食。花徑里，一番風雨，一番狼籍。
紅粉暗隨流水去，園林漸覺清蔭密。算年年，落盡刺桐花，寒無力。

庭院靜，空相憶。無說處，閒愁極。怕流鶯乳燕，得知消息。
尺素始今何處也，彩雲依舊無踪跡。謾教人，羞去上層樓，平蕪碧。

Although there were no traces of Hsin's residence in Shangjao, there *was* something south of Shangjao, and that was where I headed, by the usual indirect route: from Huwan east to Chinhsi, north via expressway to Yingtan, then east on another expressway to Yenshan, where we exited then navigated our way through that city to join Highway 202. Half an hour later, we entered the modest town of Yungping. When Hsin's house in Shangjao burned down in 1195, he moved south of Yungping. He decided to follow the example of his hero, T'ao Yuan-ming, and try his hand at country living. But the ideal of simplicity for which T'ao was famous has never been easy to realize, and Hsin found it lonely, which is evident in this poem about his new home titled simply, "To the Tune Ho-hsin-lang" 賀新郎 (Congratulating the Groom):

How far I have declined
a lifetime of despair
scattered friendships
of which too few remain
a mile of useless white hair
when I laughed at all the things people do
you asked what was it
that might make me happy
I'm attracted to mountains
I imagine mountains
likewise attracted to me

inside and outside
we're more or less the same

Drinking at the east window I scratch my head
I think about T'ao Yuan-ming
the meaning of his "Unmoving Clouds"
in tune with these times
here in the South drunkards claim fame
as if they could see the truth in dregs
I turn and shout
"Wind arise, clouds away"
I don't mind not knowing the ancients
I only mind the ancients
not knowing this madness of mine
and those who know me
but two or three

甚矣我衰矣，恨平生，交游零落，只今餘幾。
白獸空垂三千丈。一笑人間萬事，問何物，能令公喜。
我見青山多嫵媚，料青山，見我應如是。情與貌，略相似。

一樽搔首東窗裏，想淵明，停雲詩白，此時風味。
江左沈酣求名者，豈識濁醪妙理。回首叫，雲飛風起。
不恨古人吾不見，恨古人，不見吾狂耳。知我者，二三子。

In his preface to the poem to which Hsin refers, T'ao Yuan-ming wrote: "'Unmoving Clouds' is about thinking of a dear friend with a cup of new wine and a garden of new flowers but with hopes unfulfilled and a heart full of sighs" 停雲，思親友也．罇湛新醪．園列初榮．願言不從歎息彌襟．Like T'ao, Hsin had plenty of unfulfilled hopes and no shortage of sighs, and wished he had a few like-minded neighbors. It was one of the shortcomings of country living.

On our way through Yungping, we came to what looked like the town's only stoplight. As we sat waiting for it to turn, I rolled down my window and waved to the driver of the taxi next to us. I asked whether she knew the way to Chenchiachai. I told her I was looking for the grave of Hsin Ch'i-chi. I couldn't help thinking to myself, had I done this in Camden, New Jersey, could I have expected directions to Walt Whitman's grave? The woman not only nodded, she said she would lead us there for 50RMB. It was a bit steep, but I had more money than time. I waved for her to proceed. She already had three passengers, but the chance to make a bit more trumped her responsibility to them. Oddly, as we followed her out of town, her passengers stayed put. Just beyond the town limits, there was a sign pointing to Hsin Ch'i-chi's grave. It listed the distance as 9.2 kilometers. I suppose we could have made it there without her help, but roads in the countryside are often confusing, and signs for historical sites rare. The woman turned west at the sign, and we followed her.

Suddenly it was a lovely day. We were being led to our next destination without the usual delay of having to ask directions every few kilometers, and the erythromycin was kicking in. I was swallowing without wincing. I was also enjoying the incredible speed at which our guide careened down the country road, slowing only slightly for villagers when we passed through the odd gathering of houses. My driver had a hard time keeping up. Her speed probably had something to do with her passengers who, no doubt, were considering mutiny.

In a matter of minutes we left the village of Chenchiachai behind, then the village of Pengchiawan as well. Finally, where the road deteriorated into a pair of ruts, she stopped and got out. This was as far as her guide service went. The grave was another half a kilometer, she said, at the end of the road. After I paid her, one of her passengers got out and offered to take us the rest of the way. That was a surprise. Apparently his business elsewhere wasn't as pressing as I had imagined. And so we followed him down the road toward the grave. A tractor would have been helpful. Due to recent rains, the road had become a quagmire. At least it wasn't far, and the road took us past hillsides illuminated by the green-white blossoms of pear trees. How could I not be happy? The only person I knew who had been to Hsin's grave warned me it would be difficult to find, and here I was being led there. The man doing the leading said the road was the work of a bulldozer that had recently widened what was previously a mere trail. He said it would be paved in another month, which future pilgrims, I'm sure, will appreciate.

After less than fifteen minutes we arrived at the base of a hill. The grave was a hundred meters up the slope. It, too, was being torn up. Hsin Ch'i-chi was getting some respect, much like Hsieh Ling-yun. Of course, respect can go too far. Still, given the remoteness of the grave, my guess is that Hsin will be seeing only the most determined of visitors.

As I walked up the slope, I had to make my way around and over the stones that once formed a set of steps. The place was a mess. At least the grave itself was sufficiently intact for a libation and an ode. Since Hsin loved mountains and clouds, I chose "Ode to Clouds and Mountains" 對賦雲山, which he composed to the tune "Yu-lou-chun" 玉樓春 (Jade Tower Spring):

Who moved the mountains last night
seeing nothing but clouds I guess it was you
for the handful of peaks I invariably see
I searched in vain up every valley
then the west wind scared the clouds away
suddenly the pillars of the sky reappeared
an old monk clapped and laughed at this show
happy the mountains were in their old place

何人半夜推山去，四面浮雲猜是汝。常時相對兩三峰，走遍溪頭無覓處。
西風瞥起雲橫渡，忽見東南天一柱。老僧拍手笑相誇，且喜青山依舊住。

It was the old summary of Zen practice as seeing the mountains, then not seeing the mountains, then seeing the mountains again, as in Donovan's song "There Is a Mountain." In Hsin's hands, though, it was more fun, which was

Grave of Hsin Ch'i-chi

one of the attractions of his poetry. By the time I got around to sprinkling the libation on Hsin's grave, it was almost five o'clock. I was hoping I would have time to visit the place where he once lived, which was five kilometers to the east. I thought maybe there was a memorial hall and that it might be about to close. I gathered my cups, thanked the man who guided us, and told him I had to hurry, that I wanted to visit Hsin's old home. He said there was no reason to hurry – nothing was there, which somehow made me feel better. I felt even better when he added that he would be happy to show us the way. I love it when someone offers to relieve me of my usual pinball approach to finding out-of-the-way places. As if guiding us there weren't enough, the man said he knew a shortcut. Given the time of day, a shortcut was welcome.

We returned to our car and, as promised, the man directed us onto a narrow road that led through the countryside and underneath an unfinished expressway. A few kilometers later, we reconnected with Highway 202 at the Pashuiyuan bus stop. We turned south again, and six kilometers later, between the 274 and 275 road markers, our guide told us to pull over. This was the place, he said. I didn't see a sign, just a farmhouse. We all got out and walked over to a courtyard where several farmers were sitting around talking. Their work for the day was done.

Our guide explained why we were there, and the farmhouse's owner introduced himself. His surname was Chou. The place where Hsin once lived was a hundred meters behind his house. He escorted us to the base of a small hill and showed us Hsin's Gourd Spring, which flowed from the rocks next to where the house once stood. Standing there at one of the world's great sources of poetic inspiration, I was overwhelmed by my good fortune. Mr. Chou pointed out the two small pools Hsin carved into the surface of a huge monolith so that water from the spring could flow first into one pool then, via a curving conduit, into another, shallower pool. I'd never seen anything like it.

Hsin bought the spring and the land around it in 1186, and nine years later, after his residence in Shangjao burned down, he built a house next to the spring and spent most of his last decade there. Any remains of the house were long gone, but the spring was still flowing. I had already offered Hsin some rye at his grave, but I couldn't pass up a spring, especially this spring. I poured out three more cups, set them at the edge of the lower pool, and began reading "New Year's Eve" 元夕, which Hsin composed to the tune "Ching-yu-an" 青玉案 (Green Jade Tray). It was one of Hsin's best-known poems. Everyone joined in, including Mr. Chou.

In the east wind last night a thousand trees burst forth
showered down
a rain of stars
jeweled horses and carriages and incense filled the road
the tremulous sound of a phoenix flute
the transforming glow of a jade vase
all night lanterns swayed
and she of the moth eyebrows and flower-decked hair
of laughter that beguiles and the subtlest of perfumes
whom I have searched for in crowds a hundred times
as I turned my head
she was there
where the lantern light was faint

東風夜放花千樹，更吹落，星如雨。寶馬雕車香滿路。
鳳簫聲動，玉壺光轉，一夜魚龍舞。
蛾兒雪柳黃金縷，笑語盈盈暗香去。
眾裏尋他千百度，驀然回首，那人卻在，燈火闌珊處。

I poured the contents of one of the cups into the pool then handed another cup to Mr. Chou. As he sipped the 128-proof rye, his eyes lit up. He said the spring got three or four visitors every year, but there were no plans to do anything with the site. He said the other places in the area associated with Hsin Ch'i-chi, such as Chanma Bridge and Chissu Ferry, were nothing but memories. After I finished my own share of the rye, I dipped my empty cup into the pool and drank a pure-water toast to Hsin and his neo-Confucian friends. Hsin and the philosopher Ch'en Liang (1143–1194) came here in 1188 and held their own ceremony shortly after Hsin purchased the property. Their friend Chu Hsi (1130–1200) was supposed to join them, but the dean of neo-Confucian philosophers failed to show up that day. So it was just the two of them. Drinking the spring's pure water, they vowed not to rest until they realized their dream of recapturing the lands in North China lost to the Jurchens. Both men died heartbroken, but I drank to their resolve. What was life for anyway?

I thanked Mr. Chou for showing me the spring and walked back to the car. We continued south. Our guide asked us to drop him off three kilometers farther down the road, at a brick factory. I was thankful for his help and tried to give him a 100RMB note. He wouldn't take it. It turned out he owned the factory and was genuinely delighted to have escorted us to the grave and the spring.

After saying goodbye, we drove back to the expressway outside Yenshan then headed west. But I wasn't going all the way back to Linchuan. I had a ticket for a ten o'clock train from Yingtan. An hour later, the driver dropped me off outside the train station. It was only seven, and I had three hours to kill, so I rented a room at a cheap hotel across the street. The room's walls were made of plywood, and the bed took up most of the space, but the bathroom had a shower and the water was hot. I even checked my e-mail and slept for an hour before recrossing the street. The train was an hour late, but at least I was awake when it arrived.

My ticket was for a hard-sleeper, which meant six berths in an open compartment, as opposed to four in a closed compartment in the soft-sleeper section. I was grateful for any ticket with a berth, especially one for a lower berth. The upper berth was so close to the ceiling, there was barely enough room to roll over, much less sit up. And the middle berth wasn't much better. I was also grateful the smokers were asleep by the time I boarded. I slept most of the night. Even the parts where I was awake weren't bad. After all, I was on a train.

As we clickety-clacked through the night, the train slipped further and further behind schedule. It was eight thirty when we arrived in Hsuancheng the next day. The train was two hours late by then, but that worked to my advantage. The first place I wanted to visit wouldn't have been open before eight anyway. Walking out of the station, I had to squint. It was so bright. I had planned to stash my bag at the train station and take a later train to the next place on the itinerary, then a taxi. Standing in the sunshine, I changed my mind. It was going to be taxis all the way, or better yet *a* taxi all the way. I joined the queue, and when it was my turn I told the driver my plans. He dropped his meter, and we were off.

Hsuancheng was blessed with two poets laureate whose names have forever been linked with the city: Li Pai and Hsieh T'iao. I began with Hsieh T'iao (464–499). Hsieh was one of the most famous poets of the fifth century, a century he shared with his uncle, Hsieh Ling-yun, and with T'ao Yuan-ming. To distinguish between the two Hsiehs, contemporaries referred to Hsieh T'iao as "Hsieh Junior" and his uncle as "Hsieh Senior." In addition to having kinship in common, they also shared the distinction of being called cofounders of China's Mountains and Rivers school of poetry. With the exception of T'ao Yuan-ming, Chinese poets up until then wrote about court life in Xanadu. If poets wrote about life outside the city gate, it was an idealized world and not one they experienced directly. Although the Hsiehs were also members of the nobility and never really separated themselves from its influence, the world they extolled in their poetry was the world outside city walls, and it was a world they experienced firsthand.

Hsieh T'iao's father was a senior official during the Liu Sung dynasty (420–478), and his mother was a daughter of one of its rulers. However, by the time Hsieh came of age, the Liu Sung had been replaced by the Southern Ch'i dynasty (479–501), and life at court was treacherous. While Hsieh

T'iao was still in his twenties, nine potential successors to the Ch'i throne were murdered one after the other, along with their families and supporters.

This all took place in Nanking, the capital of a series of southern dynasties beginning with the Eastern Chin (317–419) and lasting until the Sui (589–618), which reunited China after 400 years of division and which itself was replaced by the T'ang (618–906). Both Hsiehs spent most of their early years either at court in Nanking or in its shadow. In the case of Hsieh Junior, he became known for hymns he composed for court ceremonies, and he would have likely remained a minor poet had it not been for an event that changed the direction of his creative life. In the spring of 495, when he was thirty-one, he was sent to serve as governor of Hsuancheng. It was only 150 kilometers away, but it was far enough for Hsieh to feel both liberated and anxious. Leaving the capital and the shores of the Yangtze behind, he described his feelings in "From Hsinlinpu River to Panchiao Bridge on the Way to Hsuancheng" 之 宣城郡出新林浦向板橋:

> River traffic keeps heading southwest
> the ocean-bound current surges northeast
> I see boats on the horizon sailing home
> and trees along the river wrapped in clouds
> thinking about this trip exhausts and deflates me
> I've journeyed alone so many times
> but it meets my need for a salary
> and accords with my interest in eremitic realms
> cut off henceforth from dust and noise
> surely I'll find what brings my heart joy
> although I lack a panther's guise
> I will disappear at last into the misty southern peaks

> 江路西南永， 歸流東北鶩。 天際識歸舟， 雲中辨江樹。
> 旅思倦搖搖， 孤遊昔已屢。 既歡懷祿情， 復協滄州趨。
> 囂塵自茲隔， 賞心於此遇。 雖無玄豹姿， 終隱南山霧。

Hsieh has been identified with Hsuancheng and its mist-shrouded peaks ever since. In fact, he is still referred to as Hsieh Hsuancheng. More than fifty of his surviving poems, or one-third, were written during the two years he served here. It was the highpoint of his far-too-short life. While he may not have been a panther, he *was* able to disappear into the surrounding hills.

My first stop was the place where he lived. It was at the top of a very small hill overlooking one of the two rivers that flowed through the city. One of the poems he wrote there, "Scenes from My Lofty Study" 高齋視事, outlines his daily work of overseeing local affairs, work that began as soon as he woke up:

As the sun breaks through the winter fog
traces of snow glitter on the mountain
villages by the river are a blur
and yet every tree is distinct
I throw on my robe and wash my face
sit at my desk then pick up a brush
I prefer simple fare to a banquet
enough room to turn around to a mansion
worrying about the country is a waste of time
the craziness I excuse here is never the same
if I could just clear a path to a hut
and get rid of these cares and troubles

餘雪映青山，　寒霧開白日。　暖暖江村見，　離離海樹出。
披衣就清盥，　憑軒方秉筆。　列俎歸單味，　連駕止容膝。
空為大國憂，　紛詭諒非一。　安得掃蓮徑，　銷吾愁與疾。

Like his famous uncle, Hsieh felt drawn to the mountains. His uncle's pursuit of the eremitic life had doubtlessly been on his mind for some time, as had the ideal of simple living represented by T'ao Yuan-ming. Although the Lofty Study where Hsieh experienced such inspiration disappeared long ago, the townspeople built a structure on the site in his honor and have referred to it ever since as Hsiehtiao Tower.

It took maybe five minutes to get there from the train station. The hill on which it stood was more of a mound, and the tower itself was modest, a two-story structure with one of those roofs that looked as if it were about to fly away with the rest of the building. In the park that surrounded the hill I stopped to look at Hsieh's statue. It was sculpted from a single monolith and depicted the poet lounging and gazing into the distance while holding a cup of wine he looked on the verge of spilling – such was his rapture. Past the statue, I walked up a long flight of steps to the tower's entrance.

I noticed a blanket someone was sunning on the railing of the second story. At the entrance I asked a group of men playing cards about it. One of the men said it was his. Taking care of the tower was his retirement job. When I asked what was on the second floor, he shook his head and told me no one was allowed up there. I said I was hoping to see the view Hsieh once enjoyed. At the mention of Hsieh, he relented, but cautioned me that the stairs were treacherous and in need of repair. He was right, but I was careful.

The second floor was packed with decorations used for civic celebrations. I squeezed through them to the balcony that faced north. One of the many poems Hsieh wrote from that very spot was "Looking Out from the Rear of My Study" 後齋回望:

> From this high up I can see in all directions
> from the window I can make out a robe and a belt
> a mountain in the clouds
> a river beyond the plains
> summer foliage forming a curtain
> autumn lotus leaves turning into a canopy
> but whenever I look toward the capital
> my heart is like a flag in the wind

高軒瞰四野，臨牖眺襟帶。望山白雲裏，望水平原外。
夏木轉成帷，秋荷漸如蓋。鞏洛常睠然，搖心似懸旆。

Hsieh may have been glad to be here and hopeful of clearing a path to a hut, but when he looked out from his study, he felt caught between the mountains and the not-so-distant capital. It was a contradiction he never lived long enough to resolve. I was hoping to see Chingting Mountain from the balcony. It was Hsieh's favorite view and appears in many of his poems. But all I saw was a curtain of green. I went back down and thanked the caretaker. When I got back to the car, I asked the driver to take me to the mountain.

Chingtingshan was only five kilometers away, and Chaoting North Road got us there in ten minutes. Chaoting was the old name for the mountain. It was changed to Chingting in the third century to avoid using the same character as an emperor's name. When we neared the turnoff for the mountain, I asked the driver to go a bit farther and to stop along the Shuiyang River. Travelers in the past said that was the best place to view the mountain. When we found a suitable spot, I walked over to the river, then turned around. The view had changed. All I could see were cranes loading gravel and sand from river barges into dump trucks. We returned to the road and entered the parking lot at the mountain's base. After paying a modest admission fee, we started up the main trail. I say "we" because the driver was intent on enjoying the day as much as I was. And we weren't alone. It was Friday, a Friday in spring, and the sun was shining.

As we started out, we passed a huge statue of Li Pai. Chingtingshan was also Li Pai's favorite mountain. Off to the side were trails to a Buddhist monastery and a pair of stupas, but we ignored them and stayed on the main trail, which passed acres upon acres of manicured hillsides. The mountain was famous for its tea. We also walked past several large rocks engraved with Li Pai's poems with the characters painted green. On one of them, of course, was "Sitting Alone on Chingting Mountain" 獨坐敬亭山:

Flocks of birds disappear into the distance
lone clouds wander away
who never tires of my company
only Chingting Mountain

眾鳥高飛盡，孤雲獨去閒。相看兩不厭，隻有敬亭山。

Not only was Chingtingshan Li Pai's favorite mountain, Hsuancheng was his favorite town. He kept coming back. Altogether, he lived here during seven periods of exile and/or imperial disdain. As we continued up the trail, the crowds thinned out. After thirty minutes we found ourselves alone at Sitting Alone Pavilion, built in honor of Li Pai's poem. Chingtingshan wasn't high as mountains go, just over 300 meters, but the pavilion provided good views of the mountain and of the town he loved best.

After catching my breath, I decided I had seen enough. I told the driver it was time to head down. When we got back to his car, I asked him to drive back to town via Chingting Road, the traditional route people took between the city's North Gate and the mountain. As we drove along, I kept looking for something, but something that wasn't there. Both sides of the road were part of a massive construction project involving the entire northern part of Hsuancheng. My driver said it was all destined to become T'ang Dynasty International City. What I was looking for was Lord Hsieh's Pavilion, where Hsieh T'iao's parting with Fan Yun (451–503) brought both men to tears. Li Pai also found it a heartbreaking place, as is clear in "Lord Hsieh's Pavilion" 谢公亭:

The place where Lord Hsieh said goodbye
everything here makes me sad
the departing travelers the moon in the sky
the deserted mountain the current in the stream
the flowers by the pond the longer spring days
the bamboo outside the window the sounds of autumn nights
today and the past are connected
in this song about a journey long ago

謝公離別處，風景每生愁。客散青天月，山空碧水流。
池花春映日，窗竹夜鳴秋。今古一相接，長歌懷舊遊。

My driver had never heard of Lord Hsieh's Pavilion. Neither had any of the people we asked. The pavilion used to be where everyone in Hsuancheng said goodbye, not only poets. Now it wasn't even a memory. I gave up and asked the driver to take me to Tangtu. I wanted to say a proper goodbye to Li Pai. I had been following him since I began this pilgrimage, and it was time for one last drink. I was glad I opted for a taxi. It spared me from leapfrogging there by train. We took the expressway and were at the Tangtu exit in less than an hour.

Li Pai spent his last two years going back and forth between Hsuancheng and Nanking, the same as Hsieh T'iao. When he finally became too ill to travel, he took refuge in Tangtu, where his uncle, Li Yang-ping, was magistrate. Li Pai died there the following year at the age of sixty-one. The story that circulated not long after his death was that he drowned while trying to embrace the moon in the nearby Yangtze. This was such a perfect story, everyone believed it. But during his last months, Li Pai was too ill to get out of bed. Fortunately, his uncle was a man of considerable literary ability and became his nephew's literary executor. It was Li Yang-ping who was responsible for the first collection of Li Pai's surviving work, which included over a thousand poems.

From the expressway exit it was only a kilometer to the grave, which was in a park-like setting near the western foot of Chingshan. When he died, in 762, Li Pai was originally buried several kilometers farther west, on Lungshan. One hundred fifty years later his remains were moved in accordance

Left: Li Pai's "Sitting Alone on Chingting Mountain" on Chingting Mountain

with his wishes to the foot of Chingshan. No matter how many times I've visited his grave, I keep forgetting to ask why he wasn't buried here in the first place.

The parking lot had big expectations. There was space for a hundred buses and cars, yet only two vehicles besides ours were there. I found that odd. The sun was shining. It was even warm. Tangtu, though, wasn't Hsuancheng, and the grave was in the countryside. Over the years it had become a park with ponds, bridges, exhibition halls, and gardens. After paying a small admission fee, I strolled through the grounds and ended up at the exhibition hall at the rear of the park. One of the display cases contained several bricks from the original grave, and the walls were covered with paintings recounting the events of Li Pai's final years — such as him lying in bed dreaming of the life of a knight-errant he wished he had lived. Despite his fame as a poet, he never relinquished his desire to right wrongs with his sword as well as with his brush. Poetry was never enough for Li Pai, though he thereby righted more wrongs than he ever could have with a sword.

At the rear of the hall, I walked through a doorway into the enclosed garden that surrounded his tomb and sat on a stone bench near his grave. The first time I visited was in 1991, with Finn Wilcox and Steve Johnson. We were sitting on the very same bench when I opened my copy of Li Pai's poems and read one to Finn and Steve. We were the only people there, so I didn't mind reading the Chinese out loud then trying to translate it on the spot. Before I'd finished, two dozen Japanese filed in and lined up in front of Li Pai's grass-covered tomb. It was like a military formation. We stood up and moved out of the way, not knowing what to think. One of the men then approached the tombstone and lit candles and incense. Once he rejoined his colleagues they began singing Li Pai's poems in unison. We discovered later they were members of a society, in Japan, devoted to the study of T'ang poetry. Even more remarkable was that they sang his poems in the ancient T'ang dialect.

While the candles and incense were still burning, the society's leader concluded their performance with a solo. He sang Li Pai's last poem, "Facing the End" 臨終哥, in which Li compares himself to a mythical bird called the P'eng, the spirit set free. He also alludes in this poem to the Chinese belief that the sun rises behind a huge tree, and to the story that Confucius burst into tears when he learned a unicorn had been captured. The form and irregular lines of his final work recall Ch'u Yuan and are a testament to Li Pai's

Right: Li Pai's grave

determination to end his life with a poem, even though he was clearly out of breath:

Soaring above the world's horizon
the P'eng's strength failed halfway to Heaven
I had enough wind for ten thousand generations
but my robe caught on the Sunrise Tree
I leave it behind for whoever finds it
Confucius is dead who'll cry for me

大鵬飛兮振八裔，中天摧兮力不濟。餘風激兮萬世，游扶桑兮掛左袂。
後人得之傳此，仲尼亡兮誰為出涕。

The singer's voice cracked at that last line, and the strangest thing happened: the sky began to cry. The entire group then bowed and filed out. Finn, Steve, and I were sitting on the grass by the grave. It was a gentle rain and actually felt good. We had a beer with us, so we each took a swig, then I got up and poured the rest over Li Pai's tombstone.

This time I was alone and had something stronger. The tomb designer had thoughtfully included a narrow trough on top of the tombstone. I hadn't seen it on my earlier visit and decided it would make a better receptacle than my little cups. However, someone had been there before me and must have emptied a whole bottle of white lightning in it. I added a couple shots of rye, but I doubt they made much of an impact. The smell of the Chinese spirits was overpowering.

I walked back to the taxi and asked the driver to head back toward the expressway. Li Pai had asked to be buried on Chingshan to be near his hero, Hsieh T'iao, whose country retreat was on the other side of the mountain. When we reached the expressway, we drove under it. A kilometer or two later, where what looked like a Buddhist stupa rose to our left, we turned north onto a cement road. The stupa turned out to be a mine shaft. Whatever was being mined, it was a big-money operation. Half a kilometer later, we turned right onto a dirt road that circled behind the mine, then began switchbacking our way up the eastern part of Chingshan. It was steep going, and my driver considered giving up several times. At my urging, he persevered, and I was glad he did. When we arrived at the site of Hsieh's old home, the car was the only thing out of breath.

In the course of his frequent travels between Nanking and Hsuan-cheng, Hsieh T'iao concluded this was the most beautiful place he had ever seen. It was also part of the region over which he was governor, and he built a villa here. It was halfway up the mountain and overlooked the Chingshan River. During his term of office, he spent more time here than he did in Hsuan-cheng, which was the prerogative of a governor, as opposed to a magistrate.

When Hsieh T'iao's assignment ended in 496, so did his life on the mountain. He was sent to far-off Hunan province to convey the emperor's respects to Mount Hengshan. One lesson I picked up in the army was to *not* learn how to do something unless it was absolutely necessary. Sooner or later, you'll be asked to do it. One's chances of survival increased with anonymity and incompetence – at least they did in the army I was in. Hsieh wasn't in the army, and he was famous for his hymns. Hence, he was the man the emperor chose to present the royal praises to the mountain that would later become China's Southern Sacred Peak. It was a long trip, and it didn't do him or the emperor much good. By the time Hsieh returned to Nanking, the emperor had died, and Hsieh was soon caught up in the aftermath of succession. When he refused to join a group of men plotting to replace the new ruler, they feared he would report them. So they took the initiative and charged him with treason. Hsieh was imprisoned in Nanking and died there the following year.

Hsieh T'iao shrine on Chingshan

No one seems to know what happened to his body, and there's no evidence of a grave in or near Nanking. Most people who care about such things think he was buried near his Chingshan residence, which was apparently why the people of Tangtu turned his home into a shrine.

As I got out of the taxi and walked up the dirt trail, it became clear that things here had changed. The shrine was now just one small building among half a dozen Buddhist shrine halls constituting Chingshan Temple. In the course of poking my head into the halls, I met the abbess. She was eighty-two, and she had lived here thirty-two years. Her name was Sheng-ying. She invited me to stay for lunch, but I told her I normally skipped that meal when traveling. Surprisingly, she understood. She agreed with my reasoning: lunch slows a person down and leads to quests for toilets that are not always easy to find. When I asked about Hsieh's grave, she said people had looked all over the mountain for it, but no one had ever found it.

She then led me to the poet's shrine. It was a small building wedged between two new Buddhist halls. The side rooms were being used for storage, but the central room still served its ancient function. It was as big as my bedroom at home, about ten by ten, and consisted of three kneeling-cushions and an altar with a portrait of Hsieh carved in relief on stone. He was flanked by half a dozen small statues representing members of the Taoist and Buddhist pantheons. On either side of the altar was a couplet: "Every seed bears a fruit" 有因必有果 and "What has no beginning has no end" 無始更無終. And above his head were the words: "May the weather be good and the harvest abundant" 風調雨順, 五谷豐登.

Given the religious aura of the place, I kept the whiskey in my bag. After three bows before the altar, I thanked Sheng-yin and said goodbye. On the way back to the taxi, I walked by the pond where devotees released fish and turtles to gain merit. Hsieh was responsible for digging the pond, which was originally quite small. Like everything else around his old home, it had been expanded. In the absence of a grave, it seemed like the most appropriate place for an offering, and I wasn't the only one who thought so. I was preceded in that regard by Li Pai, who left "Lord Hsieh's Home" 謝公宅 instead of whiskey:

As sunlight disappears from Chingshan
Lord Hsieh's home seems forlorn

Left: Altar inside Hsieh T'iao shrine

no one talking in his bamboo grove
the moon shining on his pond in vain
his deserted courtyard full of last year's weeds
his abandoned well covered with moss
only the unrestrained breeze
still rises from his mountain spring

青山日將暝，寂寞謝公宅。竹裏無人聲，池中虛月白。
荒庭衰草遍，廢井蒼苔積。惟有清風閑，時時起泉石。

Hsieh T'iao, like Li Pai, was a man who felt the wind under his wings. In addition to hymns for imperial occasions, he composed hymns for himself. While the perfume of my offering rose to the heavens, I intoned his "My Prince Is Traveling" 王孫遊, which was inspired by Ch'u Yuan's "Summoning a Hermit" 招隱士 ("My prince is traveling and hasn't returned / spring grass is growing and spreading everywhere" 王孫遊兮不歸，春草生兮萋萋):

Green grass is spreading like fine silk thread
even ordinary trees are decked out in pink
it doesn't matter you haven't returned
by the time you do spring will be gone

綠草蔓如絲，雜樹紅英發。無論君不歸，君歸芳已歇。

It was the Ides of March, and the sweet scent of spring was, indeed, fading. After toasting Hsieh and pouring what remained into the pond, I returned to the taxi. Half an hour later, the driver dropped me off at Tangtu's new East Bus Station. Two hours later, I was ensconced in the New Century Hotel, just down the street from the Nanking train station. My room looked south across Hsuanwu Lake. The court that imprisoned Hsieh Junior and executed Hsieh Senior was somewhere beneath the grass on the lake's far shore. I poured a shot of rye for myself for a change and congratulated both men on outliving their judges and executioners by 1,500 years. Poetry, it turns out, has uses poets seldom imagine.

I began the day with Wang An-shih, again. That made twice in three days. Once Wang left the family home near Linchuan, Nanking became his home away from home. It was also where he retired. I was hoping to visit the place where he lived and the adjacent mountain that inspired so many of his poems. But I had a ticket on an eleven o'clock train, so it was going to be a quick visit. I checked out of the New Century before eight and flagged down the first taxi I saw. I showed the driver a map on which I'd highlighted a small triangle of land at the northeast corner of the city. While he was looking at it, I told him I hoped he could find a way past the guards.

Wang An-shih first came to Nanking in 1037, when he was seventeen. He accompanied his parents when his father was appointed the city's controller-general, the man in charge of overseeing the man in charge, namely, the magistrate – sort of like Hsieh T'iao serving as governor and not magistrate of Hsuan-cheng. When Wang's father died two years later, Wang stayed in Nanking to be near his father's grave. Wang put his time to good use. When the obligatory three-year period of mourning was over, he took the civil service exams and placed fourth. He had his choice of jobs. However, rather than seek a position at the Sung court in Kaifeng, Wang requested an appointment in the provinces. And he stayed in the provinces for twenty years, serving as magistrate of Yangchou, Ningpo, Chienshan, and Changchou.

He resigned the last of these posts when his mother died, and returned to Nanking for another period of mourning. When that was over, he decided it was time to do what he had been thinking about for twenty years. In his provincial posts he had been testing economic reforms, and he hoped to see them carried out nationwide. His proposals won over the emperor, and within a few years he rose to the post of prime minister. Even with the backing of the emperor, Wang met intense opposition from the entrenched elite. Why would anyone loan money to farmers at a lower rate when they could demand more? And why should the state adhere to a budget? And why should military appointments not be based on relationships? For all Wang's good intentions, he was outmaneuvered by his enemies and even briefly imprisoned. The best the emperor could do was to have Wang released and allow him to return to Nanking as a sort of magistrate emeritus. The year was 1075.

Wang bought fifty acres near the foot of Chungshan, not far from his parents' graves, and he built a residence there. Because his property was halfway between the city wall and Chungshan, he called his place Halfway Garden.

The name was still there on the map I showed the taxi driver. I explained to him that the site was now part of the College of Naval Intelligence, and I suspected access would be difficult. He understood the problem, but, surprisingly, he was game.

After the driver worked his way into the area still known as Halfway Garden, he drove around looking for an entrance that might not be guarded. But every lane he tried ended at a wall, and we realized we had no choice. He drove to the college's main entrance, where there was the customary barred gate and uniformed guard. The guard looked almost cute in his sailor cap with twin tassels hanging in back. But he didn't act cute. He ordered me to leave immediately and ignored my request to call someone higher up to discuss the matter further.

My driver, though, wasn't willing to give up. Since both the college and Wang's property were just inside the expanded Ming-dynasty city wall, he drove me to a section of the wall where there were steps that led to the top. He thought maybe I would have a view of the site where Wang once lived. It seemed like a great idea. I had seen pictures on the Internet of a building that housed Wang An-shih memorabilia. There were also several pavilions and, of course, a garden. Once I reached the top of the steps I saw people walking and jogging on the section of wall to the south. It overlooked a park and was itself part of the park. However, the section to the north, the section I needed

End of the trail for the author on Nanking's Ming-dynasty city wall

to traverse, ended at a guardhouse. And beyond the guardhouse was a forest that had formed on the detritus that had accumulated over the centuries. It didn't look promising, but I walked over to the guardhouse anyway. It turned out the guardhouse wasn't manned by sailors but by two park employees. They let me continue but warned me to be careful. Beyond the guardhouse, I snaked my way through a hole in a wall built to prevent people from doing what I was doing. I then worked my way across an immense pile of garbage. Why, I wondered, would anyone dump garbage on *top* of the wall? But I didn't let this particular mystery slow me down. Beyond the pile, there was a trail that led through the forest. I began to think maybe this walking-on-the-wall idea would work. However, after 300 meters, I came to another wall – one I couldn't get past. In the middle of it was a metal door. It was locked, and clearly posted were the words "Restricted Military Area." Usually I ignored that sort of thing, but there was no way around. What I needed was a ladder or a rope with a hook on the end. Lacking either, I had no choice but to give up. I walked back through the forest, over the pile of garbage, through the hole in the wall, and thanked the men at the guardhouse for letting me have a look.

Wang spent the final decade of his life just beyond my reach. The last poem he wrote there was "One Day Home" 一日歸行, which he wrote the day his wife died:

> I ran after food and clothes when we were broke
> a hundred days gone and one day home
> simple pleasures were an endless struggle
> our hope was to have some support in old age
> in this bleakest of rooms your shroud now hangs
> in the faint light of midnight the crying has died down
> where are the voice and the smile I once knew
> will we meet again underneath the ground

賤貧奔走食與衣，百日奔走一日歸。平生歡意苦不盡，正欲老大相因依。
空房蕭瑟施總帷，青燈半夜哭聲稀。音容想像今何處，地下相逢果是非。

Heartbroken, Wang couldn't bear to remain in the home he and his wife had shared. He gave Halfway Garden to his monk friends, and they turned it into Paoning Monastery. Meanwhile, he bought a small courtyard residence along one the canals in the southern part of the city, near Inner Bridge, and stayed there until his own death, which wasn't long in coming. He was buried in his old garden next to his wife and his parents. Over the years, this was the place both friends and enemies came to pay their respects. Three hundred years later, the founder of the Ming dynasty established Nanking as his capital and decided he needed a bigger palace. So he expanded the city walls to include Wang's former property. That was when Wang's remains and those of his wife and parents were dug up and reinterred at Moon Pond, where I'd parted from him two days ago.

During that last decade, when Wang lived at Halfway Garden and before his wife died, he wore a path between his house and Chungshan, sometimes on foot, sometimes on his donkey. Since the mountain wasn't a restricted area, I asked my driver to take me there. From just outside the Ming wall, we drove up Mingling Road, which more or less followed Wang's likely route. One of his favorite spots was Plum Blossom Valley, which consisted of a crescent-shaped lake in front of a mountainside covered with plum trees. And they were in bloom! When most Chinese think of plum flowers – me, too, for that matter – they think of shimmering white petals on branches decked with snow. These are the plum trees that bloom during the Lunar New Year, when winter is ending and spring is beginning. The trees in Plum Blossom Valley were blooming in mid-March, and they weren't white. They were every shade of red and pink. There wasn't a white blossom in sight. Wang noticed this too in "Red Plum Flowers" 紅梅:

> They don't open until the middle of spring
> mostly because they don't like the cold
> northerners mistake them at first
> thinking it's apricot flowers they see

春半花纔發，多應不奈寒。北人初未識，渾作杏花看。

The driver said there were 400,000 plum trees on Chungshan. That was a lot of plum flowers. Despite the overwhelming beauty of the shimmering, red-stained lake and the hillside it reflected, we drove on. I had another destination in mind. A minute later, we reached the entrance to the section of the mountain where the first Ming emperor was buried. The place I was looking for was near his tomb. I walked through the gate – admission was free for seniors – while the driver waited in the parking lot.

It was only nine o'clock, so I had plenty of time. Still, I hurried up the pedestrian roadway known as Wengchung Road. It was the "spirit way," or path to the emperor's tomb, and was lined with larger-than-life stone statues of generals, officials, and beasts. When I didn't see any signs pointing to what I was looking for, I asked an old man. It turned out he visited the mountain every day. He said the place I was looking for was just beyond a small lake where a few hardy souls went swimming year round, even in winter. Sure enough, past the lake and a forest of cassia trees and bamboo, I saw the black-tiled roofs and white facades I was looking for.

Formerly Tinglin Temple, it was now called Tinglin Villa to distinguish it from another temple in the city that had taken over the monastery's name. Tinglin was Wang's favorite haunt, and he often lived here for extended periods. He called the temple his "study." As I crossed a stream and approached the entrance, I imagined this was the setting he had in mind for "Events on Chungshan" 鍾山既事:

> A stream winds silently through the bamboo
> flowering plants to the west reveal the softness of spring
> all day below thatched eaves I sit and face this scene
> the mountain is quieter when birds don't sing

澗水無聲繞竹流，竹西花草弄春柔。茅簷相對坐終日，一鳥不鳴山更幽。

Wang was responding here to a poet who wrote, "The mountain is quieter when birds sing." I've gone back and forth as to whose line I like better.

As I entered the "villa," I was hoping to find something I hadn't seen before. The villa was, after all, also known as the Wang An-shih Memorial Hall. In the first hall there was an exhibition, but for a literary figure named Liu Hsieh (465–520), author of China's first work on literary aesthetics, *The Literary Mind and the Carving of Dragons*. Reading *about* literature, though, has never appealed to me. Give me a poem, please. Liu lived at Tinglin Temple for the last twenty years of his life and made extensive use of its library in compiling his work on poetics—hence the exhibition. The year before he died he became a monk, and he was buried in the bamboo grove just west of the monastery. His grave, though, was gone, as were any traces of the monastery.

In the remaining halls I kept looking for something—though, in truth, I didn't know what. There were, of course, dozens of Wang's poems carved onto slate tablets along the corridors—each in a different style of calligraphy—and

I paused to read half a dozen of them. But I was looking for something else. I finally found it when a returned to the entrance. When I first walked in, I turned left but should have turned right.

As Wang lay dying and friends came to pay their respects, he asked an artist friend to paint a portrait of him riding his donkey. The donkey had enabled Wang to continue making visits to the mountain after he became too ill to walk. The artist was Li Kung-lin (1049–1106), one of the greatest painters of the Sung. But by the time Li finished the portrait and brought it to show his friend, Wang had died. The painting was hung beside Wang's coffin while his body lay in state. And here it was in his memorial hall, *Lord Wang of Ching Riding His Donkey*. Unfortunately, the glass that protected it made it impossible to photograph. In any case, it was probably a copy. Li Kung-lin's paintings sold for millions of US dollars. But whether or not it was the original didn't matter. I had found what I was looking for and conveyed my silent greeting – and thanks. Since the memorial hall was not the appropriate place, I walked back outside and poured a shot of rye into the stream that flowed past Wang's "study." After having a shot myself, I hurried to my taxi. Fortunately, the driver had the good sense to go down the mountain the back way. It was Saturday, and the roads were jammed. But I made it to the train station sufficiently early that I was able to exchange my ticket on the eleven o'clock for one on the ten-thirty express.

It was another bullet train. It left on time, and the few stops it made were brief. I was bound for Suchou, the Venice of China. The appellation was appropriate: we must have crossed a dozen canals on the way there. We were, after all, just upstream from the Yangtze delta where most of the water in China collects before heading out to sea. It was the land of fish and rice and freshwater pearls and, in the case of Suchou, gardens. The wealth, though, that made Suchou's gardens possible didn't come from fish or rice or pearls but from silk. In fact, pretty much everything in Suchou came from silk, and always has. Archaeologists have found signs of silk production there dating back 5,000 years. It was about that time Lei Tsu, the wife of the Yellow Emperor, was said to have discovered silk when a silkworm cocoon fell from a mulberry tree into her teacup. She caught hold of a filament and began unreeling. Over the centuries, Suchou's combination of weather and waterways made it the center of silk production in China. The Romans loved Suchou silk. Of course, someone had to make the silk, and it was from the sweat of those someones that Suchou prospered, as we hear in "Silk Spinners Ballad" 繅絲行:

When wheat is green and barley yellow
when the sun finally shines but the air is still cool
all the women shout it's time to get to work
through doorways you can smell the boiled cocoons in back
spinning wheels all squeak as if rain were on the way
our cocoons are fat and their threads go on forever
who had time this year to weave something for themselves
we're off to sell our silk tomorrow at West Gate

小麥青青大麥黃，　原頭日出天色涼。姑婦相呼有忙事，　舍後煮蠶門前香。
繰車嘈嘈似風雨，　蠶厚絲長無斷縷。今年那暇織絹著，　明日西門賣絲去。

Silk was the backbone of the city's — and to a large extent the nation's — economy. To make sure there was enough to meet demand, people in this part of China were required to pay their taxes in silk. Everyone either made silk or bought it from someone who did.

The poet who sympathized with the plight of these someones in the above poem was Fan Ch'eng-ta (1126–1193). Fan, not silk, was my reason for stopping in Suchou. When I exited the station, I hired a driver from the taxi queue to take me to Fan's house at Stone Lake. It was ten kilometers to the south, at the foot of Shangfangshan. The driver took the expressway, and we were there in minutes.

Since it was the weekend, and since both the mountain and the lake were prime recreation areas, I asked my driver to wait for me. Just past the entrance to Shangfangshan Park was a line of people waiting for the cable car to the top of the mountain. Fortunately, Fan's home wasn't at the top of the mountain. I turned right and walked through the grounds of Chihping Temple then followed a trail that led to Stone Lake Cottage, where poets once came for get-togethers and inspiration in ancient times. Fan's house was just below.

He wasn't born here, though. He was born in the old part of Suchou to a family that was fairly well off. At seventeen, when he was newly married and about to begin preparations for the civil service exams, his parents died within months of each other, and his life suddenly changed. Being the eldest son, he had to supervise the education of his two younger brothers, and arrange suitable marriages for his two sisters, all while supporting everyone with what remained of their parents' estate. He was twenty-eight before he was able to take the exams that opened the door to government service.

Fan passed, and his career finally began the next year with a series of minor posts. Like Wang An-shih, Fan was a hands-on administrator. After an assignment along the coast, he returned to the capital and reported on the reforms he had instituted to ease the tax burdens on the people. The emperor was impressed and ordered similar reforms throughout the empire. Suddenly Fan was an official held in high regard, which led to his being chosen to head an important diplomatic mission to negotiate changes to the peace treaty between the Southern and Northern Sung dynasties.

When Fan arrived in Beijing, he broke protocol by asking the Northern Sung emperor – *in person* – to consider changes to the treaty. The emperor was so incensed he threatened to have Fan executed for his effrontery. Fan, however, offered to die right then and there if the emperor refused to hear his request. Instead of having Fan executed, the Jurchen ruler said he wished he had such officials in his own service. Fan was hailed as a hero upon his return to Hangchou, and he has been praised ever since as a great patriot. Stronger than his patriotism, though, was his concern for the human condition, which was not exactly flourishing under the Jurchens, as we can see in his poem "Chingyuan Inn" 清遠店, to which he added this preface: "In front of an inn in Tinghsing County, there was a servant girl with the characters for 'escapee' on both cheeks. She said that her owner tattooed them there himself and that no one would have stopped him had he killed her" 定興縣中客邸前, 幽婢兩頰刺逃走二字, 云是主家私自黥涅, 雖殺之不禁.

A sweat-drenched servant girl follows a felt-curtained carriage
she says her father and brothers live down along the Huai
killing slaves or servants isn't questioned here by officials
tattooing words on their faces is still considered light

女僮流汗逐氈軺, 云在淮鄉有父兄。屠婢殺奴官不問, 大書黥面罪猶輕。

For decades, the silk-wearing Chinese and felt-wearing Jurchens contested the Huai River watershed between the Yangtze and Yellow Rivers, and the Jurchens enslaved the people who lived in the areas they conquered. The girl's father and brothers were luckier.

For his statecraft, Fan was rewarded with a series of senior posts at court, but his experience in North China only steeled his resolve to advocate a policy of confrontation with the Jurchens. This was not well received by a court bent on placating its enemy, and Fan was sent to the most distant parts of the empire: first to Kueilin in South China, then to Chengtu in the West. Being away from the constant intrigue at court was the best thing that could have happened to Fan. Rather than languishing, he flourished. He took advantage of his rustications to produce some of China's finest travel journals and geographical accounts. When he was finally summoned back to court, in 1177, he wanted nothing to do with the goings-on in Hangchou. He claimed illness and returned to the home he had made for himself at Stone Lake. He welcomed himself back with this poem, "On First Coming Back to Stone Lake" 初歸石湖:

> The rising sun turns the morning fog shades of orange and green
> on the west bank of Hengtang and Yuehcheng Bridge to the east
> the upper halves of pedestrians bob above the flowering rice
> nesting egrets illuminate a sea of water chestnuts
> I trust my feet's ability to find my former paths
> but I'm startled when I meet neighbors who've grown old
> from the willow I once planted beside the arching bridge
> countless jade cicadas swarm across the sky

曉霧朝瞰紺碧烘，　橫塘西岸越城東。　行人半出稻花上，　宿鷺孤明菱葉中。
信腳自能知舊路，　驚心時復認鄰翁。　當時手種斜橋柳，　無數鳴蜩翠掃空。

From his home Fan could see Hengtang Dike to the north and also Yuehcheng Bridge, constructed only a year earlier. And right behind his house he had a mountain where he could go hiking whenever he wished. What more could he want? To be left alone would have been nice. But he was cajoled into coming out of retirement for three more years, and he accepted two high-level appointments, first as magistrate of Ningpo then as governor of the province in which the capital was located. The combination of political backstabbing and his own poor health, though, drove him back to Stone Lake in 1183. This time he didn't leave.

His old home was now a shrine. As I entered, Fan was sitting on a large rock, holding a book in his hand and staring off toward Yuehcheng Bridge. Over his head was a plaque bestowed on his residence by the emperor: Hall of the Long-Lived Oak. Fan planted all kinds of things here and wrote books about what he planted. He wrote books about plum trees, chrysanthemums, roses — even vegetables. He also left nearly 2,000 poems. Among his best-remembered verses is a series of sixty quatrains, "The Four Seasons of

Inspiration among Fields and Gardens" 四時田園雜興. Here are quatrains 4 and 6 from the section on summer:

> Plums are golden yellow and apricots are ripe
> the flowering wheat looks like snow and the rapeseed is nearly gone
> all day beyond the fence no one passes by
> dragonflies and butterflies are the only creatures moving

梅子金黃杏子肥，麥花雪白菜花稀。日長籬落無人過，唯有蜻蜓蛺蝶飛。

> Hoeing fields during the day or spinning hemp at night
> village boys and girls all have their chores
> those too young to know how to hoe or weave
> learn to plant melons in the shade of mulberry trees

晝出耘田夜績麻，村莊兒女各當家。童孫未解供耕織，也傍桑陰學種瓜。

The sculpture of Fan sitting in the shade of his own shrine hall was quite well done. I was impressed even more by the stone tablets on the surrounding walls carved with Fan's calligraphic rendering of his own poems—namely the "Fields and Gardens" series—a remarkable treasure to have survived so many wars and thieves. The caretaker told me that in addition to being an avid gardener and garden designer, Fan was one of the principal instigators of Suchou's garden craze, a craze that continues to attract millions of visitors to Suchou every year. His own garden was, of course, gone, but at least the spot where he lived had been preserved. Like many of the poets I had been visiting, Fan modeled himself on T'ao Yuan-ming. Like T'ao, he chose to live in the countryside, and, like T'ao, he made no attempt to idealize such a life. He even made fun of it, as in "Retired Living" 幽棲:

> I was lax about my attire even before I retired
> now the autumn heat anoints my skin with sweat
> carrying on conversations is something of a chore
> and dealing with household affairs doesn't always get done
> I eat dinner while the sun still lights my walls
> and I'm in bed before my window fills with stars

Fan Ch'eng-ta in the Hall of the Long-Lived Oak at Stone Lake

don't say an idle life is lived without desires
I'm counting the days hoping for one that's cool

幽棲先自嬾衣裳，秋暑薰肌汗似漿。對客緒言多勉強，謀家生事總荒唐。
蚤眠不待星當戶，晚飯常占日半墻。莫道閒中無外慕，朝朝屈指望新涼。

It was a realistic poem. The annual heat wave still renders Suchou motion-
less and gasping for air.

Having seen the treasures of Fan's shrine, I thanked the caretaker and
walked down to the lakeside to offer Fan and his poet pals a treat from Ken-
tucky. Afterward I returned to the park entrance to find my driver. The place
was mobbed. Dozens of people were looking for taxis back to town. I was
glad I'd kept mine waiting. I had one more stop on my itinerary, the saddle
between a pair of mountains just west of the old part of town. Connecting

Lingyenshan and Tienpingshan was a small ridge named Yangtienshan (or Ma'anshan). That was where Fan was buried. Although his grave had disappeared, I wanted to visit the site.

Like Shangfangshan, Tienpingshan had become a recreation area, complete with an office where people hired guides. While my driver waited outside I went in and asked whether anyone could direct me to the saddle. They pointed me back the way I had come to a side lane that bordered the recreation area's southern boundary.

I conveyed their directions to my driver, and a few minutes later we parked outside a yurt. It belonged to a Mongolian family who rented horses. They knew nothing about Fan Ch'eng-ta but said there were hundreds of graves on the hillside. From the yurt, we followed a gravel road that ended at a dirt parking lot. I got out and continued on foot past a workshed where several men were making tombstones. The grave-making business was still going strong. I stopped and asked one of the men whether he knew anything about Fan Ch'eng-ta's grave. To my surprise, the man said the grave had been dug up during the Cultural Revolution and moved to Suchou's Hanshan Temple, to prevent its destruction by Red Guards. I should have been happy to hear this, but I doubted his story. Hsing-k'ung, the current abbot of Hanshan Temple, had shown me around the grounds on two occasions. He was a poet himself and would have mentioned anything to do with poetry. And yet, I had to wonder why the stonecutter had such a clear memory.

Despite my misgivings, I thanked him for the information and continued on until I reached a dirt trail along the fence separating the recreation area from the graves. Three women were clearing brush. When I explained my purpose, they dropped their sickles and led me farther up the slope to where the oldest graves were located. I walked past hundreds, some dating back 500 years to the Ming dynasty, but nothing from the Sung.

Even though I didn't find Fan's grave, I *did* come across the grave of Ta-hsiu (1870–1932). At the time of his death, he was the abbot of Hanshan Temple. Buddhists throughout China still recite his teaching: "It's not bigger than you or smaller than you, it's not inside you or outside you / work on yourself, know yourself, it's all up to you" 無大無小無內外 / 自休自了自安排. One can never be reminded too often of the obvious. In addition to being a Zen master, Ta-hsiu was also a master of the one-string zither.

Since his grave was in such great condition, and since there was a large altar in front for offerings, I decided this was the perfect place to send word to Fan how much I loved his poems. The ladies who led me there looked on with interest as I filled a single cup with rye. I figured Ta-hsiu would appreciate

Grave of Zen Master Ta-hsiu on Suchou's Lingyenshan

the joke: one-cup Zen. I decided to let Hanshan Temple's departed abbot act as my intermediary to the spirit world, just in case there was some truth to the stonecutter's tale.

I only stayed long enough to send my message. I had a bus to catch as usual. After drinking what was left of my offering, I said goodbye to Ta-hsiu, Fan Ch'eng-ta, and my three bemused onlookers. I walked back down and asked the taxi driver to take to me to whichever bus station had buses that went to Huchou. He took me to the new South Station, and I was on a Huchou-bound bus in less than thirty minutes. The bus driver told me we would be there in one hundred minutes, and exactly one hundred minutes later we arrived. On the way I called my friend Ta-ch'a, and he was waiting at the station. Before I could stop him, he grabbed my bag then took me to a hotel on an island in the middle of the river that flowed through town. I went to bed early, listening to the water. I knew the next day was going to be a big day. Little did I know how big.

This was going to be a different kind of day, one in the company of friends who weren't yet dead. Martin Merz, who joined me earlier for my day with Hsueh T'ao, took another break from his shoe business in Hong Kong. I was also joined by Wu Chen, known to his friends as Ta-ch'a, or Big Tea, a tea aficionado and member of a tea network that extended throughout China.

I met him on a previous trip when I was taking some American friends to Hsiamushan south of Huchou, and halfway there the road was torn up. We parked our van at a barricade, and I walked ahead to find out whether there was some other way to the mountain. Ta-ch'a was advising the road crew about possible historical relics in the area where they were digging, and he and I struck up a conversation. It turned out he knew more about Hsiamushan than anyone I had ever met. What's more, he offered to guide us there by an alternate route. That was in 2011. This time, in addition to Martin and Ta-ch'a, our group included Ms. Chao Hsien, the editor-in-chief of the tea magazine *Haihsia Chatao*. She wanted to interview me later that day about my interest in tea.

I liked to start my days around eight o'clock, but on this occasion I wasn't really in charge. It was nearly ten when the taxi Ta-ch'a had hired arrived at the hotel. The four of us crowded in, and we headed south. When we reached the southern edge of the city we turned west onto Highway 306. Just past the 7 km marker, we turned south again, this time on a local road. As we did, we drove past a statue of Lu Yu (733–804), China's Tea Sage.

In 2011, Ta-ch'a led me and my companions to the nearby village of Shushan to visit Lu Yu's grave. After paying our respects to China's most famous tea master, we did the same at an adjacent grave that belonged to his best friend, the monk Chiao-jan (730–799). It was Lu Yu's work on Chiao-jan's tea farm that provided Lu Yu with the hands-on experience that formed the basis of his *Chaching*, or *Book of Tea*. Chiao-jan was a direct descendant of Hsieh Ling-yun and also a poet. Although he was a Zen monk, he saw himself more in the mold of T'ao Yuan-ming, as in this "Occasional Poem" 偶然:

> I hide my mind not my footprints
> I prefer to live around people
> if a place lacks trees I plant one in spring
> if there aren't any mountains I paint one

I've never regretted living near noise
the truth is present right here

隱心不隱蹟，卻欲住人寰。欠樹移春樹，無山看畫山。
居喧我未錯，真意在其間。

Ironically, the one Chiao-jan poem that made it into the anthology *Three Hundred Poems of the T'ang* is titled "Looking for Lu Yu, Finding Him Gone" 尋陸鴻漸不遇:

Your new home is inside the outer wall
but the path still winds through mulberry and hemp
the chrysanthemums you planted along your fence
haven't yet flowered this fall
when I knocked on your gate and the dog didn't bark
I asked your neighbor to the west
he said you were off in the mountains
and you never come back before sunset

移家雖帶郭，野徑入桑麻。近種籬邊菊，秋來未著花。
扣門無犬吠，欲去問西家。報道山中去，歸來每日斜。

Lu Yu liked to hike. It was part of his never-ending search for the best water. He discovered that the water he used to brew tea was just as important as the leaves and how they were processed. And so he roamed the mountains south of Huchou comparing springs. I was headed into the same mountains to visit someone who appreciated springwater just as much as Lu Yu but who *didn't* come back at sunset. His name was Shih-wu Ch'ing-kung (1272–1352), or Shih-wu (Stonehouse) for short. I had known him since 1982, the year I discovered his poems.

Like Chiao-jan, Stonehouse was a monk, but a monk who preferred solitude. He built a hut on Hsiamushan ten kilometers south of Chiao-jan's grave, and he lived there for thirty-five years. Hsiamushan wasn't that high — its summit was only 560 meters — but it was the highest mountain in the area, which was why there was a road to the top: it was a good place for a radar station.

Less than an hour after leaving Huchou, we arrived where the radar station used to be. My first time here was in 1991, when it was still a restricted

Grave of Lu Yu, China's Tea Sage

area. I was with my friends Finn and Steve, and within a minute of stepping out of our taxi, we were surrounded by soldiers holding rifles fixed with bayonets. I showed the officer in charge a copy of Stonehouse's poems and told him we were looking for where the monk lived. After the officer read a few of the poems, he waved the soldiers away, pulled out his machete, and led us into the bamboo. It was incredibly thick, but he hacked his way through, and we followed. Even with him leading the way, we had to struggle to move our arms and legs.

After about twenty minutes, we emerged at a small farmstead. We were covered with scratches and thought the officer might have led us through the bamboo as punishment for entering a restricted area. In truth, he had our best interests at heart. He pointed to the farmhouse and said that before the radar station was built, the farmhouse was the only structure on the mountain. Just then, the farmer who lived there appeared in the doorway and waved for us to come inside.

The farmer told us he had been living on the mountain for the past twenty years. He moved there shortly after the Red Guards chased the monks away. The farmhouse was all that remained of their temple, which itself was one of many incarnations of Stonehouse's original hut. Stonehouse often referred to a spring behind his hut, and the farmer showed it to us. It was still flowing, as it does in number 55 of Stonehouse's *Mountain Poems* 山居詩:

> The Way of the Dharma is too singular to copy
> but a well-hidden hut comes close
> I planted bamboo in front to form a screen
> from the rocks I led a spring into my kitchen
> gibbons bring their young to the cliffs when fruits are ripe
> cranes move their nests from the gorge when pines turn brown
> lots of idle thoughts occur during meditation
> I gather the deadwood for my stove

法道寥寥不可模，一菴深隱是良圖。門前養竹高遮屋，石上分泉直到廚。
猿抱子來崖果熟，鶴移巢去澗松枯。禪邊大有閒情緒，收拾乾柴向地爐。

The farmer invited us inside for a cup of tea. He lived there alone. His children had grown up, and his wife lived in the village at the foot of the mountain. He didn't have much to say the whole time we were there. Sitting on a stool just smiling and content with not talking, he reminded me of Stonehouse's number 183:

> I built my hut at the top of Hsia Summit
> plowing and hoeing make up my day
> half a dozen terraced fields
> two or three hermit neighbors
> I made a pond for the moon
> and sell wood to buy grain
> an old man with few schemes
> I've told you all that I own

結屋霞峰頭，耕鉏供日課。山田六七坵，道人三兩個。
開池放月來，賣柴糴米過。老子少機關，家私都說破。

Since that 1991 visit, the radar station had been replaced by Hsiawu Springs, a water-bottling plant. And the farmer's hut was a monastery once again, Yunlin Temple. In the interim, I had also learned that the mountain had two names. The northern summit, where we parked, is Hsiawushan — hence, Hsiawu Springs. Three hundred meters away, the southern summit, where the farmhouse and the temple were located, is called Hsiamushan. Since the southern summit is slightly higher, it got all the credit on maps. During his thirty-five years on the mountain, Stonehouse lived near both summits and used both names. Wherever he lived, he never regretted choosing a mountain hut over a monastery — as he says in number 18:

My meditation hut sits on rocks near the summit
clouds fly past and more clouds arrive
a waterfall hangs in space beyond the door
a mountain ridge rises like a wave in back
I drew three buddhas on a wall
I put a plum branch in a jar for incense
the fields down below might be level
but can't match a mountain home's freedom from dust

岳頂禪房枕石臺，　白雲飛去又飛來。門前瀑布懸空落，　屋後山巒起浪堆。
素壁淡描三世佛，　瓦瓶香浸一枝梅。下方田地雖平坦，　難及山家無點埃。

This time there were no soldiers. Ta-ch'a paid the driver and told us he had arranged for another taxi to take us down in the afternoon. He had also arranged for us to have lunch on the mountain and led us to a group of buildings where we met Mo Shih-ch'in, the woman whose plantation had made the mountain's tea famous. Her parents were cooking and said lunch wouldn't be ready for another hour. She suggested that we go for a walk. Since hiking around the summit was what I had in mind, that was what we did.

We walked back down the road a hundred meters to a sign for Hsiamushan Cemetery. Somewhere below were the graves of some of the monks who had lived on the mountain over the centuries, the first of whom was Stonehouse. On my earlier visits, I didn't know about the graveyard or about his second hut. I was looking forward to seeing both, and Ta-ch'a led the way.

There was no trail. We had to snake our way through thickets of bamboo, ease ourselves over rock ledges, and avoid getting tangled in the vines that covered everything. Ta-ch'a pointed out wild tea bushes, suggesting the ledges were man-made and the area was once a terraced tea orchard. After about 200 meters, we came to the gravesites. All that remained were broken stones half-buried beneath vines. Although no one had found the stupa that contained Stonehouse's cremated remains, the stones of which it was made must have been within a few feet of where we stood. He died shortly after he wrote this poem, number 114 in his *Mountain Poems:*

> Corpses don't stink in the mountains
> there's no need to bury them deep
> I might not have the fire of samadhi
> but enough wood to end this family line

青山不着臭屍骸，死了何須掘土埋。顧我也無三昧火，光前絕後一堆柴。

About fifty meters north of the graveyard was his second hut. That was where he died. While I was poking around the stones, thinking I might find something with Stonehouse's name on it, I stepped onto what looked like leaf-covered ground. My foot and lower leg disappeared into a hole, and I heard something snap. I tried to pull my foot out, but it was entangled by roots. When I finally managed to free it, my foot was pointing 45 degrees to the left of where it normally pointed. When I tried to walk on it the pain was excruciating, like nothing I'd ever experienced before. I sat on the ground and with both hands tried to straighten my foot—which seemed like the right thing to do at the time. When I did, the tendons along my leg popped like rubber bands in a model airplane when they're wound too tight. All I could do was sigh. At least it wasn't raining. Ta-ch'a had said heavy rain was in the forecast.

I shouted to Martin, who called Ta-ch'a and Ms. Chao over, and I explained to them what had happened. Something broke, and I couldn't walk. Ta-ch'a tried to call an ambulance on his cell phone, but the signal was too weak. He and Ms. Chao headed back up to the road to find a stronger signal, and Martin waited with me. Fortunately, I had

Stonehouse's second hut

my flask of Thomas H. Handy Holywater. Over the next hour I emptied all four ounces of its 128-proof contents. As I did, I explained to Martin how this was really no problem, just a minor detour on the pilgrim trail. I could still complete my journey. I would get a cast on my leg in Huchou then hire a taxi for the rest of the trip so I wouldn't have to deal with buses or trains. I could use crutches or even a wheelchair to visit the remaining places on my itinerary. I just blabbered on. I've always suffered from optimism. Now I was suffering from shock.

When the rye and the blabber ran out, I just lay there on the ground and stared at the sky. About ninety minutes after they'd gone, Ta-ch'a and Ms. Chao reappeared with two policemen. Soon after that, two medics arrived. Their ambulance, they said, was parked about 200 meters uphill. One of the medics found a stick and bandaged it to my leg to form a splint. Then he cut a vine and used it to lash me to their stretcher. In the meantime, four workers from Ms. Mo's tea factory appeared. Together, they began the ordeal of carrying me up to the road. Lying on my back, all I could see were the tops of trees just beginning to leaf out and branches of bamboo feathering a darkening sky that looked like it was about to rain.

As there was no trail, they had to carry me through the same bamboo thickets we had negotiated earlier and hoist me above the same ancient tea

Author awaiting transport to Huchou

terraces a meter or more high. Given the angle, the slipperiness of the slope, and my weight – the last time I checked, it was 205 pounds – it was very slow going. According to Martin, it looked like a caterpillar whose back legs couldn't get any traction. I winced with every movement. After nearly an hour they finally got me to the road and put me in the ambulance. Just then, it started to rain. I thought the gods were just amusing themselves and this was a dream.

The ride down the mountain made it clear it wasn't a dream. I was there, in this body, for every excruciating bump. I was still there an hour later, when we arrived at the Huchou Military Hospital. Ta-ch'a said it was the best hospital in Huchou. But after I was carried into the emergency room, the doctors there said they didn't treat foreigners. Back I went into the ambulance and off to the next hospital. It was now pouring, but at least I wasn't on the mountain. This time the ambulance turned on its siren, which made me feel better. As we worked our way through downtown traffic, I felt like a celebrity.

Finally, we arrived at the Huchou Central Hospital. After I paid for the ambulance, the ambulance medics turned me over to hospital medics, who took me to register and get X-rays. Once that was over, a doctor put a cast on my leg. The heat given off by the plaster provided the first relief I had felt from the pain, but it only lasted a few minutes. Then I was wheeled to the orthopedic ward, where I was given the last available bed, and it was in a two-person room. My luck was changing. The other patient was a man whose legs had been crushed by a truck. He had been in the ward for three months and expected to stay another three. While Ta-ch'a, Martin, and Ms. Chao chatted and waited for the doctor, all sorts of people came into the room – out of curiosity. While I lay on my back with my leg elevated on two large pillows, an IV was hooked up to my arm to introduce medications for inflammation and, I hoped, pain. I concluded this was a pretty good hospital. There were no stains on the ceiling tiles, and all the lights worked.

Eventually, Dr. Shen arrived and showed me the X-rays. I had a trimalleolar fracture: all three bones connecting the lower leg to the ankle were either broken or shattered. He asked whether I wanted to go somewhere else for surgery, maybe Shanghai or America? I told him I wasn't going anywhere. Just lying there was pain enough. I couldn't face another ambulance ride, let alone a flight across the Pacific. He agreed to operate when the swelling went down, which he estimated would take three or four days.

Meanwhile, one of the nurses came in and opened a binder with hundreds of photographs of hospital aides. She told me to choose one. The cost, she said, was 100RMB, or fifteen dollars a day. I told her to choose one for me. She selected Mrs. T'ao. In China, nurses take care only of a patient's medical needs. Family members take care of everything else. Patients without family members have to hire someone. Mrs. T'ao arrived a few minutes later and set up her cot in a corner of the room. The idea was that she would be there twenty-four hours a day in case I needed to pee, which was easy enough, or shit, which was not so easy, or I wanted something to eat or drink.

My friends accompanied me through all of this, but they finally called it quits around eight o'clock, and I began my first night in the hospital. Thinking I might be able to sleep, I asked my roommate to turn down the TV. Every room had a set, and my roommate controlled the remote. He was amenable, but it didn't matter. If I slept, I didn't notice.

The next morning they took me to have a CT scan. Dr. Shen wanted something more detailed than X-rays. Three days later they wheeled me in for surgery. It was the spring equinox – an auspicious day. Light and dark were in balance. I was hoping when I came to there would be a new kind of pain. I was tired of the old kind that kept me awake all night.

When I woke up, I had a titanium plate and a dozen screws in my ankle, and I was hooked up to a morphine drip. For the first time since breaking my ankle, I wasn't in pain. It was such a relief. Unfortunately, the morphine lasted only until nightfall. When it ran out, I pressed the call button and asked for more. But that was it for the morphine. It was pills from there on out. The pills, whatever they were, were useless. For the next three days, my only comfort was during the day when Martin and Ta-ch'a and his tea friends came by to chat. Chatting about nothing was a welcome distraction. Dr. Shen also made my life easier by sharing the password to his wireless Internet account. With my laptop, I was able to send e-mails and check on what was happening at Spring Training. Finally, a week after I arrived, Dr. Shen said I could leave. I had been pressuring him for days. I wasn't looking forward to the plane ride, but I wanted to go home.

The day before I left, through the combined generosity of Martin, Ta-ch'a's tea friends, a real estate broker, and my Chinese publisher, I managed to pay the hospital bill, which was US$3,500. It was not part of my budget, and I was surprised and grateful that I was able to come up with that much money so quickly. The next challenge was getting to the airport in Shanghai. Once again a friend came to my aid. His name was Li Hsin. Two years earlier, he saw an article about me in the *China Daily* and came to visit me at my home in America. When I called him from the hospital, he sent his car and driver to pick me up—a very swank Buick van. And so I made it back home and learned to be grateful for the provisions of the Americans with Disabilities Act. A month later in Seattle, Dr. Stephen Benirschke added another titanium plate to my ankle and a dozen more screws. Suddenly, the pain was gone. Two months later, I started walking without crutches. Four months after that, I returned to Huchou to finish Day 25.

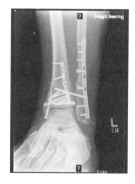

X-ray of author's ankle post second surgery

March was long gone. So was summer. It was November. I was with Ta-ch'a again and we were joined by Yin Yun, the real estate broker who had helped pay my hospital bill and who had taken it upon herself to cover my travel expenses in China. I wondered what good deed I had done to deserve such generosity.

Once again we ventured forth from Huchou later than I would have liked, and once again we turned west on Highway 306. This time we turned south on a different, and much narrower road. We weren't driving to the top of Hsiamushan. I wanted to hike to the top, and this was the old route between Huchou and the foot of the mountain that farmers had been using for centuries. Where the asphalt had worn away, I could see the old paving stones. We drove until we were about two kilometers from the base of the mountain and stopped next to a sign for Yangfu Bridge. Ta-ch'a said the bridge was built 300 years ago in the Ch'ing dynasty. I saw only weeds, no bridge. Ta-ch'a paid the driver and said we would be walking up the mountain from there. That was welcome news. I was looking forward to testing out my new ankle. Ta-ch'a turned his attention back to the bridge and pointed it out for me. I would never have distinguished it from the vegetation. I stepped carefully to avoid getting my feet tangled in the vines.

Once we were across the bridge, we followed a dirt trail past row after row of tea bushes, then past a reservoir, and finally into a bamboo forest. Just after the trail crossed the stream that fed the reservoir, we turned onto a side trail that led to the front steps of Fuyuan Temple. It was the kind of Buddhist temple I wished there were more of—namely, modest. It looked like a farmhouse. When we walked up the steps, the temple's lone resident appeared in the doorway of the shrine hall. His name was Tao-jen. He looked to be about sixty years old and never stopped smiling. After we exchanged introductions, he led us into the shrine hall and showed me what Ta-ch'a brought me here to see. Tao-jen lifted a tarp and revealed the broken remains of a stele. On one of the pieces was Stonehouse's name: Shih-wu. Apparently, Stonehouse

Fuyuan Temple

had some sort of relationship with this temple. My guess is that he lived here before he moved to the top of the mountain, or he used it as a place for giving Zen talks. In any case, this would have been the temple whose bell was always reminding him that there was, in fact, another world down below, as in number 9:

> Green gullies and red cliffs wherever I look
> and my thatch hut in between
> beneath a patched robe my body stays warm
> I've forgotten my worries along with the date
> rushes grow thin where the soil is rocky
> bamboo shoots grow tall where it's deep
> sometimes at midnight I hear a bell
> and remember there's a temple down below

翠竇丹崖列四傍，茅菴恰好在中央。一身布衲衣裳煖，百念消融歲月忘。
石瘦種來蒲葉細，土深迸出筍芽長。有時夜半聞鐘磬，知有招提在下方。

After showing me the stones, Tao-jen went into the kitchen and started preparing us an early lunch. I tried to stop him, but to no avail. While he was cooking, he said that when he arrived, eight years ago, the buildings were knee-deep in weeds. The ruins of the original temple covered the slopes on either side of the farmhouse and must have housed hundreds of monks. All that remained were the stone foundations, still visible in places where the bamboo hadn't obscured the hillsides.

Lunch was simple: stir-fried winter melon, stir-fried taro and cabbage, and sun-dried honey-covered pumpkin, which was more of a dessert. It reminded me of Stonehouse's number 67:

Lunch in my mountain kitchen
there's a shimmering springwater sauce
a well-cooked stew of preserved bamboo
a fragrant pot of hard-grain rice
blue-cap mushrooms fried in oil
purple-bud ginger vinaigrette
none of them heavenly dishes
but why should I cater to gods

山廚修午供， 泉白似銀漿。 羹熟筍鞭爛， 飯炊粳米香。
油煎清丁蕈， 醋煮紫芽薑。 百味皆難及， 何須說上方。

It was all good. A Stonehouse meal. After lunch, Tao-jen showed us the ruins of the old temple, then we followed him back to the vine-covered bridge and started walking up the road toward the mountain. Along the way, I stopped to talk with some farmers who were harvesting rice. They said they used to harvest two rice crops a year. Now it was rapeseed in late May or early June and rice in late October or early November. The market had changed, they said. They now earned more from rapeseed, which was made into cooking oil, than they did from rice.

The road soon petered out into a dirt trail. When we came to a fork, we stayed right. Just past the fork, we met some men walking down the trail holding long bamboo poles with nets attached. One of them also had a cage and lifted the covering to show us two thrushes they had caught and which they planned to sell in town. Lots of people in China, especially old people, keep thrushes. They take them out in the morning and hang their cages in trees so the birds can practice their singing. Once when I was living at

Hai-ming Monastery in Taiwan, I ran into some men with their nets on one of my daily walks and actually chased them off the mountain. Now I just nodded and sighed.

A few minutes later we came to Hsiamushan Reservoir. A guardhouse and a gate prevented access, but no one was there. We followed Tao-jen's lead and eased ourselves around the building, being careful not to fall into the reservoir. Just past the far shore Tao-jen stopped and pointed to a wall of grass at the left side of the road. He said that was where the trail to the summit began. Disappearing into the grass, he yelled for us to follow. The grass was taller than us, and I was surprised to find stone steps under my shoes. I know my ankle appreciated the footing. I'm sure Stonehouse was grateful, too, assuming the trail included steps in his day. As we made our way up the mountain, number 11 came to mind:

> My hut is at the top of Hsia Summit
> few visitors brave the cliffs or ravines
> lugging firewood to market I slip on the moss
> hauling rice back up I drip with sweat
> with no end to hunger less is better
> with limited time why be greedy
> this old monk doesn't mean to cause trouble
> he just wants people to let go

菴住霞峰最上頭，巖崖巇嶮少人遊。擔柴出市青苔滑，負米登山白汗流。
口體無厭宜節儉，光陰有限莫貪求。老僧不是閒忉怛，只要諸人放下休。

While I was trying to imagine lugging firewood down the mountain, two farmers appeared on the trail doing just that. We stepped to the side to let them pass. Working our way up the mountain was like walking through a tunnel. We had to hunch over and keep our heads below the bamboo that hemmed in the trail from either side and from above. Eventually, the steps were replaced by rocks alongside a stream, which we crossed and recrossed half a dozen times. Finally, we reached the stream's source, the spring next to Stonehouse's second hut. The hut had gone through many generations of recluses and was now just a rock-wall shell. While we paused to catch our breath, I thought to myself that it wouldn't take much to fix up. There were plenty of trees and bamboo for building material, and the overgrown tea terraces could be replanted. And surely the mountain's remaining thrushes would stop by to wake me in the morning. It was a brief reverie. Ta-ch'a pointed in the direction of the cemetery where I broke my ankle and asked whether I wanted to revisit the hole that did me in. I suggested we keep moving. A few minutes later, we reached the road.

I wasn't surprised that Tao-jen and Ta-ch'a made it to the top. Yin Yun and I, though, were a different story, but a story with a happy ending. We made it too. Once we were all on the road, we walked together toward the water-bottling plant. After about fifty meters Tao-jen pointed to another trail of stone steps on the right. He said that was the trail to Stonehouse's meditation rock. It was too tempting to pass up. I asked him to show us the way. The steps lasted only a few meters. After that we had to scramble the rest of the way up a leaf-covered slope. Eventually, we reached an outcrop of huge boulders, and one of them had a flat top. We all clambered up and sat down. Ta Ch'a's life revolved around tea, and he was always prepared for such occasions. He took out a tea set from his arm bag and made us tea with hot water from a

Ta-ch'a serving tea on Stonehouse's meditation rock

thermos. We sat there for a long time enjoying the tea and the boulder and the sky. So did Stonehouse, on full-moon nights, as he relates in number 36:

> I was a Zen monk who didn't know Zen
> so I chose the woods for the years I had left
> a robe made of patches over my body
> a belt of bamboo around my waist
> mountains and streams explain Bodhidharma's meaning
> flower smiles and birdsongs reveal the hidden key
> sometimes I sit on a flat-topped rock
> after midnight cloudless nights when the moon fills the sky

我本禪宗不會禪，甘休林下度餘年。鶉衣百結通身掛，竹篾三條驀肚纏。
山色溪光明祖意，鳥啼花笑悟機緣。有時獨上臺盤石，午夜無雲月一天。

It would have been a fine place to meditate. The boulders were higher than the surrounding jungle, and sitting here under the full moon must have been an exceptional experience. Tao-jen thought so too and folded his legs as if getting ready to meditate. He was a true practitioner and clearly at home on the mountain. Before he reclaimed Fuyuan Temple from the weeds, he lived for many years at Yunlin Temple, which replaced the farmhouse at the site of Stonehouse's first hut. People like Stonehouse and Tao-jen were rare. So was Ta-ch'a: in addition to his tea gear, he brought Stonehouse's poems with him, and we all read our favorites. Little did Stonehouse know the karmic winds he was stirring when he wrote those poems, which he advised people not to chant, but to sit on, which was what we did.

When we ran out of tea, Ta Ch'a gathered his cups and his teapot, and we returned to the road. We thanked Tao-jen and kept waving until he disappeared back down the trail. A few minutes later, Ms. Mo showed up with her car, and we, too, headed down the mountain. A bigger, longer day I could never have imagined.

It took a while, but I finally got past Stonehouse. Next up was Meng Chiao (751–814), again. I had already searched for his grave on Day 5 near the airport in Loyang. I was hoping to have better luck with his home. He grew up south of Huchou, and I thought maybe I would find more there than where he was buried.

DAY

26

Ta-ch'a was waiting for me early this time, and with him were two tea brothers, Yang Fan and Lin Hsiao-p'ing. Mr. Yang was providing directions, and Mr. Lin was providing the car. I intended to end the day in Hangchou, but there were several places in between I hoped to visit, and a car and someone familiar with the area were essential. I was fortunate to have such indulgent companions. It was just after seven when we left Huchou, and I couldn't have been happier.

Once more we headed south. This time, we didn't turn off. We kept going on what became Highway 104. Sixty kilometers and an hour later, we arrived in Teching. Since that was where Mr. Yang worked, he took over navigation and told Mr. Lin to go around the first traffic circle that greeted us and to turn down the second lane on the left, which was Chunhui Street. The name means "spring sunshine" and came from Meng Chiao's most famous poem, "Song of a Wayfaring Son" 游子吟:

> The thread in the hand of a loving mother
> the coat on the back of a wayfaring son
> before he left she stitched it tight
> worried he wouldn't return soon
> what can a blade of grass do
> to repay the sunshine of spring

慈母手中線，遊子身上衣。臨行密密縫，意恐遲遲歸。
誰言寸草心，報得三春暉。

When he was young, Meng Chiao was, indeed, a wayfaring son. He traveled throughout the middle reaches of the Yangtze. But until he was forty, he kept coming back to the family home, which was somewhere off the street we were driving on. After a few blocks, we parked just short of the train tracks in front of the town's Meng Chiao Shrine. Finally, something better than a cornfield. But we were early. It wasn't quite eight. The doors were locked, and no one answered when we knocked.

While my tea brethren waited in the car for the person with the key, I felt the need to do something more and tried the dirt trail between the side of the building and the train tracks. Perhaps there was an entrance in the rear. The place, though, was surrounded by a high wall—there was no way in. While I was looking around, I saw a woman working in a field and asked her when the shrine opened. Without bothering to answer, she walked out to the street and disappeared into a store. A minute later, she returned with the caretaker.

The doors swung open to a single large hall. Against the far wall was a standing statue of the man we had come here to see. He was over three meters high, painted gold, and in one hand he held a book—a volume of poetry, I presumed. Poetry was Meng Chiao's life. He also wore an official's hat, the kind with butterfly wings on either side. It was a silly-looking hat, but that was what they wore in those days. In front of the statue, a dozen red candle stubs lined a cement altar. Since that was the appropriate place, I set out my whiskey, and Ta-ch'a did the same with tea. Among Meng Chiao's friends were Lu Yu, the Tea Sage, and the Tea Sage's best friend, Chiao-jan. They were all members of a poetry society that met regularly in Huchou. No doubt, Meng Chiao drank his share of tea, but he preferred something stronger, which presumably helped distract him from the suffering that dogged his life. Somewhere down the street, he and his wife had three children, none of whom survived childhood. I tried to cheer him up with his "Inspired by a Spring Day" 春日有感:

> Rain falls and new grass appears
> day after day it grows taller
> wind blows and willow catkins sway
> every branch swaying together
> only the face of a worried man
> makes it through spring unfazed
> come fill your cup with wine
> let's sing and laugh without restraint

雨滴草芽出，一日長一日。風吹柳線垂，一枝連一枝。
獨有愁人顏，經春如等閒。且持酒滿杯，狂歌狂笑來。

Judging from what we know of Meng Chiao's life, he didn't take his own advice, at least not as often as he should have. Singing and laughing without restraint was more of a fantasy. When life got him down, his solution was to travel or to head for the hills.

While Ta-ch'a and I were letting him choose between our offerings, we walked behind his statue and discovered another building connected to the shrine by an awning. It was Huatiao Temple, and it was full of statues, large and small, to all the major deities of the Buddhist and Taoist pantheons – something for everyone and for all occasions. The caretaker said that was the primary function of the place. The temple and the shrine hosted all sorts of village get-togethers and celebrations.

Ta-ch'a offering tea at Meng Chiao shrine

After Ta-ch'a and I returned to reclaim what was left in our respective cups, we walked back to the car. While my tea brothers continued talking with the caretaker, I spotted a sign on the other side of the street pointing toward Chengtao Temple. I decided to follow it, thinking it might lead to where Meng Chiao's mother fell into the Yuying River or maybe even to the well her son dug for her. On my map, I could see that the river was only a few hundred meters away. The story of the well began when Meng Chiao was off on one of his adventures. He got word that his mother almost drowned while washing clothes. When he got home, he dug a well in the family courtyard so she wouldn't have to risk washing clothes in the river anymore. Twenty years ago, the well's capstone was found, and I was hoping the residence was still there. So I followed the sign, first down one alley then down another.

About 200 meters down the second alley, I came to the temple. It had been rebuilt and was much larger than I expected. Inside the entrance, a woman was folding paper money for parishioners to burn for their departed loved ones. I asked her whether she knew anything about Meng Chiao's well or his home. I figured why not ask. She put down the small sheets of shiny gold paper and led me back out into the alley. She pointed in the direction I had come and said Meng Chiao's home was a hundred meters away at No. 22

Chinghofang. The well, she said, had been cemented over, and the compound was now home to three families.

Finding Meng Chiao's home was *that* easy. It was now a compound with three separate dwellings surrounded by a wall. While I was standing outside the gate, my tea brothers caught up to me and talked with the neighbors. After assuring ourselves that this was, in fact, the location of Meng's home, we walked back to the temple, across some fields, and down to the river where Meng's mother almost drowned. It was no longer a river. Both ends had been blocked off, and it was being filled in. One of the farmers working in the fields said there were plans to build a factory on the site. That was another way to keep people from drowning.

We responded to the news with a four-person sigh and returned to the car. However, I wasn't quite done with Meng Chiao. I had read about another well Meng dug, and it was only a few minutes away. We returned to the highway and turned south again. Five kilometers later, at a sign for Chengshan village, we turned right. Less than a kilometer later, we stopped beside a large pond that separated the upper and lower sections of Wentsun Village.

We walked over to one of the farmhouses that bordered the pond and talked to the owner. He confirmed the story about the discovery here of a stele dating back to 1260, which recorded Meng's digging of a second well. The researchers who found the stele concluded that this was probably the site of the poet's hermitage, which explained the need for a well. There were hills nearby, and Meng was known to have spent much of his twenties and thirties cultivating a life of seclusion when he wasn't traveling. The farmer said the authorities had taken the stele away and that the pond had formed as a result of excavations where the well used to be. I poured Meng Chiao yet another shot of rye.

If I had had more time, I would have wandered a bit in the hills to the west. In addition to his home in Teching and his hermitage in the countryside, Meng built a hut there. And he wasn't alone. At least one other family member joined him. In 790, when Meng was forty, he wrote "In the Mountains Seeing Off Uncle Meng Chien Leaving for the Exams" 山中送從叔簡赴舉:

> Below hundred-foot firs rooted in rocks
> from springs that flow from the mountain's eyes
> you lived on the ethereal force of the Tao
> and drank the rarest of inspired verse

now where you wandered in freedom
suddenly hearing the music of farewell
you laugh at this vine-bound recluse
not joining in praise of your big year

石根百尺衫，山眼一片泉。依之道氣高，飲之詩思鮮。
於此逍遙場，忽奏別離弦。卻笑薛蘿子，不同鳴躍年。

Although Meng Chiao poked fun at his uncle for exchanging the life of a recluse for that of an official, his uncle's success in the exams inspired Meng to do the same. The exams, though, were harder than expected. It took Meng three tries. And passing the exams didn't result in a position. When an opportunity finally did materialize, it wasn't much of a position. But Meng took it and stuck it out as long as he did in order to be near the friends he had made. When they left on assignments, he lost heart, as he reveals in his "Letter-in-Reply Song" 歸信吟:

I wrote a letter with ink and tears
addressed to a friend a thousand miles away
when the letter left my spirit left too
suddenly this body is an empty shell

淚墨灑為書，將寄萬裏親。書去魂亦去，兀然空一身。

The last thing Meng thought about was work. His superiors noticed. At his last post, his boss simply gave up and hired someone else to perform the work, reducing Meng's salary by half. Alas, there were no university teaching jobs for poets in those days.

Having tracked down what traces there were of Meng's life in and around his hometown, we returned to Teching, dropped off Mr. Yang near the place where he worked, then headed for our next destination. From Teching, we followed Highway 304 east. At least, we tried to follow it. It appeared and disappeared as we crossed the southernmost corner of the Yangtze delta. After an hour, we traded 304 East for 60 North, an expressway with road signs and marked exits. Thirty minutes later we took the exit for the Tung-hsiang train station then headed southeast. The place I was looking for was only five kilometers from the exit. But since neither Mr. Lin nor Ta-ch'a had been there, it took a while to find. We persevered, though, and two hours after leaving Teching, we arrived at Luchung, the hometown of Chu Shu-chen (1135–1180).

Chu was one of China's most famous female poets, and Luchung was where she was born. It was a canal town. Most of the canal towns between Shanghai and Hangchou had been taken over by factories or turned into tourist attractions, but Luchung was an exception, if only because it was so small. Since its stone-lined streets weren't wide enough for cars, we parked just inside its southwest corner at the Haining Farm Cooperative Credit Union then began walking along Chenhsi Road, which ran parallel to Tinghsi Canal. The two-story houses on both sides of the narrow street were made of wood, with the upper stories on the canal side extending out over the waterway and red lanterns hanging from the upper stories on the street side. It looked quite picturesque. After about a hundred meters, we passed the stone arch of Teyi Bridge, and after another fifty meters we came to No. 38, the Chu Shu-chen Exhibition Hall. It was easily the nicest building in the village. Someone in Luchung clearly loved her. Not only was the building in good condition, the design of the exhibits inside was also well done. Her poems lined the walls, as did photographs of scenes around the village. I had read about the hall online and I expected to find books of her poetry for sale, but there weren't any. Nor was there anyone to guide us or regale us with stories only a person from Luchung would know.

After reading the poems and explanations in the exhibition hall, I walked outside. There was a small dry-goods store across the street, run by an old couple, and I thought maybe they had books for sale. They didn't, but the man surprised me by suggesting I have a look at Chu Shu-chen's old house. I didn't know her house had survived – or at least a descendant of her house. The man said to go back the way we had come, turn right, then left, then right. Her house, he said, was next to a pavilion that overlooked a much smaller canal. Five minutes later, I returned and asked him whether he could guide me. I must have taken a left when I should have taken a right. He hadn't been there in a while himself, but he agreed. He was ninety-one and had to retrace his steps several times, but he found it. After telling the people who lived there what I was doing, he went back to his store.

Like Meng Chiao's home, it was occupied by several families. But unlike Meng Chiao's home, they all lived in a single building. It was fairly large and probably dated back to the end of the Ch'ing dynasty, if not earlier.

Chu Shu-chen's house at Luchung

The address was No. 49/50 Hsishih Street. The residents were friendly and invited me in, but I didn't feel like intruding. A few minutes later, Ta-ch'a and Mr. Lin also found their way there. While they talked to the residents, I walked around to the pavilion in back that overlooked the canal. I could imagine Chu sitting here, writing "Events on a Spring Day" 春日即事:

> It's teeth-clenching cold and the flowers are late
> green ripple upon ripple joins the distant waves
> fish rise from river grass showing off their jade flanks
> orioles weave through trees like shuttles made of gold
> I look through drafts of my poems by the railing
> and listen to fishermen singing across the shore
> all day by the window my heart beats in silence
> with nothing here to do how will I survive spring

輕寒噤瘁花期晚，皺綠參鱗接遠波。躍藻白魚翻玉尺，穿林黃鳥度金梭。
閑將詩草臨軒讀，靜聽漁船隔岸歌。盡日倚窗情脈脈，眼前無事奈春何。

In ancient China, women were called *nei-jen* 內人, "interior persons."
They lived inside, behind the walls, where their lives were likewise "interior."

After my companions joined me at the pavilion, we walked over to Tefeng
Bridge, which spanned the canal behind her house. It was the perfect place
for our respective ceremonies. Big Tea got out his tea, and I did the same with
my whiskey. After thanking Chu for her poems, we poured what we didn't
drink into the canal. I was amazed by our success in finding her exhibition
hall *and* her home. I would have liked to have wandered around the village
and along its canals, but as usual, I had a train to catch. Ta-ch'a and Mr. Lin
left me at the Tunghsiang station we passed earlier on our way there. Once
again I was in debt to my tea brothers. I was on a bullet train fifteen minutes
later, and it was just after two when I reached Hangchou, where Chu Shu-
chen spent the second half of her life, the married half.

Before I knew it, it was my turn in the taxi queue. I told the driver the
name of my hotel, but added that I wanted to stop on the way, in the old part
of town, and walk down Chungshan Middle Road. The street dated back to
the Sung dynasty, and its southern section had been fixed up to look as it
might have 900 years ago during Chu Shu-chen's time. Her house was report-
edly off the pedestrian-only part of the street in Paokang Lane. While the taxi
driver waited, I walked up and down Chungshan Middle Road. But none of
the shopkeepers had heard of Paokang Lane or Chu Shu-chen's home. I gave
up. But I wasn't quite done. Since her house was said to have been near the
city's Yungchin Gate, I asked the driver to go there as well.

The gate was built in 936, 200 years before Chu Shu-chen's birth. But
it wasn't your standard city gate. It was a water gate, for letting water into
the city from West Lake. It was only later expanded to include road traffic.
Although the gate was gone, there was a stele that summarized its history.
I paused long enough to read it, but I was distracted by the sheer loveliness
of the view beyond it: the mountain-ringed, placid waters of West Lake and
its willow-lined shore.

Oddly enough, I returned to Hangchou less than a week later, the day after
I completed my pilgrimage and the day before I left China. I wanted to walk
down Chungshan Middle Road once more. This time I got lucky. It turned
out the online account I had relied on mistyped the first character of Paokang
Lane. It wasn't Precious Health Lane, it was *Protecting* Health Lane. I could

see, though, how I missed it. Just north of Kaiyuan Road, it was barely wide enough to walk down and less than fifty meters long. Just before the end of the lane, at No. 14, I found the current incarnation of Chu Shu-chen's house. All the residents were distinctly proud of living in, or next to, or across from it. Apparently, the knowledge of its existence never made it to the street. Given her failed marriage, I imagine Chu was grateful to have a residence near the lake and the friendships that such a city made possible. I could imagine her writing "Around the Stove" 圍爐:

Sitting around a glowing stove singing silly songs
straining more new wine reciting more new poems
none of us regretting getting drunk tonight
this time won't come again once we say goodbye

圍坐紅爐唱小詞，旋篘新酒賞新詩。大家莫惜今宵醉，一別參差有幾時。

Her house was less than a kilometer from Yungchin Gate. It would have been easy walking distance, assuming her feet weren't bound – it was around that time that this cruelest of customs began. After tearing myself away from Yungchin Gate and the view Chu, no doubt, also enjoyed, I returned to the taxi. I had one more stop, and the day was getting on. I asked the driver to take me to my hotel and to wait while I divested myself of my bag. My Chinese friend Simeng was waiting in the lobby. She had offered to guide me to my final destination of the day: the Hangchou Botanical Gardens.

It was only ten minutes from the hotel, but it was already after four when we walked through the main gate. The place closed at five thirty, so I walked quicker than usual. I was trying to squeeze this last destination into the day because this was where Chu Shu-chen was buried. That much was known. People had written about visiting her grave. But the grave seems to have disappeared during the last century – at least, until recently. I read an online account by someone claiming to have found it in the Lingfeng Tanmei section of the park. That part of the park was also one of Simeng's favorite places, which was why I asked her to be my guide. When I made up my itinerary, I knew I would be looking for Chu Shu-chen's grave at the end of the day, in fading light, and couldn't afford a wrong turn.

In English, *ling-feng* means "spirit peak" – the ridge that formed the western border of the park was known for its graves – and *t'an-mei* means "looking for plum blossoms." During the Sung dynasty, when the North was lost to the Jurchens, the plum blossom came to represent the Chinese spirit of resilience. It bloomed when the weather was at its coldest. One of the many poems Chu wrote on the subject was "I Send This Quatrain to the Poorly Located Plum Tree at the Foot of the Mountain Bereft of Sunlight and Finally Budding in Late Winter" 山腳有梅一株, 地差北陽冬深初結蕊, 作絕句寄之:

Near the store by the bridge plum buds are bursting
it's late winter here but still isn't cold
I'm sending this to the plum flowers asking them to wait
without snow on the branches who's going to look

溪橋野店梅都綻, 此地冬深尚未寒。寄語梅花且寧奈, 枝頭無雪不堪看。

For Chu Shu-chen, the plum flower represented not only the dynasty's resilience but also *her* resilience. She was a plum flower. That was why she asked to be buried here, where the people of Hangchou come every year, especially after a snowfall, in search of plum blossoms.

After passing under a stone archway bearing the words Tanmeiyuan (Looking for Plum Blossoms Garden), we walked across a huge, grassy bowl to the foot of Lingfeng, or Spirit Peak. It was November: Lunar New Year was two months away. The mountain's plum blossoms were still dreaming. As we walked along the foot of the mountain, we paused at every pavilion and grave to read any and all inscriptions, but we saw nothing with Chu's name on it. As we began working our way up the slope to the top of the ridge, we followed a trail that led past dozens of thousand-year-old camphor trees. The trees were as old as Chu Shu-chen's grave, if not older. Suddenly, I noticed that some of the paving stones we had been walking on were tombstones. I slowed down and looked more carefully.

I also kept looking at my watch. The park was about to close, and the light was disappearing from the sky. Finally, I called it quits. If I had stepped on her tombstone, I wouldn't have known. There wasn't enough light. As we headed down the slope, I glanced to my left and noticed several hundred narrow steps leading to the top of the north side of the ridge. Even though we were out of time, I thought *what the hell* and started up. But halfway to the top, I stopped. I was out of breath and wondering why I had started up in the first place. I turned to go back down, but Simeng urged me to keep going. So I kept going, feeling almost embarrassed that she was more determined than me. A minute later, as we reached the top, there was the tombstone whose photo

I had seen online. Whatever was originally carved on its surface had been worn away by centuries of rain. Someone had scrawled some words on it with red paint, but they were equally illegible. That someone had dared to write on the tombstone – there wasn't graffiti on any of the others – I took as confirmation that there was something special about it. No doubt, the person who posted the photo felt the same. Whether it really was Chu Shu-chen's grave didn't matter. This was her favorite place, and that was good enough for me.

Once I caught my breath, I took out the whiskey and thanked Chu for her poems. They were hard-won, and we were fortunate to have them. Her parents were so embarrassed by her talent, they burned all the poems they could find after she died. Lucky

Chu Shu-chen's grave on Lingfeng

for us, someone gathered copies she had shared with friends, over 300 verses, and titled the collection *Poems of a Broken Heart*. It was an apt title. The only good thing about her marriage was that her husband left her alone. And the only good thing about her relationships with other men was that she survived them, except the last one. The most repeated story about her death is that she drowned herself in West Lake after one heartbreak too many. The truth is, all we really know is what we can find in her poems. And, of course, different people find different things.

By the time I was done thanking her with my little offering, the park gates had closed. Simeng said not to bother going back down and trying to climb the fence. She led me to a weather station above Chu's grave then along a dirt trail that wound past hundreds of Muslim graves, most of them dating back to the late nineteenth and early twentieth centuries, when Hangchou was called the "Stronghold of Islam" in China. It was nearly dark when we finally came off the hill to a street lined with fancy restaurants and brightly lit nightspots. It was a startling, and unwelcome, change of scenery.

Fortunately, we were still on Simeng's turf, and she led me on another series of paths through hillsides of bamboo, which circumvented the neon and the traffic and which brought me back to my hotel. It was such an exhausting yet exhilarating day, I shared two bottles of wine with Simeng over dinner. Later that night, just before letting the day go, I read one more poem of Chu's, "Looking for Plum Blossoms" 探梅:

> The weather was so warm it could have been spring
> looking for plum blossoms we found a whole slope
> breaking off a twig and sticking it in my hair
> I laughed and asked is anyone more shameless

溫溫天氣似春和，試探寒梅已滿坡。 笑折一枝插雲鬢，問人瀟灑似誰麼。

No one, Chu Shu-chen. Certainly not a plum blossom.

I woke to a fine mist outside the window and took my time getting out of bed. I had an easy day planned, and it was all in Hangchou. What could be better? Hangchou was home to many of China's greatest poets, especially from the ninth through fourteenth centuries. They all loved it, even when they were sent here as punishment, which was admittedly like tossing Br'er Rabbit into the briar patch. When Marco Polo visited Hangchou in the thirteenth century, he called it the world's greatest city. Long before that, the Chinese extolled it as the best place to be born. I, too, was pleased whenever my travels brought me here. On this occasion, I was going to limit myself to one very small corner of the city's beloved West Lake. Hence, I took my time getting up.

The place where I was easing into the day was the Huapei Hotel. Before it opened to the public, the Huapei's guests were limited to senior military officers and party officials. Such places were invariably dreary, and the Huapei was no exception. However, its location was more important to me than its dreariness. It was on the lake's north shore, a ten-minute walk to my one and only destination of the day, and set back from the road far enough to render traffic noise imperceptible.

I savored a second cup of coffee in bed, and it was almost ten before I finally left my cozy sanctuary. Despite the mist, I decided to leave my umbrella behind. But I did put on galoshes. My shoes were made of canvas and got wet even in fog. Thus outfitted, I walked down to the main road, ignoring the two major tourist destinations at hand: Yuehfei Temple, which honored an unfortunate Sung-dynasty general, and Su Causeway, which connected the lake's north shore with its south shore, much to the appreciation of anyone on foot or on a bicycle. Instead, I followed the lakeside promenade toward the western edge of the city. West Lake was always lovely, but I liked it best when it was only half-visible, as it was that day. At the short, ancient span of Hsiling Bridge, I left the promenade and crossed to Kushan Island. The island's name means "lone peak," and until modern times it was the residence of those who preferred a solitary existence. It was also the setting of hundreds, if not thousands, of poems.

Among the poets inspired by the island was Su Tung-p'o, who crossed the same bridge on horseback during the winter of 1071. He had been rusticated to the provinces due to his opposition to the reforms introduced by Wang

An-shih. Fortunately, he was on friendly terms with the prime minister, and his punishment was to serve as magistrate of Hangchou. It wasn't even a slap on the wrist. After Su returned home one evening from a visit to the island, he wrote "On Winter Solstice Visiting the Monks Hui-ch'in and Hui-ssu during an Outing to Kushan" 臘日遊孤山訪惠勤惠思二僧:

> Snow about to fall
> clouds upon the lake
> mountains and pavilions visible then not
> streams so clear I could count the fish
> woods too thick for people but not for birds
> today on winter solstice I left my wife at home
> I said I was visiting monks but was indulging myself instead
> and where pray tell did these prelates live
> up a winding path on Jewel Cloud Hill
> and who dared live on lonely Lone Peak Isle
> two followers of the Way who thought it not lonely at all
> their paper-window bamboo hut was warm enough
> and wrapped in robes we dozed on cushions made of straw
> until my servants grumbled it's cold and the road home's long
> and readied the horses so I'd be home by dusk
> I turned as we left and watched the trees merge with clouds
> hawks circling a pagoda was the last thing that I saw
> such a simple outing yet filled with so much joy
> by the time I got home it was a fading dream
> I rushed to write a poem before it all had fled
> but once it was gone I couldn't find that scene again

天欲雪，雲滿湖，　樓臺明滅山有無。　水清石出魚可數，　林深無人鳥相呼。
臘日不歸對妻孥，　名尋道人實自娛。　道人之居在何許，　寶雲山前路盤紆。
孤山孤絕誰肯廬，　道人有道山不孤。　紙窗竹屋深自暖，　擁褐坐睡依團蒲。
天寒路遠愁僕夫，　整駕催歸及未晡。　出山回望雲木合，　但見野鶻盤浮圖。
慈遊淡薄歡有餘，　到家恍如夢蘧蘧。　作詩火急追亡逋，　清景一失後難摹。

I followed Su along the island's south shore: past the steps that led to its famous seal-carving society, past the even more famous Louwailou Restaurant, and past the provincial museum and the museum of fine art. Just short of where the island ended and Pai Causeway began, I entered the Shrine to Lords Pai and Su. It was built in the manner of a Sung-dynasty villa, with white walls and black-tiled roofs, to honor the two men who, more than any others, made West Lake what it was – the most beautiful, the most painted, the most photographed, the most walked around, the most rowed upon lake in China.

The two lords were, of course, Pai Chu-yi and Su Tung-p'o. Pai came here first. He was appointed governor in 822. Chientang Lake – West Lake's earlier incarnation – was often overwhelmed with silt, rendering it useless for drinking water, much less for fishing or boating. And once it silted up, the slightest influx from the nearby estuaries of the Chientang River flooded the city, especially when the tidal bore came upstream every autumn. To solve such problems, Pai, and later Su, carried out large-scale dredging projects, using the mud and sand to form the causeways later named for them, causeways that have since provided people with the most splendid of promenades from which to enjoy the lake.

Pai also repaired the dikes south of the city and built a dam to control the flow of water into the lake. Both men also had dozens of wells dug inside the city proper to improve access to drinking water. Appropriately, the shrine on Kushan was built on the former site of the Water God Temple. At one time the water god had several shrines around West Lake. As the townspeople's appreciation for Pai and Su grew, the god had to start sharing his shrines with the two poets. Now, there was only one shrine, to Pai and Su.

The walls of the shrine's halls were covered with their poems, among them Pai's "Springtime Promenade on Chientang Lake" 錢塘湖春行:

> From Kushan Temple in the north to Chiating Pavilion in the west
> the lake is perfectly calm and the clouds are low
> orioles everywhere contest the sunniest branches
> to whose homes now are swallows carrying mud
> the profusion of flowers never fails to enchant
> the veil of new grass finally masks the hoof prints
> I love the east shore and could stroll there forever
> along the sandy causeway in the green willow shade

孤山寺北賈亭西，水面初平雲腳低。幾處早鶯爭暖樹，誰家新燕啄春泥。
亂花漸欲迷人眼，淺草才能沒馬蹄。最愛湖東行不足，綠楊陰裏白沙堤。

Another poem on display was the last one Pai wrote in Hangchou, "Saying Goodbye to the Townspeople" 別州民, in which he refers to a legendary ruler who governed his subjects while sitting under a pear tree:

> Elders crowded the road leading out of town
> at the farewell banquet the wine overflowed
> I didn't sit under a pear tree
> I don't understand this torrent of tears
> people here were poor yet my taxes were heavy
> farmers were hungry and their fields were parched
> all I'm leaving is a lake full of water
> to help when the years turn bad

耆老遮歸路，壺漿滿別筵。甘棠無一樹，那得淚潸然。
稅重多貧戶，農饑足旱田。唯留一湖水，與汝救凶年。

Pai's tenure began the transformation of Hangchou's lake from an eyesore into its principal attraction. Two hundred and fifty years later, when Su Tung-p'o ended his assignment to Hangchou, he drew a comparison to the famous beauty Hsi Shih (Lady Shih West) in "Drinking on the Lake as It Clears Then It Rains" 飲湖上初晴后雨：

> The shimmering of the water in sunshine is lovely
> the veiling of the hills in the rain is divine
> I think of West Lake as Lady Shih West
> with or without makeup either way it's perfect

水光激灩晴方好，山色空蒙雨亦奇。欲把西湖比西子，淡妝濃抹總相宜。

The poems on display were written out by some of China's most famous calligraphers, including Tung Ch'i-ch'ang (1555–1636), whose calligraphy I once used as the model for my own laughable efforts with the brush. The whole place was magnificent, and I had it all to myself, which was both precious and a shame. There were, however, no poems by the poet who led me to Kushan.

After I had seen enough of the shrine, I followed the path that led along the island's east and north shores. The south shore saw thousands of visitors every day, but I found myself alone on the other side. It was an isolation I always appreciated when visiting someone whose spirit still hung in the air. The poet I was looking for was Lin Pu (967–1028), aka Lin Ho-ching. The latter name was bestowed upon him by the emperor and is the name by which most people still refer to him. I knew I was getting close when I reached Crane Releasing Pavilion. The crane was Lin Ho-ching's favorite bird. It was an ancient symbol for the cultivation of stillness and solitude. Lin's early biographers said he considered cranes his children – he never married. He trained the birds to dance and to come find him when visitors arrived. He referred to them as "Marsh Callers" 鳴皋:

The name "marsh birds" goes back to ancient times
alone at midnight bringing forth from their perfect throats
cries that shatter the stillness of the sky
and yet they have no interest in reaching the distant clouds

皋禽名祇有前聞，孤引圖吭夜正分。一唳便驚寥汱破，亦無閒意到青雲。

Like his cranes, Lin saw himself shattering the island's stillness with his poems and likewise disdaining the quest for high office or immortality, represented here by the clouds. He was the quintessential refined recluse. Born near Hangchou to a family that had for centuries provided the government with officials, he received a good education. However, his branch was in decline by the time he was born. He grew up with refined sensibilities but not the wherewithal to indulge them. Still, he saw himself in a heroic light and sought to put into practice the ideals of his mentors, men such as Confucius and Lao-tzu. He spent much of his youth traveling in search of employment commensurate with such aspirations, but with little success.

Finding the Sung court in Kaifeng rife with deception and indulgence, he finally gave up and returned to Hangchou. Shortly afterward, in 1008, he moved outside the city's west wall to Kushan. Not coincidentally, that same year Emperor Chen-tsung "received" a series of "letters from Heaven" ordering lavish sacrifices to be conducted at places of potency throughout the empire. The following year, the emperor ordered the construction outside the capital of the largest Taoist temple ever built. Its purpose was to ensure his own long life as well as that of his reign. He then ordered all districts in the realm to construct similar, though smaller, temples dedicated to his longevity. Lin responded to such excess with "A Quatrain Written to Commemorate Construction of My Own Hall of Longevity" 自作壽堂因書一絕以志之：

> The mountains beside the lake all face the hut I built
> the bamboos before my grave all bend in mourning
> letters of praise were once requested for imperial tombs
> I'm glad at least I never suggested a sacrifice

湖上青山對結盧，墳前修竹亦蕭疏。茂陵他日求遺稿，猶喜曾無封禪書。

Lin built his "Hall of Longevity" on the hillside above Crane Releasing Pavilion. From the pavilion, I followed a trail of stone steps up the slope to his tomb. As I approached, I heard music. It was very faint and seemed to be coming from the grave. As I got closer, I saw a red plastic lotus on the stone altar in front of the tomb. It rose from a white plastic pedestal with a dozen burned-out candles around its edge. Instead of "Om Mani Padme Hum," the lotus was playing "Happy Birthday." I couldn't help laughing. Who had left such an offering? I smiled in appreciation and set out my own less ostentatious tribute.

Once Lin settled on Kushan, he lived here as a recluse for the rest of his life. He didn't make a big deal of it, though. He even joked about the life he chose, all the while extolling it. The Chinese say the minor recluse lives in the mountains, but the great recluse lives in town. With this in mind, Lin wrote his "Self-Portrait of a Minor Recluse" 小隱自題：

> My hut is surrounded by a forest of bamboo
> it feels so wonderfully secluded
> cranes stand unmoving at the water's edge
> bees never stop searching for flowers
> hangovers interrupt my time with books
> I'm out hoeing lotuses on cloudy spring days
> in my favorite paintings by the ancients
> there's a woodcutter or a fisherman somewhere

竹樹繞吾盧，清深趣有餘。鶴閒臨水久，蜂懶得花疏。
酒病妨開卷，春陰入荷鋤。嘗憐古圖畫，多半寫樵漁。

Landscape paintings with a tiny figure — hauling firewood down a mountain path, say, or hunched over in a fishing boat in winter — put a human life in perspective. It was that perspective that Lin admired in paintings and that he admired about the life he chose. If he couldn't be a heroic figure at court, he would be a heroic figure in the mists of West Lake. A grave robber who opened Lin's tomb at the end of the Sung-dynasty reportedly found only an inkstone and a hairpin. That pretty much summed up Lin's connection to the world of red dust. He lived alone and never married. He told people his cranes were his children and his plum trees were his wives.

Grave of Lin Ho-ching on Kushan

As I toasted Lin with rye, and the little gizmo played "Happy Birthday," it started to rain. Umbrellaless, I drained what was left of the whiskey, put away my cups, and walked down to the main path that continued along the shore. I was wearing my wool hat, so at least my head stayed dry, as did my rubber-encased shoes.

Although Lin lived on Kushan as a recluse, he didn't have the island to himself. There were several Buddhist monasteries in his day, as there were when Su Tung-p'o was magistrate. Lin was on good terms with the monks, but he preferred solitude: just himself and his crane children and his plum-tree wives. Lin said he planted 365 of them so that the fruit produced by each tree would provide enough money to support him for one day. They not only supported him, they inspired him, as in "Small Plum Tree in a Mountain Garden" 山園小梅:

> When flowers all have fallen this tree alone shines forth
> usurping entirely my little garden scene
> its thin reflection slanting across a pristine pond
> its subtle scent floating below the moon at dusk
> winter birds about to land can't keep from looking
> if butterflies knew it would break their hearts
> luckily my modest tune is intimate enough
> no need to beat a clapper or raise a golden goblet

眾芳搖落獨暄妍，占盡風情向小園。疏影橫斜水清淺，暗香浮動月黃昏。
霜禽欲下先偷眼，粉蝶如知合斷魂。幸有微吟可相狎，不須檀板共金尊。

The remarkable thing about Lin's twenty-year island residency is that once he moved to Kushan, he never entered Hangchou again. He did, however, enjoy the company of other like-minded individuals, and he visited friends in the surrounding hills. As I approached Hsiling Bridge, where I began my Kushan excursion, the rain turned to mist again, and I imagined Lin rowing home under the bridge's lone arch singing "Summoning a Hermit" 招隱士, a poem by Ch'u Yuan which lists all the terrors of living alone in the mountains. It ends, "O my prince come home / you can't stay in the mountains" 王孫兮歸來，山中兮不可以久留. After singing Ch'u Yuan's poem, Lin sang his own "In My Boat on West Lake Encountering Snow" 西湖舟中值雪：

> An empty void above a vast expanse
> it was snowing all the way to the shore
> rowing my boat I turned to look
> as I neared Kushan it still wasn't clear
> my zither was too frozen to tune
> my little stove's warmth was faint
> singing "Summoning a Hermit" I paused
> why would I regret leaving the crowd behind

浩蕩彌空闊，霏霏接水濆。舟移忽自卻，山近未全分。
凍軫閒清泛，溫爐把薄薰。悠然詠招隱，何許歎離群。

Why, indeed?

This was not a sleep-in morning. I was up at seven to catch a nine o'clock train. That sounds a bit excessive, but I wasn't sure how long it would take to find a taxi and to reach the train station during rush hour. My fears were unfounded. I arrived with nearly an hour to spare, which gave me time for some hot soy milk — at KFC, of all places. Twenty minutes after I left Hangchou, I stepped out of the Shaohsing station. Shazam. Three hundred kilometers an hour made distances seem unreal. And there were patches of blue in the sky.

For the second time during my trip, I was checking in at a hotel before ten. Since this was the last hotel I would be staying in, I decided to splurge. I reserved a room at the Hsienheng. The taxi driver asked me, twice, was I sure I wanted to go to the Hsienheng. When I entered the lobby, the bell-boys stared. While they were trying to decide whether to take my bag, I walked past them to the front desk and handed the desk clerk my passport and credit card. I told the desk clerk I had a reservation. I wished his smile of disbelief had lasted longer. I was enjoying this. The room I had reserved was a hundred bucks, which was a lot, but not for something as special as the Hsienheng. The place was a palace. After the clerk found my reservation, he returned my passport and credit card and gave one of the bellboys my room key. A minute later, I was in my suite. The bedroom was as big as my living room at home, and it was divided from a sitting room that was even larger. The bathroom was equally impressive, especially the bathtub. It was big enough for two. But what impressed me the most was the pencil and pad of paper next to the toilet. Shaohsing was a writer's town, which was, of course, why I was there. And I wasn't there to spend the day in my room.

I walked back out to the cobblestone street in front of the hotel and turned east. It was a pedestrian-only street, but I soon discovered walking on cobble-stones wasn't as easy as it looked, especially with an ankle no longer as flexi-ble as it was when I began this pilgrimage. As I hobbled along, a series of touts came up and showed me photograph albums of all the places they would be happy to take me in their rickshaws. I waved them off. Shaohsing was even more ancient than Hangchou, and there were dozens of places worth visit-ing, if one had the time. But there was only one place on my itinerary, and it was straight ahead. Two hundred meters from the hotel, I passed Lu Hsun's old house. Lu Hsun (1881–1936), I presumed, was one of the reasons for the pencil and paper next to the toilet. He was China's favorite twentieth-century writer, and this was his town. Next to his home was a Lu Hsun museum, and next to that was a museum for Shaohsing wine – the city's most famous product. Five hundred meters of cobblestones later – maybe I should have opted for a rickshaw – I reached my destination: Shen Garden.

Just inside the front gate, there was one of those wave-eroded rocks, the kind no Chinese garden is complete without. Carved onto its surface and painted green were the characters 詩境 for "poetry world." The calligraphy was that of the man I was here to see, Lu You (1125–1210). Most Chinese know the story of Lu You and his cousin, T'ang Wan: how they grew up together and developed a mutual love of poetry, and how they married, and how Lu You was forced to divorce T'ang Wan because his mother thought she was distracting him from his studies, and how eight years later they met by chance one day in Shen Garden, and how T'ang Wan presented Lu You with a cup of wine, and how he responded with a poem to the tune "Ch'ai-t'ou-feng" 釵頭鳳 (Phoenix Hairpin). It was written on the garden wall:

> Your plain pink hands
> this fragrant yellow wine
> the city in spring the willows by the temple wall
> the cruelty of the east wind
> the fading of our joy
> the constant thoughts of sorrow
> all the years apart
> and yet and yet and yet again
> spring is still the same
> though you're thinner now
> the tear-streaked red eyes behind silken sleeves
> the peach petals falling
> the deserted pond pavilion
> the vows that remain
> the letters we can't send
> no and no and no again

> 紅酥手，黃藤酒，滿城春色宮墻柳。
> 東風惡，歡情薄，一懷愁緒，幾年離索。錯，錯，錯。
> 春如舊，人空瘦，淚痕紅邑鮫綃透。
> 桃花落，閑池閣。山盟雖在，錦書難托。莫，莫，莫。

Shen Garden in Shaohsing

T'ang Wan died the following year, and Lu You went off to fight the Jurch-ens. Beyond the poem was a gallery lined with thousands of tinkling bells from which hung messages left by people hoping that love might prevail.

I walked through the gallery, and the garden, and past a pond where hundreds of desiccated lotuses were bent over, done for the year. Beyond the pond, I passed through an opening in the garden's rear wall and entered the grounds of the Lu You Memorial Hall. The walls inside the hall were covered with his poems, including several in his own hand. Few poets wrote as many poems as Lu You. He left over 9,300. And that astonishing number doesn't include the poems of his youth, which he burned. The hall also included a map of all the places he traveled to. In addition to poems, he wrote journals. Especially celebrated is his account of his trip to Szechuan. As he sailed up the Yangtze and approached the towering form of Wushan near Paiticheng, he wrote "Three Gorges Song" 三峽歌:

> Of Wushan's twelve peaks from my boat I see nine
> their bright-green shapes fill the autumn sky

and morning clouds and evening rain it goes without saying
and the howls of gibbons all night in the moonlight

十二巫山見九峰，船頭彩翠滿秋空。朝雲暮雨渾虛語，一夜猿啼月明中。

Outside in the courtyard were more poems and also a statue of Lu You looking incredibly thin and bony. He often referred to himself as Lone Crane. This was the neighborhood where he grew up and lived with T'ang Wan during the three years they were married, down some lane not far from his statue – but no one knows exactly where. His parents were émigrés from the north who fled to Shaohsing after the Jurchen invasion and brought their infant son with them.

After an hour, I felt I had seen enough and decided to visit the places where we know he lived. Although Lu You held several government posts, such as the one in far-off Szechuan, he spent most of his life near Shaohsing. I walked out to the road and hailed a taxi. I told the driver I wanted to go to Yunmen Temple. He looked puzzled. He said he knew all the temples in Shaohsing and had never heard of Yunmen. I told him it was fifteen kilometers south of Shaohsing and showed him my map. He nodded, and off we went.

Once we worked our way through city traffic, we headed south on Highway 32. After ten kilometers, we entered the newly constructed town of Pingshui, whose previous incarnation was now at the bottom of a reservoir. As we exited New Pingshui, we came to a traffic circle and turned west. Five kilometers later, we saw a sign for Yunmen Temple. The temple was just above a small village of the same name.

Lu You lived near the temple with his father until he was thirty-two. Father and son each had his own hut. Lu You was here to study, and Lu You's father was engaging in the ancient Chinese practice of choosing retirement over service to a government in which he had no confidence.

Over the centuries, a number of poets wrote about visiting Lu You's hut. The hut was long gone, but the temple was still here, or at least a recent version. As I walked into the courtyard, I heard a group of laywomen chanting in the main shrine hall. The abbot saw me and came out to greet me. I told him why I was there, and he proceeded to show me around. I tried to look interested, but all I wanted to see was where Lu You's hut used to be. The abbot, however, was quite proud of what he'd been able to accomplish in such a rustic setting, considering that his devotees were farmers. He insisted on showing me each and every hall. As we walked from building to building, a recording of monks and nuns chanting "Omitofo" – the name of Amitabha, the Buddha of Infinity – followed us everywhere.

When the temple tour finally ended, the abbot pointed beyond the bamboo grove behind the buildings. He said Lu You's hut was originally on the hillside to the south, and he led me across a series of just-harvested rice fields for a closer look. I've always thought if I ever decided to live in a hut, I, too, would want to live close enough to a monastery to hear the dinner bell. No doubt, Lu You and his father chose the locations for their huts with similar thoughts in mind. It would have been a good place to study. I thanked the abbot for showing me the spot and started walking back to the taxi. When I told him I was off to look for Lu You's grave, he said he knew the area and offered to help.

He got in the front seat, and I got in back. When we reached the main road, he told the driver to head south. A hundred meters later, he directed us to turn left onto a road that followed the base of a forested hillside locals called Lu Family Garden. This was where Lu You was buried. The abbot added that no one had ever found the poet's grave. I knew that, but I had read that someone had recently found the grave of one of Lu You's sons. After a few hundred meters, the driver stopped where a landslide had destroyed enough of the road that we couldn't proceed. I got out and continued along what was left of the road, looking for a trail or a sign of a grave. After a few unsuccessful forays up trails that led nowhere, I took out a poem that Lu You wrote a few months before he died. At the base of the hill where he was buried, I read "To My Sons" 示兒:

> Of course I know once I die it's all empty
> still I regret not seeing our land united
> the day our armies reclaim the Central Plains
> at the family sacrifice don't forget to tell me

死後元知萬事空，但悲不見九州同。王師北定中原日，家祭無忘告乃翁。

Just in case they had forgotten, I told Lu the barbarians had been swept from the plains and the Middle Kingdom was at peace once again.

I walked back to the taxi, and we returned to the main road. The abbot wanted to talk with a farmer working in a nearby field, so we dropped him off. As he got out, he handed me a set of beads and an electronic device that gave me a choice of chants, "Homage to the Buddha of Infinity" or "Homage to Kuan-yin Bodhisattva." How could I refuse? As long as it wasn't "Happy Birthday."

On our way back to Shaohsing, I told the driver I had one more stop to make. I wanted to visit Chinghu, or Mirror Lake. The driver knew where it was. Once we returned to Shaohsing, we headed west on Shengli West Road. After about five kilometers, we turned north on Shaochi Boulevard and were soon driving along the lakeshore. After a kilometer or so, I asked the driver to pull over next to a factory. According to my map, we should have been near Tangwan Village. A factory worker confirmed that was, indeed, where we were. When I told him I was looking for where Lu You used to live, he pointed to a muddy road next to the factory. Behind the factory there were rows of plastic-canopied fields. And between the fields and the factory was a small, white picket fence surrounding a stele that said this was the site of Lu You's old home. The stele was new, erected in 1985. On the back was Lu You's "My Hut" 吾盧:

Here in my hut on Mirror Lake hut
my door opens onto the water
it's early autumn and the leaves still aren't red
at sunset the mountains look even greener
a lone crane flew here from the west
foraging on a sand spit it keeps calling
I too have known hardship and hunger
but won't swallow anything that stinks
although my diet includes no meat
with chopsticks and spoon I find enough treats
at a darkening window beside a flickering lamp
I pour unstrained wine into a broken jug

吾盧鏡湖上，　傍水開雲扃。　秋淺葉未丹，　日落山更青。
孤鶴從西來，　長鳴掠沙汀。　亦知常苦饑，　未忍吞膻腥。
我食雖不肉，　匕箸窮芳馨。　幽窗燈火冷，　濁酒倒殘瓶。

Lone Crane moved here in 1166. He was forty-two, and this was the only home he ever owned. He called it Sanshan Piehyeh (Three Hill Retreat) after the three hills southeast of his property. The hills weren't more than 200 meters high, but they were still there, and his hut wasn't. While I was reading the poem on the back of the stele, several farmers walked over out of curiosity. One of them suggested I walk farther down the road. He said that was where the residence was originally located. I followed his directions and about 200 meters later, next to a garbage dump, I stopped. There was a statue of Lu You. He was seated in a chair reading a book.

During the thirty-eight years Lu You lived at Mirror Lake, he wrote over 6,000 poems – two-thirds of his surviving work. Like T'ao Yuan-ming before him and his friend Fan Ch'eng-ta, Lu You was inspired by country living. Below his statue, I arranged my cups and read him a poem he wrote the year after he moved here, "Visiting a Village West of the Hill" 游山西村:

> Don't laugh at the farmers' cloudy solstice wine
> their year was good and they have enough food for guests
> hemmed in by hills and water and seemingly cut off
> theirs is another paradise of willow shade and flowers
> they greet the gods of spring with flutes and drums
> wearing simple robes and hats they've kept the old ways intact
> beginning today whenever there's a moon
> I'm grabbing my staff and knocking on their doors

莫笑農家臘酒渾，豐年留客足雞豚。山重水復疑無路，柳暗花明又一村。
簫鼓追隨春社近，衣冠簡樸古風存。從今若許閒乘月，柱杖無時夜叩門。

Despite his intention to follow the path of simple living, it took Lu You a while to learn to accept what he couldn't change – namely, government policies aimed at appeasing the Jurchens. It was only in the last twenty years of his life, after he was sixty-five, that he finally stopped trying and turned his attention to frequenting his neighbors' doors on moonlit nights.

Although it didn't rain that day, it must have been raining for days before I got here. As I walked back to the taxi, I had to keep stopping to scrape mud from my shoes. When I reached the stele again, one of the farmers came over and pointed out two ponds just beyond the fields. He said they were part of Lu You's old garden and used to be full of lotuses but now were choked with weeds. He said the local government had been talking about dredging the ponds, tearing down the factory, and building a park. I asked him what he

Former site of Lu You's home outside Shaohsing

grew under the plastic. He said strawberries and vegetables, depending on the time of year. I think Lu You would have preferred strawberries and vegetables to a park.

By the time I returned to the hotel, it was only two o'clock, and my day, at least the pilgrimage part, was done. After all my running around, the meter read only 211RMB. The driver was such a congenial fellow, I gave him 300 and asked him if he would drive me the following day. I finally noticed his dashboard ID. His surname was Chou, and Mr. Chou said he would see me in the morning.

Instead of going to my room, I proceeded to the hotel basement. The price of the room included a sauna, so I indulged. After half an hour of alternating between the sauna and the hot pools, I shampooed and put on a set of pajamas, provided by the attendant, then I went into a room where several other guests were relaxing in huge reclining chairs, each with its own TV. A girl brought me a fizzy orange drink and a plate of watermelon slices and cookies. For a pilgrim, I was living large.

When I returned to my room, I decided why not continue? I called the concierge and asked for a bucket of ice. I had a bottle of Woodford bourbon I'd bought at the Seattle duty-free. The good stuff, the Thomas H. Handy, was for the poets. The Woodford wasn't bad with ice. It made me feel like I was on a business trip. After a few pours, I dozed off for an hour. Two days in a row with a nap! I should have planned more naps. It was after four when I finally woke. Instead of getting up, I decided to work on revisions to my translations of Stonehouse's poems. I had been carrying them with me across China and was just about finished.

Although I hadn't done much that day, I had somehow worked up an appetite. Around six I realized it was time for dinner and went no farther than the Kungyichi, next door to the hotel. Its name first appeared as the title of a story Lu Hsun wrote in 1919, shortly after finishing *A Madman's Diary*. It was about an unsuccesful scholar named K'ung Yi-chi who frequented the restaurant. The story became so well known, the scholar's name replaced the restaurant's, and the restaurant's earlier name became the hotel's.

The restaurant was divided into two parts. There were tables outside, just off the pedestrian street, and inside, through sliding doors, more tables and the counter where diners ordered their food. I walked inside and ordered stinky tofu, a specialty of the town, Shaohsing meatballs, for which it was even better known and which came with taro, and spinach, just to have something green. Since it wasn't that cold, I sat outside at one of the rustic wooden tables that hadn't changed since K'ung Yi-chi sat there. He wasn't allowed to sit inside because he failed to pass the exams and was too poor. While I waited for my food, a waitress in equally rustic attire asked whether I wanted a bowl of wine. How could I not? Shaohsing was the most famous producer of rice wine in China. It included millet in addition to rice and went through two fermentations, then pasteurization, and finally aging in pottery jars for ten, twenty, or even fifty years. Unlike sake, which ranged from clear to the palest of yellows to cloudy-white, Shaohsing wine ranged from amber to red to brown, depending on how much millet was used in the mash. The variation also resulted in four categories of flavor from dry to sweet. I asked for a bowl of the restaurant's own semisweet brew.

When I first started traveling in China in the 1980s, beer and rice wine were served in rice bowls. The practice had since disappeared in favor of glasses. But not at the Kungyichi. The waitress returned with a bowl brimming with a liquid so dark it could have passed for a porter or a stout, but thicker. When I asked how strong it was, she said it was 14 percent. The taste was surprisingly complex. I tasted licorice and dates, and the sweetness was ever so slight. It reminded me of a very fine oloroso, one made with PX grapes. After I emptied my bowl, I noticed the date of the restaurant's founding stamped on the bottom, 1894. When my food arrived, I ordered a second bowl, one to share with Lu You, who wrote "Drinking at Night" 夜酌 not far from where I was sitting:

> I have a ladle of wine
> to share with you tonight
> a new year rain drums on the roof
> an ancient wind sings in the fields
> considering the world's springtime and fall
> this body's decay and emptiness
> the destruction of the tombs on Peimang
> let us sigh for all our heroes

我有一瓢酒，與君今夕同。鳴簷社公雨，卷野沛歌風。
閱世花開落，觀身却壞空。北邙丘壟盡，太息幾英雄。

In honor of my own pantheon, I ordered one more bowl, for dessert. It was a good thing I arrived in Shaohsing near the end of my trip and not at the beginning.

I actually turned down the free breakfast at the palace.
It was a small gesture, but one that made me feel better. I used to
lose weight when I traveled in China. Not anymore. And at home
it wasn't any easier, with my wife doing the cooking and me in
charge of leftovers. It was just after eight when I walked past the
bellboys for the last time and began another day on the pilgrim
trail. Mr. Chou was waiting outside, parked on the pedestrian
street – there were exceptions for taxis and delivery vehicles. I didn't see him
at first, because he wasn't driving a taxi. He brought his own car, which he
used for his other job at a driving school. He told me to be careful of the brake
pedal on the passenger's (or instructor's) side. We hadn't discussed a price
the day before, and we didn't discuss one now. I was more interested in mak-
ing sure my feet were on either side of the brake pedal. I guessed it would be
a 500, maybe even a 600RMB day, and I was fine with that.

Once we navigated Shaohsing's morning traffic, we headed east on the old
highway that connected Shaohsing with Ningpo. About twenty kilometers
later, shortly before we reached Shangyu, we entered the G15 expressway
and headed south. After another twenty kilometers, we exited at Shangpu,
then crossed the Tsaoeh River. At the east end of the bridge, we turned south
again and drove along the top of a dike. Two kilometers later, we turned off at
a sign for the Tungshan Scenic Area. Tungshan, according to the sign, was
two kilometers away, and the grave of Hsieh An (320–385) was three. Two
kilometers later, we were greeted by a Li Pai poem someone had carved on a
cliff at the base of the mountain. It was "Recalling Tungshan" 憶東山:

> It's been so long since I've been to Tungshan
> how many times have the wild roses bloomed
> or the white clouds come and gone
> on whose house now does the moonlight fall

不向東山久，薔薇幾度花。白雲還自散，明月落誰家。

Li Pai came here on three occasions to visit places along the Tsaoeh where
Hsieh An and his nephew and his nephew's nephew once lived. The moun-
tain was at the center of Hsieh An's old estate, and the shrine honoring him
and his esteemed descendants was less than a kilometer away, just below the

Li Pai's "Recalling Tungshan" at the foot of Tungshan

summit. It was called Taifu Shrine and was my first destination of the day.

As promised, the road ended a kilometer later, at Kuoching Monastery. Inside the monastery gate I asked a workman how to get to the shrine. He directed me through a side gate and down a flight of steps. The shrine's current incarnation was new, and I was the only person there other than the caretaker. He guided me to the main hall, and I paid my respects before the statues of the three Hsiehs: Hsieh An, whose grave was back up the steps, his nephew Hsieh Hsuan (343–388), and his nephew's nephew, Hsieh Ling-yun (385–433), whose grave and memorial hall I had visited a week earlier.

The entire mountain and all the land as far as the river was part of Hsieh An's Shihning Estate, where he lived between the ages of twenty and forty. Despite the remoteness of his residence, his reputation for moral integrity and unbiased judgment spread far beyond the mountain. He was eventually called out of his self-imposed retirement to serve at the Eastern Chin dynasty court in Nanking, where he quickly rose to become prime minister. It was a role at which he excelled. He was especially noted for his impartiality. China has had thousands of prime ministers, but few have had shrines built for them. Hsieh's had gone through many restorations, and its most recent was only a few years old. It was worthy of the man it honored. I especially liked the combination of slate-gray roof tiles and dark-brown walls and pillars. It was elegant yet understated. The caretaker said it cost a million renminbi to build and was the work of artisans from Ningpo.

Hsieh An, though, wasn't the reason I was there. I was there because of his grandnephew, Hsieh Ling-yun, who lived on his granduncle's estate as a youth and later lived just south of here on the estate he inherited from his uncle, Hsieh Hsuan. Although Ling-yun's various residences were long gone, I wanted to see what he loved so much about this area. Since I wasn't going to see that at a shrine, I headed back to my taxi. There were more mountains on the itinerary.

On my way back through the temple courtyard, I met the abbess. In the course of conversation, I mentioned that I was visiting places where Hsieh Ling-yun once lived. She said his residence on his granduncle's estate was up a side valley not far from the monastery — that was the kind of news I was always happy to hear. Local knowledge often never made it into historical accounts. When I expressed an interest in going there, she asked one of the monks to guide me. The monk, she said, had lived as a hermit in the same area and knew the trail. So, off we went: me, the monk, Mr. Chou, and another man doing some work at the temple who said he had climbed mountains all over China and never passed up a chance for a hike.

From the monastery, the monk led us northeast along a dirt road. A few minutes later, we came to a reservoir whose water had drained out. The monk said there was something wrong with its construction. He scrambled up a dirt slope and motioned for us to follow. At the top he disappeared into a bamboo thicket, and we followed. Fortunately, the monk knew to bring a machete and was able to clear enough of the bamboo for us to reach the trail that he had once used as a hermit. It wasn't much of a trail. It came, and it went. We had to stop repeatedly and wait until the monk found it again.

At one point, while he was looking for the trail, he stopped and broke off some pine needles and ate the tips. He said they were effective for preventing illnesses, and he offered me some. They were so bitter I spit them out, which amused him. When the trail passed through a hillside of ferns, he said they were one of his favorite foods when he lived on the mountain, but added it was too late in the year to eat them: spring and summer was fern season. Whenever we passed mushrooms, he also let us know which ones were edible. He said it was good we were hiking in November. We didn't have to worry about snakes. The monastery, he said, kept half a dozen peacocks to hold the snake population in check.

After we had hiked for more than an hour, the monk pointed to a mist-filled valley. He said that was where Hsieh lived when he was young. It was a perfectly beautiful spot. But I couldn't help wonder at Hsieh's fortitude in trying to make it through winter in such a remote place. I could see him writing "Year End" 歲暮:

> These worries won't let me sleep
> when will this night ever end
> the snow-covered world in the moonlight
> the withering and relentless north wind
> the season that leaves nothing behind
> at the end of the year I feel helpless

殷憂不能寐，苦此夜難頹。明月照積雪，朔風勁且衷。
運往無淹物，年逝覺已催。

The spot where he lived wasn't that far below us, but there was no trail leading down. We had to continue along the ridge. At some point we went through a clear-cut where the ground was covered with the slash left from logging. We had to climb over and under the debris. Our guide took a wrong

Valley in which Hsieh Ling-yun's hermitage was located

turn but didn't realize it for half an hour. It had been eight years since he had been back to this part of the mountain. Instead of going back, he continued on. He said it would take longer if we went back and we could still get there, he added, in another hour or so. That was too much for me. Before we set out, the nun told us it used to take her thirty minutes to reach Hsieh's place, and she estimated it should take us forty. We had already been hiking two hours. I spotted a dirt trail far below us and told the monk I was calling it quits. My ankle was beginning to hurt, and there were more mountains on the day's agenda. I took advantage of an old landslide and slid down the dirt parts and scrambled over the rocky parts. When I reached the trail below, I waved for the others to follow. Sometimes you have to know when to fold 'em. When the monk finally caught up with me, he told me I shouldn't be disappointed. Right trail, wrong trail, both were trails on the Path. Of course, he was right. Still, I wished this particular wrong trail hadn't taken such a big bite out of the day.

The dirt trail eventually widened into a logging road, and thirty minutes later we were out of the mountains. When I asked the monk how much longer it would take to walk back to the monastery, he said at least an hour. I hadn't realized our mountain meandering had taken us so far from where we started. While I was adding this news to my earlier disappointment, we passed a farmhouse with a stable of donkeys. I thought maybe a donkey would get us there quicker. When I suggested this to the monk, he said the donkeys were used for carrying provisions to the hermits in the area, not for riding. Hsieh Ling-yun wasn't alone in his appreciation of Tungshan's seclusion. I also noticed that the farmer was filling his van with produce. I approached him and asked whether he could ferry us back to the temple. He was reluctant but acquiesced when the monk seconded my request.

The farmer dropped us off at the base of Tungshan, not far from Li Pai's poem. He said his van couldn't make it up the mountain with us and his produce. That was as far as he could take us. I was grateful to squeeze an hour back into the day and tried to give him 100RMB, but he wouldn't take it. After the farmer drove off, my monk guide and the other man headed up the road to the monastery. Mr. Chou said it didn't make sense for us both to walk to the car and proposed that I wait there. My ankle appreciated his insight. Thankfully, my trip was almost over. Thirty minutes later, Mr. Chou drove down, and we returned the way we came.

After we recrossed the bridge at Shangpu, we turned south on the old highway: Highway 104. As we did, it started to rain. I was glad the skies waited until we were out of the mountains. Getting lost on the Path was one thing. Getting soaked was quite another. It was pouring, and I was dry. Suddenly I felt much better.

Ten kilometers later, we turned off the highway and crossed the Tsaoeh again. Once we were on the other side, we turned south and continued into the town of Changchen, less than a kilometer away. The place was a mess. Everything was being torn down – even the mountain at the north edge of town. The mountain was called Chiangshan and was shaped like a pyramid. I asked Mr. Chou to drive a bit farther so I could get a better view of it. Less than a kilometer later, we stopped at Lingyun Village. It was named for Hsieh Ling-yun and was at the northern edge of the property he called Shihning Villa, to distinguish it from Hsieh An's Shih-ning Estate. In one of the many quatrains that make up his "Ode to Mountain Living" 山居賦, he wrote:

> As for my two north and south homes
> they're accessible by water not by land
> unless you examine the wind and the clouds
> you won't know where they are

若乃南北兩居，水通陸阻。觀風瞻雲，方知厥所。

His northern residence was located near the foot of Chiangshan, not far from where we parked. Although I wasn't planning to go hiking in search of it, I got out for a closer look. Mr. Chou loaned me his umbrella – not expecting rain, I had packed mine. I walked up and down the road looking at the mountain and the surrounding landscape. I talked to several villagers, but questions about where Hsieh Ling-yun might have lived were met with blank stares.

I got back in the car, and we recrossed the Tsaoeh and resumed our southward journey. I reluctantly checked Shihmenshan (Stone Gate Mountain) off my itinerary. It was one of Hsieh Ling-yun's favorite haunts, up a side valley west of the river. I'd planned to take a look, but my Tungshan sortie made that impossible. Besides, it was raining. All I could do was imagine the source of "Overnight at Stone Gate" 夜宿石門, which Hsieh wrote after a night at the hermitage he maintained at the foot of the mountain:

> I moved the orchids from my garden this morning
> fearing they wouldn't survive the frost

I spent the night with the returning clouds
lit by the moon at the top of Stone Gate
hearing crows call I knew the birds were roosting
hearing leaves fall I knew the wind was rising
the different sounds I heard as one
they were different yet equally transporting
but no one was here to share such wonders
no one to praise this fragrant wine
the person I love didn't come
I dried my hair in the sunshine in vain

朝搴苑中蘭，畏彼霜下歇。暝還雲際宿，弄此石上月。
鳥鳴識夜棲，木落知風發。異音同致聽，殊響俱清越。
妙物莫為賞，芳醑誰與伐。美人竟不來，陽阿徒晞髮。

The first and last couplets were inspired by one of Ch'u Yuan's "Nine Songs," in which Ch'u used orchids to represent the unperceived virtue of seclusion. Ch'u too waited in vain for his loved one's return. Chu's was a shaman's song, and so was Hsieh's. Mountains have always been home to spiritual seekers in China. In the case of shamans, in addition to the solitude, they also went there in search of the plants and fungi that made their spiritual flights possible. In "Overnight at Stone Gate," though, Hsieh is transported by the sounds he hears. Mountains made him high, and he felt at home in their presence. But his life in the mountains was hardly like that of a recluse or a hermit. Wherever Hsieh went, his retainers went, too. While we never see them in his poetry, they're there, like so many stagehands, arranging the scenery for his next performance. We can sense them in the hut's shadow in "Climbing to the Summit of Stone Gate" 登石門最高頂:

I set off at dawn for precipitous cliffs
I rested at dusk in a mountain hut
a lofty lodge set among scattered peaks
perched above a winding stream
the door opened onto towering pines
the front steps and foundation were piled-up stones
with no apparent route across the cliffs
no clear trail through the thickets of bamboo
those who hike up forget the way they came

those who go down can't make out the path
mountain torrents gush at dusk
gibbons howl all night long
the unspoken truth isn't other than this
the Way I follow isn't somewhere else
my mind is one with every tree in autumn
my eyes smile at every sign of spring
living a normal life waiting for the end
I just go along and everything is perfect
and yet I regret the absence of friends
no one to join me on this ladder through the clouds

晨策尋絕壁，夕息在山棲。疏峰抗高館，對嶺臨迴溪。
長林羅戶穴，積石擁階基。連巖覺路塞，密竹使徑迷。
來人忘新術，去子惑故蹊。活活夕流駛，噭噭夜猿啼。
沈冥豈別理，守道自不攜。心契九秋幹，目翫三春荑。
居常以待終，處順故安排。惜無同懷客，共登青雲梯。

Even an army of retainers could never make up for the absence of friends. Everyone Hsieh knew was busy in town or at court. It was the isolation of mountains that attracted Hsieh, yet it was also their isolation that drove him back to the capital and to his demise. Maybe if he had been poorer, he would have lived longer. Unfortunately, he was not poor. And he did not live a normal life.

Beyond the turn off to Stone Gate, the Tsaoeh Valley grew narrower, and the expressway that paralleled the highway quickly consumed whatever space the highway didn't. At the village of Yaoyao, we crossed the Tsaoeh one last time and started up a mountain road – directions courtesy of villagers. The road wound all over the place, but we kept stopping to ask farmers, and they kept encouraging us to continue on. After thirty minutes of this, Chechishan finally came into view. Suddenly the rain stopped.

The mountain was named for Hsieh Hsuan, Hsieh Ling-yun's uncle, who was called Ch'e-chi-chiang, the Cart-Riding General. In 383, at the Battle of Fei River, Hsieh Hsuan led an army of 80,000 against an enemy force numbering over a million, and crushed it. His victory immortalized Hsieh in Chinese annals – hence the name of the mountain (Cart-Riding Mountain). It formed the southern border of Hsieh Hsuan's vast estate, which Hsieh Ling-yun inherited when he was three years old. Once Ling-yun came of age, the estate became the base of his many explorations, and he maintained residences at both ends of the property. It was a landscape of narrow valleys and thickly forested mountains divided by an endless array of streams, waterfalls, and lakes. It was only recently that the forests began giving way to tea plantations, which accounted for the paved road.

Not long after we passed through the tiny village of Chuangchiao, I asked Mr. Chou to pull over. There was a clear view of Chechishan, and it looked like the perfect place to share some "fragrant wine." I waded into the waist-high tea bushes that covered the slope until I found a clear spot to set out my cups. As I was filling them with the last of the Thomas H. Handy, the fog rolled in and shrouded the peak – still shy after all these years. While the perfume of my offering drifted up to the poetry world, I read Hsieh a poem he wrote just north of there, on the other side of Chechishan, "Written While Coming Back by Boat from Shihpi Hermitage" 石壁精舍還湖中作:

> From dawn to dusk the sky keeps changing
> mountains and rivers have their own inner light
> an inner light that can be so entrancing
> travelers forget to go home
> the day was beginning when I left the valley
> the light was fading when I reached the boat again
> forested ravines were gathering darkness
> red clouds were returning with the dusk
> the caltrop and lily pads shimmered
> the marsh grass and rushes were dense
> pushing through I hurried up South Trail
> happy to spend the night in East Cottage
> an untroubled person doesn't care about possessions
> a contented person doesn't offend reason
> for those who would guard their lives here's a message
> why not give this Path a try

昏旦變氣候，山水含清暉。清暉能娛人，遊子憺忘歸。
出谷日尚早，入舟陽已微。林壑斂暝色，雲霞收夕霏。
芰荷迭映蔚，蒲稗相因依。披拂趨南徑，愉悅偃東扉。
慮淡物自輕，意愜理無違。寄言攝生客，試用此道推。

Offering Hsieh Ling-yun whiskey at Chechishan

Shihpi Hermitage, where Hsieh studied, was on the south shore of Wuhu Lake. His villa was on the north shore. According to my calculations, the lake was five kilometers north of where I stood. Just after I finished reading the poem, the rain returned. I hurried to wrap up my little ceremony and rejoined Mr. Chou in his car. But in my haste, I dropped my eyeglasses and didn't discover they were missing until an hour later. I added them to the offering. Right trail, wrong trail. Glasses, no glasses. Lots of opportunities to practice on the pilgrim trail. At least it wasn't raining inside the car.

Once we returned to the highway, it wasn't long before we left the Tsaoeh watershed behind. I could see why Hsieh loved it. There were mountains in all directions. And where there weren't mountains, there was water. It was, after all, the birthplace of the Mountains and Rivers school of poetry. Half an hour later, we arrived at the Shengchou bus station, just in time for the 3:10 to Tientai, my final destination. I paid Mr. Chou 700RMB, which surprised him, but he earned it. I couldn't have accomplished such a whirlwind visit to Hsieh's old haunts without his help.

Mr. Chou waved goodbye, and I boarded my bus. Tientai wasn't that far, maybe sixty kilometers. I thought it might take an hour. Unfortunately, the bus took the old highway up and over the mountains, rather than the expressway through them. I arrived in Tientai two hours later, but at least I arrived without incident. A five-minute taxi ride brought me to Kuoching Monastery (different characters from the one on Tungshan). The rain had stopped, and I could see some blue sky. Before I got out, I asked the driver for his phone number. I told him I would be calling later to talk about my plans for the next day. He was amenable and headed back to town. Since it was after five, and the monastery's main gate had already closed, I entered through the side gate. I had stayed at the monastery a dozen times and knew the way to the guest hall. When I got there, I asked a monk where I could find the guest manager. He pointed to a window. He said to talk to the layman on the other side. The layman was in charge of registering guests. As soon as my request for lodging was out of my mouth, the man said the monastery was full and that they didn't accept outsiders anyway. When I told him I had stayed there before, he abruptly closed the window. That was surprising, and disappointing. I walked back out to the courtyard, wondering what to do. While I was wondering, another monk saw me and asked what I was doing there. After a brief conversation, he told me to follow him. He led me to the guest quarters at the back of the monastery. Once he found the laywoman in charge, he asked her to unlock a room and register my passport information.

After filling out the registration form and dropping my bag in my room, I walked back out the monastery's side gate and told the monk in charge of the gate that I would be back in an hour. It was always embarrassing to bang on a monastery gate once it was closed for the night. After he assured me it would be open for another hour or so, I walked up the road to the Tientai Hotel, the only hotel inside what was now a national park. Waiting for me in the lobby was Robin Chang.

When I returned to Shanghai to finish the last part of my journey, the Stonehouse–Cold Mountain section, I was invited to give a talk at Futan University. Before the talk began, Robin came up and introduced himself. He said his name was Chang Ch'i and he was Gary Flint's technical adviser and responsible for maintaining Gary's website, Mountainsongs.net.

Gary had traveled all over China visiting mountains where poems were written. At last count, he had visited over 200. He posted photos of them as well as more than a thousand poems inspired by the mountains – translated by me and Burton Watson and a dozen others. It was a labor of love: all the great mountains in China and all of its great poets together in one place. I saw Gary whenever I passed through Shanghai, to compare notes on mountains and poets. He was the one person I had met whose passion for such things exceeded mine. So I was surprised that he hadn't answered my e-mails or phone calls. I'd last seen Gary in 2008, in Shanghai. He gave me a self-produced CD of country-western music he recorded with some local musicians titled *Shanghai Cowboys*. I played it whenever I felt like feeling blue, which was the effect country-western music always had on me. After the talk, Robin told me Gary died of pancreatic cancer in 2009. I went back to my hotel and thought about Gary. Cold Mountain was the first poet I translated and the last poet I planned to visit on this trip, and Gary Flint and I were both connected with him through Gary's friend and classmate at Reed College, Gary Snyder, who also translated Cold Mountain. So I called Robin and asked him to join me. I thought it would be a good way of thanking all those we loved and admired, not just China's greatest poets but also those who loved them.

While we were eating dinner, Robin called the taxi driver who brought me to the monastery and told him our plans for the following day. It was all arranged. My last day.

After dinner, I walked back to the monastery and got ready for bed. It was only seven o'clock, but it had been a big day, and I was tired. What I really wanted was a bath. Monasteries, of course, don't have bathtubs. In the old days, at the monasteries where I lived in Taiwan, I had to make do with a bucket of cold water. We got hot water once a week. But at Kuoching, there was a new electric hot water tank in the bathroom, and there was a hose with a handheld showerhead. It hardly compared to the previous night at the Hsienheng. Still, the hot water helped soothe the scratches on my arms from my mountain excursion. The room didn't come with a towel, but my bandanna worked just fine. Indeed, everything was, as Hsieh said, *perfect*. I opened the window and air-dried what the bandanna didn't then lay down on one of the room's two beds. It was just as hard as the monastery's old beds that had boards for mattresses, but it didn't matter.

It was so quiet, all I could hear were the faint sounds of frogs and crickets. The year was getting late. Everyone was going to sleep. Before I joined them, I got out my backup eyeglasses and my Stonehouse translations. I thought I'd work on a few revisions. I opened the manuscript, and my eyes settled on number 151. The first line was enough: "After meditation I chant a Cold Mountain poem" 禪餘高誦寒山偈. I suddenly realized I had one more day and it was going to be with Cold Mountain. I thought back to the first time I met him. It was in 1976, and the abbot of the monastery where I was living gave me a copy of Cold Mountain's poems. Cold Mountain and I have been friends ever since.

The sound of someone banging the monastery's early
morning wake-up board had the intended effect. I looked at
my travel alarm on the table next to the bed. It was three thirty.
I tried to go back to sleep but couldn't. I turned on the light and
got out my Stonehouse translations and spent an hour on revi-
sions. It was a distraction-free time, but I fell asleep again. The
next thing I knew, someone in the hallway was calling my name,
my Chinese name, Ch'ih-sung (Red Pine), and knocking on doors. It was
six thirty. I hadn't intended on making the early morning chanting cere-
mony, which began at four thirty, or breakfast either, which began at six.
Maybe I was supposed to. Maybe the rules for guests had changed. I put on
my shorts and T-shirt and opened the door. Standing there was the monk
who had led me to the guest quarters the night before. He said he was the
monastery's *yi-po,* the abbot's personal secretary, and handed me a bag with
two coconut-filled croissants. He also handed me a book. It was an old-style
string-bound edition titled *Han-shan-tzu shih-chi* 寒山子詩集 (The Collected
Poems of Han-shan). It was a limited edition published by the monastery.
The book and croissants were gifts from the abbot, Master Yun-kuan, who
was away when I arrived the night before. I was dumbfounded and just nod-
ded my appreciation.

Croissants and earliest extant edition of Cold Mountain's poems

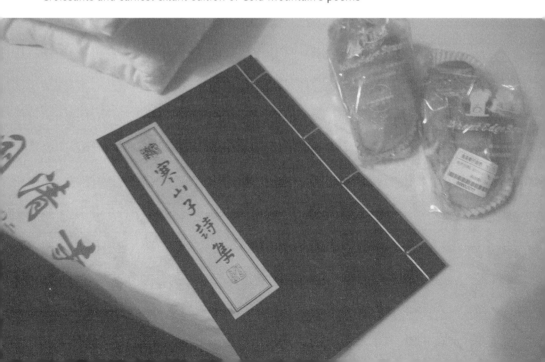

After the monk left, I made myself a cup of coffee and ate one of the crois-sants — it was unexpectedly delicious. Then I opened the book. It turned out to be a special reprint of the earliest extant woodblock edition of Cold Moun-tain's poems. I had heard of the edition but had never seen a copy. Accord-ing to the publication information inside, it was originally printed in 1201 and was now part of the rare book collection of the Chekiang Provincial Museum. What a treasure! And there it was in what I hoped were my coconut-filling-free hands. When I opened the book, staring up at me was poem 299:

> People laugh at my poems
> but my poems are refined enough
> they don't need Cheng Hsuan's comments
> much less Mao Heng's explanations
> I don't mind few understand them
> true friends alas are rare
> if we got rid of tonal rules
> no one could stop my disease
> one day I'll meet a clear-eyed person
> then it will infect the world

> 有人笑我詩，我詩合典雅。不煩鄭氏箋，豈用毛公解。
> 不恨會人稀，只為知音寡。若遣趁宮商，余病莫能罷。
> 忽遇明眼人，即自流天下。

Who exactly that clear-eyed person was remains a mystery. It's not as though Cold Mountain had a publisher. But the bigger mystery was, who made the croissants? I never found out. A few years earlier, when I was vis-iting Chenju Monastery, China's most renowned Zen training center high in the mountains of Kiangsi province, a monk invited me into his room for a cup of espresso, which he made with a Rube Goldberg contraption imported from Belgium. I didn't ask how or why and just enjoyed the espresso. In the same spirit, I decided to accept the croissant mystery for what it was. I didn't have time to ponder mysteries anyway. It was the final day of my pilgrimage, and I needed to get an early start.

I began with the monastery. There were two places I wanted to visit before eight o'clock, which was when the monks opened their gates to the public. Kuoching was one of the best-preserved monasteries in China. Looking at the blue sky out my window, I could see it was going to be a big day for the

Three Sages

monks as well as for me. I left my bag in the room and navigated the maze of corridors and steps to the monastery's main courtyard. I always enjoyed standing there. The setting, for me, was one of the most inspiring in China. The ginkgos and cedars were a thousand years old, and the trees beyond the temple walls weren't far behind. Tientai was declared a national park in 1988, and both the mountain and the monastery had benefited. The shrine halls dated back over 300 years and were as impressive as any in China. Standing there, I felt as if I were in the T'ang.

After spending a few minutes in the eighth century, I crossed the court-yard and descended a flight of steps to the monastery's shrine for its Three Sages. These three friends were the reason I was here. In fact, they were the reason I came to China in the first place. Their statues were about two-thirds scale, carved out of wood and gilded. The artistry was remarkable. So was the effect. Even though the hall was unlit, they radiated light. Feng-kan was standing in the middle holding a staff taller than he was, Shih-te was on the left holding a broom, and Han-shan was on the right leaning on a short hiking staff. They were all laughing.

Feng-kan came to Kuoching first. He showed up at the monastery one day in the second half of the eighth century, riding a tiger — or so the story goes. Because he was tall and skinny, people called him Feng-kan, meaning "big stick." Whenever anyone asked him about Buddhism, all he would say was, "Whatever works" 隨時. Shih-te, whose name means "pickup," was abandoned on Tientaishan as a child. Feng-kan found him crying on the mountain, picked him up, and brought him back to Kuoching. Although Shih-te lived at the monastery, he never became a monk. He was content to work in the kitchen and sweep the monastery grounds. Han-shan was the last to arrive. He took his name, meaning "cold mountain," from the cave he lived in, which was called Hanyen, or Cold Cliff. He, too, never became a monk, but he visited the monastery often enough. To this day, no one knows much more than this about any of them. All we know is that they were friends and practitioners of the Anything Real Dharma, as Feng-kan called it in this poem of his:

> Whenever Cold Mountain stops to visit
> or Pickup pays his usual call
> we talk about the mind or the moon
> or wide-open space
> reality has no limit
> so anything real includes it all

寒山特相訪，拾得常往來。論心話明月，太虛廓無礙。
法界即無邊，一法普偏該。

It must have been quite a monastery back in those days, namely the last decades of the eighth century and the first few of the ninth. After paying my respects to its Three Sages, I went to visit the monastery's other treasure, a plum tree. I was always relieved to see it. It had been there over 1,400 years and looked like plum trees always did in winter: lifeless. The Lunar New Year was still two months away, and somehow it always remembered what to do when the time came. I envied it its memory. I wished the plum tree another thousand springs and walked back to my room. After finishing the second croissant and another cup of coffee, I packed my bag and returned my room key to the caretaker. Then I set off to pay my respects to the man who planted the plum tree.

As I made my way toward the exit, I met the abbot in a side courtyard. He had just returned from his travels. We exchanged greetings, and I thanked him for his kindness and generosity. He had been talking to the monks about the rice. Under the eaves that surrounded the courtyard were dozens of huge baskets of grain the monks had harvested from their fields. They were sending the rice off to be milled. There were 130 monks living at the temple, and they ate a lot of rice. So they grew a lot of rice. It was November, and now that the rice had been harvested, they were about to replant the same fields with rapeseed to make cooking oil. Kuoching was a functioning monastery and had been ever since that plum tree was planted there.

After saying goodbye to the abbot, I passed through the main gate and crossed the ancient stone archway of Fengkan Bridge, named for the eldest of the Three Sages. In addition to the previous poem, Feng-kan also left this one, which he began by quoting the response of Hui-neng, Zen's Sixth Patriarch, to a monk who thought Buddhist practice amounted to wiping dust off a mirror:

Actually there isn't a thing
much less any dust to wipe away
who can master this
doesn't need to sit there stiff

本來無一物，亦無塵可拂。若能了達此，不用坐兀兀。

Once across the bridge, I walked up the road to the hotel. Robin was waiting in the lobby, and a few minutes later our driver showed up. I told him I wanted to begin with a visit to Chihche Tayuan, Chih-che's Stupa Cemetery. Even though the driver was from Tientai, he hadn't heard of the place. I had been there once about fifteen years earlier and wasn't too sure of its exact location myself. All I knew was that it was halfway up the mountain, so we started up on the one and only road.

It was a winding road with lots of hairpin turns. Thankfully it was in good condition – one of the advantages of being in a national park. The stupa cemetery I hoped to visit housed the remains of Chih-che (538–597). It was Chih-che who first built a hut where Kuoching Temple now stood. He was also the man who planted the plum tree. As we wound higher and higher, I thought surely there would be a road sign. But no. Just past the 9km marker, I asked the driver to pull over. A roadside trail of narrow stone steps looked familiar. Robin and I decided to give the trail a try, and we followed it about 200 meters until it forked. We went right. When we came to a farmhouse, the farmer pointed us to a different trail that eventually connected with the trail we should have taken.

A few minutes later, we reached the temple that housed Chih-che's stupa. Few monks were more important in the development of Chinese Buddhism than Chih-che. The only others of similar stature were Hui-neng, who helped establish Zen in China, and Hsuan-tsang, who helped spread the teachings of Yogacara – that everything is made of mind. The school of Buddhism established by Chih-che was different. It was named for the mountain, Tientai, and it was syncretic. It sought to harmonize and explain the different teachings attributed to the Buddha by assigning them to different periods in his ministry. To this end, Chih-che arranged all the sutras in an order of increasing transcendence, culminating with the *Lotus Sutra,* which he considered the Buddha's most profound teaching.

Chih-che was also known for the system of meditation he developed. He called it "stopping and looking," as it involved cessation of discursive thought and contemplation of fundamental reality. In his "Commentary on the Benevolent King Sutra" 仁王經疏, he explained it this way: "When formless wisdom illuminates the formless world, both inside and out are still, for both are seen as empty" 謂無相妙慧照無相境，內外并寂，緣觀共空. I've always preferred Han-shan's summary in number 82 of his 307 surviving poems:

> Springwater is pure in an emerald stream
> moonlight is white on Cold Mountain
> silence thoughts and the spirit becomes clear
> contemplate emptiness and the world becomes still

碧澗泉水清，寒山月華白。默知神自明，觀空境逾寂。

Robin and I lit incense outside the shrine hall – lighting it inside was forbidden as a safety precaution – then we entered and bowed before the stupa. I told Chih-che his plum tree was doing fine. Unlike that of most monks, Chih-che's body wasn't cremated. It was placed inside a large ceramic pot, and the pot was placed inside the stupa. It was a very impressive stupa, about seven meters high and carved completely out of white marble.

Cold Mountain Cave

After paying our respects, Robin and I returned to the taxi and asked the driver to take us to Cold Mountain. Han-shan often visited Kuoching, and I'm guessing it was where he spent his winters, but he spent most of the year twenty-five kilometers south of Tientai.

Two kilometers north of town we turned west onto Highway 62. It was a four-lane divided highway. In the past it didn't even have a number, much less pavement. Whenever we came to crossroads, there were traffic lights – traffic lights in the middle of nowhere and no traffic. When I first traveled this road in 1989, it was nothing but dirt and gravel, and I was in the back of a three-wheeled carryall that went no more than twenty kilometers an hour. Times had changed. Twenty minutes and not a single pothole later, we arrived in Chiehtouchen. The village was only three streets deep. Still, it was always tricky finding the road that went to Cold Mountain's cave. My memory got us through the village, and we soon found ourselves on the narrow road that led along a dike, then through an opening in the adjacent mountains. Whenever I passed through that opening, I thought of Han-shan's number 16:

> People ask the way to Cold Mountain
> but roads don't reach Cold Mountain
> in summer the ice doesn't melt
> sunny days the fog is too dense
> so how did someone like me arrive
> our minds are not the same
> if they were the same
> you would be here

人間寒山道， 寒山路不通。 夏天冰未釋， 日出霧朦朧。
似我何由屆， 與君心不同。 君心若似我， 還得到其中。

Once we came out of the defile, I remembered the remaining turns. We didn't have to ask a single farmer. Ten minutes later, we pulled over at the side of the road. Hanyen (Cold Cliff) was 200 meters away. As Robin and I started down the trail, our driver decided to join us. He had never been here. I'd been to the cave at least ten times, though never so late in the year. Usually the fields were full of corn, beans, and sunflowers. This time all that remained was stubble from the harvest.

The cave where Han-shan lived was at the base of the cliff. It was roughly fifty meters across, just as deep, and over ten meters high, with an assortment of holes in the roof where bats lived. Once we reached it, we walked to the back of the cave, where devotees had set up several shrines to the Three Sages. We lit incense at all of them, just in case one had an active connection. Then we walked back to the cave entrance and over to the doorway of a two-story roofless building. It didn't have a roof because it was inside the cave. It had gone through a lot of transformations, but ever since I had been coming here it was home to a hermit. For the past ten years, that hermit was a lay-woman. She was about sixty-five years old, but I never learned her name. I called her Butterfly Woman, because she seemed to flit and float. I thought maybe she had been an opera singer: she had the presence and mannerisms of someone who had been on a stage. Also, she didn't speak – I presumed she'd taken a vow of some sort.

She was standing by the stove when we entered and waved for us to sit on the stools next to her table. There was now another woman living with her, about the same age. I just wanted to say a quick hello, but that was impossible. We had to sit down and have tea. And it wasn't ordinary tea. It was ginseng tea. Her disciple was very proud to tell us the ginseng was from America.

How Han-shan ended up at Hanyen is a mystery. In fact, everything about him is a mystery. No one knows where he came from or who he was. He was just that crazy hermit who wrote poems on trees and rocks and temple walls. His dates, too, are a mystery. My best guess is that he came to Tientai to escape the aftermath of the An Lu-shan Rebellion (755–758), and he

Author reading Cold Mountain poems in Cold Mountain Cave

died around 850, which was when people started writing stories about him. It's said he lived to be 120, which would mean he was born around 730 and arrived at Cold Cliff around 760. Poem number 131 recounts his arrival here:

Born thirty years ago
I've traveled countless miles
along rivers where the green rushes swayed
to the frontier where the red dust swirled
I've made elixirs and tried to become immortal
I've read the classics and written odes
and now I've retired to Cold Mountain
to lie in a stream and wash out my ears

出生三十年，常遊千萬里。行江青草合，入塞紅塵起。
錬藥空求仙，讀書兼詠史。今日歸寒山，枕流兼洗耳。

The first printed edition of his poems was published in 1189. The second edition, a reprint of which was in my bag, appeared in 1201. There was something about his craziness that impressed others, something that wasn't crazy at all, which made people see the craziness going on in their own lives and in their own times. His was the fearless attitude of a bodhisattva doing everything he could to help others, as he himself noted in number 234:

Cold Mountain speaks these words
as if he were a madman
he tells people what he thinks
thus he incurs their wrath
a straightforward mind speaks straight words
a straightforward mind holds nothing back
crossing the River of Death
who is that jabbering fool
the road to the grave is dark
and karma holds the reins

寒山出此語，復似顛狂漢。有事對面說，所以足人怨。
心直出語直，直心無背面。臨死渡奈河，誰是嘍囉漢。
冥冥泉臺路，被業相拘絆。

It wasn't the kind of poetry officials exchanged with each other, nor was it the kind most people wanted to hear. But someone did, and someone wrote it down. Han-shan has never been considered a great poet in terms of poetic craft, but poetry is not simply about getting the tones and the rhymes and the metaphors right. Poetry is also about the message and where that message comes from. As Mao Heng said in the earliest known commentary to the Book of Poetry, "Poetry is what the heart holds dear put into words" 在心為志, 發言為詩. Of course, there are many kinds of poetry, and plenty of it is disconnected from the heart. But the poets whose graves and homes I had been visiting agreed with Mao Heng. And of those who spoke from the heart, few have had the impact of Han-shan. It isn't surprising that Han-shan, not Li Pai or Tu Fu, became the patron saint of the Beat generation, or that Jack Kerouac would dedicate *The Dharma Bums* to him. And it isn't surprising that Robin and I were here, sitting where Han-shan wrote number 180:

> Once I reached Cold Mountain all my cares stopped
> no idle thoughts remained in my head
> with nothing to do I write poems on rock walls
> trusting the current like an unmoored boat

一住寒山萬事休, 更無雜念掛心頭。 閒於石壁題詩句, 任運還同不繫舟。

After a second cup of tea, we hid some money under a plate, thanked our hosts, and returned to the taxi. Halfway back to the mountain defile that led back to Chiehtouchen, we turned right and followed a different road, one that led to Mingyen. Both Mingyen and Hanyen consisted of cliffs and caves on opposite sides of a huge massif but only a kilometer apart as a magpie might fly. Mingyen was where Han-shan lived when he got older, and it was also where Shih-te lived when he wasn't at Kuoching. Of the poems Shih-te left about his life at Mingyen, my favorite is number 49:

> Woods and springs make me smile
> no kitchen smoke for miles
> clouds rise up from rocky ridges
> cascades tumble down
> a gibbon's howl makes the path clearer
> a tiger's roar transcends the world

pine wind sighs so softly
birds discuss singsong
I walk the winding streams
and climb the peaks alone
sometimes I sit on a boulder
or lie down and gaze at trailing vines
but when I see a distant town
all I hear is noise

可笑是林泉，　數里勿人煙。　雲從巖嶂起，　瀑布水潺潺。
猿啼暢道曲，　虎嘯出人間。　松風清颯颯，　鳥語聲關關。
獨步繞石澗，　孤陟上峰巒。　時坐盤陀石，　偃仰攀蘿沿。
遙望城隍處，　唯聞鬧喧喧。

Mingyen felt different than Hanyen. It looked different, too. It consisted of a gorge 300 meters long and 40 meters wide, with a cave at the far end and

Shrine to Three Sages in Mingyen Cave

a nunnery at the near end. The nunnery was Mingyen Temple, and different versions of it had been here for the past thousand years. Beyond the nunnery were half a dozen shrine halls lining the gorge, all of them built since my first visit. A lot of money was being invested to make the place a major pilgrimage site. We walked past them all until we reached the cave at the end of the gorge. I wanted to show Robin the place where Han-shan and Shih-te were said to have disappeared, where the rocks closed behind them when an official made an attempt to pay his respects. There was a small shrine, and we lit incense and bowed. Then we headed back to the nunnery. I had one last place to visit, one last ceremony to perform before going home.

When we reached the nunnery, I saw several nuns and laywomen spreading wild vegetables in the sun to dry. I recognized the abbess, Master Wu-hsien. I didn't think she'd remember me, so I introduced myself and told her I had recently heard that Cold Mountain's remains were preserved in a stupa somewhere near her temple. She said that was true and pointed back toward the gorge. She told us to walk to the pond where there was a statue of Kuan-yin, the Goddess of Mercy, then take the trail that led up the mountain. At the pond we saw steps going up the rock face and followed them. The trail was steep, but it took only a minute for us to reach the ridge and another minute to reach the stupa.

The villagers in the surrounding area had been conducting ceremonies here for centuries, and I was surprised I hadn't heard about it earlier. A professor I contacted at the provincial university, who was from Tientai and specialized in Buddhist studies, confirmed the stupa's existence and its centuries-old association with Han-shan. Seeing it for the first time, I was startled. Over the original stupa, someone had erected another structure made of aluminum and painted it pale yellow, with tin eaves on each of its nine stories and tiny bells hanging from their corners. I had never seen anything like it. Cold Mountain would have loved it. It was so him.

Once we recovered from our astonishment, Robin and I took out our offerings. I set my cups on the cement altar inside the railing that was designed to protect the stupa. Figuring that Cold Mountain could take a joke, I left them empty. Next to the cups I placed my newly acquired Sung-dynasty edition of his poems. I thought he'd get a kick out of that, too. Then Robin took out his laptop and set it down at the base of the railing and played "Listening to the Wind," a country-western song that Gary Flint used on his website. Robin also brought along Gary's copy of Gary Snyder's *Danger on Peaks*. Snyder and Flint had stayed in touch over the years. Snyder, of

Cold Mountain's stupa at Mingyen

course, had translated several dozen Cold Mountain poems and had helped introduce a generation of Westerners to Han-shan. Robin handed me Snyder's book and asked me to read a poem. The book opened to "Give Up":

> Walking back from the Dharma-talk
> summer dry madrone
> leaves rattle down
>
> "Give up! give up!
> Oh sure!" they say

I put down the book, and we just stood there, listening to Merle Haggard — and, when he was done, to the bells. That seemed like enough.

LEXICON

The following list includes the modified Wade-Giles romanization used in this book for Chinese names, places, and terms followed by the Pinyin romanization and the traditional Chinese characters. Although it is no longer fashionable, the Wade-Giles system was designed as a compromise for speakers of various European languages in the mid and late nineteenth century, while the Pinyin system was designed for Russian speakers in the mid-twentieth century.

Ai Ch'ing / Ai Qing / 艾青
An Lu-shan / An Lushan / 安祿山之亂
Anchuanshan / Anquanshan / 安全山
Ankuo / Anguo / 安國寺
Anlu / Anlu / 安陸
Anyueh / Anyue / 安岳
Baidu / Baidu / 百度
Chaching / Chajing / 茶經
Chaisang / Chaisang / 柴桑
Ch'ai-t'ou-feng / Chaitoufeng / 釵頭鳳
Chang Chi / Zhang Ji / 張繼
Chang Ch'i / Zhang Qi / 張琪
Ch'ang-an / Changan / 長安
Ch'ang-o / Chang-o / 嫦娥
Changan (street) / Changan / 長安路
Changchen / Zhangzhen / 章鎮
Changcheng (hotel) / Changcheng / 長城大酒店
Changchiang / Changjiang / 長江
Changchiangchi / Changjiangji / 長江集
Changchiangpa / Changjiangba / 長江壩
Changchih / Changzhi / 長智
Changchiu / Zhangqiu / 章丘
Changchou / Changzhou / 常州
Changsha / Changsha / 長沙
Changshu / Changshu / 常熟
Chanma / Zhanma / 斬馬
Chanyu / Zhanyu / 單于
Chao Hsien / Zhao Xian / 趙嫻
Chaoling (tomb) / Zhaoling / 昭陵
Chaomienching / Zhaomianjing / 照面井
Chaoting / Zhaoting / 昭亭
Chaoyang / Chaoyang / 潮陽

Ch'e-chi-chiang / Chejijiang / 車騎將
Chechishan / Chejishan / 車騎山
Chekang / Zhegang / 柘岡
Chen (lady) / Zhen / 甄
Chen Wu / Zhen Wu / 真武
Ch'en (surname) / Chen / 陳
Ch'en Liang / Chen Liang / 陳亮
Ch'en Po-ta / Chen Boda / 陳伯達
Ch'en Tzu-ang / Chen Zi'ang / 陳子昂
Chen-tsung / Zhenzong / 真宗
Chenchiachai / Chenjiazhai / 陳家寨
Cheng (surname) / Zheng / 鄭
Ch'eng Tzu-an / Cheng Zi'an / 成子安
Chengchou / Zhengzhou / 鄭州
Chenghu / Chenghu / 城湖
Chengshan / Chengshan / 城山
Chengtao / Zhengdao / 正道
Chengtu / Chengdu / 成都
Chenhsi / Zhenxi 鎮西
Chenju / Zhenru / 真如
chi / ji / 寄
ch'i / qi / 氣
(Southern) Ch'i / Qi / (南) 齊
ch'i-kung / qigong / 氣功
Chia Tao / Jia Dao / 賈島
Chiahsien / Jiaxian / 郟縣
Chialing / Jialing / 嘉陵
Chiangchou / Jiangzhou / 江州
Chiangling / Jiangling / 江陵
Chiangnan / Jiangnan / 江南
Chiangshan / Jiangshan / 姜山
Chiangyou / Jiangyou / 江油
Chiao-jan / Jiaoran / 皎然

Chiaotso / Jiaozuo / 焦作
Chiawutai / Jiawutai / 嘉午台
Chiehtouchen / Jietouzhen / 街頭鎮
Chien Chin-sung / Jian Jinsong / 簡錦松
Chienshan / Qianshan / 潛山
Chientang / Qiantang / 錢塘
Chienyuan / Qianyuan / 乾元
Chih-che / Zhizhe / 智者
Chih-yi / Zhi'yi / 智顗
Ch'ih-sung / Chisong / 赤松
Chihche Tayuan / Zhizhe Tayuan / 智者塔院
Chihhsiting / Zhixiting / 至喜亭
Chihping / Zhiping / 治平
Chihsien / Jixian / 杞縣
Chihta / Zhida / 直大
Chikou / Qikou / 郪口
(Eastern) Chin / (東)晉
Ch'in (state, dynasty) / Qin / 秦
Chinan / Jinan / 濟南
Chinchiang / Jinjiang / 錦江
Chinchiangchi / Jinjiangji / 錦江集
Ch'ing (dynasty) / Qing / 清
Ch'ing-ming (festival) / Qingming / 清明
Chingcheng / Qingcheng / 青城
Chingchou / Qingzhou / 青州
Chingchuanhu / Qingzhuanhu / 青磚湖
Chinghofang / Qinghefang / 清河坊
Chinghu / Jinghu / 鏡湖
Chinghua / Qinghua / 青華
Chingkung / Jingkong / 景空
Chinglien / Qinglian / 青蓮
Chinglung / Qingong / 青龍
Chingshan / Qingshan / 青山
Chingte / Jingde / 敬德
Chingting / Jingting / 敬亭
Chinhsi / Jinxi / 金溪
Chinhua (mountain, temple) / Jinhua / 金華
山/觀
Chinjenming / Jinrenming / 金人銘
Chinling (mountain) / Qinling / 秦嶺
Chinling (capital) / Jinling / 金陵
Chinsha / Jinsha / 金沙
Chiputsun / Qibucun / 七步村
Chissu / Qisi / 期思
Chiuchiang / Jiujiang / 九江
Chou (dynasty, surname) / Zhou / 周

Chou En-lai / Zhou Enlai / 周恩來
Choukoutien / Zhoukoudian / 周口店
Choukueili / Zhouguili / 胄貴里
Ch'ou-nu-er / Chounuer / 醜奴兒
Ch'u (state) / Chu / 楚
Chu Hsi / Zhu Xi / 朱熹
Chu Shu-chen / Zhu Shuzhen / 朱淑真
Ch'u Yuan / Qu Yuan / 屈原
Chu-ke Liang / Zhu-ge Liang / 諸葛亮
Chuanchen / Quanzhen / 全真
Chuang Yen / Zhuang Yan / 莊嚴
Chuang-tzu / Zhuangzi / 莊子
Chuangchiao / Zhuangjiao / 庄角
Chuanhui / Chuanhui / 川惠
Chuchou / Chuzhou / 滁州
Chufu / Qufu / 曲阜
Chungching / Chongqing / 重慶
Chungnan / Zhongnan / 終南
Chungshan (street) / Zhongshan / 中山
Chungshan (mountain) / Zhongshan / 鍾山
Chunhui / Chunhui / 春暉
Chunshan / Junshan / 君山島
Chuntientai / Juntiantai / 鈞天台
Chupo / Zhupo / 朱坡
Chussu (academy) / Zhusi / 諸思書院
Chutang (gorge) / Qutang / 瞿唐
Chutzu (book) / Chuci / 楚辭
Chutzu (shrine) / Quci / 屈祠
Chuyuanchen / Quyuanzhen / 屈原鎮
Echou / Ezhou / 鄂州
Emei / Emei / 鵝眉
Fan (river) / Fan / 樊川
Fan Ch'eng-ta / Fan Chengda / 范成大
Fan Shan-feng / Fan Shanfeng / 范山峰
Fan Yun / Fan Yun / 范雲
Fancheng / Fancheng / 樊城
Fankungting / Fangongting / 范公亭
Fei (river) / Fei / 淝水
Feng (river) / Feng / 澤河
Feng-cha / Fengzha / 鳳閘
Feng-kan / Fenggan / 豐干
Fengchieh / Fengjie / 奉節
Fenghuangshan / Fenghuangshan / 鳳凰山
Fenghuangtai / Fenghuangtai / 鳳凰台
Fengshan / Fengshan / 鳳山
fu (ode) / fu / 賦

Fu Hsi / Fu Xi / 伏羲
Fuchiang (Szechuan river) / Fujiang / 涪江
Fuchiang (Kiangsi river) / Fujiang / 撫江
Fuhe (river) / Fuho / 府河
Fulin / Fulin / 福臨
Futan / Fudan / 復旦
Fuyang / Fuyang / 阜陽
Fuyuan / Fuyuan / 福源
Haihsia Chatao / Haixia Chadao / 海峽茶道
Haiming / Haiming / 海明
Haining / Haining / 海寧
Han (dynasty) / Han / 漢
Han (manor) / Han / 韓庄
Han (river) / Han / 漢江
Han Hsiang / Han Xiang / 韓湘
Han Yu / Han Yu / 韓愈
Han-shan / Hanshan / 寒山
Hangchou / Hangzhou / 杭州
Hankukuan / Hanguguan / 函谷關
Hanshan / Hanshan / 寒山
Hanyen / Hanyan / 寒巖
Hengshan / Hengshan / 衡山
Ho Shih-p'ing / He Shiping / 何世平
Hochicheng / Heqizheng / 何其正
Honan / Henan / 河南
Hsi Shih / Xi Shi / 西施
Hsiamushan / Xiamushan / 霞幕山
Hsiang (Hunan river) / Xiang / 湘江
Hsiang (Hupei river) / Xiang / 襄水
Hsiang Yu / Xiang Yu / 項羽
Hsiangchou / Xiangzhou / 襄州
Hsiangyang / Xiangyang / 襄陽
hsiao / xiao / 嘯
Hsiao T'ai / Xiaotai / 嘯台
Hsiaotien / Xiaotian / 小田
Hsiawu (springs) / Xiawu / 霞霧甘泉
Hsiawushan / Xiawushan / 霞霧山
Hsieh An / Xie An / 謝安
Hsieh Hsuan / Xie Xuan / 謝玄
Hsieh Hsuancheng / Xie Xuancheng / 謝玄城
Hsieh Ling-yun / Xie Lingyun / 謝靈運
Hsieh T'iao / Xie Tiao / 謝朓
Hsiehtiao (tower) / Xietiao / 謝朓樓
Hsien Yu-shu / Xian Yushu / 鮮于樞
Hsienheng / Xianheng / 咸亨大酒店
Hsienshan / Xianshan / 峴山

Hsiengyang / Xianyang / 咸陽
Hsilin / Xilin / 西林寺
Hsiling (bridge) / Xiling / 西泠
Hsilinghsia / Xilingxia / 西陵峽
Hsin Ch'i-chi / Xin Qiji / 辛棄疾
Hsin-yi / Xinyi / 心一
Hsinan (river) / Xinan / 新安江
Hsincheng / Xinzheng / 新鄭
Hsing-chien / Xingjian / 行簡
Hsing-k'ung / Xingkong / 性空
Hsingchiao / Xingjiao / 興教
Hsintien / Xindian / 辛店鎮
Hsishih / Xishi / 西市街
Hsiushui / Xiushui / 修水
Hsiwang / Xiwang / 希望小學
Hsu (driver) / Xu / 許
Hsu Cheng-tuan / Xu Zhengduan / 徐正端
Hsuan Kung / Xuan Gong / 宣公
Hsuan-tsang / Xuancang / 玄藏
Hsuan-tsung / Xuanzong / 玄宗
Hsuancheng / Xuancheng / 宣城
Hsuanwu / Xuanwu / 玄武湖
Hsueh T'ao / Xue Tao / 薛濤
Hsuehchiahsiang / Xuejiaxiang / 薛家巷
Hsuehtang / Xuetang / 雪堂
Hsuehtien / Xuedian / 薛店鎮
Hsuliangchen / Xuliangzhen / 許良鎮
Hsunyang / Xunyang / 潯陽樓
Hu Chien-yin / Hu Jianyin / 胡建銀
Hua-tzu Ch'i / Huazi Qi / 華子期
Huai (river) / Huai / 淮河
Huai (king) / Huai / 懷王
Huaiyang / Huaiyang / 淮陽
Huang (driver, travel agent) / Huang / 黃
Huang T'ing-chien / Huang Tingjian / 黃庭堅
Huang-po / Huangbo / 黃檗
Huang-ti / Huangdi / 黃帝
Huangchou / Huangzhou / 黃州
Huangchuehshu / Huangjueshu / 黃桷樹
Huangkang / Huanggang / 黃岡
Huangtzupo / Huangzipo / 皇子陂
Huangyuan / Huangyuan / 黃源
Huanhua (creek, village) / Huanhua / 浣花溪/村
Huapei / Huabei / 華北大飯店
Huatiao / Huadiao / 華吊

Huayang (gazetteer) / Huayang / 華陽志
Huayen / Huayan / 華嚴
Huchou / Huzhou / 湖州
Huhsien / Huxian / 戶縣
Hui-neng / Huineng / 慧能
Huichou / Huizhou / 惠州
Huihsien / Huixian / 輝縣市
Hunan / Hunan / 湖南
Hung Yai / Hong Yai / 洪崖
Hung-lin / Honglin / 宏林
Hupei / Hubei / 湖北
Huwan / Huwan / 滻灣
Innca (hotel) / Yingjia / 盈嘉
ju / ru / 汝
ju-chia / ru-jia / 儒家
Ju-meng-ling / Rumengling / 如夢令
Juan Chi / Ruan Ji / 阮籍
Juanchuang / Ruanzhuang / 阮庄
Juchou / Ruzhou / 汝州
Jungyang / Rongyang / 榮陽
Jurchen / Nuzhen / 女真
Kaifeng / Kaifeng / 開封
Kansu / Gansu / 甘肅
Kanyu / Ganyu / 感遇
Kechoupa / Gezhouba / 葛洲壩
Khitan / Qidan / 契丹
Kiangsi / Jiangxi / 江西
k'o / ke / 客
k'uai-t'ing / kuai-ting / 快艇
kuan / guan / 觀
Kuang-hung-ming-chi / Guanghongmingji / 廣弘明集
Kuangshan / Kuangshan / 匡山
Kuangte / Guangde / 廣德
Kuanyin (pavilion) / Guanyin / 觀音閣
Kueichih / Guichi / 歸池
Kueichou / Kuizhou / 夔州
Kueifeng / Guifeng / 圭峰
Kueilaitang / Guilaitang / 歸來堂
Kueilin / Guilin / 桂林
Kung-lu / Gonglu / 公路
Kuo-yi / Guoyi / 果一
Kuoching (Shangpu) / Guoqing / 國慶
Kuoching (Tientai) / Guoqing / 國清
Kuotien / Guodian / 郭店
Kushan / Gushan / 孤山

Kuyin / Guyin / 谷隱
K'ung Li / Kong Li / 孔鯉
K'ung Yi-chi / Kong Yiji / 孔乙己
K'ung-chi / Kongji / 孔伋
Kungtzulunshih / Kongzilunshi / 孔子論詩
Kungyichi / Kongyiji / 孔乙己
Laichou / Laizhou / 萊州
Langyashan / Langyashan / 琅玡山
Lankavatara (sutra) / Lengqie / 楞伽經
Lantien / Lantian / 藍田
Lantienshan / Lantianshan / 藍天山
Lao (river) / Lao / 牢河
Lao-tzu / Laozi / 老子
Laoyehtzu / Laoyeci / 老爺祠
Lei Tsu / Lei Zu / 嫘祖
Lepingli / Lepingli / 樂平里
Leyou / Leyou / 樂遊原
li / li / 里
Li Ch'ing-chao / Li Qingzhao / 李清照
Li Hsin / Li Xin / 李昕
Li K'o / Li Ke / 李客
Li Kung-lin / Li Gonglin / 李公麟
Li Pai / Li Bai / 李白
Li Shang-yin / Li Shangyin / 李商隱
Li Sheng-liang / Li Shengliang / 李盛良
Li Yang-ping / Li Yangping / 李陽冰
Liangfushan / Liangfushan / 梁甫山
Licheng / Licheng / 歷城
Lichuan / Liquan / 里泉
Lin Ho-ching / Lin Hejing / 林和靖
Lin Hsiao-p'ing / Lin Xiaoping / 林曉平
Lin Pu / Lin Bu / 林逋
Lin-chiang-hsien / Linjiangxian / 臨江仙
Linchi / Linji / 臨濟
Linchuan / Linchuan / 臨川
Ling-hu Ch'u / Linghu Chu / 令狐楚
Lingfeng Tanmei / Lingfeng Tanmei / 靈峰探梅
Lingpao / Lingbao / 靈寶
Lingyenshan / Lingyanshan / 靈巖山
Lingyun / Lingyun / 靈運
Linkaoting / Lingaoting / 臨皋亭
Lishan / Lishan / 驪山
Lisao / Lisao / 離騷
Liu Hsieh / Liu Xie / 劉勰
Liu Sung / Liu Song / 劉宋

Liu Tsung-yuan / Liu Zongyuan / 柳宗元
Liu Yu-hsi / Liu Yuxi / 劉禹錫
Liuchou / Liuzhou / 柳州
Liuli / Liuli / 琉璃
Liuyi Shuyuan / Liuyi Shuyuan / 六一書院
Lo (river) / Luo / 洛河
Louwailou / Louwailou / 樓外樓
Loyang / Luoyang / 洛陽
Lu (state) / Lu / 魯
Lu (Eric, driver) / Lv / 呂
Lu Hsun / Lu Xun / 魯迅
Lu You / Lu You / 陸游
Lu Yu / Lu Yu / 陸羽
Luchung / Luzhong / 路仲
Luling / Luling / 盧陵
Lumen / Lumen / 鹿門寺
Lumenshan / Lumenshan / 鹿門山
Lungcheng / Longcheng / 龍城大道
Lunghsi / Longxi / 隴西院
Lungmen / Longmen / 龍門石窟
Lungpao / Longbao / 龍寶
Lungpaoshan / Longbaoshan / 龍寶山
Lungshan / Longshan / 龍山
Lushan / Lushan / 盧山
Luyuan / Luyuan / 鹿苑寺
Ma (driver) / Ma / 馬
Ma'anshan / Ma'anshan / 馬鞍山
Ma-tsu / Mazu / 馬祖
Man-chiang-hung / Manjianghong / 滿江紅
Mao Heng / Mao Heng / 毛亨
Maoping / Maoping / 茅坪
Meihuachuan / Meihuaquan / 梅花泉
Meipo / Meipo / 渼陂水庫
Meng Chiao / Meng Jiao / 孟郊
Meng Hao-jan / Meng Haoran / 孟浩然
Meng Kuang / Meng Guang / 孟光
Mengchou / Mengzhou / 孟州
Milo (river) / Miluo / 汨羅江
Min / Min / 岷江
Mingling / Mingling / 明陵路
Mingyen / Mingyan / 明巖
Mingyuehshan / Mingyueshan / 明月山
Mo Shih-ch'in / Mo Shiqin / 莫仕琴
Mokanshan / Moganshan / 莫干山
Mu Tan / Mu Dan / 穆旦
nan-hu / nan-hu / 南胡

Nanchang / Nanchang / 南昌
Nanchu / Nanqu / 南渠
Nang / Nang / 瀼
Nanking / Nanjing / 南京
Nanpu / Nanpu / 南浦賓館
nei-jen / nei-ren / 內人
Ningpo / Ningbo / 寧波
Nishan / Nishan / 尼山
Niutoushan / Niutoushan / 牛頭山
Nu Wa / Nu Wa / 女媧
Omitofo / Amituofo / 阿彌陀佛
Ou-yang Hsiu / Ouyang Xiu / 歐陽修
Pa / Ba / 巴
Pachen / Bachen / 八陳村
Pai (causeway) / Bai / 白堤
Pai (garden) / Bai / 白園
Pai Chu-yi / Bai Juyi / 白居易
Pai-chang / Baizhang / 百丈
Paichaoshan / Baizhaoshan / 白兆山
Paichiaping / Baijiaping / 白家坪
Paichiayen / Baijiayan / 白家巖
Paichuan / Baiquan / 白泉勝景
Paihuatan / Baihuatan / 白花潭
Paimochuan / Baimoquan / 百脈泉
Paiticheng / Baidicheng / 白帝城
Paiyun / Baiyun / 白雲泉
P'ang Te-kung / Pang Degong / 龐德公
pao-tzu / bao-zi / 包子
Paochi / Baoji / 寶雞
Paokang / Baogang / 寶康巷/保康巷
Paokuo / Baoguo / 報國寺
Paolin / Baolin / 寶林寺
Paoning / Baoning / 報寧寺
Paotuchuan / Baotuquan / 趵突泉公園
Pashuiyuan / Bashuiyuan / 八水源
Patung / Badong / 巴東
Payi / Bayi / 八一路
Pei Ti / Pei Di / 裴笛
Peihsin / Beixin / 北新街
Peimang / Beimang / 北邙
P'eng / Peng / 鵬
P'eng (river) / Peng / 彭水
P'eng Hsien / Peng Xian / 彭咸
Pengchiawan / Pengjiawan / 彭家灣
Penglai / Penglai / 蓬萊
Pengtse / Pengze / 彭澤

pieh / *bie* / 別
Pingchiang / Pingjiang / 平江
Pingshui / Pingshui / 平水
Pipa (ballad, pavilion) / Pipa / 琵琶行/琵琶亭
Pishan / Bishan / 碧山
Po Mao-lin / Bo Maolin / 柏茂琳
Poaihsien / Boaixian / 博愛縣
Poshan / Boshan / 博山
Pu-suan-tzu / Busuanzi / 卜算子
P'u-sa-man / Pusaman / 菩薩蠻
Pute / Pude / 普德廟
Putissu / Putisi / 菩提寺
Sanlu / Sanlu / 三閭
Sanshan Piehyeh / Sanshan Bieye / 三山別業
Santai / Santai / 三台
Sanyoutung / Sanyoudong / 三游洞
Saotan Lienyungchi / *Saotan Lianyongji* / 騷壇
　聯詠集
Saotan Shihshe / Saotan Shishe / 騷壇詩社
se / *se* / 瑟
Shaho / Shahe / 沙河
Shan Chien / Shan Jian / 山簡
Shangfangshan / Shangfangshan / 上方山
Shanghai / Shanghai / 上海
Shangjao / Shangrao / 上饒
Shangli / Shangli / 上梨
Shangpu / Shangpu / 上浦
Shangyin (road) / Shangyin / 商隱路
Shangyu / Shangyu / 上虞
Shantung / Shandong / 山東
Shanyin (town) / Shanyin / 山陰
shao-ping / *shao-bing* / 燒餅
Shaochi / Shaoji / 紹齊公路
Shaohsing / Shaoxing / 紹興
Shaoling / Shaoling / 少陵原
Shehung / Shehong / 射洪
Shen (doctor, garden) / Shen / 沈
Shentu / Shendu / 神都大廈
Sheng-sheng-man / Shengshengman / 聲聲慢
Sheng-ying / Shengying / 聖英
Shengchou / Shengzhou / 嵊州
Shengfeng / Shengfeng / 盛豐路
Shengli / Shengli / 勝利街/勝利西路
Shensi / Shaanxi / 陝西
shih / *shi* / 詩
Shih-te / Shide / 拾得

Shih-wu / Shiwu / 石屋
Shih-wu Ch'ing-kung / Shiwu Qinggong / 石
　屋清珙
Shihching / *Shijing* / 詩經
Shihma / Shima / 石馬河
Shihmenshan / Shimenshan / 石門山
Shihning (estate, villa) / Shining / 始寧別墅/
　始寧墅
Shihshuo Hsinyu / *Shishui Xinyu* / 世說新語
Shoushan / Shoushan / 壽山
Shuangching / Shuangjing / 雙井村
Shuiyang / Shuiyang / 水陽江
Shushan / Shushan / 杼山
Sian / Xi'an / 西安
Simeng / Simeng / 思夢
Ssu / Si / 思溪
Ssu-feng-chia / Sifenzha / 四鳳閘
Ssu-ma Ch'ien / Sima Qian / 司馬遷
Ssu-ma Hsiang-ju / Sima Xiangru / 司馬相如
Ssuchichiao / Sijiqiao / 四季橋
(West) Ssuma / Sima / 西司馬村
Su (causeway) / Su / 蘇堤
Su Ch'e / Su Che / 蘇轍
Su Hsun / Su Xun / 蘇洵
Su Shih / Su Shi / 蘇軾
Su Tung-p'o / Su Dongpo / 蘇東坡
Su Tzu-you / Su Ziyou / 蘇子由
Suchou / Suzhou / 蘇州
Sui (dynasty) / Sui / 隋
Suining / Suining / 遂寧
Sumenshan / Sumenshan / 蘇門山
Sun Teng / Sun Deng / 孫登
sung / *song* / 送
Sung (dynasty) / Song / 宋
Sung Chih-wen / Song Zhiwen / 宋之問
Sungchou / Songzhou / 松州
Szechuan / Sichuan / 四川
Ta-ch'a / Dacha / 大茶
Ta-hsiu / Daxiu / 大休禪師
T'ai-tsung / Taizong / 太宗
Taichung / Taizhong / 台中
Taifu / Taifu / 太傅祠
Taihang / Taihang / 太行山
Taipei / Taibei / 台北
Taiping / Taiping / 太平
Taishan / Taishan / 泰山

Taiyuan / Taiyuan / 太原
Tamien / Damian / 大面中路
Taming / Daming / 大明寺
T'an Hou-lan / Tan Houlan / 譚厚蘭
T'ang / Tang / 唐
T'ang Wan / Tang Wan / 唐婉
Tangpai / Tangbai / 唐白河
Tangtu / Dangtu / 當涂
Tangwan / Tangwan / 塘灣村
Tanmeiyuan / Tanmeiyuan / 探梅園
Tanpuchen / Tanbuzhen / 潭埠鎮
(Mrs) T'ao / Tao / 陶太太
T'ao Yuan-ming / Tao Yuanming / 陶原明
Tao-jen / Daoren / 道忍
Taoteching / Daodejing / 道德經
Taoyuanko / Taoyuanke / 桃源窠
Te-an / De'an / 德安
Teching / Deqing / 德清
Tefeng / Defeng / 德風橋
Teng Hsiao-p'ing / Deng Xiaoping / 鄧小平
Teng Li-chun / Deng Lijun / 鄧麗君
Tengfenglin / Dengfenglin / 東風林
Teyang / Deyang / 德陽
Teyi / Deyi / 德義橋
Tienchenlou / Tianchenlou / 天辰樓
Tienchin / Tianjin / 天津電視台
Tienchushan / Tianzhushan / 天柱山
Tienning / Tianning / 天寧寺
Tienpingshan / Tianpingshan / 天平山
Tienshih / Tianshi / 天師
Tienshui / Tianshui / 天水
Tientai (mountain, sect) / Tiantai / 天台
Tinghsi / Tingxi / 淳溪港
Tinghui / Dinghui / 定惠院
Tinglin (temple, villa) / Dinglin / 定林寺/定
林山庄
Tingling / Dingling / 丁零塞
Ts'ai Ch'in / Cai Qin / 蔡琴
Ts'ao Chih / Cao Zhi / 曹植
Ts'ao P'i / Cao Pi / 曹丕
Ts'ao Ts'ao / Cao Cao / 曹操
Tsaoeh / Cao'e / 曹鵝江
Tsaopao Paotzupu / Caobao Baozipu / 草包
包子鋪
Tsaotang (temple, river) / Caotang / 草堂寺/
草堂河

Tseng Hsi / Zeng Xi / 曾晳
Tsulai / Culai / 徂徠
Tsung-mi / Zongmi / 宗密
Tu Fu / Du Fu / 杜甫
Tu Ku-ch'ung / Du Guchong / 獨孤崇
Tu Mu / Du Mu / 杜牧
Tuan Wen-ch'ang / Duan Wenchang / 段文昌
Tuanwuchieh / Duanwujie / 段午節
Tung Ch'i-ch'ang / Dong Qichang / 董其昌
Tung-shan / Dongshan / 洞山
Tunghsiang (Sian) / Tongxiang / 通向
Tunghsiang (Kiangsi) / Dongxiang / 東鄉
Tunghsiang (Chekiang) / Tongxiang / 桐鄉
Tunghsu / Tongxu / 通許
Tungkuossu / Dongguosi / 東郭寺
Tunglin (monastery, buddha) / Donglin / 東林
寺/東林大佛
Tungpo / Dongpo / 東坡
Tungshan / Dongshan / 東山景區
Tungtachieh / Dongdajie / 東大街
Tungting / Dongting / 洞庭湖
Tungtun / Dongtun / 東屯茅屋
Tutiling / Tudiling / 土地陵
Tutsuoshan / Duzuoshan / 獨坐山
Tzu-kung / Zigong / 子貢
Tzuchou / Zizhou / 梓州
Tzuke (peak, monastery) / Zige / 紫閣峰/寺
Tzukeyu / Zigeyu / 紫閣峪
Tzukuei / Zigui / 秭歸
Wainan / Wainan / 外南街
wan-yueh / wan-yue / 婉約
Wanchou / Wanzhou / 萬州
Wang An-shih / Wang Anshi / 王安石
Wang Chao-chun / Wang Zhaojun / 王昭君
Wang Chao-yun / Wang Chaoyun / 王朝雲
Wang Tzu-you / Wang Ziyou / 王子猷
Wang Wei / Wang Wei / 王維
Wangchianglou / Wangjianglou / 望江樓
Wangchuan / Wangchuan / 輞川
Wantsai / Wanzai / 萬栽
Wanyuehting / Wanyueting / 玩月亭
Wei (dynasty) / Wei / 魏
Wei (district) / Wei / 韋曲
Wei (river) / Wei / 渭河
Wei Hsiung / Wei Xiong / 韋夐
Wei Kao / Wei Gao / 韋皋

Wei Ying-wu / Wei Yingwu / 韋應物
Wei-chih / Weizhi / 微之
Weichu / Weiqu / 韋曲北街
Weishih / Weishi / 尉氏
Wenchou / Wenzhou / 溫州
Wenchuan / Wenchuan / 溫泉村
Wengchung / Wengzhong / 翁仲路
Wenhsuan / Wenxuan / 文選
Wentsun / Wencun / 溫村
Wu (state) / Wu / 吳
Wu Chen / Wu Zhen / 吳鎮
Wu Ts'e-t'ien / Wu Zetian / 武則天
Wu-hsien / Wuxian / 悟賢
Wu-k'o / Wuke / 無可
Wu-pen / Wuben / 無本
Wuchang / Wuchang / 武昌
Wuhan / Wuhan / 武漢
Wuhsiang (temple) / Wuxiang / 無相寺
Wuhsing / Wuxing / 吳興
Wuhu / Wuhu / 巫湖
Wushan / Wushan / 巫山
Wushihkang / Wushigang / 烏石岡
Wutangshan / Wudangshan / 武當山
Wutzu / Wuzi / 午子綠茶
Wuyin / Wuyin / 無隱庵
Wuyishan / Wuyishan / 武夷山
Yang (pass) / Yang / 陽關
Yang Fan / Yang Fan / 楊帆
Yang Hu / Yang Hu / 羊祜
Yang Wan-li / Yang Wanli / 楊萬里
Yangchihshan / Yangchishan / 楊崎山
Yangchou / Yangzhou / 揚州
Yangfu / Yangfu / 楊富橋
Yangtienshan / Yangtianshan / 仰天山
Yangtze / Yangzi / 揚子 (長江)
（West) Yangwanpo / Yangwanpo / 西楊萬坡
Yao Ho / Yao He / 姚合
Yaoyao / Yaoyao / 姚岆村
Yehlang / Yelang / 夜郎
Yen (river) / Yan / 剡溪
Yen Wu / Yan Wu / 嚴武
Yenshan / Yanshan / 鉛山
Yi (Chufu river) / Yi / 沂河

Yi (Loyang river) / Yi / 伊河
Yi-ai / Yi'ai / 遺愛湖
Yi-an (studio) / Yi'an / 易安室
Yi-an Chu-shih / Yi'an Jushi / 易安居士
yi-po / yi-bo / 衣鉢
Yichang / Yichang / 宜昌
Yiching / Yijing / 易經
Yin (Ningpo) / Yin / 鄞
Yin Yun / Yin Yun / 殷雲
Yinchen / Yinzhen / 引鎮
Ying (city) / Ying / 郢
Yingpin / Yingbin / 迎賓賓官
Yingtan / Yingtan / 鷹潭
Yinshihlou / Yinshilou / 吟詩樓
Yitu / Yidu / 驛都大道
Yiyang / Yiyang / 宜陽
Youchou (capital, tower) / Youzhou / 幽州
Yu Hsien-k'ai / Yu Xiankai / 于仙凱
Yuan (river) / Yuan / 沅江
(Master) Yuan / Yuan / 圓上人
Yuan Chen (friend of Pai Chu-yi) / Yuan Zhen / 元稹
Yuan Shu / Yuan Shu / 袁术
Yuanming / Yuanming / 淵明路
yueh-fu / yue-fu / 樂府
Yuehfei / Yuefei / 岳飛廟
Yuehtang / Yuetang / 月塘
Yuehyang (town, tower, river) / Yuehyang / 岳陽
Yun-kuan / Yunguan / 允觀
Yungchia / Yongjia / 永嘉
Yungchin / Yongjin / 湧金門
Yungchou / Yongzhou / 永州
Yunghuai / Yonghuai / 詠懷
Yungping / Yongping / 永平
Yungyang / Yongyang / 永陽
Yunlin / Yunlin / 雲林寺
Yunmen (monastery) / Yunmen / 雲門寺
Yunnan / Yunnan / 雲南
Yuntaishan / Yuntaishan / 雲台山
Yushan (hill) / Yushan / 魚山
Yuyangshan / Yuyangshan / 玉陽山
Yuying (river) / Yuying / 余英溪

ABOUT THE AUTHOR

Bill Porter was born in Van Nuys, California, on October 3, 1943, and grew up in northern Idaho, where his parents moved in 1954. Since his father was often away on business, Porter attended boarding schools in Los Angeles and the San Francisco Bay Area, where he graduated from high school in 1961. After a tour of duty in the US Army (1964–67), he attended UC Santa Barbara and majored in anthropology. In 1970, he entered graduate school at Columbia University and studied anthropology with a faculty that included Margaret Mead and Ruth Benedict. While he was living in New York, he became interested in Buddhism, and in 1972 he left America and moved to a Buddhist monastery in Taiwan. After more than three years with the monks and nuns, he struck out on his own and supported himself by teaching English and later by working as a journalist at English-language radio stations in Taiwan and Hong Kong. During this time, he married a Chinese woman, with whom he has two children, and began working on translations of Chinese poetry and Buddhist texts. In 1993, he returned to America so that his children could learn English, and he has lived ever since in Port Townsend, Washington. For the past twenty years, he has worked as an independent scholar and has supported himself from book royalties and speaking fees. He has given talks on Zen at dozens of Zen centers throughout the United States and has lectured on Chinese history, culture, religion, and poetry at many of the major universities in the United States, England, and Germany. His translations of texts related to these subjects have been honored with a number of awards, including two NEA translation fellowships, a PEN translation award, the inaugural Asian Literature Award of the American Literary Translators Association, and more recently a Guggenheim Fellowship, which he received to support work on this book.

Terrace of pools on Stone Mountain Gate where Li Pai and Tu Fu said goodbye.

Copper Canyon Press is grateful to the following individuals whose extraordinary support and funding made publication of *Finding Them Gone* possible.

With special thanks to longtime friends of the Press
LESLIE AND JANET COX.

Joseph Bednarik and Liesl Slabaugh
Jeffrey and Jill Bishop
Vince and Jane Buck
Daniel Gerber
Mark Hamilton
Jim Harrison
Steven Myron Holl
Phil Kovacevich and Eric Wechsler
David Novros
Walter Parsons and Linda Fay Gerrard
John Phillips and Anne O'Donnell
Li Xin
Brice Marden
James Richardson
Kim and Jeff Seely
Yang Yongwang
Yun Yin

Poetry is vital to language and living. Since 1972, Copper Canyon Press has published extraordinary poetry from around the world to engage the imaginations and intellects of readers, writers, booksellers, librarians, teachers, students, and donors.

WE ARE GRATEFUL FOR THE MAJOR SUPPORT PROVIDED BY:

THE PAUL G. ALLEN
FAMILY FOUNDATION

CULTURE

Anonymous

John Branch

Diana Broze

Beroz Ferrell & The Point, LLC

Janet and Les Cox

Mimi Gardner Gates

Linda Gerrard and Walter Parsons

Gull Industries, Inc.
on behalf of William and Ruth True

Mark Hamilton and Suzie Rapp

Carolyn and Robert Hedin

Steven Myron Holl

Lakeside Industries, Inc.
on behalf of Jeanne Marie Lee

Maureen Lee and Mark Busto

TO LEARN MORE ABOUT UNDERWRITING
COPPER CANYON PRESS TITLES,
PLEASE CALL 360-385-4925 EXT. 103

WE ARE GRATEFUL FOR THE MAJOR SUPPORT PROVIDED BY:

Brice Marden

Ellie Mathews and Carl Youngmann as The North Press

H. Stewart Parker

Penny and Jerry Peabody

John Phillips and Anne O'Donnell

Joseph C. Roberts

Cynthia Lovelace Sears and Frank Buxton

The Seattle Foundation

Kim and Jeff Seely

David and Catherine Eaton Skinner

Dan Waggoner

C.D. Wright and Forrest Gander

Charles and Barbara Wright

The dedicated interns and faithful volunteers of Copper Canyon Press

The Chinese character for poetry is made up
of two parts: "word" and "temple."
It also serves as pressmark for
Copper Canyon Press.

This book is set in Farnham Text with
Chinese in Adobe Kaiti Std. Display type set
in Classica, with sans serif details in
Scala Sans. Book design by VJB/Scribe.
Printed on archival-quality paper.

Finding Them Gone is also issued in a signed,
limited edition of 126 copies. These copies
are available exclusively through donation to
Copper Canyon Press. Please e-mail
poetry@coppercanyonpress.org
for more details.